Cultures of Representation

Cultures of Representation
DISABILITY IN WORLD CINEMA CONTEXTS

EDITED BY
BENJAMIN FRASER

WALLFLOWER PRESS
LONDON & NEW YORK

A Wallflower Press Book

Wallflower Press is an imprint of
Columbia University Press
publishers since 1893
New York

cup.columbia.edu

Copyright © 2016 Columbia University Press
All rights reserved

Wallflower Press® is a registered trademark of Columbia University Press

A complete CIP record is available from the Library of Congress

ISBN 978-0-231-17748-1 (cloth : alk. paper)
ISBN 978-0-231-17749-8 (pbk. : alk. paper)
ISBN 978-0-231-85096-4 (e-book)

Cover image: *Yo, También* (2009) © Olive Films

Columbia University Press books are printed on permanent
and durable acid-free paper.
This book is printed on paper with recycled content.
Printed in the United States of America

Contents

ACKNOWLEDGEMENTS vii
NOTES ON CONTRIBUTORS ix

Introduction
Disability Studies, World Cinema and the Cognitive Code of Reality
Benjamin Fraser 1

Global In(ter)dependent Disability Cinema
Targeting Ephemeral Domains of Belief and Cultivating Aficionados of the Body
David T. Mitchell and Sharon L. Snyder 18

'Beyond Forgiveness'?
Lee Chang-dong's *Oasis* (2002) and the Mobilisation of Disability Discourses in the Korean New Wave
Paul Petrovic 33

Refusing Chromosomal Pairing
Inclusion, Disabled Masculinity, Sexuality and Intimacy in *Yo, también* (2009)
Michael Gill 47

Dunce! Duffer! Dimwit!
Dyslexia in Bollywood's *Taare Zameen Par* (2007)
Sanjukta Ghosh 63

Landscapes of Children
Picturing Disability in Buñuel's *Los olvidados* (1950)
Susan Antebi 78

Fearful Reflections
Representations of Disability in Postwar Dutch Cinema (1973–2011)
Mitzi Waltz 93

'People Endure'
The Function of Autism in *Anton's Right Here* (2012)
José Alaniz 110

Displaying Autism
The Thinking and Images of *Temple Grandin* (2010)
Katherine Lashley 126

More than the 'Other'?
On Four Tendencies Regarding the Representation of Disability
in Contemporary German Film (2005–2010)
Petra Anders 141

The Other Body
Psychiatric Disability and Pedro Almodóvar (1988–2011)
Candace Skibba 157

On the Road to Normalcy
European Road Movies and Disability (2002–2011)
Anna Grebe 173

Re-envisioning Italy's 'New Man' in *Bella non piangere!* (1955)
Jennifer Griffiths 187

'Get Your Legs Back'
Avatar (2009) and the Re-booting of American Individualism
Susan Flynn 200

Through the Disability Lens
Revisiting Ousmane Sembène's *Xala* (1975) and *Camp de Thiaroye* (1988)
Ken Junior Lipenga 216

Homes Wretched and Wrecked
Disability as Social Dis-ease in Kurosawa's *Dodes'ka-den* (1970)
James A. Wren 230

Leprosy and the Dialectical Body in Forugh Farrokhzad's
***The House is Black* (1964)**
Rosa Holman 247

INDEX 263

Acknowledgements

I have drawn inspiration and received encouragement from many teacher-scholars and colleagues during my years at College of Charleston and now East Carolina University who deserve my thanks, whether for collaborative efforts on disability film series, conversations or both: Nancy Ausherman, Martha Chapin, Liz Johnston, Morgan Koerner, Cindy May, Marylaura Papalas, Alison Piepmeier, Steve Sligar and Alison Smith. Thanks also to the Film Studies folks at ECU, particularly Anna Froula, Amanda Klein and Justin Wilmes. Special thanks to all those seeking to bring Hispanic Studies into dialogue with Disability Studies as an interdisciplinary area – above all Susan Antebi, Encarnación Juárez Almendros and Matthew Marr, but also Julie Avril Minich and Victoria Rivera-Cordero. Thanks too to the graduate students and faculty at the University of Illinois for an invitation to speak there on disability and Spanish cultural production in 2015, which proved very encouraging. I am most grateful to Abby, Ben and Judd, from whom I continue to learn much about disability and society outside of academic contexts.

Notes on Contributors

JOSE ALANIZ is associate professor in the Department of Slavic Languages and Literatures and the Department of Comparative Literature (adjunct), and director of the Disability Studies Program at the University of Washington – Seattle. He is the author of *Komiks: Comic Art in Russia* (University Press of Mississippi, 2010) and *Death, Disability and the Superhero: The Silver Age and Beyond* (University Press of Mississippi, 2014).

PETRA ANDERS is a lecturer at Ostfalia University of Applied Science, Wolfenbüttel, Germany. She is the author of *Behinderung und psychische Krankheit im zeitgenössischen deutschen Spielfilm. Eine vergleichende Filmanalyse* (Königshausen & Neumann, 2014).

SUSAN ANTEBI is associate professor of Spanish and director of the Latin American Studies Program at the University of Toronto. She is the author of *Carnal Inscriptions: Spanish American Narratives of Corporeal Difference and Disability* (Palgrave Macmillan, 2009) and co-editor, with Beth Jörgensen, of *Libre Acceso: Latin American Literature and Film through Disability Studies* (SUNY Press, 2016).

SUSAN FLYNN is a doctoral graduate of the Equality Studies Centre at the School of Social Justice, University College Dublin, and a lecturer in media and cultural studies at the University of the Arts, London. She has published in a range of international journals including the *American, British and Canadian Studies Journal* and *Considering Disability Journal*.

BENJAMIN FRASER is professor of Hispanic Studies and chair of Foreign Languages and Literatures at East Carolina University in North Carolina. He is the author of, amongst other publications, *Deaf History and Culture in Spain* (Gallaudet University Press, 2009) and *Disability Studies and Spanish*

Culture: Films, Novels, the Comic and the Public Exhibition (Liverpool University Press, 2013). His articles on disability themes have appeared in such journals as *Cultural Studies, Journal of Literary and Cultural Disability Studies, Arizona Journal of Hispanic Cultural Studies, Bulletin of Spanish Studies, Hispanic Issues Online, Hispania* and *Dieciocho*.

SANJUKTA GHOSH is professor in the Department of Communication and the Women's and Gender Studies Program at Castleton University in Vermont. She has published in a variety of international journals such as *Alternatives* and in anthologies on race, gender and sexuality.

MICHAEL GILL is assistant professor of Disability Studies in the School of Education at Syracuse University. He is the author of *Already Doing It: Intellectual Disability and Sexual Agency* (University of Minnesota Press, 2015) and the co-editor, with Cathy Schlund-Vials, of *Disability, Human Rights, and the Limits of Humanitarianism* (Ashgate, 2014).

ANNA GREBE is a lecturer at the University of Vienna and the Johannes-Kepler-Universität in Linz, Austria. She is an associate member of the DFG research group 'Media and Participation: Between Demand and Entitlement' at the University of Konstanz and member of the Chilean research group 'Arte y Nuevos Medios' at the University of Valparaíso.

JENNIFER S. GRIFFITHS is a lecturer at Iowa State University College of Design Rome and the American University of Rome. Her articles on issues of gender and representation have appeared in *Gastronomica, Women's Studies Quarterly*.

ROSA HOLMAN is a researcher with the Alfred Deakin Institute for Citizenship and Globalisation at Deakin University in Melbourne. She is the author of various publications, with her research on Iranian cinema appearing in the journals *Senses of Cinema* and *Screening the Past*.

KATHERINE LASHLEY is a PhD candidate in English at Morgan State University and an adjunct in the English Department at Towson University. She has published a memoir about growing up with an older autistic sister entitled *My Younger Older Sister* (2001).

KEN JUNIOR LIPENGA is a lecturer in the English department at Chancellor

College, University of Malawi. He has published articles on disability in several journals, including the *African Journal of Disability, Journal of African Cultural Studies* and *Agenda: Empowering Women for Gender Equity*.

DAVID T. MITCHELL AND SHARON L. SNYDER are the co-authors of *Narrative Prosthesis: Disability and the Dependencies of Discourse* (University of Michigan Press, 2000), *Cultural Locations of Disability* (University of Chicago Press, 2006) and *The Biopolitics of Disability: Neoliberalism, Ablenationalism, and Peripheral Embodiment* (University of Michigan Press, 2015). They are also the creators of three award-winning films about disability arts, history and culture. Together they helped found the Committee on Disability Issues in the Profession at the Modern Languages Association as well as researched, wrote and curated a Chicago Disability History Exhibit for Bodies of Work: Disability Arts and Culture Festival, and also are producing a new film on the social and surgical issues involved with esophageal atresia.

PAUL PETROVIC is a lecturer at the University of Tulsa and Oklahoma Wesleyan University. He is the editor of *Representing 9/11: Trauma, Ideology, and Nationalism in Literature, Film, and Television* (Rowman & Littlefield, 2015) and has been published in the journals *Critique, Studies in American Naturalism* and *Journal of Graphic Novels and Comics*.

CANDACE SKIBBA is an Assistant Teaching Professor of Spanish in the Department of Modern Languages at Carnegie Mellon University. She is the author of 'Equally Authentic: Illness and Disability in the Films of Pedro Almodóvar – Blindness and the Voyeur', included in the anthology *Otherness in Hispanic Culture* (Cambridge Scholars Publishing, 2014).

MITZI WALTZ is a Senior Researcher with Disability Studies in Nederland and Hogeschool van Rotterdam. She is the author of *Autism: A Social and Medical History* (Palgrave Macmillan, 2013).

JAMES A. WREN is a retired professor of Japanese and comparative literature at San Jose State University. His monographs include *Epidemics and Pandemics* and *The Himalayas*, and has had essays published in *Microscopia, Critique,* and *disClosure*. He is also the editor of *Reconstruction 16.1: Regionalism, Regional Identity and Queer Asian Cinema*.

Introduction

Disability Studies, World Cinema and the Cognitive Code of Reality

Benjamin Fraser

A discussion is brewing about disability in world contexts that might best be summed up through a series of questions. Is Disability Studies limited by an association with Anglophone origins and contexts? Should the theoretical tools and perspectives associated with the political project of Disability Studies in such contexts transfer to the analysis of other spaces and struggles across the globe? Does this political project necessarily reaffirm paradigms of the globalized West or the Global North? To what degree do state practices and national imaginaries construct disability? Or inversely, to what degree does disability inflect the construction of nationhood? Should we be wary of a tendency to compartmentalize disability as definable only within the boundaries of certain national, cultural and/or linguistic contexts? Or should we be suspicious of approaches to disability that take cross-cultural similarities for granted and tend to ignore the specificities of embodied space/place? Are there, in fact, commonalities in how disabilities are conceived, perceived and lived cross-culturally? Is there evidence of a universal disability culture? Or does any such evidence serve to naturalize a suspect disciplinary formation and uncritically accept existing dynamics of able-bodied geopolitical power?

Although the selections published here may encourage readers to think through such questions, *Cultures of Representation: Disability in World Cinema Contexts* provides no definitive answers. This volume is not devoted to advocating a single position on the state of this progressively globalising field of inquiry. Nor, even, is it envisioned as a direct commentary on the disciplinary questioning I have tried to approximate in the above paragraph.

Moreover, because it is my conviction that such questions have not been systematically asked, I do not believe they can be answered at this time. And, of course, I am not sure that any future answer would be or should be definitive. My own inclination is to affirm that *in the end, it may be best to conceive of Disability Studies as a disciplinary formation whose sustained political force requires constant methodological innovation and political commitment if it is to respond to struggles that appear, morph and reappear in specific places and at specific times – always with specific human consequences.*

This book's central proposition is simple enough: the time has come to think more globally about both disability in general and Disability Studies in particular. Film is one point of entry into this global discussion – one toward which many gravitate because of a deceptive accessibility, the potential that moving images hold to capture the imagination of the widest possible public. One cannot sidestep an important issue of spectatorship in this regard. Analysis of moving images implies the requisite risks and rewards associated with what has been called 'mass' or 'popular culture', as previous scholarship on disability has made clear. That is, the most brute reduction would have it that cinematic representations may reinforce 'positive' or 'negative' images of disability. They advance characterisations that are certainly not always as welcome or as simple as they may seem. In the end, what is important is to acknowledge the power of filmic images as representations. As such, they are a visible counterpart to the less-often visible social representations that mediate the way disability is conceived, perceived and lived.

For the viewing public that approaches disability and film within the context of teaching and learning, within the context of scholarship, within the political project of Disability Studies, I believe the rewards of attending to filmic representations of disability will always outweigh the risks. And because films are increasingly screened globally, the greater risk is that of ignoring such representations. If we do so, we thus also ignore the questions that surface with their production and reception. Anglophone publications, in my estimation, have shown far too little documented scholarly interest in disability in non-Anglophone contexts – and it is quite simply to this reality that this book responds in conception and design. While elsewhere one can find a significant number of article-length publications that touch on disability contexts throughout the world – with more or less success depending on the place and time sought – we might take the pulse of existing interest in the topic of disability in non-Anglophone contexts by assessing the relative quantity of book-length products alone. Despite the growing, and perhaps vast, number of book publications on disability in general, there are only a small handful of these each year that relate to non-Anglophone contexts.¹ And when one asks how many of these books systematically deal with artistic representations or humanities cultural products – films or otherwise – the total number of relevant publications is greatly lessened indeed.

Humanities-trained scholars interested in film, literature and cultural production continue to believe that artistic and cultural representations are inextricable from political struggles. The history and significance of previous work on this theoretical or methodological question is far too vast to rehearse here, but one can start by saying this: at the largest scale – the one most pertinent to introductory discussions – it matters not whether one considers art forms to be reflections of society, mediations of the social, or products indistinguishable in any meaningful sense from the larger society in which they are produced and consumed. Similarly to all manner of extra-artistic practices and products, artistic works teach, inspire, model, habituate, norm, entertain, distract, anesthetise, engage, challenge, contest, subvert, critique and even potentially re-norm. Moreover, they are constructed, viewed, circulated, appropriated and re-appropriated from divergent perspectives and according to diverse interests that all merit scrutiny. Although this summary of the significance of art obscures important nuances that distinguish different approaches to cultural production, my hope is that general readers will find its basic assertion to be glaringly self-evident: representations matter.

In all likelihood, to approach disability and film from a global perspective brings new considerations to light while also confirming old suppositions. I leave it for readers of this volume to sift the former from the latter as may suit them. What is most important to note is that, to date, there has been no volume published dedicated expressly to a global perspective on disability and film.² The first edition of Lennard J. Davis's *The Disability Studies Reader* (1997) – a touchstone for the field that has been re-edited three times since its original publication – included no essays on film and spoke more to Anglophone contexts than to a global engagement of disability studies.³ Of course, disability and film has been addressed directly in a number of book publications, all of them laudable, but also, all too often, insufficiently global.⁴

What I have found particularly interesting as I seek to connect my disciplinary Hispanic Studies work on disability with the wider field of Disability Studies is that sources originally published in Spanish themselves have viewed Anglophone disability cinema as a touchstone, eschewing a more direct exploration of disability in Spanish-language films themselves.⁵ This was in essence, a recapitulation of a discovery I had made a decade earlier while researching deaf culture in Spain, where I had found similar evidence of the continuing cultural capital enjoyed by Anglophone work on deafness.[6] To my eyes, such evidence – which remains to be explored and confirmed across this and other linguistic contexts as well as Area Studies disciplines and Language and Literature fields – would corroborate the assertions of those who associate global Disability Studies with an Anglophone project. This association, as I see it, presents both advantages and challenges that must be acknowledged if the field is to acquire a more global resonance.[7] Leaving aside, for the time being, the important matter of Disability Studies work as published in languages other than English, the motivation behind this edited volume is to underscore that Anglophone scholarship on disability itself should – and, in fact, must – seek to globalise itself more extensively than it has up until now.

A strong note toward globalising Anglophone Disability Studies was sounded in 2010 with Sharon L. Snyder and David T. Mitchell's special issue of the *Journal of Literary and Cultural Disability Studies* titled 'The Geo-Politics of Ablenationalism' (2010a) and Clare Barker and Stuart Murray's special issue of that same journal titled 'Disability Postcolonialism: Global Disability Cultures and Democratic Criticism' (2010).[8] Attentive to the nuances of studying disability in concrete contexts of ablenationalism, Snyder and Mitchell's issue offered 'an opportunity for scholars to pursue a new paradigm for theorizing disability among other cross-cultural experiences of bodies identified as deviant' (2010a: 119). In their introduction, Barker and Murray wrote that 'as a whole, contemporary Disability Studies is not especially perceptive in its articulation of global dynamics' and cautioned that 'Disability Studies problematically transports theories and methodologies developed within the Western academy to other global locations, paying only nominal attention to local formations and understandings of disability' (2010: 219).[9] These approaches did not delve sufficiently into the question of artistic representation, but in their global orientation and large-scale thinking they did pave the way for the contents of the present volume.

Cinematic Representation: Indexical, Iconic and Symbolic Signification

It is worth asking: why film? Although he did not discuss film in *Disability Aesthetics* (2010), it is important to remember Tobin Siebers' more general proposition. Disability, he wrote, was present even if 'rarely recognized as such' throughout the history of modern art, where the presence of disability – of 'strangeness' and the 'convulsive'; of 'misshapen and twisted bodies' – allowed 'the beauty of an artwork to endure over time' (2010: 4, 5). Though there may be nuances that distinguish disability in aesthetics in general and disability in film in particular, there should be no reason to consider the story of film to stand wholly outside of this analysis of modern art. As a visual medium, cinema – like painting and sculpture for example – has been focused on the representation of bodies: bodies in specific locations, real and/or imagined. While I do not want to overemphasise the importance of this assertion or to present it unproblematically, I do believe it is important to understand film's unique representational significance as it relates to ableism, disability and the interdependence of all human lives. It is this: film inherits from photography an ontological assertion that should not be ignored – and from which it draws its potential and its risks; in sum, its representational force.

Early films captured everyday moments and their peculiar form of artistic representation was governed, I would say, by an expressly ontological quality that has never left cinema. The events famously captured by the Lumière brothers on their cinematograph and by others on comparable machines – the arrival of a train, workers leaving a factory, for example – in a simple sense re-presented daily routines or activities for consideration in a new light. Such relatively simple representations asserted the brute reality of an extra-cinematic (social and political) existence for the cinematic sign whose theorisation was to grow in complexity throughout the twentieth century.

The noted director and cinema theorist Pier Paolo Pasolini once made an astute observation I consider imperative for discussions of representations of disability in film: 'if we see in the sublime *Man of Aran* [Robert J. Flaherty, 1934] a woman and a boy on the rocks, we recognize them because the cognitive code of reality as such comes into play' (1988: 250). This was no passing anecdote for Pasolini, but a comment encapsulating his entire approach to cinema. Paraphrasing his perspective, we can say that the semiotic code of cinema is the semiotic code of reality. One can find echoes of Pasolini's 'cognitive code of reality' in other samples of canonical film theory – for example, in Siegfried Kracauer's theory of film as the redemption of physical reality (1968), or, for that matter, in the value given to the indexical and iconic qualities of the filmic sign as signaled by Peter Wollen: 'The cinema contains all three modes of the sign: indexical, iconic and symbolic. What has always happened is that theorists of the cinema have seized on one or more of these dimensions and used it as the ground for an aesthetic firman' (1972: 125).[10] The indexical and iconic qualities of film signs – in the interests of brevity we might say that these result from the direct impression of light onto a receptive surface (in celluloid film), and from a correspondence in form or shape between the representation and the original – together point to the extra-filmic (socially and politically inflected) existence of a thing, an object, a person.

These forms of signification co-exist with the symbolic and arbitrary, conventional forms of signification that arguably drove film theory throughout the twentieth century.[11] It is, then, the complex interplay between index, icon and symbol – between motivated and arbitrary/conventional representation – that makes film so important to disability studies today.

As illustration, we might take Belgian filmmaker Jaco van Dormael's intriguing short film *The Kiss* (1995). Made to commemorate the 100th anniversary of the first Lumière screening, *The Kiss* was included in the collection *Lumière et compagnie* (*Lumière and Company*, 1995), a project where forty directors from around the world were asked to shoot a short film using a model of the original cinematograph machine employed by the Lumière brothers.[12] Van Dormael's 52-second black and white film opens with actors Pascal Duquenne and Michele Maes looking directly at the camera in a mid-close-up. Although not much of the background can be seen, the presence of a building and the movement of passers-by clearly demonstrate the public-ness of the space in which they are captured. From a perspective that acknowledges the relevance of the same 'cognitive code of reality' to both film and life, it is significant that viewers will note both actors have the physical traits associated with Down syndrome. After eight seconds, they turn toward each other, smile and kiss. Their kissing becomes more passionate and, in between caresses, they once again smile and look at the camera.

There are many ways to view this short film. Two jump immediately to mind. One may see it, for example, as part of a tradition of 'objectifying ethnography',[13] or else as a subversion of the way disabled bodies more routinely serve as a 'vehicle of sensation' (Snyder and Mitchell 2006: 163) related to trauma and threats to able-bodiedness. We should not overlook the way disability has been harnessed for exploitation by narratives – filmic, literary or otherwise – that reaffirm the denigrating discourse of disability as lack from the perspective of a medical model or as a product of an ableist imaginary. Nor should we ignore that disability has been systematically differentiated from a socially and politically constructed able-bodied or neurotypical norm. It may be relevant to keep in mind, too, that narratives of disability – filmed or otherwise – rarely incorporate sexuality, preferring a sanitised image of platonic or amorous love instead. Many of the contributions to this volume in fact deal with these very points, issues that have shaped important strata of Disability Studies criticism. Neither should we forget, more generally, the problematic on-screen portrayal of disability by ablebodied actors, a topic that has also rightly received much attention in Disability Studies scholarship, a continuing historical tendency that is seemingly counteracted here. Nor still, however, should we ignore the risks of even categorising van Dormael's production as a 'disability film', given advances in intersectionality theory that warn of the dangers of adhering too closely to identity politics, narrowly defined (see Siebers 2008: 27–30).

Cinematic representation, as noted above, is not just about the indexical or iconic meaning of images, but also about its symbolic signification. Thus another perspective on this particular film might tie *The Kiss* to cinema's oft-cited ability to turn images into metaphors; this is cinema as a form of thinking, and specifically as a form of thinking through, via, by way of, representations. This is a visual form that stages for us the way we think through, via, by way of, concepts – keep in mind Pasolini's notion of the 'cognitive code of reality'. From this perspective, cinema becomes a reflective mirror, a productive expression or a theoretical ground for the integration of perception and concepts that informs our socially negotiated understanding of disability. Because of the way indexical, iconic and symbolic/arbitrary signification blend together in the cinematic sign, film becomes, like reality, a cognitive code that actively requires questioning, understanding, and perhaps decipherment. This might be said of all art, or of all artistic representation and engaged spectatorship, of course. But in this case and in this volume we deal in cinematic representation. To deal with film's symbolic signification is always to deal with social convention/social history one one hand, and individual consciousness/individual interpretation on the other. Viewers are perhaps encouraged to assess where van Dormael's film – considered as represented thought, images as socially mediated concepts – coincides with their own thinking. For some viewers, the significance of *The Kiss* thus may seem to come from the way it reconciles two times as well as the perceived distance between the real and the 'reel'.

Restaging the equipment, limitations and stylistic conventions of 1895 for modern audiences, the film boasts an organic simplicity – a black and white image, length of approximately one minute, static camera, no editing or postproduction, unity of time and place, everyday topic, situated in public space, natural lighting, no sound. With the knowledge of when it was filmed assured, however, the moment captured speaks to a more contemporary moment. Van Dormael's film seems to take on greater meaning in light of the growing awareness of disability in Europe toward the end of the twentieth century. Given the metaphorical value of cinema stemming from the symbolic signification of the filmic image, one might see the film as a vehicle for abstraction. From the stark reality of the couple's moment viewers can easily move toward consideration of the abstract and embattled concepts through which they make sense of this image: public-ness? emotions? relationships? love? nationhood? progress? rights? humanity? But such abstraction is always held in tension with the indexical and iconic aspects of film, which assure that such a moment is not abstract but embodied. From this perspective, one might suggest that the question posed by van Dormael's film is precisely how far the socially mediated concept of disability – perceived through the ontological assertion of bodies captured in cinematic representation – intertwines with other concepts such as community, nation and human-ness.

To ask this question is to consider the imbrication of indexical, iconic and symbolic modes of signification in the filmic image. But it is also to fuse together notions of existence and interpretation – which of course can never fully be pulled apart from one another. The application of Pasolini's notion of the 'cognitive code of reality' to film should not be seen in limited terms as an essentialisation of disability, but rather as a call to recognise that viewers call upon the same socially mediated concepts, categories and representations in analysing van Dormael's screen images as they do in making sense of extra-filmic perceptions. It is to recognise that, whether in art or in 'real life', thought influences perception and vision affects knowledge. Through film, viewers may confront their own socially mediated perceptions of disability in other cultures, and they may potentially form knowledge of how concepts of disability are embedded in social environments. The vehicle for this engagement with disability on film is the notion of representations as a presence. The individual and social forces that construct and shape the presence of disability on film draw their power – whether seen as pernicious, progressive or neutral – from those forces that construct and shape the presence of disability off of film. In dismissing this on-screen presence – however problematic it may be – we risk dismissing the presence of disability in arguably less-artistic, but similarly socio-political, contexts off-screen.

The filmic presence of disability, its on-screen representation, is – it seems to me – always significant, but until now it has never been approached in a range of global contexts. Interrogating this range of contexts may prompt us to think further about the connections between ontology and epistemology as they relate to disability as a product of social relationships. In doing so, we must understand that there are always risks, just as there are also opportunities.[14] As scholarship on disability in film testifies, and as the contributions to this volume themselves suggest, cinematic representation can be reductively violent and normative, on one hand, or potentially transformative on the other. Moreover, it may be conflicted and contradictory. As with other forms of artistic representation, the representation of disability on film may push viewers to advocate integration, full inclusion and the dismantling of ableist concepts or it may play into discourses of ablenationalism, locational exceptionality or a cleansed global universality. I hope that readers will agree with me on one point: no matter what the textures of cinematic representation discussed, and no matter where they unfold across the globe, it is in discussing, critiquing and understanding the concepts through which film is produced and viewed – it is via the interrogation of social formations of visual knowledge – that viewers may move toward other ways of seeing. In this way global film becomes the start of a conversation concerning representation – and representation is, of course, a process that unfolds also outside of the discourse of art in our everyday social worlds (consider Siebers' remark that 'representation is the difference that makes a difference' [2008: 17]). The cognitive codes we use to discern (said a different way, construct) reality are necessarily mediated by social representations – and as such they are also potentially impacted, shaped, grounded, re-calibrated by artistic representations. Put quite simply, without a global approach to these dynamics, Disability Studies as a discipline will have contented itself with a mere reflection of its Anglophone origins.

Toward World Cinema Contexts

As David T. Mitchell and Sharon L. Snyder suggest toward the end of their contribution to this volume, 'film's most significant, potential innovation' may be that it provides a partial answer to an important question: 'how do we affect peoples' belief systems, the attitudes, their ideas and their conceptualisation of people with disabilities?' The staging of disability for global audiences and readerships thus begins an important conversation on attitudinal change. At the same time, my hope is that this collection on disability in world cinema contexts will further push scholars, students and general readers to think more globally about the limitations and the potential of Anglophone Disability Studies. If 'disability enlarges our vision of human variation and difference' (Siebers 2010: 3), then consideration of disability across world cinema contexts will have enlarged our world a great deal more indeed.

In composing this volume I first struggled to find global 'coverage' only to content myself with the understanding that this is not the end but the mere beginning of a more global discussion of disability. Nevertheless, the inclusion here of films from Belgium, France, Germany, India, Italy, Iran, Japan, Korea, Mexico, Netherlands, Russia, Senegal, Spain, and of a pair of Anglophone films with global resonance, assures me that this discussion is off to a good start. The contributors – primarily drawn from institutions in the United States but also from Australia, Austria, Canada, the United Kingdom, Germany, Ireland, Italy, Malawi and the Netherlands – have had the autonomy to approach their chosen subject in whatever way they feel is best. Fearing that structuring the volume along national or regional lines would encourage essentialising conclusions, I had hoped to organise the films into mutually exclusive categories – such as Physical Disability, Cognitive Disability, Illness and Psychiatric Disability, Gender and Sexuality, Marxism and Politics/Social Reform, Cultural Construction of Disability, Documentary Film, Fiction Film, Auteur Approaches, Overviews and so on… Such a principle was impossible, however, since so many of the contributions gathered here speak to multiple, overlapping considerations. In the end, the contents of this volume have themselves suggested a more organic organisation based on the readerly flow from each contribution to the next. Rather than map out those considerations here, my hope is that a brief statement on each chapter will direct readers toward specific cultural locations and/or themes.

David T. Mitchell and Sharon L. Snyder's 'Global In(ter)dependent Disability Cinema: Targeting Ephemeral Domains of Belief and Cultivating Aficionados of the Body' both asserts the value of film festivals as embodied events and covers a range of films from diverse contexts (Australia, France, Poland, Russia, UK, US) released over the span of more than a decade (2002–14). In the end they assert that 'art gives us access and tries to transform public consciousness'.

Paul Petrovic's '"Beyond Forgiveness"?: Lee Chang-dong's *Oasis* (2002) and the Mobilisation of Disability Discourses in the Korean New Wave' asserts that the fiction film spans 'two gendered modalities, simultaneously spotlighting a male crisis while anticipating a more expansive take on female subjectivity'. The representation of cerebral palsy is explored with particular attention to matters of identity formation and sexuality in situations shaped by familial and economic ties.

Michael Gill's 'Refusing Chromosomal Pairing: Inclusion, Disabled Masculinity, Sexuality and Intimacy in *Yo, también* (2009)' looks at a Spanish film that stages a meditation on the consequences of ableist assumptions that limit the sexual rights of those with intellectual disabilities. In particular, the representation of the relationship between the characters Daniel, who has Down syndrome, and Laura, who does not, is read against others in the film (of two intellectually disabled partners, and of two able-bodied partners), suggesting that more needs to be done to secure 'wider participation in sexual and reproductive rights' both on- and off-screen.

Sanjukta Ghosh's 'Dunce! Duffer! Dimwit!: Dyslexia in Bollywood's *Taare Zameen Par* (2007)' looks at intellectual disability in the context of contemporary India. The story of eight-year-old Ishaan Awasthi, who lives with his parents in Mumbai, prompts the author's exploration of larger social, cultural, educational and political circumstances: 'For disability film politics to be truly transgressive and potentially revolutionary, impairment cannot be examined in isolation from the larger social system from which it emerges'.

Susan Antebi's 'Landscapes of Children: Picturing Disability in Buñuel's *Los olvidados* (1950)' joins physical disability and juvenile delinquency within a wider paradigm of societal ills in Mexico. Blending a close reading of the film with the era's discourse on abnormality – with which Buñuel was familiar – she argues that 'the combined display of, on one hand, corporeal difference as moral cruelty, and on the other, violent action determined by conditions of socioeconomic inequality, reveals bodies at odds with their surroundings'.

Mitzi Waltz's 'Fearful Reflections: Representations of Disability in Post-war Dutch Cinema (1973–2011)' turns to films in the Dutch language (Nederlands or Vlaams/Flemish) from either the Netherlands or Belgium. Contextualising more recent cinema within a broader post-war turn in filmmaking, this approach brings representations of illness, physical disability and intellectual disability together to argue that 'with notable exceptions, disability is typically used as a dramatic and often tragic plot point, or as shorthand for a character flaw'.

José Alaniz's '"People Endure": The Function of Autism in *Anton's Right Here* (2012)' blends close analysis of documentary film form with Stuart Murray's exploration of the idea of function. The socio-political background of Putin's Russia informs discussion of the representation of a boy with autism as neurotypical bias is interrogated both on- and off-screen. In the end a productive ambivalence towards the film leads readers to ask whether 'a conventionally functional cinema [is] at odds with the experience of autism?'

Katherine Lashley's 'Displaying Autism: The Thinking and Images of *Temple Grandin* (2010)' employs such notions as disability drag and the supercrip to explore the representation of autism in a widely screened Anglophone film. She draws from Grandin's own explanation of 'thinking in pictures', and prompts readers to take director Mick Jackson's autism into account. While 'the film breaks some boundaries in disability film' is it not unproblematic, but still has a pedagogical value that can potentially open doors between autistic communities and neurotypical audiences.

Petra Anders' 'More than the "Other"?: On Four Tendencies Regarding the Representation of Disability in Contemporary German Film (2005–2010)' explores a range of films, disabilities and perspectives. She concludes that 'although disability is predominantly "othered" in contemporary German film in various ways, there are cases in which films have attempted to go beyond this notion'.

Candace Skibba's 'The Other Body: Psychiatric Disability and Pedro Almodóvar (1988–2011)' takes on three films by the noted international director (*Mujeres al borde de un ataque de nervios, Átame!, La piel que habito*). Working on two levels at once, she argues that 'by seeing Almodóvar's films through a disability lens it is possible to dialogue with existing discourses of gender/sexuality and social marginalisation in his work from Spanish Peninsular studies while also working to correct the insufficient work on psychiatric disability in the wide interdisciplinary field of Disability Studies from Spain'.

Anna Grebe's 'On the Road to Normalcy: European Road Movies and Disability (2002–2011)' looks at three recent German and Belgian films through the conventions of an understudied cinematic subgenre – the 'Behinderten-Roadmovie' (disability road movie). In this chapter, the road movie is transformed by its specifically European context, through which it differs from its North American counterpart, and by a focus on disabled protagonists who 'confront and potentially transgress the social boundaries of the normalcy that governs their lives'.

Jennifer Griffiths' 'Re-envisioning Italy's 'New Man' in *Bella non piangere!* (1955)' analyses the cinematic representation of physical disablilty in a narrative framing Enrico Toti as a national war hero. Folding the historical myth that coalesced around the soldier together with his on-screen representation reveals insights into how a discourse of disabled masculinity resonated with post-war Italian nationalism. Toti's embodiment of a political martyrdom, she writes, 'exemplifies how, in the Italian context, disabled bodies after 1916 came to symbolise the national community and its struggle toward victory'.

Susan Flynn's '"Get Your Legs Back": *Avatar* (2009) and the Re-booting of American Individualism' takes on an extensively screened global Anglophone film by connecting the individualist myth and narratives of personal responsibility with a problematic portrayal of disability. Seen here from a perspective that links a Marxian critique of ideology with the film's abelist character construction, she explores how biotechnology/genomic capital 'facilitates American individualism; providing the opportunity to escape from the imperfect body'.

Ken Lipenga's 'Through the Disability Lens: Revisiting Ousmane Sembène's *Xala* (1975) and *Camp de Thiaroye* (1988)' asserts the existence of disability as an 'embedded concept' relative to postcolonial African contexts.

Taking on two noted films, this chapter mobilises a widely social perspective on disability and explores its intersections with ableism, colonisation, racism, illness and impotence – as well as witchcraft and the role of supernatural/cosmological forces as a dominant theme characteristic of Nollywood productions.

James A. Wren's 'Homes Wretched and Wrecked: Disability as Social Dis-ease in Kurosawa's *Dodes'ka-den* (1970)' takes on the internationally acclaimed director's work as both 'an enthralling and richly textured portrait of the downtrodden' and a film that 'exposed the unsavory side of a "new" Japan'. Drawing from early quasi-historical accounts and contemporary discourses of family and nation, he explores the multi-faceted presence of disability in the film as a product of wider social forces.

This volume's splendid final chapter, Rosa Holman's 'Leprosy and the Dialectical Body in Forugh Farrokhzad's *The House is Black* (1964)', interrogates lyrical representations of physical suffering in a black and white film read against 'the poetic realism of contemporary Iranian cinema'. In particular, the director's cinematic use of rhythm and sound ties images of individual bodies to the wider social environment in which they are enmeshed. The film is interpreted at once in the context of the Shah's programme of modernisation and its consequences for women as well as the filmmaker's style and the Iranian New Wave cinema of the 1960s.

NOTES

1 See Garland 1995; Plann 1997; Cohen 1998; Silla 1998; Biesold 1999; Petryna 2002; Ryan and Schuchman 2002; Weiss 2002; Kohrman 2005; Metzler 2006; Nakamura 2006; Antebi 2009; Fraser 2009; Poore 2009; Addlakha 2013; Fraser 2013a; Marr 2013; Minich 2014; Rao and Kalyanpur 2014; Rasell and Iarskaia-Smirnova 2014; Scalenghe 2014. Certainly it should be emphasized that i) this listing may not include books on embodiment that may also overlap with or tie-in to disability studies from related disciplines (whether literary studies, gender and sexuality studies, psychology, sociology, and so on), and that ii) I have suspended consideration of the degree to which each of these listed texts relates to a disciplinary formation of Disability Studies proper.

2 *Disability Studies: Enabling the Humanities* (2002), edited by Sharon L. Snyder, Brenda Jo Brueggemann and Rosemarie Garland-Thomson, was a landmark text for its robust humanities contribution to the field, but was overhwlemingly Anglophone in conception despite a handful of laudable chapters on non-Anglophone contexts – and did not feature film in its composition.

3 Although the fourth edition published in 2013 includes several sustained accounts of films, these are films produced for Anglophone audiences.

4   For example: Klobas 1988; Norden 1994; Pointon and Davies 1997; Enns and Smit 2001; Riley 2005; Bhugra 2006; Chivers and Markotić 2010; Richardson 2010; Smith 2011; Mogk 2013 (importantly, here five essays – by Sally Chivers, Sarah Dauncey, Eunjung Kim & Michell Jarman, Russell Meeuf and Joyojeet Pal – do discuss non-Anglophone contexts); Wijdicks 2015.

5   In the course of my research for *Disability Studies and Spanish Culture* (2013a), for example, I was pleased to discover Olga María Alegre de la Rosa's book, *La discapacidad en el cine* (2003) only to find out that it consisted almost entirely of references to Anglophone and Hollywood cinema. On cognitive disability and visual representation see also Fraser 2010b; 2013b. In Hispanic Studies see also Plann 1997; Antebi 2009; Marr 2013; and Juárez Almendros 2013.

6   For more on this nuance, see the introduction to my *Deaf History and Culture in Spain* (2009) which is due – of course – to the global recognition afforded Gallaudet University and the Deaf President Now! movement of 1988 and its more recent resurgences (see also Fraser 2007; 2010a).

7   It is also reasonable to suggest that the Modern Language Association as a whole, dominated as it is by English department faculty, has not finished its work of globalising itself.

8   Susan Reynolds White and Benedicte Ingstad's edited volume *Disability in Local and Global Worlds* (2007) featuring work by anthropologists was also an early salvo; Erevelles (2011) is a more recent project from the field of education.

9   The introduction to this special issue draws motivation from Snyder and Mitchell's *Cultural Locations of Disability* (2006) and momentum from a special issue of *Wagadu* (2007) on 'Intersecting Gender and Disability Perspectives in Rethinking Postcolonial Identities' edited by Pushpa Naidu Parekh.

10 Stephen Prince (1999) continues and updates Wollen's line of thought on the indexical and iconic modes of the filmic sign, which are also important for the geographical film criticism of Jeff Hopkins (1994). See Fraser (2010c) for more discussion of these threads in film scholarship.

11 Prince (1999) covers quite a bit of ground in illustrating how arbitrary signification outweighed the indexical/iconic in twentieth-century film theory.

12 The film can also be viewed online at https://www.youtube.com/watch?v=cXz_TNZAVFk .

13 'Film spectators arrive at the screen prepared to glimpse the extraordinary body displayed for moments of uninterrupted visual access – a practice shared by clinical assessment rituals associated with the medical gaze' (Snyder and Mitchell 2006: 158).

14 Snyder and Mitchell put it well: 'The analysis of film images of disability provides an opportune location of critical intervention, a form of discursive rehab upon the site of our deepest psychic structures mediating our reception of human differences' (2006: 158). See also the discussion of what I would describe as a necessary ambivalence regarding representation in humanities texts that appears in Mitchell and Snyder 2000: 40–5).

FILMOGRAPHY

Van Dormael, Jaco (1995) *The Kiss*. Included on: *Lumière et compagnie*. 88 minutes. Cinétévé/Fox Lorber. Belgium.

BIBLIOGRAPHY

Addlakha, Renu (2013) *Disability Studies in India: Global Discourses, Local Realities*. New Delhi: Routledge India.

Alegre de la Rosa, Olga María (2003) *La discapacidad en el cine*. Tenerife: Octaedro.

Antebi, Susan (2009) *Carnal Inscriptions: Spanish American Narratives of Corporeal Difference and Disability*. New York, NY: Palgrave Macmillan.

Bhugra, Dinesh (2006) *Mad Tales from Bollywood: Portrayal of Mental Illness in Conventional Hindi Cinema*. New York, NY: Psychology Press.

Biesold, Horst. 1999. *Crying Hands: Eugenics and Deaf People in Nazi Germany*. Washington, DC: Gallaudet University Press.

Chivers, Sally (2011) *The Silvering Screen: Old Age and Disability in Cinema*. Toronto: University of Toronto Press.

Chivers, Sally and Nicole Markotić (eds) (2010) *The Problem Body: Projecting Disability on Film*. Columbus, OH: Ohio State University Press.

Cohen, Lawrence (1998) *No Aging in India: Alzheimer's, the Bad Family, and Other Modern Things*. Berkeley, CA: University of California Press.

Davis, Lennard J. (ed.) (1997) *The Disability Studies Reader*. New York: Routledge.

Enns, Anthony W. and Christopher R. Smit (eds) (2001) *Screening Disability: Essays on Cinema and Disability*. Lanham, MD: University Press of America.

Erevelles, Nirmala (2011) *Disability and Difference in Global Contexts: Enabling a Transformative Body Politic*. New York, NY: Palgrave Macmillan.

Fraser, Benjamin (2007) 'Deaf Cultural Production in Twentieth-Century Madrid', *Sign Language Studies*, 7, 4, 431–57.

____ (2009) *Deaf History and Culture in Spain: A Reader of Primary Documents*. Washington, D.C.: Gallaudet University Press.

____ (2010a) 'Spain, 1795: A Reconsideration of Lorenzo Hervás y Panduro (1735–1809) and the Visual Language of the Deaf', *Dieciocho*, 33, 2, 259–77.

____ (2010b) 'The Work of (Creating) Art: Judith Scott's Fiber Art, Lola Barrera and Iñaki Peñafiel's *¿Qué tienes debajo del sombrero?* (2006) and the Challenges Faced By People With Developmental Disabilities', *Cultural Studies*, 24, 4, 508–32.

____ (2010c) *Encounters with Bergson(ism) in Spain: Reconciling Philosophy, Literature, Film and Urban Space*. Chapel Hill, NC: University of North Carolina Press.

____ (2011) 'Toward Autonomy in Love and Work: Situating the Film *Yo, también* (2009) within the Political Project of Disability Studies', *Hispania*, 94, 1, 1–12.

____ (2013a) *Disability Studies and Spanish Culture: Films, Novels, the Comic and the Public Exhibition*. Liverpool: Liverpool University Press.

____ (2013b) 'Disability Art, Visibility and the Right to the City: The Trazos Singulares [Singular Strokes] (2011) Exhibit at Madrid's Nuevos Ministerios Metro Station', *Arizona Journal of Hispanic Cultural Studies*, 17, 245–61.

Garland, Robert (1995) *The Eye of the Beholder: Deformity and Disability in the Graeco-Roman World*. Ithaca, NY: Cornell University Press.

Hopkins, Jeff (1994) 'Mapping of Cinematic Places: Icons, Ideology, and the Power of (Mis)representation', in Stuart C. Aitken and Leo E. Zonn (eds) *Place, Power, Situation, and Spectacle: A Geography of Film*. Lanham, MD: Rowman and Littlefield, 47–65.

Juárez Almendros, Encarnación (2013) 'Disability Studies in the Hispanic World: Proposals and Methodologies', special issue of the *Arizona Journal of Hispanic Cultural Studies*, 18, 151–261.

Kohrman, Matthew (2005) *Bodies of Difference: Experiences of Disability and Institutional Advocacy in the Making of Modern China*. Berkeley, CA: University of California Press.

Kracauer, Siegfried (1968) *Theory of Film: The Redemption of Physical Reality*. Oxford: Oxford University Press.

Marr, Matthew J. (2013) *The Politics of Age and Disability in Contemporary Spanish Film: Plus Ultra Pluralism*. New York, NY, Routledge.

Metzler, Irina (2006) *Disability in Medieval Europe: Thinking about Physical Impairment during the High Middle Ages*. London: Routledge.

Minich, Julie Avril (2014) *Accessible Citizenships: Disability Nation and the Cultural Politics of Greater Mexico*. Philadelphia, PA: Temple University Press.

Mitchell, David T. and Sharon L. Snyder (2000) *Narrative Prosthesis: Disability and the Dependencies of Discourse*. Ann Arbor, MI: University of Michigan Press.

Mogk, Marja Evelyn (2013) *Different Bodies: Essays on Disability in Film and Television*. Jefferson, NC: McFarland.

Murray, Stuart and Clare Barker (eds) (2010) 'Disability Postcolonialism', special issue of the *Journal of Literary and Cultural Disability Studies*, 4, 3.

Nakamura, Karen (2006) *Deaf in Japan*. Ithaca, NY: Cornell University Press.

Norden, Martin F. (1994) *The Cinema of Isolation: A History of Physical Disability in the Movies*. New Brunswick, NJ: Rutgers University Press.

Parekh, Pushpa Naidu (2007) 'Intersecting Gender and Disability Perspectives in Rethinking Postcolonial Identities', special issue of *Wagadu*, 4.

Pasolini, Pier Paolo (1988) *Heretical Empiricism*, ed. Louise K. Barnett, trans. Nem Lawton and Louise K. Barnett. Bloomington, IN: Indiana University Press.

Petryna, Adriana (2002) *Life Exposed: Biological Citizens after Chernobyl*. Princeton, NJ: Princeton University Press.

Plann, Susan (1997) *A Silent Minority: Deaf Education in Spain 1550–1835*. Berkeley, CA: University of California Press.

Poore, Carol (2009) *Disability in Twentieth-Century German Culture*. Ann Arbor, MI: University of Michigan Press.

Prince, Stephen (1999) 'The Discourse of Pictures: Iconicity and Film Studies', in Leo Braudy and Marshall Cohen (eds) *Film Theory and Criticism*, 5th ed. Oxford: Oxford University Press, 99–117.

Rao, Shridevi and Maya Kalyanpur (2014) *South Asia and Disability Studies: Redefining Boundaries and Extending Horizons*. New York: Peter Lang.

Rasell, Michael and Elena Iarskaia-Smirnova (eds) (2014) *Disability in Eastern Europe and the Former Soviet Union*. New York: Routledge.

Reynolds White, Susan and Benedicte Ingstad (2007) *Disability in Local and Global Worlds*. Berkeley, CA: University of California Press.

Richardson, Niall (2010) *Transgressive Bodies: Representations in Film and Popular Culture*. Burlington, VT: Ashgate.

Riley II, Charles (2005) *Disability and the Media: Prescriptions for Change*. Lebanon, NE: University Press of New England.

Ryan, Donna and John Schuchman (2002) *Deaf People in Hitler's Europe*. Washington, D.C.: Gallaudet University Press.

Scalenghe, Sara (2014) *Disability in the Ottoman Arab World, 1500–1800*. Cambridge: Cambridge University Press.

Siebers, Tobin (2008) *Disability Theory*. Ann Arbor, MI: University of Michigan Press.

——— (2010) *Disability Aesthetics*. Ann Arbor, MI: University of Michigan Press.

Silla, Eric (1998) *People Are Not the Same: Leprosy and Identity in Twentieth-Century Mali*. Portsmouth: Heinemann.

Smith, Angela M. (2011) *Hideous Progeny: Disability, Eugenics and Classic Horror Cinema*. New York, NY: Columbia University Press.

Snyder, Sharon L. and David T. Mitchell (2006) *Cultural Locations of Disability*. Chicago, IL: University of Chicago Press.

——— (eds) (2010) 'The Geo-Politics of Ablenationalism,' special issue of the *Journal of Literary and Cultural Disability Studies*, 4, 2.

Snyder, Sharon L., Brenda Jo Brueggemann and Rosemarie Garland-Thomson (2002) *Disability Studies: Enabling the Humanities*. New York, NY: Modern Language Association.

Weiss, Meira (2002) *The Chosen Body: The Politics of the Body in Israeli Society*. Stanford, CA: Stanford University Press.

Wijdicks, Eelco F. M. (2015) *Neurocinema: When Film Meets Neurology*. Boca Raton, FL: CRC Press.

Wollen, Peter (1972) *Signs and Meaning in the Cinema*, 3rd ed. Bloomington, IN: Indiana University Press.

Global In(ter)dependent Disability Cinema:

Targeting Ephemeral Domains of Belief and Cultivating Aficionados of the Body

David T. Mitchell and Sharon L. Snyder

The topic with which we would like to begin is a contemplation of some overarching modes and methods operational in international in(ter)dependent disability films – particularly within the genre of disability documentary; although it's important to point out that we believe one cannot fully understand the form of disability documentary alone without a necessary juxtaposition alongside disability fiction films. Thus, we will move back and forth between two genres throughout this analysis.

Independent disability films when contextualised and screened in a meaningful way within international disability film festivals allow for a crucial alternative approach to imagining disability: namely, these visual works provide opportunities for not only raising public awareness about inclusion (i.e. the sharing of public space) but, even more importantly, global disability cinema now provides viewers with an alternative ethical map of living interdependently with each other. This key shift in representational approaches to disability has the potential to exponentially escalate audience understanding of disability as a productive social identity in its own right – one that complicates previous social model efforts to merely argue disabled people should be able to live as non-disabled people do (see Mitchell and Snyder 2015: 4).

The Founding Sexual Prohibition

For instance, one fiction film by Stephen Lance, *Yolk* (2008), explores the narrative of a post-adolescent girl with Down syndrome moving toward maturity and exploring her own sexuality. One of the ways we introduce this film to students and general audiences is to explain that the film is about the sexual prohibition of pursuing active experiences of pleasure – particularly for cognitively disabled women. A primary point to understand about the social management of people with disabilities in post-industrialised western cultures revolves around sexual prohibition as a foundational cultural exclusion. As Tobin Siebers argues, reproductive withdrawal of sexual opportunities serves as a key impetus for most socially perpetuated violence against disabled people: why disabled people are institutionalised, why marriage laws develop at the end of the nineteenth century and why disabled people are coercively sterilised by nations practicing eugenic beliefs (2012: 38). The argument of eugenics, in the most straightforward gloss of its structure as a discriminatory belief system, was for states to remove forcibly disabled people from the reproductive pool of the country (Snyder and Mitchell 2006: 98).

During an audience Q&A at the 2015 DisArts Film Festival in Grand Rapids, Michigan (19–22 April 2015), an individual made the earnest observation that he didn't see *Yolk* as about the sexual oppression of disabled people. Instead he only saw a film about a mother naturally concerned about her daughter's naïve interest in becoming sexually active. This comment seemed completely right except for the fact that the film only shows up at disability film festivals and is informed by the historical sexual prohibition of disabled women as the cultural backdrop against which its narrative unfolds. We also pointed out that the comment distorted the fact that we framed the film with respect to explorations of 'sexual prohibition' and not 'sexual oppression'. Those are different magnitudes of order for us and we needed to make that correction. We said that 'this could be a film about sexual oppression, there's plenty of sexual oppression experienced by disabled people (disabled women in particular), but this film is not the vehicle for that topic'. *Yolk* is more in the family melodrama genre of film that requires one to bring the content of sexual prohibition to its story.

But, nonetheless, this exchange reminded the audience that the stakes are very high in these films. One key to understanding in(ter)dependent disability film is to recognise that these works understand serious social dangers and attempt to imagine more habitable worlds for members of multiple marginalised communities (racial, queer, female, cognitive, sensory, psychiatrically and physically disabled people). A pressing need to diminish feelings of audience alienation with embodied differences serves as their foundational political platform. There's an urgent social background against which all of these films develop. That, we believe, is incredibly important to acknowledge in part because it's easy to miss this facet of their politicised objectives beneath the surface of their aestheticised presentations.

So, for instance, in the United States we're in the middle of racial antagonisms where largely able-bodied, white, working-class police officers shoot with impunity non-normatively embodied, African American youth (particularly young men). The killing in Ferguson, Missouri of Michael Brown (a large man), for instance, or Eric Garner in New York City (also a large man who had asthma), represent the destruction of racialised young men with anomalous bodies. They're also about people who live within great proximity to poverty. Disability cinema allows us one important forum to contemplate the incredibly serious repercussions of these extreme able-bodied reactions in the midst of encounters of anomalous bodies. Thus, their film messages help to bring home the representational stakes of what we're after.

A 'Lack' of Cinematic Urgency

When viewing independent disability film one does not necessarily get a sense of that urgency. In general, the degree of desperation they conjure up within their plots exists on a relatively small scale. One can critique and/or feel dissatisfied with this absence of urgency given the violence of current circumstances, but disability film tries to ease audiences into a comfort with non-normative functionality and the appearance of non-normative bodies. Each film brings audiences into the lives of their disabled characters and helps us negotiate these difficult social questions brought on by the historical exclusion of disabled people from social participation in a fairly gentle way. This is what independent disability film offers us at this historical moment of which we write (i.e. largely films made between 2000 and 2014). Expressing the desperate circumstances of many disabled peoples' lives is not the terrain that disability film inhabits. But, perhaps paradoxically, this desperation forms the complete background of the film narrative they generate.

So, for instance, in a film such as the Russian documentary *O Lubvi* (*About Love*, 2003) we are introduced to a cast of cute disabled kids going to school in a segregated special education environment. The subjects talk about the relationships between boys and girls (both heterosexual and 'agnostic'), define their understanding of 'love' and sexuality, etc. But like many in(ter)-

dependent disability films, *O Lubvi* is a celebration of Russian culture because the film features a celebration of their special education programmes; in fact, one could easily argue *O Lubvi* is, in fact, about the love of devoted teachers and extended family caregivers. It captures scenes of teachers carrying kids who can't walk to the chalkboard where they have to write their letters like everybody else. In portraying these scenes the film offers a truly beautiful vision of a supportive educational system focused, appropriately, on academics and socialisation for disabled children.

Yet, as the film unfolds, one might suddenly say to oneself: 'Oh, I understand, the content here is actually about the abandonment of disabled children and how common that neglectful situation has become.' Also, there's the fact that nations – this happens in the US as well as Russia – have to create these massive support systems in order to take up care for disabled children rejected by their families. Such children are commonly left at hospitals or in orphanages by their parents, or the parents just can't provide the level of care needed given lack of social supports and the economic demands on their lives: abandonment can now be recognised as part of contemporary austerity measures under neoliberalism. Likewise, *O Lubvi* also helps audiences take into account the commonality of men who leave relationships as a result of the birth of a disabled child.

On 28 December 2012 Russia's President Putin passed a law stating the country would no longer allow people in countries such as the United States to adopt Russian children … with the exception of disabled kids. Disabled children could continue to be adopted but all other Russian children were off the international adoption market. So everywhere in these films one finds an incredibly urgent, desperate situation informing their materials. And yet despite this hazardous social terrain, these films ease us into their materials with little fanfare; you could watch them without ever taking note of the desperate circumstances to which they give voice. In many ways these works encourage viewers to feel free to watch their narratives without attending to the alarm of social neglect and violence residing in the background. But, at bottom, independent disability cinema wants the seriousness of materials to slowly emerge and make an impression on audiences without throttling them, so to speak: this is their deal with the social devil of ableism in many ways. The urgency of the issues are downplayed in order to secure a wider general audience and/or to depend upon the knowledge nature of their audiences across in(ter)dependent disability film networks.

Since these films are often financed by nationally sponsored arts funding organisations, they are, to a certain extent, expressions of the state's desirability.

When we speak of in(ter)dependent disability films, we refer to predominantly video-based works created on low budgets (less than USD$100,000 but in many cases below USD$10,000) and without the backing of multi-national corporations that often promote other minority film festivals. Independent disability films derive largely from local community contexts but speak globally to people with disabilities living around the world. To some degree, one could extrapolate their collective message as a voicing of paternalistic states; they seem to say: 'We even take care of our disabled populations no matter how little they have to contribute to the robust life of the citizenry.'

The tenuous line that must be navigated between personal story and public critique is exemplified most powerfully in documentary films such as *goodnight, liberation* (2003) by the African American filmmaker Oriana Bolden, which serves as an example of what we refer to as 'Introduction to My Disability' films. Many films screened at disability film festivals are about introducing audiences to disability conditions through discussions of symptom clusters and the negotiation of stigmatising public responses. Collectively these work offer an entry into the unique experiences of living within non-normative bodies by saying, 'here's what it's like to exist in my particular kind of body'. Consequently, these works have an unabashedly diagnostic impulse behind them. Effectively they argue that if we understand a particular disability from the point of view of the bearer audiences will have an easier time relating with and accepting other disabled people who share a particular medical label.

This journey into a certain level of medical complexity represents a significant impulse in in(ter)dependent disability documentary films. Except that in the case of *goodnight, liberation*, Bolden's film gives you a taste of the 'Introduction to My Disability' genre only to turn the tables on the scenario completely. The documentary uses a search for the diagnosis of what is troubling the narrator physically (bleeding gums, unexplained bruises on her abdomen, chronic stomach upset) in order to expose a lack of systemic access to public healthcare in the United States. So once again a film such as *goodnight, liberation* reverses its more individualistic trajectory while having a serious message couched in minoritarian terms.

Alternative Disability Universes

A significant alternative to the 'Introduction to My Disability' genre (nearly always an expression of documentary form) are disability films that use all-disabled ensembles of actors. The employment of disabled actors proves highly uncommon in the US but, for instance, in the UK there is now a stipulation that companies may not hire a non-disabled actor to play a disability part. Among all of the things that such an employment practice allows is the creation of film worlds wherein the exclusionary isolation most people with disabilities experience is inverted. One may think this practice leads to the portrayal of significant stories about collective action (and this does happen to an extent such as in the first film discussed below). However, the works about alternative disability universes tend to narrate the tensions and fissures that exist across and between disability groupings.

For instance, in the ensemble cast of the short French fiction film *Sang Froid* (*Cold Blood*, 2002), one views deaf people cast as animalistic predators chasing a hysterical able-bodied human prey across a snowy landscape. The prey and predators arrive at a church near the end of the chase, the person being pursued hides behind a life-sized Jesus crucified on the cross, and much mayhem ensues. The deaf vampires are stopped at the sight of the cross as if the overwhelming Christianity of the symbol halts them from their pursuits (this is also a law of vampire films). After realising this protection, the once-pursued hearing character begins to laugh hysterically at the deaf vampires' inability to continue their attack. In the middle of a 360-degree shot things change and the vampires begin pointing and laughing at the Christ-like figure on the cross who comes to life with fanged teeth and devours the figure of their pursuit from above.

So no sanctuary within the religious setting is allowed and the church – which has been historically presumed as a social sanctuary for disabled people – turns out otherwise in this reversal of fortunes (and able-bodied to disabled bodies performance ratios). In fact, the film goes on to show other people asleep in their beds in a nearby rural village also being attacked in a similar way by smaller bronze-and-silver Jesuses jumping in commando-like fashion from their stations on tiny wooden crucifixes nailed above their beds for protection. The horrified shrieks of unsuspecting villagers fill the night air. There is nothing made of the fact that the vampires are deaf in the film but they survive while the hearing world continues to experience the assault of their own imprisoning religious tradition.

In general what one comes to understand about disability films is their primary emphasis on the removal of stigma from disabled bodies and the transfer of that social debasement onto those who would perpetuate it. They are, in other words, about depathologisation at their most basic level. Within such an effort to gather up those on the margins of the margins, the alternative disability universes on display in in(ter)dependent disability films expose cultural norms for what they really are: inelastic standards of homogeneity incapable of accommodating a wide array of human diversity. In contrast, international in(ter)dependent disability film festivals have become new spaces of social collectivity-making: as people with disabilities find themselves denied ways to narrate viable futures for themselves, in(ter)dependent disability cinema allows an exploration of alternative modes of transmission and the creative exploration of non-normative modes of being (see Kafer 2013: 2).

In a UK short such as Martin Taylor's *Berocca* (2005), the main story is told through interactions of an all-disabled cast. This genre of film (almost always fiction but usually drawing upon disabled actors who share congregate settings) often shows up at disability film festivals in the form of a plot puzzle. It's hard to say what many of these films are about as they thrive on experimental, allegorical and the mysteries of unfamiliar, non-normative life forms. *Berocca*, for instance, forwards a plot about a disabled guy with cerebral palsy who is illegally selling after-market Viagra to a pharmacist who also happens to be parenting a young boy. The young boy – who turns out to be the son of Kohl, the film's disabled protagonist – has been removed by the state to live with a foster family due to a charge of negligence on the part of Kohl who has no legal, gainful employment to support him. In undertaking this plot the film also points out that parenting a disabled child provides the basis for state removal of children from the home.

Near the conclusion Kohl and his mute companion (one is tempted to read the child as a symbolic fragment of the adult protagonist's psyche) arrive at the beach. The differences between the two characters prove intense: the father's neurological differences contrasting with the son's intensity of introspection and muteness (some reviews of the film identify the boy as autistic). Ultimately the film becomes about the struggle to identify, communicate and establish some meaningful connection between these two very different disabled bodies. The two characters inhabit distinct, and certainly not automatically overlapping, neuroatypical worlds and the challenge is to see if the film can create a bridge between them. This connection fails in some significant ways and one is left contemplating the degree to which disability film is about incomplete, imperfect and missed opportunities for connection between non-normative human actors.

The matter of minority group solidarity is at stake with respect to disabled people, disability communities and everyone who cares and works on these issues. The issue now plaguing various social movements is – and we want to argue this must be recognised as an alternative strength within crip/queer collectivities – the degree to which we can search for unity across differences without jettisoning their content-specific cargo. For instance, in the Scottish autism film *I'm in Away From Here* (2007), the audience awakens with Archie, suddenly and without warning along a Scottish beach. Signaled by distortions on the audio and video tracks, the world crashes in upon viewers as well as the protagonist; we cannot interpret the story amidst these sensorial intrusions coming from every direction. Disability films employ experimental narrative techniques such as these as ways to *simulate interior subjectivities* that offer access to disabled people's ways of experiencing the world directly.

The alternative disability universe of *I'm in Away From Here* helps to underscore a key element in the earlier film *Berocca*, in that they both attempt to situate audiences within the perspectives of their disabled characters. So, for instance, in the latter film we sensorily experience events through the autistic protagonist, Archie, in order to understand his life through a series of interruptions he experiences throughout his daily travels. Thus, the best way to describe the plot of this film might be through our exposure to the discomfort of the myriad intrusions that enter into his personal space. His inability to control these unwanted interruptions of his personal space become part of our own annoyance and hindrance to pleasure but they also provide an alternative simulation of embodiment as an opportunity to widen audience perspectives on this corner of the disability experience.

Early on in the film Archie takes up with a friend named Bruno, who also has a disability (likely CP and he uses a wheelchair) and they spend most of their days together within the limited options offered by life in a Day Centre. The two grow frustrated with the adherence to arbitrary rules, incomprehensible social cure and the deadening pursuits prescribed by the Day Centre staff. Rejecting these limited options they go off to pursue more adventurous worlds on their own – such as life at a nearby pub that includes Archie gambling on a brightly colored Lotto machine and sex with a prostitute for Bruno. As in the earlier films mentioned above, the two characters struggle to make a connection and at the conclusion they roll off toward the harbour with the sun glinting in the background and tell each other in a simple, yet reassuring manner something that the outside able-bodied world refuses to say: 'You're all right.' This sentiment is echoed by Archie's mother awaiting anxiously at the Day Centre when they return worried that her autistic son has walked off and the staff has no idea regarding his whereabouts. When his mother sees him return safely, her relief is spoken by words that echo Bruno's words: 'It's all right, Archie.'

In other words, the film asks us to contemplate whether a strictly regulated form of institutionalised care is necessary to protect disabled participants.

Like the other characters in the film, audiences are also reassured that Archie has his own strategies for navigating a turbulent life as others must negotiate them. Rather a socially paternalistic protectionism seems more on behalf of protection for the able-bodied world rather than the other way around.

Who Owns Disability Representations?

Even in mainstream media it's very uncommon to find stories about the relationship between mothers and daughters. As an example of the immersion and exposure to atypical lives that in(ter)dependent disability films offer, the short fiction film *What It Is Like To Be My Mother* (2007) uses a family drama to stage a now common political conflict about the necessity of policing the borders of disability representation between disabled people and non-disabled image-makers. In the film, a non-disabled daughter makes a film about the life of her newly disabled mother who is a double amputee. The film gets selected for screening at 'the last minute' by a disability arts festival in Warsaw and the story unfolds based on the mother's ensuing reluctance to allow her to screen her double amputee body for a public audience. A debate erupts about who owns the disability image and whether or not even an intimacy such as mother and daughter is enough to allow respectful entry into the disabled character's life.

During the festival screening of the film, the mother hastily rolls out of the theatre and decides to manually propel herself home (miles away from the theatre) in a torrential rainstorm. Whereas the mother's character appears relatively unlikable to this point of the film (both a bit tyrannical and exhibitionistic), she tells the daughter that she became upset while watching the film. The reason for this emotionality is that she realises how mature the daughter is becoming (certainly capable of telling her story in a moving way) and that she inevitably will have to leave her someday to pursue her own life.

As with all of the independent disability films discussed above, a real-life urgency at the bottom of the film emerges in that many disabled people – like the mother – need caregivers to navigate their lives and that care is often most effectively and comfortably provided by family members. The mother's prospects at developing her own romantic relationship appear slim. For instance, she tells her daughter a story about a disabled female friend of hers who is rejected by a male partner because 'he cannot trust himself to not leave her in ten years'. If she were not disabled, he explains, he would never have had this thought. Thus, the mother becomes suddenly more sympathetic in revealing these personal details and making herself vulnerable to the daughter.

In turn, the daughter – through whose eyes we have watched the action unfold – uses the opportunity of this private revelation to reject the mother's efforts at renewed intimacy between them. She calls her a 'stupid cow' and tells her taxi-cab driver, Yurek, that he should refuse to drive her around Poland in the future. In the culminating scene in the mother's bedroom after the emotion-filled night, the mother removes her prosthetic legs with great delicacy for the audience and asks the daughter to hug her. The daughter grows stiff and refuses to return the show of affection. A stalemate develops and the film ends in discomforting irresolution.

One of the things that disability film allows audiences to do is to comprehend the degree to which they allow us to sit with non-normative bodies in public spaces. Such an opportunity remains relatively rare in that we usually don't get to share public space with those with severe impairments. The fact that film is very much the kind of imaginative site where one can gain intimacy with people who inhabit different bodies and that opportunity, in-and-of-itself, is a very powerful political emphasis within disability film. If you go to disability film festivals you quickly realise that these works are global vehicles; they do not simply originate in the US or the UK or Australia, the usual triumvirate of disability 'savvy' western post-industrial nations. Instead, in(ter)dependent disability cinema represents a global phenomenon where disabled people think about what people within one national boundary have done to make their lives more manageable and then attempt to export some of those strategies to their home towns in order to affect transformations in their own local arenas.

We want to think about this wider principle of disability access and the creation of multiple accessible spaces as the advent of more habitable forms of living and environments for disabled people. Consequently, we've been arguing that we need to understand disability as a baseline model of interdependency rather than a tangential or exceptional situation. The kinds of inclusion on display in in(ter)dependent disability films are much more than outside efforts to include four or five more people in a culture; rather they help us think about disability as a foundational cultural model for re-imagining how human beings might inhabit the Earth together. In April 2015, during a presentation to a Chinese disability delegation at George Washington University (where we teach) we remarked: 'We're not particularly good at getting along with each other in the world, inhabiting the world with other human beings is not particularly our forte, and we think disability culture has something to teach us about that because of the degree to which interdependency is an in-built, very consciously created, intergenerational necessity.'

That value of in(ter)dependency is what disability culture has to teach us in a much wider sense about better inhabiting the Earth with each other. Thus, this unveiling of alternative possibilities within disability universes turns disability into not only a target of oppression, attitudinal prejudice and exclusions through social barriers, but rather a productive value of non-normative embodiment. Audiences discover alternative ethical maps by which to live their lives in contrast to the majority of others pursuing normative habitudes.

Afficionados of Human Variation

This innovative, alternative cultural value of interdependency also plays a key role in films about disability dance. We call the primary thematic of these films, 'disability in motion'. The works within this category prove significant in the sense that one often hears, 'Well, disabled people, they don't move and they certainly don't dance! We all know that.' In other words this is a foundational paradox at the heart of much independent disability film. One of the best examples of films sharing this central concern about disability movement is the British film *The Cost of Living* (2004), a work made by the UK mixed disabilities theatre and dance company DV8. All of the primary dancers and performers in DV8 have significant disabilities and that fact in and of itself makes DV8 an incredible originator. This film is one of the most powerful and interesting to come out of the independent disability cinema movement since 2000.

When we originally viewed this film we had the good fortune of watching it in the company of disability performance studies professor Carrie Sandahl from the University of Illinois at Chicago. As we were watching the film we were asking ourselves, 'Why is this film so amazing?' Carrie made this insightful comment: 'Watch the way the film uses the alternative bodily movements, rhythms, and flows of the disabled performance artists rather than the other way around [i.e. disabled peoples' bodies mimicking the movements of the more graceful able-bodied performers around them]. The plane of disabled existences and the movement of very disabled bodies sets the rhythm, the score, the shape, the texture of the film itself.' And that's one of the truly powerful things about the film.

The other thing we want to argue is that we began this chapter with an observation about the rare instance of inhabiting public space with disabled bodies. This observation is at the basis of most independent disability film. These events are now held all over the world in nearly every major urban cosmopolitan urban centre: Helsinki, Milan, London, Paris, Brazil, New Zealand, and there are several in the United States, Canada, Australia, and Japan. In other words independent disability film is a serious global phenomenon. And when you go to other disability film festivals, just like other events, they're like marathon events – events that no disabled person can quite do successfully! Three days of film programming, running disability film after disability film, they run for eight, nine, ten hours at a time, and by the end of the day one has to try to rest in order to struggle and endure the following day of programming.

But we think there's a powerful effect of spending that much time with disabled bodies in a theatre for that long. By the end of this continual exposure to non-normative bodies at the disability film festival one becomes a connoisseur of the body different. One starts to think of oneself as a kind of aficionado of human variation in much of its dissimulated richness in the outside world. One comes away from the disability film festival thinking: 'One of the values I took away from this experience was getting incredibly comfortable with the massive variation that human bodies show up in.'

Consider, for instance, Christian von Tippelskirch, who was the primary creator of the disability film *Invitation to Dance* (2014), which is a documentary about the life and times of disability scholar, activist and dance advocate Simi Linton. One of the most important things about a film such as *Invitation to Dance* is that filmmakers allow us to consider the fact that in many ways we don't know how to do this awkward, world-fragmenting dance of disability. Linton's film allows us to admit that and yet keep going with this invention as a guiding value. There are so few things in the world of able-bodiedness that can help disabled people more effectively manage their own lives. As Alison Kafer says in the film: 'We're all uncomfortable with the way our bodies move.'

At the 2010 Society of Disability Studies conference a flash dance erupted out in the main intersection of the campus. The impromptu event stopped traffic in order to allow disabled people to celebrate their bodies. The day after the conference ended the conference programme director was called to the Dean's office and asked why participants had been allowed to block a major intersection in order to perform outrageous displays of their bodies? This was one university administrator's response to one of the most successful disability studies conferences in the sense that the conference brought around five hundred disabled people, scholars, activists, advocates and allies to a major US university campus. The Dean made it clear during the meeting that he was livid about the whole 'spectacle', as he called it.

What struck us about this unexpected expression of outrage about the conference participants is that the world of disabled people continues to be experienced as the violation of powerful taboos about displaying the disabled body in public on disability terms. It's not an artifact of the past – this was the year 2010. And the event led to an incredibly complex, uncomfortable, harassing situation. This response accompanied, at the same time, an organisation of disabled people trying to create an alternative public space, a way of life that might prove more sustaining, creative and enjoyable than anything that non-disabled culture would provide for them. The flash dance offered nothing less than a glimpse at an alternative way to be disabled in the world. *Invitation to Dance* takes up this very project in a serious, unfinished, imperfect pursuit of crip/queer bodies, almost like a Cubist experiment. As Rosemarie Garland-Thomson says on screen: 'This is broadest invitation to dance that has ever been issued in the history of the world!' Yet it turns out to be an incredibly fraught subject in so many ways.

Disability movements (including the independent international film festivals they help spawn) have to re-imagine exclusionary public spaces including alternative theatre seating layouts, presentation formats and projection techniques. Yet, ultimately, what independent disability film seeks to target is the domain of public consciousness. It's one thing to be able to get on the bus and enter into public space – this is a huge innovation of global disability rights movements – but it's another to change the attitudinal reception of disabled peoples' entry into the world. Film, ultimately, tries to transform the realm of public consciousness. The medium tries to change our perspective by giving us access to disabled peoples' subjectivities. It's this targeting of the attitudinal domain that's so difficult to get at from anywhere other than art. Getting disabled people into the public is definitely part of this transformation; just the fact of getting us to share public space in a way that has rarely happened in history is part of the change of our moment. It's the reason why the disability rights movement is so significant to the way we live now (to borrow the theme of Germany's 2007 disability short film festival). However, in and of itself, that's not enough. There's an entire other domain that's often off limits to us: how do we affect peoples' belief systems, the attitudes, their ideas and their conceptualisation of people with disabilities? That's where we see film's most significant, potential innovation.

One last point on which to end regarding the accessibility of film festivals to disabled people. Films, like other products such as books once one produces them, have a life of their own. They go out into the world without you, like children or students, and you don't always know how they'll turn out or how they will be received. Getting disabled people to a film festival such as the one in Grand Rapids, Michigan is very difficult. Many people can't travel; if you travel on airlines they commonly damage power wheelchairs due to inadequate handling procedures – there's a great deal one has to exchange in order to participate in it. One of the things about film is that it travels in a rectangular box on a round disc. So it goes really easily without the participants in an envelope. We think this is one of the key reasons why disability film festivals have become so significant – they offer a kind of tiny mobility across national borders that disabled people themselves do not enjoy. If you try to move across borders as a disabled person, as we did in March 2015 with a group of students studying the T4 Program in Germany, you could find yourself pulled out of line by a guard suggesting a BiPAP machine might have a bomb in it. You might find yourself (as we did) taken off into an interrogation room and nearly made to miss your flight. Disability film festivals serve as a key way in which disabled people might be able to communicate through the physical barriers of mass transit inaccessibility, intensive immigration restrictions and poverty.

But even all of those hassles aside, we'd rather see the world and participate in it than observe it from the sidelines where so many disabled people are sequestered. That risk of going out into the world is worth it, but it's highly draining at the same time. So when that cannot happen film also does that for us. It gets disabled people into the space with an audience and gives us access to their lives. An intimacy with disabled persons' perspectives becomes available even when they live in radically divergent corners of the globe.

Conclusion

While each film discussed here wrestles with its own particular struggles with ableist nationalist practices and beliefs, its own ensnarement within neoliberal orders of reproductive sameness resulting from more meagre forms of inclusion, the ensemble of films available for viewing across the space of multi-day international film festivals significantly pluralise encounters with human variations. They tend toward a diminishment of audience alienation with embodied differences while avoiding the alternative problem of flattening the field with platitudes of claims to universally shared identities in disability. We suggest, in drawing upon these multivalent media portrayals of disability in various global locations, that the exploration of subjectivities wrought within neoliberalism unveil alternative possibilities for an ethics of living interdependently with others developed within disability subcultures.

Such plumbings of experiential navigations involve the opening up of formerly prohibited interactions based on sexuality, body care, arts/cultural programming, shared access to public and private spaces, intrusions upon bodies and the ambivalences of disability inclusion projects. In each of the examples provided, disability 'failures' to meet ableist expectations result in inversions that challenge the assumed positivity of heteronormative practices, beliefs and capacities provisioned for able bodies.

FILMOGRAPHY

Bolden, Oriana (dir) (2003) *goodnight, liberation*. 7 minutes. USA.
Lance, Stephen (dir) (2008) *Yolk*. 14 minutes. Head Pictures. Australia.
Levacher, Pierre-Louis (dir) (2002) *Sang Froid (Cold Blood)*. 6 minutes. France.
MacInnes, Catrona (dir) (2007) *I'm in Away From Here*. 16 minutes. Scotland.
McGettigan, Norah (dir) (2007) *What It Is Like To Be My Mother*. 30 minutes. Poland.
Murphy, Ryan (dir) (2014) *American Horror Story: Freak Show*: 'Photo's Bullseye'; Episode 5, Season 4. 52 minutes. USA.
Newsom, Lloyd (dir) (2004) *The Cost of Living*. DV8 Films Ltd. 35 minutes. UK.
Shakhverdiev, Tofik (dir) (2003) *O Lubvi (About Love)*. 26 minutes. Russia.
Taylor, Martin (dir) (2005) *Berocca*. 13 minutes. UK.
Von Tippelskirch, Christian (dir) (2014) *Invitation to Dance*. 86 minutes. USA.

BIBLIOGRAPHY

Kafer, Alison (2013) *Feminist, Queer, Crip*. Bloomington, IN: University of Indiana Press.
Mitchell, David T. with Sharon L. Snyder (2015) *The Biopolitics of Disability: Neoliberalism, Ablenationalism, and Peripheral Embodiment*. Ann Arbor, MI: University of Michigan Press.
Siebers, Tobin (2012) 'A Sexual Culture for Disabled People', in Robert McRuer and Anna Mollow (eds) *Sex and Disability*. Durham, NC: Duke University Press, 37–52.
Snyder, Sharon L. and David T. Mitchell (2006) *Cultural Locations of Disability*. Chicago, IL: University of Chicago Press.

'Beyond Forgiveness'?

Lee Chang-dong's *Oasis* (2002) and the Mobilisation of Disability Discourses in the Korean New Wave

Paul Petrovic

While South Korean filmmaker Lee Chang-dong's films are central to the narrative of the new *hallyu* of Korean cinema, specific critical narratives unfold depending on which of Lee's films receives consideration. His breakthrough, *Bakha Satang* (*Peppermint Candy*, 1999), a film that moves backwards from the IMF economic crisis of 1997 to the military's aggressive suppression of the 1980 Gwangju Uprising, remains the work that has attracted the most scholarly attention. The majority of criticism analyses its innovative approach to reverse-chronology narration even as the film highlights the impotence of individual masculinity amidst South Korea's contemporary history.[1] Critics often judge Lee's filmography by foregrounding his early films' insistence on their male protagonist's traumatic experience. Soyoung Kim, for example, contends that *Peppermint Candy* is 'predicated on male trauma, privileging a sense of a gendered trauma of Korean society, rather than universal human trauma. This gendered trauma, hidden under the veil of universalist narration and the weight of history, prevents women's trauma from being exposed' (2010: 180). However, Lee's films have undergone a gender inversion.

The tropes of masculinity and male anxiety that foreground Lee's first two films *Chorok Mulgogi* (*Green Fish*, 1997) and *Peppermint Candy*, which critic Kyung Hyun Kim explores expertly in *The Remasculinization of Korean Cinema*, contract as Lee expands his oeuvre (2004: 45). *Milyang* (*Secret Sunshine*, 2007) and *Shi* (*Poetry*, 2010), Lee's two most recent films at the time of writing, concentrate on women's experiences and relegate male trauma to the margins. As a result, *Oasiseu* (*Oasis*, 2002) exists as the connective tissue between these two gendered modalities, simultaneously spotlighting a male crisis while anticipating a more expansive take on female subjectivity. *Oasis* frames discourses of disability, especially visual rhetorics of physical disability, articulating a longing for societal acceptance for those non-able-bodied citizens ostracised by their family, community and nation even as those same forces materially prey upon them. To dismiss the film, then, as advocating for a male hegemony or power fantasy alone, as a first reading may suggest, is to overlook the rigour with which it indicts a patriarchal system of abuse.

As *Oasis* begins to be critically understood within the apparatus of disability studies, seen especially in the scholarly work of Eunjung Kim and Katarzyna Rukojć, its reception has been likewise marked by opposition. This critical perspective is perhaps not unexpected. Lee's film, concerning the relationship between the mentally stunted ex-con Hong Jong-du (Sol Kyung-gu) and the physically handicapped Han Gong-ju (Moon So-ri), who has cerebral palsy, is abrasive and inherently problematic, framed around an attempted rape that then develops into a romantic relationship. *Oasis*'s sexual politics deserve to appear at the head of any discussion of the film, as do Gong-ju's five separate fantasy sequences where she transforms reality and often re-imagines herself as able-bodied. Often filmed as single-takes, these sequences amend the inherent melodrama of such wish-fulfilment, but nonetheless open up Lee's film to charges of victim-blaming. *Oasis*'s filmic challenge with these sequences lies in the uneasy balance they establish between subjective representation and the semblance of desire regulated through normative bodily experiences, such as flirting, dancing and singing. Yet more nuanced criticism on *Oasis* is needed to complicate the early readings on the film since these treatments often neglect key particulars of the narrative structure. For example, Gong-ju does not at first conjure for herself greater command of her voice or mental intelligence in these fantasy sequences. Rather, the only change in her character in these scenes is her ability to stand and clarify intent that she already possesses. Her last fantasy sequence even incorporates the wheelchair that has been an avatar of her disability throughout the film, but, significantly, relocates Jong-du as the necessary recipient for the device. This transplanting of physical agency, with Jong-du represented as the disabled occupant, allows Lee to critique the constructedness of essentialist privilege.

The push to protect minorities' rights has been central in contemporary South Korea. Nonetheless, rhetorical gaps and areas of slippage have proliferated in the rush to secure protection for those with disabilities. Disabilities critic Eunjung Kim, for one, laments how the 2006 National Human Rights Commission of the Republic of Korea defines disability 'as the complete lack of capability' (2009: 231). This designation lobotomises the selfhood of those with physical disabilities and codifies a negative value onto those with mental handicaps. These citizens are thereby cast as marginal subjects, reified as vulnerable and lacking power. Representing disability on film carries with it a great responsibility since film is a cultural apparatus that legitimises cultural practices, including how the Other, that is, the non-normative, is perceived. With a transgressor like Lee Chang-dong, however, film can also criticise the societal conditions that lead to what Harlan Hahn terms the 'asexual objectification' (in Garland-Thomson 2002: 18) of those with disabilities. Lee's film works to record the abject powerlessness that the disabled can feel, and though it relies on normalising the disabled body via fantasy to secure a romantic courtship, *Oasis* pointedly refuses to represent sexual intimacy through the façade of a fantasy sequence. Jong-du's early attempted rape captures the grotesque brutality of sexual assault on people who cannot easily repel such attacks. Similarly, the culminating sex scene that testifies to the fulfilment of their courtship is misinterpreted by Gong-ju's family, who walk in to celebrate her birthday, precisely because they cannot fathom subjective desires for sex in Gong-ju. *Oasis* thus records the cultural and social abuse that lead to Jong-du and Gong-ju's status as marginalised subjects, documenting the caustic reaction that the disabled receive from Korean society.

A summary of the film is necessary before continuing. It opens on Jong-du, who has been released from prison after serving a sentence for a hit-and-run killing that, in point of fact, his elder brother committed. Even after Jong-du receives a brick of tofu from a kind storeowner, a cultural tradition connoting society's offering of a fresh new start to ex-convicts (see Fenkl 2007: 340), his family continues to view him as a social pariah. Lerita Coleman Brown highlights how inhibiting is the general stigmatisation 'of treating people, such as the ex-con and ex-mental patient who are attempting to reintegrate themselves into society, as if they still had the stigma' (2013: 154). Jong-du struggles to navigate within this toxic climate and, in a spectacular bid of misunderstanding, elects to visit the family home of the man 'he' killed, bearing flowers and asking forgiveness. There, he sees Gong-ju and her brother Sang-shik, the latter of whom is understandably disturbed and runs him off. The apartment where she stays is a suburban space that has atrophied, becoming a place of waste and decay. Lee frames the space so that whenever Jong-du walks up the stairway to Gong-ju's apartment, someone is always leaving or transitioning away from the building. Jong-du returns, sensing some connection with Gong-ju, and tries to force himself upon her. When she passes out, he flees. Gong-ju, for her part, has been preyed upon by her brother and his wife for the monetary benefits paid out by the South Korean government to the disabled. Her brother co-opts the house that the state provides, designates that space for himself and his family and deposits Gong-ju in the squalid apartment complex where she starts the film, visiting only rarely, paying a neighbour to look in on her. Those neighbours, though, look upon Gong-ju as subhuman and use her apartment for their own ends, having sex in front of her. That encounter causes Gong-ju to sift through her emotions regarding Jong-du's attack on her, and she calls him up and invites him back to the apartment. From there, their relationship nurtures, to such an extent that Jong-du introduces her to a family birthday celebration for his mother, generating distaste from his elder brother. When they finally culminate their relationship sexually, Gong-ju's family walks in on them and call the police; Jong-du is arrested and the film ends with him corresponding with her by mail while Gong-ju cleans the apartment.

Most pieces of scholarship on *Oasis* compartmentalise their analysis of Lee's film into cross-cultural studies of disability-related issues. Eunjung Kim and Katarzyna Rukojć operate within this critical lens, submitting comparative readings on how gender and the nation-state complicate *Oasis* amidst other texts. Their critical approach, however, runs the risk of denying them the room necessary to register and respond to more minute aspects of the filmic text. In their assessment concerning the representation of disability in the film, Kim and Rukojć do not analyse how the cinematic elements of the film challenge, synthesise or complicate earlier iterations of disability within the narrative structure of *Oasis*. These moments, however, are vital in documenting how *Oasis* resurrects a counter-narrative to the repressed silence imposed on them by society and family. For example, Kim Young-jin, a Korean film critic, suggests that *Oasis* 'is not stylized' (2007: 36), but that contention neglects how Lee's film utilises the quotidian nature of urban environment to signify how these characters are segmented apart from it.

Oasis announces its concern for Seoul's social milieu in its opening frames, focusing on newly released convict Jong-du as he gazes out of a bus window while the cityscape reflects in the window. Cinematically, this scene operates as shorthand for Jong-du and his re-entrance into an alienated city, where the physical boundaries of the bus obstruct any organic engagement with the

Fig. 1: Jong-du on the bus, partitioned from the city around him.

culture. The visuals that Jong-du sees are at a remove, partitioned by the bus windows so that he is passive and immediately positioned apart from the city culture, even as he longs to integrate himself back into the nation. This sense echoes midway through the film, when Gong-ju's brother and sister-in-law take her from her dank apartment; stricken with continual spasms, she presses against the car window and gazes out at a world that her family denies her from knowing. After Sang-shik presents Gong-ju in front of state officials and pacifies them that the funds they allocate to him are a material benefit to Gong-Ju, he discards her back in the apartment. When she cannot fulfill any economic purpose, her brother's apathy is transparent, for he states curtly: 'Call me if the neighbours don't feed you properly or anything else.' Her resignation to this embarrassing reality is evident, as she struggles to articulate her first translated words: 'Alright, you go now.' In each circumstance before they meet each other, Jong-du and Gong-ju acquiesce to a worldview in which they are tossed and flung about, relegated to insignificance by their families because of their respective disabilities.

While *Oasis* charts the ways in which the South Korean nation does not step in to repel the stigma levelled at those with disabilities, the film's biggest perpetrator remains the prejudiced and predatory capitalistic family across South Korean society. Rukojć contends that such a shift 'points out that the misuse is on the side of the family, whereas the Korean Government does a lot to provide decent standard of living and rehabilitation. The State guarantees accommodation, money in a form of a disability pension and, most of all, it ensures that there is and will be a guardian in the vicinity of the disabled one' (2013: 345). In this manner, Lee's film refuses to objectively lessen the experience of the disabled. Rather, it is the family members alone who revel in devaluing and marginalising their kin. This negotiation allows *Oasis* and Lee's script a narrative pathway in which to record interactions but never to justify their fallow perspective. Lee's films since *Oasis* – that is, *Secret Sunshine* and *Poetry* – have similarly defended the marginalised in the face of overwhelming misconduct and oppression.

For her part, Gong-ju especially internalises the projections of shame and humiliation emanating from her family. Susan Wendell powerfully writes about the disabled body in order to assess the discomfiture that can arise, for 'disabled people can participate in marginalizing ourselves. We can wish for bodies we do not have, with frustration, shame, self-hatred. We can feel trapped in the negative body; it is our internalized oppression to feel this' (1989: 113). Gong-ju's fantasising an able-bodied persona for herself epitomises this trend, but *Oasis* also wisely circumvents the disability-related issues with this ethical choice when Gong-ju stops relying on the fantasy sequences to represent her romantic awakening. Her refusal to embed reality within the regulatory politics of subjective fantasy during the mutually desired sex with Jong-du testifies to her newfound acceptance and delight in her body. As Brown writes: 'For stigmatized people, the idea of normality takes on an exaggerated importance. Normality becomes the supreme goal for many stigmatized individuals until they realize that there is no precise definition of normality except what they would be without their stigma' (2013: 155). In *Oasis*, Gong-ju negotiates a path for herself away from what she had perceived as the essentialist negativity levelled at the disabled.

In order to understand the ways in which social economies are working within Lee's film, it is wise to first contextualise how network societies – which is to say, global capitalist societies – segment and territorialise first identity and then social relations. In his text *The Power of Identity*, social theorist Manuel Castells conceives of identity as 'arrangements between individuals and ... institutions and organizations', wherein the root of identity is negotiated through a 'process of individuation', becoming an identity 'only when and if social actors internalize them, and construct their meaning around this internalization' (1997: 7). At the time in which people certify their identity, they typically lock themselves into that relationship with the social collective. Castells sees this range of identity as a triangulation, offering three main types, or forms, of identity building: legitimising identity, resistance identity and project identity, though this last form is least possible in the stratified world that *Oasis* chronicles. As such, this chapter focuses more on the other two forms, since Jong-du and Gong-ju attain project identity only briefly before the dominating institutions of society shove them back into an inferior social economy. The sense of a constant regulation that enforces lesser identities is key to Castells as he summarises the principles between the earlier forms: 'legitimizing identity: introduced by the dominant institutions of society to extend and rationalize their domination *vis à vis* social actors' (1997: 2). The second form is summarised as a 'resistance identity: generated by those actors that are in positions/conditions devalued and/or stigmatized by the logic of domination' (1997: 8). Insofar as society allocates agency to these actors, society nonetheless polices that sense of power, so that disabled individuals remain overmatched by the social relations that circumscribe their internalised identity. Tying Castells' theorising into Lee's *Oasis*, then, allows us to see Jong-du and Gong-ju as confined to the embryonic stage of resistance identity, always delineated and exerted upon by societal and institutional forces.

Indeed, Jong-du's family similarly alienates him from its social and cultural economy. They try to secure him a job as a food deliveryman, thereby ingraining in him the ethos of a legitimising identity, but Lee films the scene in a way that repudiates any sense of familial attachment. Jong-du is nothing to them other than the capital that he might bring them. His eldest brother, Jong-il, verbally ridicules Jong-du at the job interview in front of his new boss, verifying that he is only suffering Jong-du's existence. Indeed, Jong-il positions Jong-du as an adult, yet he maligns Jong-du's mental faculties, locking him into a liminal space, a liminal economy. Jong-du wipes out the work delivery motorcycle on a night excursion chasing down a production crew filming an ostentatious car sequence that bears no semblance to the reality that he and other marginalised citizens recognise. This transgression ends his job prospects, and his sister-in-law cleans the blood and grime from his knees and matter-of-factly tells him: 'I'm sorry to tell you this [but] I really don't like you' [and that] with you out of the way, I felt good about life.' During this confession Jong-du's mother sits and silently watches the television, symbolically forsaking her son. Even the sister-in-law's candid critique is not an authentic representation of honesty, for her reproach is regulated by the fact that it does not occur until after Jong-du proves incapable of bettering their social condition. Only after she receives validation that Jong-du is an unstable worker does she articulate her coldness towards him. Thereafter, Jong-du's family divorce themselves from direct contact with him by coercing him to stay the nights at his brother's car repair shop.

Amidst Jong-du's victimisation at the hands of his family, his attempted rape of Gong-ju can seem accidental rather than part of a pathological repetition. However, Jong-du has exhibited dangerous social mannerisms before. His legal record includes bouts of indecency and attempted rape, and early in the film he leers at two teenage schoolgirls giggling on a pay phone. *Oasis* also highlights the potential threat of Jong-du by showcasing him threatening a woman on the street for a cell phone. *Oasis* challenges spectators because the film never reconciles whether Jong-du's legal charges were misinterpreted by a society that never noticed his mental inhibitions enough to pardon his oddness or whether they were legitimate transgressions. Eunjung Kim adopts this latter reading and assesses how that perspective leads to the film's representation of Gong-ju, such as how 'the non-disabled audience is supposed to see the attack as one of the benign mistakes of a fool that makes his antisocial characteristics more humane' (2010: 150). Kim, though, glosses over particular moments of agency that are afforded to Gong-ju's character. For example, after Gong-ju calls Jong-du back to her dilapidated apartment, he expresses misgivings and yearns to be pardoned for his attempted sexual assault. He promises to relax 'Only if you'll say you forgive me'. However, Gong-ju never affords him this luxury. She remains silent on this issue and even though the two move on approximating a normal romantic relationship, his efforts are always predicated on his earlier interaction with Gong-ju. Jong-du's treatment of her thereafter is as a real subject, wherein she is not marginalised or used for profit through any social exchange, and leads to his assertion that 'From now on I'm going to call you Your Highness'. Gong-ju returns the honorific terminology, giggling as she says that 'Then I will call you … General'. This consideration is not intended sardonically but is instead an investment in constituting each other apart from the cultural logic of Seoul's stratified society. Indeed, during this encounter, Lee's camera appraises them in a medium long shot, with Jong-du and Gong-ju each afforded half of the frame. This shot places them on equal footing, a setting which *Oasis* maintains for the rest of its duration.

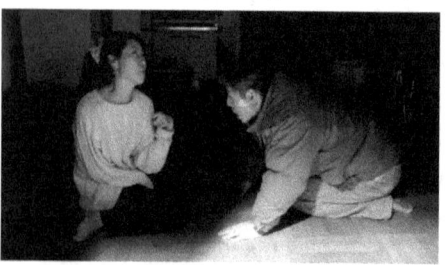

Fig. 2: Gong-ju and Jong-du occupy equal placement in the frame.

In turn, Jong-du and Gong-ju demonstrate in this sequence the strongest correlative back to Castells' third form of identity building: 'project identity: when social actors, on the basis of whichever cultural materials are available to them, build a new identity that redefines their position in society in society and, by so doing, seek the transformation of overall social structure' (1997: 8). Jong-du not only re-names Gong-ju, reconstructing and prioritising her worth in his social imagination apart from her disability, but he also begins to entrench in himself economies of authentic behaviour. Afterward, the two go onto the apartment's rooftop, which is the first sense of spatial liberation that she experiences. Lee's camera frames her smiling through the cerebral palsy as she gazes up at the expansiveness of the open blue sky. This moment is not only spatially transformative, for here Jong-du is seen counteracting any aggressiveness as the two discursively find in each other the real sense of interdependence, wherein they mobilise a resistance to the orthodoxy.

Even as Jong-du and Gong-ju mobilise their strength, though, the hegemonic social institutions work to regulate differentials of power and exploit their authority over these disabled outcasts. Representing just one instance is a scene that explicitly renders the city culture of Seoul itself as repudiating any legitimate connection to Jong-du and Gong-ju. When the two enter a restaurant and settle in to be served, a waitress comes over to them and deprives them of the ability to eat there, manufacturing a claim about closing after lunch in order to circumvent their customers having to endure the sight of Gong-ju in spasm. Here the restaurant asserts full hierarchal exertion, territorialising its social economy as the antithesis of Jong-du and Gong-ju's marginalised culture. Though Jong-du lingers in the restaurant and incenses a few customers, the two devalued outcasts ultimately settle on a meal delivered to his brother's car repair shop, accepting of their alienated cultural status.

Gong-ju orchestrates a fantasy sequence here, disrupting the social realist space that otherwise informs her fears and anxieties. The first instance was benign enough, with Gong-ju early on playing with sunlight with a broken handheld mirror in her apartment. Spots of light project onto the ceiling from the mirror and transform from objective reality, reflecting the outside sunlight, to subjective reality, with the spots mutating into doves or butterflies in flight. Other instances have her imagining herself healed from her cerebral palsy and innocently flirting with Jong-du in the subway or in his brother's car repair shop. This latter incident, however, is more complicated than it first appears. Kyung Hyun Kim writes how this scene compounds exclusively realist expectation, since spectators must reconcile 'the fact that the boundary between reality and fantasy has collapsed (the reality in which Jong-du is talking on the phone merges with the fantasy in which Gong-ju gets out of her wheelchair and walks), but Jong-du must also participate in Gong-ju's illusion in order to fully realize their romantic union' (2011: 160). In turn, *Oasis* complicates the strictly subjective, and thus essentialist, perspective that it had earlier adopted regarding Gong-ju's internalisation of fantasy. As Jong-du likewise places himself into this reverie, the film situates how Gong-ju's fantasy pervades and incorporates his subjective experience into it as well. The last two instances are the most exhaustive fantasy sequences and utilise single-takes with Gong-ju kissing Jong-du while real-life images of an oasis art tapestry dance around them or have her placing Jong-du into her wheelchair and singing him a South Korean pop song.

This final fantasy sequence also adds a layer in that Gong-ju places Jong-du in the wheelchair and definitively treats his condition as worthy of the same victimisation status that are more overtly signalised in Gong-ju's physical

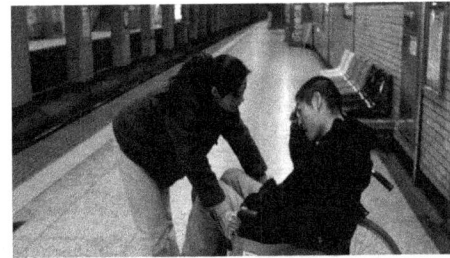

Fig. 3: Gong-ju places Jong-du in her wheelchair and highlights the constructedness of disability.

appearance. Lee's approach with a single-take legitimises the unity between Gong-ju's and Jong-du's representational space, signifying an alternate economy of knowledge that cannot be otherwise objectively revealed.

When Jong-du brings Gong-ju to his mother's birthday in a surprise that makes public his attraction to her, Lee's script engineers the first true revelation of the narrative. Jong-du's intentions here may be virtuous, for he is not physically cognisant of any social repercussions or discomfiture, but for Lee they also act as an ideological indictment. When Jong-du's brothers object to her presence, he validates his decision to bring her because he felt guilty. Jong-il, however, responds by saying: 'If anyone should feel guilty, it should be me!' The film in turn discloses its chief narrative conceit, that Jong-du accepted jail time for the hit-and-run in order to save his older brother's business prospects in the city. In this personal acquiescence to better the family name, *Oasis* situates how Hong's family produces authenticity. To return to Castells' phrasing, with the family having conceived of Jong-il as a legitimising identity, it falls on Jong-du to assume the social stigmatisation and feign liability.

Jong-du's younger brother, Jong-sae, while ostensibly a gentler relative who is willing to engage his disabled brother, administers a harsh psychological rebuke in private. As he tells Jong-du, shadowed by Jong-il: 'Listen to me carefully. No one forced you to go to prison. You volunteered, didn't you? After Jong-il ran over that guy, you were the first to say it. That he had a family to feed and had a future. So you'd go in for him. You also said you had prior convictions, had no job. And knew the way to jail. Isn't that what you said?' Jong-sae underpins his rhetoric so that Jong-du is presented with false agency, colouring Jong-du's decision, deceptively, as being his own. This subterfuge ultimately allows Jong-sae the ability to act with more aggression and underhanded belligerence toward his brother. Jong-du's self-sacrifice, then, is not merely a familial decision, but it is also an institutional decision, so that, as Castells writes, matters of inequality are normalised through a 'political logic' (1978: 19). By authoring Jong-du's liability, which includes with it all the various prescripts of social construction, the Hong family retains the larger family unit, sacrificing their underachieving, disabled sibling and in turn projecting publicly their resentment of him so that both Jong-du and Gong-ju are ostracised from the dinner.

Lee's directorial choices embed a symbolic echo in this larger narrative event. During the family's birthday celebration for Jong-du's mother, a young child in a white sweater and blue cap sits in a chair, his face slack-jawed and altogether ignored. This character, who has no lines in the film, nonetheless operates as another indictment regarding the position of the disabled in

South Korean society: he is physically present but effectively eliminated from their public record. When the family gathers together for a picture to commemorate the occasion, this child never appears, a cultural omission itself occasioned by the family's refusal to incorporate Otherness into their record. Jong-du's attempt to include Gong-ju in the picture as his significant other is similar rebuffed. The disabled are denied access to the cultural record by those who perpetuate their own legitimacy.

Late that night, Gong-ju stops Jong-du from leaving her apartment to catch the bus home and instead asks him to sleep with her, entreating him with the pained statement: 'You said I was quite pretty.' Jong-du acquiesces to her plea and the two make love. As it happens, though, the day is her birthday and Gong-ju's brother shows up with both a guilty conscience and a birthday cake. Naturally, when he and his wife stumble upon his sister's intimacy they misinterpret it as rape and the institutional domination again rises up to suppress Gong-ju and Jong-du's redefined and liberated identities. While the rage he feels at his sister's perceived violation is authentic, it can also be read more simply as guarding his sacred cash-cow, for the operating profit that he secures from her habitual encounters with the city officials sustains him and his wife. This economic sense is further facilitated at the police station, where Gong-ju's brother talks to Jong-du's brothers about compensation for his sister's emotional anguish, trying to transfigure emotional scars into economic profit. Tellingly, Jong-du's family does not mention any prior exposure on their part to Gong-ju, faking innocence to the whole affair and abandoning him to the police bureaucracy; worse, Gong-ju's brother ends up trying to coax capital from the man who genuinely murdered his father, even as Jong-il declares that Jong-du has gone 'beyond forgiveness', an irony that is built into Lee's narrative.

Jong-du is able to get his handcuffs removed and flees the jail cell through an act of serendipity predicated on manipulating a pastor's trust. Escaping to the streets, there is little surprise that he returns to Gong-ju's even if he cannot visit her directly. Early in the narrative Gong-ju had complained about how a tree perpetually scrapes against her apartment window and terrorises her at night, stretching out its shadows over the tranquil oasis art tapestry that she finds solace in, and indeed the opening credits focus on this abstract scene. Thus, the tree becomes the catalyst for effecting change. Armed with a handsaw, Jong-du cuts off each tree branch that threatens to terrorise her, hailing her with ecstatic shouts of 'Your Highness!' Lee's camera flashes back to Gong-ju, giddy by her window, and she communicates to him by turning up a pop song on her radio. In this way, despite the physical partitions of society that keep them apart, a metaphor that *Oasis* invoked in the opening images with Jong-du on the bus, the two nonetheless resist the social institutions and organisations together. While the tree branches are admittedly a small gesture, they allow him a last act of mobilisation against the prevailing social economies, enabling him to reclaim the project identity that he had had denied by those around him before the police haul him away.

Lee's film, then, examines not just the characterisation of the disempowered in *Oasis*, but also interrogates the ways in which the social economies of Seoul construct and stratify the weak and vulnerable. As Saskia Sassen concludes in her text *Cities in a World Economy*, the global city, which Seoul now belongs to, concentrates 'a disproportionate share [of corporate power on] the disadvantaged and [is] one of the key sites for their devalorization' (2006: 198). In legitimising their corporate and institutional identity, social economies monopolise the national consciousness and frame the traditional narrative. As one of the foremost films in the Korean New Wave, *Oasis* works as a filmic depiction of Jean-François Lyotard's famous declaration of an 'incredulity toward metanarratives' (1984: xxiv). Rather than letting the social and corporate forces gentrify their depiction of the marginalised, *Oasis* acts as a counter-narrative to the social hegemony, privileging the authenticity found in disabled, marginalised society rather than the fakery that is dominant in the city economy. Ultimately, Lee Chang-dong's film does not uncritically study the conditions or discourses of disability. Rather, *Oasis* works to underscore how the context of disability can overpower social realist conventions and strengthen the partnership and communion of knowing another with disabilities. Jong-du and Gong-ju are both resistant in small ways to the domination inherent to society, and together author a discourse of cultural resistance.

NOTE

1   See criticism by Chung and Diffrient (2007), McGowan (2007) and Choe (2008), among others.

FILMOGRAPHY

Chang-dong, Lee (dir) (1997) *Chorok Mulgogi (Green Fish)*. 111 minutes. CJ Entertainment/ East Film Company. South Korea.
____ (dir) (1999) *Bakha Satang (Peppermint Candy)*. 129 minutes. East Film Company. South Korea.

___ (dir) (2002) *Oasiseu* (*Oasis*). 133 minutes. UniKorea Pictures/East Film Company. South Korea.

___ (dir) (2007) *Milyang* (*Secret Sunshine*). 142 minutes. CJ Entertainment/Pine House Film. South Korea.

___ (dir) (2010) *Shi* (*Poetry*). 139 minutes. UniKorea Pictures/Pine House Film. South Korea.

BIBLIOGRAPHY

Brown, Lerita Coleman (2013) 'Stigma: An Enigma Demystified', in Lennard J. Davis (ed.) *The Disability Studies Reader*, 4th ed. New York, NY: Routledge, 147–60.

Castells, Manuel (1978) *City, Class and Power*, Elizabeth Lebas (trans). London: Macmillan Press.

___ (1997) *The Power of Identity*. Malden, MA: Blackwell.

Choe, Steve (2008) 'Catastrophe and Finitude in Lee Chang Dong's *Peppermint Candy*: Temporality, Narrative, and Korean History', *Post Script: Essays in Film and the Humanities*, 27, 3, 132–44.

Chung, Hye Seung and David Scott Diffrient (2007) 'Forgetting to Remember, Remembering to Forget: The Politics of Memory and Modernity in the Fractured Films of Lee Chang-dong and Hong Sang-soo', in Frances Gateward (ed.) *Seoul Searching: Culture and Identity in Contemporary Korean Cinema*. Albany, NY: State University of New York Press, 115–39.

Fenkl, Heinz Insu (2007) 'On the Narratography of Lee Chang-dong: A Long Translator's Note', *Azalea: Journal of Korean Literature & Culture*, 1, 338–56.

Garland-Thomson, Rosemarie (2002) 'Integrating Disability, Transforming Feminist Theory', *NWSA Journal*, 14, 3, 1–32.

Kim, Eunjung (2009) 'Minority Politics in Korea: Disability, Interraciality, and Gender', in Emily Grabham, Davina Cooper, Jane Krishnadas and Didi Herman (eds) *Intersectionality and Beyond: Law, Power and the Politics of Location*. Abingdon: Routledge Cavendish, 230–50.

___ (2010) '"A Man with the Same Feelings": Disability, Humanity, and Heterosexual Apparatus in *Breaking the Waves*, *Born on the Fourth of July*, *Breathing Lessons*, and *Oasis*', in Sally Chivers and Nicole Markotic (eds) *The Problem Body: Projecting Disability on Film*. Columbus, OH: Ohio State University Press, 131–56.

Kim, Kyung Hyun (2004) *The Remasculinization of Korean Cinema*. Durham, NC: Duke University Press.

___ (2011) *Virtual Hallyu: Korean Cinema of the Global Era*. Durham, NC: Duke University Press.

Kim, Soyoung (2010) 'Gendered Trauma in Korean Cinema: *Peppermint Candy* and *My Own Breathing*', *New Cinemas: Journal of Contemporary Film*, 8, 3, 179–87.

Kim, Young-jin (2007) *Lee Chang-dong*, trans. Park Sang-hee. Seoul: Korean Film Council.

Lyotard, Jean-François (1984) *The Postmodern Condition: A Report on Knowledge*, trans. Geoff Bennington and Brian Massumi. Minneapolis, MN: University of Minnesota Press.

McGowan, Todd (2007) 'Affirmation of the Lost Object: *Peppermint Candy* and the End of Progress', *Symplokē*, 15, 1/2, 23–43.
Rukojć, Katarzyna (2013) 'An Ostracized Minority Silently Facing Denial of Social Acceptance: The Depiction of Disabled People in South Korean and Japanese Movies', *Forum for World Literature Studies*, 5, 2, 342–53.
Sassen, Saskia (2006) *Cities in a World Economy*, 3rd ed. Thousand Oaks, CA: Pine Forge Press.
Wendell, Susan (1989) 'Toward a Feminist Theory of Disability', *Hypatia*, 4, 2, 104–24.

Refusing Chromosomal Pairing

Inclusion, Disabled Masculinity, Sexuality and Intimacy in *Yo, también* (2009)

Michael Gill

Antonio Naharro and Álvaro Pastor's film *Yo, también* (*Me Too*, 2009) allows viewers to question expectations of competence, citizenship, ability and sexual attractiveness. The protagonist, Daniel (Pablo Pineda) falls in love with his co-worker, Laura (Lola Dueñas). Despite the standard formula of the film – man meets woman and falls in love – Daniel's intellectual disability and Laura's lack of such means that viewers are allowed to imagine how disability enhances and complicates expectations of love, intimacy and sexual activity. During a moment of illustrative dialogue in the film, where Daniel and his older brother, Santi (Antonio Naharro) are discussing Daniel's love of (and attraction to) Laura, Santi bluntly tells him that no woman with 46 chromosomes will ever love Daniel. Santi advises him to fall in love with another woman with Down syndrome. Daniel's chances at love are clinically reduced to genetics, where chromosomal matching is assumed to be necessary in order to obtain companionship. Tellingly, Daniel refuses to let this sexually ableist assessment direct his chances for love and intimacy. Daniel's continual assertion of his desire, while working with and against systems that seek to qualify his competence, helps to complicate reductive assumptions about which types of partners are appropriate for disabled individuals.

In this chapter, expanding on the work of Benjamin Fraser (2013), Victoria Rivera-Cordero (2013) and Rachel Adams (2015), I argue that Daniel's assertions of his heterosexual masculinity work to secure him as a desiring and desirable subject. More explicitly, Daniel's statement that he is Down syndrome from head to toe centres his medical diagnosis allowing for a disidentification between the assumptions about the condition to foreground Daniel's epistemological insights. In addition, the film challenges assumptions of inclusion and citizenship based solely on economic or political means; rather, the film argues that the sexual and reproductive desires of intellectually disabled individuals have to be recognised as valid and are central to discourses of citizenship and rights. In this chapter, I compare three pairings that appear in the film: a disabled couple, a non-disabled couple and a couple where one individual has an intellectual disability and the other does not. I argue that while the film transgresses representational patterns by showing a love story between an intellectually disabled protagonist and his non-disabled partner, ultimately, their relationship is not granted wider familial and cultural legitimacy.

Questions of Identity and Inclusion

Alongside questions of inclusion – one of the central themes in *Yo, también* – the film also invites a critique of how assumptions of ability and labels of disability impact attempts to secure rights under the banner of a common humanity. As such, the film begins with Daniel's voiceover, as part of a speech he is giving:

> Es como el cuerpo humano. ¿Qué sería del cuerpo sin sus miembros? Sí, son frágiles. Porque aquellas sociedades que dividen y apartan a las minorías son sociedades mutiladas. No están unidas. Parece como si cada uno fueran islas desiertas. Eso es lo que no se pretende. Lo que se quiere es todo lo contrario. Es unir. Aquí no hay ni mujeres, ni negros, ni homosexuales, ni nada. Aquí todos somos personas. Por eso, el trabajo nos ayuda a sentirnos parte de esta sociedad, porque lo somos, siempre lo hemos sido, y queremos tener voz en esta sociedad que para eso se llama democrática. Muchas gracias.

> (It is like a human body. What would it be without limbs? They're fragile. Because all those societies that divide and isolate minorities are mutilated societies. They're not united. It's like each one was a desert island. That is not what we're aiming for. We want just the opposite, we want to unite. Here there aren't men or women or Blacks or homosexuals or anything. Here, we are all people. So, work helps us to feel part of this society. Because we are. We have always been. And we want to have a voice in this society. That's why it's called democratic. Thank you.)[1]

His speech, which lasts a little over three minutes, is intercut with shots of commuters in the present (including Daniel), sights and sounds of Seville, audience members listening to his speech in the past and a dance class attended by disabled dancers. Daniel's speech blurs temporalities where he addresses past failed democracies ('desert islands'), while also advocating for a more equitable and accessible future. In between these gestures to the past and future, the camera shows the present with his commute to work and the shots of the dance class. The mixing of temporalities signals the political project of the film to explicitly argue for equity and inclusion under the banner of human rights; in addition, the film highlights how discourses of human rights, which often depend on discourses of a more repressive past and equitable future, can obfuscate how various minorities are not able to access full rights.

Of Daniel's speech, Fraser writes: 'The topic of disability, here, is not explicit, but instead implicit in the speech – it is embodied in Daniel's performance' (2013: 5). One could argue that Daniel's speech doesn't mention disability, perhaps because the audience during his address, and the viewer through the camera, make an explicit link between markers of Down syndrome and Daniel. Yet Fraser's analysis highlights the tension in the film: to what extent does disability matter? Or, more explicitly, how does a democratic society centre the needs and concerns of a diverse population, including those with intellectual disabilities, when citizenship might be predicated on an ability to work, live independently, or be constructed as 'rational'? Tellingly, assumptions of intellectual disability are central to this scene in the film given what Adams has identified as 'an immediately legible signifier of a disabled mind and body' (2015: n.p.). She continues: 'The most visually recognizable and deeply stigmatized of all intellectual disabilities, Down syndrome brings questions about consent, sexual rights, and ableist disgust sharply into focus' (ibid.). The disabled embodiment of both the actor and the character he plays results in a verisimilitude where Pineda's disability adds to the realness of the performance, and perhaps also to the veracity of the claims in the film.

In his speech, Daniel does mention gender/sex ('men' and 'women'), racial categories and sexual minorities ('homosexuality'). His language of impairment ('mutilated') constructs an experience of oppression or discrimination as not only isolating, but also harming the integrity and unity of the body politic. Daniel's call for inclusion, here the ability to work, becomes part of the project of unity. Beyond a call for inclusion, his speech is also a call for recognition: 'Here, we are people. So, work helps us feel part of this society.

Because we are. We have always been. And we want to have a voice in this society. That's why it's called democratic.' An argument linking work (and its association with productivity, paying of taxes and, in a time of austerity, not being supported by welfare) to humanness and citizenship thus becomes one of the central themes of the film. Daniel's speech prompts an interrogation of the relationship, if any, between disability and citizenship.

Discussing citizenship in the United States, Allison C. Carey remarks:

> Despite the long history of exclusion, the story of citizenship and intellectual disability is not one-sided. If people with intellectual disabilities were in fact naturally and categorically unable to exercise rights, we would see no significant debate about rights for this population. This is not the case, however; throughout the twentieth century advocates for people with intellectual disabilities and people with intellectual disabilities themselves engaged in many successful attempts to claim rights and support their active participation in society. (2009: 6)

Carey then proceeds to illustrate how various actors, even during moments of segregation and sterilisation, sought to make citizenship claims for people with labels of intellectual disabilities (2009: 6–11). She writes that often efforts to expand rights and citizenship are set up against efforts to restrict rights: 'At no point in history has there been a clear resolution of the "problem" of intellectual disability as related to rights, toward exclusion or inclusion' (2009: 9). In *Yo, también*, Daniel is the first person in Europe with Down syndrome to have graduated from university (see Fraser 2013: 1). The film invites an interrogation of how discourses of rights, citizenship and inclusion are only available to those that work (or graduate from university) or if the promises of citizenship are available to all regardless of labels of disability (or other markers of identity). In addition, it highlights the failures of securing sexual and reproductive rights, especially for those labeled with intellectual disabilities (see Gill 2015). Individuals with labels of intellectual disabilities often are sterilised, prescribed birth control without their knowledge or forbidden from participating in sexual activities (see Shildrick 2009; Desjardins 2012; Gill 2015). Fraser compellingly argues that the success of *Yo, también* 'lies in its ability to use the themes of love to draw attention to the way in which the needs, desires, and the very autonomy of people with disabilities are habitually subjugated to a clinical view of disability' (2013: 13).

As an opening framing mechanism, Daniel's address nicely illustrates Sharon L. Snyder and David T. Mitchell's examination of 'ablenationalism' that 'involves the implicit assumption that minimum levels of corporeal, intellectual, and sensory capacity, in conjunction with subjective aspects of aesthetic appearance, are required of citizens seeking access to "full benefits" of citizenship' (2010: 124). Snyder and Mitchell continue: 'As such, most people with disabilities are excluded by falling short of this participatory bottom line and, as such, key guiding principals of democracy are left unrealized' (ibid.). It is tempting to read Daniel's success as a university graduate and temporary worker as a marker of inclusion, and by extension, citizenship, especially if his employment can become more permanent. The most hopeful reading of the film, as a text, makes an argument that disabled individuals can *access* the academy and workplace. In the age of the United Nations Convention on the Rights of Persons with Disabilities (UNCRPD), we might assume that the academy has expanded its admissions procedures to include those with labels of Down syndrome, and by extension, shifted ableist assumptions of rationality that in the past have actively excluded cognitively disabled individuals from participation and success (see Price 2011: 25–57). However, these assumptions are predicated on a narrative of progress where the expansion of rights facilitates new levels of engagement and inclusion.

As Snyder and Mitchell assert, in this process, there is the potential to uphold 'crip normativities' which signal the 'able disabled' (2010: 118) – 'celebrated by capitalist commodity cultures and communist governments alike as symbols of the success of systems that further marginalise their "less able" disabled kin in the shadow of committed researchers conjoined to "creaming" practices for the non-impaired' individual (2010: 117).[2] Fraser remarks how the film is 'far from presenting a self-congratulatory view of the state of Spanish integration. Integration, after all, may not be enough if it is accompanied by a perspective that denies true autonomy and independence to people who become systematically identified by their disability alone' (2013: 7). This tension between the state's desire to celebrate the disabled subject as covered under (and protected by) human rights regimes, including the UNCRPD and optional protocol, which Spain ratified and signed in 2007, and the various levels of segregation that exist alongside discourses of inclusion illuminate how a discourse of rights is selectively applied. Is the category of 'human', in human rights regimes, flexible enough to include those constructed as 'unfit to work' and 'undeserving'? Are intellectually disabled individuals afforded citizenship in practice, or just in name? And, as explored below, does the promise of citizenship extend to expressions of sexuality?

Down Syndrome from Head to Toe

After graduation, with a degree in teaching and educational psychology, Daniel works as a temporary employee in the General Office for Disabled Persons. Initially, his duties consist of clerical work including answering phones and making copies. On his first day, he is sitting at a desk looking through a smoking cessation manual and listening to a motivational speech, via headphones. As the voice on the tape announces to 'concentra tu inteligencia en tu frente' ('concentrate your intelligence in your forehead') and to do the same in the eyelids, we first encounter Laura entering work late. The camera first shows her high heels and legs covered in jeans, before panning up to show her back and dyed blonde hair with dark roots showing. Her pace is rushed as Laura sees Daniel sitting in her desk. Laura immediately tells Daniel he is lost, as she doesn't seem to remember that Daniel would be her co-worker. After Consuelo (Consuelo Trujillo), the head of the office, corrects the misrecognition, Laura apologises to Daniel.[3]

In a matter of minutes we are introduced to both Laura, through her late arrival and correction of dress, and Daniel, through his speech and exploration of Laura's desk. Daniel is the disabled university graduate asking for inclusion and Laura is the wild, seemingly unreliably social service worker. While narratives of reformation are standard cinema fare, usually where an 'active' bachelor settles down with a 'moral' woman, or a 'wild' woman is tamed by the unconditional love of a man, *Yo, también* alters this narrative slightly where Daniel's intellectual disability (and Laura's lack of such) have to be negotiated as part of Laura's reformation and redemption.

The film quickly contrasts Daniel's work goals with those of marriage/companionship and sexual intercourse. For example, after Daniel's first day of work, his parents, María Ángeles (Isabel García Lorca) and Bernabé (Pedro Álvarez-Ossorio), give him a new briefcase. After receiving the gift, Daniel remarks, 'Ya solo falta casarme' ('Now I just have to get married!'). Next, the camera cuts to Daniel opening a folder on his computer labeled 'Daniel's personal file' and two sub-folders titled, 'Apuntes Facultad' ('faculty notes') and 'Diagnóstico en Educación 2 elementos' ('educational diagnosis'). We next see Daniel, in his room, watching pornography presumably hidden in these computer files. Later Daniel has an erotic dream about his female co-workers, including Laura. When two of his co-workers see him laughing at work, they comment to each other how 'cute' he is, not realising, of course, that the previous night they were actors in his erotic dream. The comment regarding his 'cuteness' helps illustrate the ableist assumption of Daniel's innocence at the expense of his sexual desire. These brief moments work to assert Daniel as an individual with sexual (and relationship) desires, which then become a key driving force as he actively flirts and develops a friendship with Laura.

Away from work, Laura is shown drinking and having seemingly unfulfilling sexual encounters with men she meets at local bars. The differences between Laura and Daniel's lives are striking: Daniel lives with his parents, both educated individuals who have taught Daniel how to appreciate art, speak English and have an ostensibly well-rounded social life. Daniel is also close to his brother Santi and his wife, Reyes (María Bravo). Laura is estranged from her father and brothers. She tells Daniel at one point she is an orphan, although her father's hospitalisation and death provide much of the dramatic conflict in her life during the film. In addition, while the details are unclear, it seems Laura was sexually abused when she was younger.[4] Laura's world is presented as wild, while Daniel's parents (and their educational and class privilege) protect (or shelter) Daniel. While a reading of the gendered relationship between Laura and Daniel could be made that argues Daniel's disabled heterosexual masculinity tames (or reforms) Laura's 'fallen' femininity, I want to make a more nuanced argument about their relationship where both are mutually constructing an interdependent relationship based on expressions of love. This reading would ignore Laura's declaration that she does not want a relationship with Daniel. In fact, the uniqueness of their relationship is what renders it as simultaneously temporary, but also as timeless in a sense: both are working against ableist assessments of the appropriateness of their relationship, and the film suggests that this will be one of the greatest loves of both characters' lives.

After the initial case of mistaken identity at work, Daniel and Laura's friendship quickly develops partially because Daniel feigns 'ignorance' to be close to Laura. As part of his ruse, she helps him find another copy machine, when the one in the office is broken, and how to manoeuvre the operating system on his work computer. Daniel accompanies Laura on her smoke breaks and the two share a meal at a local restaurant. And while Daniel is increasingly attracted to Laura, telling his brother all about her virtues during their workout sessions, Laura continues her social habits, especially after news of her father's hospitalisation.

At a pivotal moment in their friendship, Laura and Daniel take a daytrip to the beach. Under the watchful protective eye of his mother, Laura picks Daniel up for their outing. After a drive in her car, the two are shown frolicking in the water. An upbeat soundtrack adds to the playfulness of their interactions. From a distance the two seem like any other couple on the beach

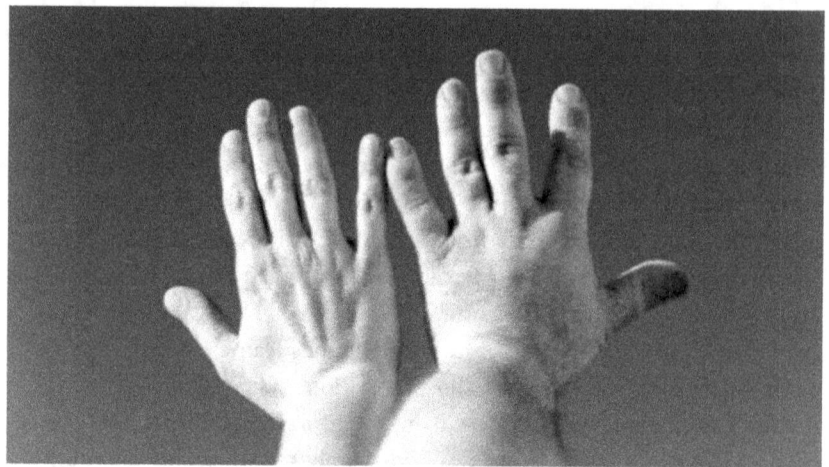

Fig. 1: Daniel and Laura holding up their hands to the blue sky to compare the size and shape of their fingers.

playing and flirting. Among diegetic sound of waves crashing and seagulls calling, both Laura and Daniel are holding up one hand to the blue sky. Laura remarks, about Daniel's fingers, 'Son gorditas, no?' ('They're chubby, aren't they?'); 'Si, bueno, ese es un rasgo de síndrome de Down, una característica' ('Yes, but that's a feature of Down syndrome, a characteristic'), Daniel replies. 'Luego, también tenemos más características, sabes? Por ejemplo el paladar, es más estrecho. Eso también afecta al habla, porque se nos pueda se nos traba la lengua, y nos cuesta mucho hablar' ('And we've got other characteristics, too, you know. For example, the palate. It's narrower, and that affects how we speak because it makes us tonged-tied and it's hard for us to talk'). Laura questions, 'Por qué eres … así?' ('Why are you … like this?'). As Daniel is discussing the impacts of his impairment on his embodiment, Laura is reconciling her assumptions of Down syndrome with her experience of Daniel. Her question about origin and cause is also one about intelligence as she wonders why Daniel is 'smart'.

Daniel shares with Laura how his mother talked to him throughout his childhood, discusses art, politics and history and fought to get him into school. Daniel's inclusion into Spanish society was enabled by his mother's advocacy and will. The call for universal inclusion, regardless of identity, from Daniel, in the beginning, is marking a time in the future, not in the present or past. His goal of inclusion has not yet arrived. Laura discloses that she thought Daniel had slight mosaicism (a potentially 'mild' version of Down syndrome). Daniel, refusing her assessment, asserts, 'No, no, para nada. Yo soy síndrome de Down de los pies a la cabeza. No ... entero, entero' ('I'm Down's syndrome from head to toe. I mean ... the whole way'). He continues: 'Y eso que dicen muchas veces de que hay dos edades, que si la cronológica, que si la mental. Eso, qué va, ni mucho menos. Yo teñgo 34 anos y sé atarme ... los cordones, pues desde los 10' ('And they often say there are two ages, the chronological and the mental, but that's not true. I'm 34 years old, and I've been tying ... my shoelaces since I was 10').[5] Clearly surprised (and perhaps feeling duped), Laura tells Daniel he has 'morro' ('nerve'). He replies that nerve, too, is another characteristic of Down syndrome.

This moment of dialogue is striking in that Daniel refuses to downplay his diagnosis – or even distance himself from assumptions, even ableist ones, about Down syndrome. His declaration of 'head to toeness' of Down syndrome, rather, means that Laura must confront her expectations of intellectual disability as she negotiates Daniel's sexual desire (and later her own). This isn't a story where one protagonist enters into a relationship 'despite' another being disabled, or where one remarks to the other that they didn't realise the other person was disabled. Fraser remarks that this scene, in particular, powerfully disrupts 'the clinical paradigm of disability' allowing Daniel the 'opportunity to control his own self-representation' (2013: 11, 12). Rivera-Cordero writes that the 'directors here invite viewers to look more carefully at the body of this young man in order for us to see in a neutral way his slightly different hands. These hands are presented neither as especially attractive nor unattractive, they simply are' (2013: 67). As such, Daniel's Down syndrome is rendered 'visible', in a sense – as corroborated through his response to Laura – making disability legible. As such, the continual reminders of Daniel's intellectual disability mean that when the protagonists engage in sexual relations, the camera is unable to document their actions because of the potentially jarring and controversial nature of their relationship.[6]

A later scene involves Laura and Daniel photocopying their hands thus carrying on the comparison between these two protagonists. Later, in the mirror to herself, Laura manipulates her eyes and tongue to approximate the visual markers of an embodiment sculpted by Down syndrome. These comparisons, importantly, are not simulations where Laura (and potentially the viewer by extension) is allowed to 'experience' intellectual disability. Rather, as Laura and Daniel's relationship develops and becomes more complicated, because of external assessments from family and co-workers about the appropriateness or potential success, Laura explores her own embodiment (and what she assumes is Daniel's) before they have a sexual encounter near the end of the film. Laura and Daniel are disidentifying with clinical assumptions, especially around 'mental age', associated with a diagnosis of intellectual disability.[7] In a society that constructs cognitive or intellectual disability as needing ableist protections, often in the name of paternalism, disidentification becomes not only a survival strategy, but also perhaps an effective mechanism to counter ableist assumptions that too often deny rights. As explored below, this mode of disidentification allows for Daniel and Laura to transgress cultural prohibitions of sexual activity, perhaps provided they only engage in sexual activity once.

Toward Inclusion?: Comparisons Between and Among

In the introduction, I briefly mentioned a moment of dialogue between Daniel and his brother, where Santi tells Daniel no woman with 46 chromosomes is ever going to love Daniel. This moment of dialogue occurs tellingly after Daniel tries to kiss Laura while they dance at a club, and then asks to come home with her. Laura tells him she wants to go home alone, effectively denying his invitation for sexual activity and seemingly the opportunity for a relationship. Drunk and rejected, Daniel attempts to enter a brothel where the bouncer refuses him entry. Daniel replies that he has two credit cards, seemingly a sign of his independence, adulthood and financial security. Despite these assurances, the bouncer calls him a 'kid' and refuses his entry into the brothel. Daniel replies: 'Tengo 34 anos! ¡No soy un niño! ¡Soy un hombre! ¡Soy un hombre! Soy un hombre … y puedo entrar ahí, si quero. ¡Soy un hombre!' ('I'm 34! I am not a child! I am a man! I am a man! I am a man … I can go in there if I want. I am a man!'). Despite his protest, Daniel is not allowed to access the brothel. Adams writes that in this scene, 'it is clear how the denial of sexual agency is tied to the denial of his status as a person' (2015: n.p.). Daniel's repetition of his status as a man illuminates how sexually ableist assumptions of intellectual disability function to actively deny opportunities for sexual activity, especially with women without intellectual disabilities.[8] These relationships accordingly 'raise concerns about the exploitation of a partner who may not fully understand the meaning or implications of his or her actions. They also elicit ableist disgust at the capacity of people with intellectual disabilities to feel, act on, and become the subjects of erotic desire' (ibid.).

Daniel's inability to enter the brothel serves to contrast his ability to act on his desires with that of his brother. After Daniel's attempt to enter the brothel, the camera fades to show Santi and Reyes engaging in sex on the couch in their living room before being interrupted by Daniel's late night knock on the front door. The disabled brother is denied the ability to engage in sexual activity, while the bodies of the couple without intellectual disabilities are shown engaged in passionate, apparently pleasurable sexual activity.[9] Visually, then, the sexually ableist prohibitions are confirmed where Daniel's isolation and sexual desire not only show him alone on the street but also interrupting the sexual activities of his brother and sister-in-law.

It is at this moment when Santi tells Daniel: 'Mira Daniel ninguna mujer con 46 cromosomas se va a enamorar de ti, y tú no paras de fijarte en mujeres así, ¿cómo no vas a sufrir? Enamórate de mujeres a tu alcance, hombre. Porque es que así no vas a conseguir nada' ('Look, Daniel, no woman with 46 chromosomes is going to fall in love with you, but you keep going after them. You're bound to suffer. Fall in love with women you can get, because you'll get nowhere like this'). Santi is reducing Daniel's chances at partnership ('love') and sexual encounters to an issue of chromosomal pairing. Daniel's impairment, here as a marker of an extra chromosome on the 21st pair, according to Santi, is the central issue that disqualifies Daniel's chance with Laura (or another individual without an intellectual disability). Recalling Daniel's opening address of inclusion puts into question how the process of attainment of rights and general discourses of inclusion can be actualised when sexually ableist forces constrain one's ability to be considered as having rights, when discourses of protection (or even more repressively suppression) emerge to limit sexual, reproductive and marriage focused desires.

Daniel's brother and sister-in-law run a dance company for disabled individuals, based on Danza Mobile, a contemporary dance company of disabled and non-disabled dancers in Seville. As part of his job, Daniel convinces his brother to accept Pedro (Daniel Parejo) into the dance company, despite not being authorised to accept him because of funding limitations and waitlists. It is at Danza Mobile that Pedro meets Luisa (Lourdes Naharro). Both Pedro and Luisa have intellectual disabilities. Almost immediately they also become attracted to each other and sensually dance, while also being reprimanded by Reyes for making out. Reyes simultaneously calls Pedro and Luisa 'chicos' (kids) and tells them it is fine to want to kiss and touch each other but that they need to do so in private. Her use of 'kids' is significant in that because of their status as being labeled intellectually disabled neither is automatically afforded privacy or given status as an adult. In fact, Luisa's mother refuses to tell her about the death of her father further linking Luisa's status as needing to be 'protected' from news of death. Luisa's mother pulls her daughter out of the dance programme because of concerns of her daughter's interest in Pedro (and his sexual desire for Luisa).

The lack of privacy, family support and cultural legitimacy for their relationship forces Luisa and Pedro to run away. In one of the more comical but also poignant moments of the film, Pedro shows up outside the bakery run by Luisa's mother. Luisa takes money out of the cash register and a display wedding cake and runs off with Pedro. At the dance company, Luisa's mother confronts Reyes. Looking down on the scene of confrontation, Daniel and Santi discuss sexual rights and access. Referring to Pedro and Luisa, Daniel tells Santi: 'Solo quieren estar juntos' ('They just want to be together'). Santi replies that they didn't go to university, effectively linking levels of rights (and inclusion) to education. Daniel remarks: 'Pero no hace falta estudiar para tener necesidad!' ('You don't have to study to have needs!'). Santi replies that they can masturbate if they have needs. As Daniel responds, we get the sense he is talking about his own desires in addition to Luisa and Pedro: 'Pero eso no es todo. Es tener compañía, es tener afecto, es tener algo' ('That isn't everything. It's having company, having affection, having something'). Santi is acknowledging their right to solitary sexual release through masturbation, but this articulation further extends sexually ableist assumptions where sexual activity (read: masturbation) becomes a solution to 'needs'. Daniel, rather, challenges this limited construction to link discourses of inclusion to only non-reproductive solitary sexual activity. Daniel even challenges his brother as 'having it all' with his wife and baby. At this moment we are forced to recount Daniel's speech in the past about the future of inclusion: being employed or graduating from university, while also being unable to marry or participate in sexual activity with partner(s), means the promise of citizenship, inclusion and acceptance, regardless of identity, has yet to materialise.

During their moment of escape Pedro and Luisa end up at a hotel. Daniel and Laura find them at the hotel and instead of immediately informing Santi, they give the two lovers a quick sex education lesson and discussion of consent. After Luisa states her love for and commitment to Pedro, Laura begins to cry softly. The two disabled lovers are able to finally be together in a private space purchased with stolen funds from the bakery. Tellingly, we are not shown their encounter; rather the camera shows Daniel and Laura sitting on the steps outside their room during Pedro and Luisa's tryst. Only after their sexual encounter is Luisa able to confront her mother and demand recognition as an adult. Minutes later in the film we see Pedro and Luisa in her mother's bakery, and it appears the matriarch accepts their relationship as legitimate.

After the night of Luisa and Pedro's escape, Laura travels to Madrid to attend to her ailing estranged father and two brothers. Following a Christmas day phone call to Daniel when she lets him know her father is dead and he confesses his love, the two meet in Madrid. Daniel accompanies Laura as she sells her share in her father's home. Later, we see Daniel and Laura at a New Year's Eve celebration eating twelve grapes before sharing a kiss at midnight. This scene transitions to one in a hotel room where Laura and Daniel negotiate the expectations of their impending sexual encounter. Daniel asks Laura if she is planning to have sex with him 'out of pity'. It is at this moment where she confesses her love for Daniel. Daniel replies, 'Yo no he hecho nunca al amor' ('I've never made love'). 'Yo tampoco' ('Me neither'), Laura answers: 'Me he acostado con muchos hombres en mi vida, pero nunca he hecho el amor' ('I've slept with lots of men in my life, but I've never made love'). Daniel tells Laura he doesn't care about her past sexual experiences: 'Te quiero como eres' ('I love you as you are'). There are no expectations of anything other than what these two are. Daniel's and Laura's labels, identities, assumptions and baggage are all present, and because of the openness and acceptance the two are free to express love. Despite the temporal nature of this encounter and the mutual recognition that this event does not signal they will become a couple or will ever have sex again, the two embrace as the camera fades to black.

In light of how Robert McRuer (2006) has linked heterosexuality and able-bodiedness, one might conclude that the film's 'chromosomal mismatch' between its protagonists is rendered unsustainable because of how Laura views Daniel's disability. While the film allows for Daniel and Laura to express their love – and participate in sexual activity together, despite their chromosomal

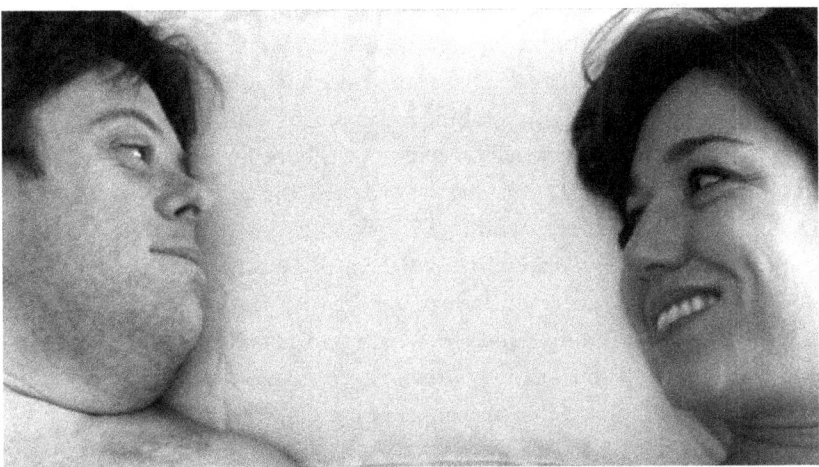

Fig. 2: Daniel and Laura smile at each other after their sexual encounter, which is undocumented in the film.

mismatch – viewers are not given access to the sexual activity, unlike Laura's previous encounters and the interrupted moment between Santi and Reyes. Although viewers see the two protagonists in a post-coital shot with heads on pillows smiling and laughing, their union proves too transgressive to document. Unlike those moments, the film allows Daniel and Laura to narrate their emotions and intent before engaging in sex. Both communicate their feelings of love and desire to each other. In addition, they also set the parameters of the interaction. This moment then is marked by both an emotional attachment as well as carefully communicated ground rules. Because the camera fades to black before showing the activity, viewers are not given clues about the passionate or pleasurable nature of their interaction. Similarly, Pedro and Luisa's sexual relationship is not visually documented. Read together, the directorial intent in these two scenes illustrates how intellectually disabled sexual activity remains too controversial to document. As such, despite the efforts of universalism in Daniel's opening address, the film suggests that labels of disability continue to disallow sexual rights, beyond a limited narrative of exceptionalism.[10]

Yo, también challenges sexually ableist assumptions as Daniel's disabled heterosexual masculine performance makes him a desirable subject. In addition, Pedro and Luisa seem to gain wider familial (and cultural) recognition of their relationship. Yet the narrative of inclusion is not sustaining in that these characters' successes depend on individual acceptance as opposed to larger social forces that Daniel calls for in his opening address. As a text of cultural criticism, the film acknowledges that calls for inclusion might be easier to obtain for arenas of employment, as opposed to wider participation in sexual and reproductive rights. Rachel Adams remarks that the film 'makes apparent that an absence of sexual access is tied to broader failures to fully recognize people with disabilities as persons' (2015: n.p.). It would appear that despite interpersonal acceptance, the hope for a democratic society lies in the future in a space that has yet to be actualised. The broad promise of citizenship and greater recognition of those labeled with intellectual disabilities, as well as their greater participation in all aspects of society, remains a goal for which some societies strive under the rhetoric of the UNCRPD. Tellingly, there remains a mismatch between rhetoric and access regarding the appropriateness of intellectually disabled sexuality, one informed by sexually ableist assumptions that may appear both on and off-screen.

NOTES

1. Interestingly, in the subtitles for the deaf and hard of hearing in the Region 2 Spanish DVD I used to obtain the Spanish text for citation, Daniel's speech is transcribed word for word, but in the Region 1, English version, his mention of racial minorities (Blacks) is not transcribed.
2. Snyder and Mitchell are discussing individuals like Aimee Mullins, whose high-tech prosthetic legs are 'promising all of the transcendent capacity a hyper-medicalized culture could offer' (2010: 117). While Daniel is not seen to be enabled by the advance of technology, there is a risk that he could be celebrated as 'able disabled' where his success marks an exception that his disabled contemporaries cannot achieve. Some viewers might see Daniel as 'deserving' of employment (and potentially a fulfilling social life), while not extending these opportunities to other disabled characters.
3. Consuelo also buttons one of the buttons on Laura's shirt announcing 'Sevilla, día laborable' ('Seville, working day').
4. Near the end of the film, her sister-in-law lets Laura know that near the end of his life, Laura's father asked for forgiveness confusing the sister-in-law with Laura. It is unclear if her father abused Laura or if he just knew about the abuse but didn't stop it. This disclosure happens in the company of her two brothers and Daniel. In addition, it is almost immediately preceding Daniel and Laura's sexual encounter.
5. Twice before the discloser of his ability to tie shoelaces, Daniel lets Laura tie his shoelaces. These moments illustrate her construction of him as unable to complete tasks requiring some hand-to-eye coordination because of his disability and Daniel's willingness to play up assumptions of disability for physical closeness.
6. Unlike *Idioterne* (*The Idiots*, 1998), where the protagonists engage in sexual relations while faking intellectual disability, here Daniel's intellectual disability is constructed as more 'real' because of the actor's identity, thus to document sexual activity might be too radical (or even illegal.) While the representation in *Yo, también* marks a shift in trends of representing intellectual disability; visualising sexual activity remains too controversial.
7. José Esteban Muñoz's point about disidentification as 'survival strategies the minority subject practices in order to negotiate a phobic majoritarian public sphere that continuously elides or punishes the existence of subjects who do not conform to the phantasm of normative citzenship' (1999: 4) illuminates how Daniel's insistence on Down syndrome as central to his experience demands a challenge to traditional ableist assumptions of the impairment.
8. Adams refers to this as a prohibition against discegenation: 'consensual erotic relations in which one partner is intellectually disabled' (2015: n.p.).
9. Earlier we learn Santi and Reyes are having a child. While they are not only able to reproduce without visible restrictions or judgements on their relationship, they also are shown having pleasurable sex.
10. Daniel's experiences are constructed as exceptional because of his economic and educational privileges, and Luisa and Pedro's acceptance depends on a willing matriarch, not wider cultural legitimacy.

FILMOGRAPHY

Naharro, Antonio and Álvaro Pastor (dirs) (2009) *Yo, también* [Me Too]. 103 minutes. Alicia Produce/Promico Imagen. Spain.

BIBLIOGRAPHY

Adams, Rachel (2015) 'Privacy, Dependency, Discegenation: Toward a Sexual Culture for People with Intellectual Disabilities', *Disability Studies Quarterly*, 35, 1. Available at http://dsq-sds.org/article/view/4185/3825 (accessed 1 May 2015).

Carey, Allison C. (2009) *On the Margins of Citizenship: Intellectual Disability and Civil Rights in Twentieth-Century America*. Philadelphia, PA: Temple University Press.

Desjardins, Michel (2012) 'The Sexualized Body of the Child: Parents and the Politics of "Voluntary" Sterilization of People Labeled Intellectually Disabled', in Robert McRuer and Anna Mollow (eds) *Sex and Disability*. Durham, NC: Duke University Press, 69–88.

Fraser, Benjamin (2013) *Disability Studies and Spanish Culture: Films, Novels, the Comic and the Public Exhibition*. Liverpool: Liverpool University Press.

Gill, Michael (2015) *Already Doing It: Intellectual Disability and Sexual Agency*. Minneapolis, MN: University of Minnesota Press.

McRuer, Robert (2006) *Crip Theory: Cultural Sign of Queerness and Disability*. New York, NY: New York University Press.

Muñoz, José Esteban (1999) *Disidentifications: Queers of Color and the Performance of Politics*. Minneapolis, MN: University of Minnesota Press.

Price, Margaret (2011) *Mad at School: Rhetorics of Mental Disability and Academic Life*. Ann Arbor, MI: University of Michigan Press.

Rivera-Cordero, Victoria (2013) 'The Self Inside and Out: Authenticity and Disability in *Mar adentro* and *Yo, también*', *Hispania*, 96, 1, 62–70.

Shildrick, Margrit (2009) *Dangerous Discourses of Disability, Subjectivity and Sexuality*. New York, NY: Palgrave Macmillan.

Snyder, Sharon L. and David T. Mitchell (2010) 'Introduction: Ablenationalism and the Geo-Politics of Disability', *Journal of Literary & Cultural Disability Studies*, 4, 2, 113–25.

Dunce! Duffer! Dimwit!

Dyslexia in Bollywood's *Taare Zameen Par* (2007)

Sanjukta Ghosh

Though Bollywood films have long been dismissed as extravagant fantasies, as mere escapist entertainment for the masses, they have always had a historical resonance. Since the earliest days of the industry, the films have tackled social, political, moral and nationalist causes. In recent years, a spate of films has been released that represent the needs of differently-abled people. Rather than use disability as a visual metaphor to showcase the physical and moral standing of the 'normal' protagonist, these new films centre the marginalised identities of those facing physical, mental or intellectual challenges.

One of these films, released in 2007 to critical and popular acclaim, was *Taare Zameen Par* (*Like Stars on Earth*), which focuses on the life of an eight-year-old boy who happens to be dyslexic. The film not only scrutinises the issue of dyslexia, but also gives us a wider critique of contemporary Indian society that values outcome over process and of an education system that has its roots in British colonialism. Thwarting Eurocentric and American notions of cinematic conventions that are accepted as normative, and using common Bollywood codes and conventions of star power and song-and-dance sequences, *Taare Zameen Par* succeeds in deconstructing the discourses of pity and deviance so prevalent in filmic representations of disability.

Bollywood Conventions

'Bollywood Cinema' is a highly contested and much debated nomenclature. While some have used it as a trivialising, pejorative and dismissive term, there are others who have not problematised the term at all (see Basu 2010). At the very least, it is a fluid concept that is both a shorthand and a contradiction. As a shorthand, the moniker refers to the extravagant Hindi-language melodramas emerging from the western Indian city of Mumbai (formally Bombay). As a contradiction, scholars and journalists alike point out that though 'Bollywood Cinema' is seen as an entirely indigenous product, the phrase has its origins in the English-language media (see Ganti 2013). Madhava Prasad (2003) argues that it is an empty signifier that can be applied to a range of signifieds within the realm of Indian cinema. Jyotika Virdi and Corey K. Creekmur (2006) remind us that the parallels in the construction of its name with the globally dominant 'Hollywood' highlight elements of both mimicry and resistance. In other words, the term 'Bollywood Cinema' simultaneously celebrates difference even as it mocks it.

Locationally, Sangita Gopal and Sujata Moorti (2008) use 'Bollywood Cinema' to refer to the Bombay-based Hindi film industry. Despite the particularities of its language or place of origin, they see this cinema as unquestionably national in its scope and transnational in its reach and influence. Ashish Rajadhyaksha makes a clear distinction between Indian commercial cinema that 'has been in existence as a national industry of sorts for the past fifty years' and Bollywood that 'has been around for only about a decade now' (2003: 28). For him 'Bollywood' films are characterised by their high-budget gloss, very specific visual and sensory maps and transnational themes. He expands the definition further, arguing that because of its global audience, the sobriquet also covers a range of distribution and consumption activities from websites to music rights, and the ancillary digital production and distribution channels. Ajay Gehlawat (2013) reminds us that Bollywood Cinema is a hybrid cultural form that fuses together theatrical and cinematic elements and Western and indigenous genres, such as the musical, dance drama and melodrama. Added to this multiplicity of meanings is the fact that some scholars do not problematise the term at all using it interchangeably and synonymously with Bombay cinema (see Mishra 2008).

For the purposes of this chapter, I use Gehlawat's and Rajadhyaksha's notion of the Bollywood archetype as a highly stylised, high-budget Hindi-language production. It has its own cinematic style that diverges from hegemonic Hollywood cinema in important ways. Chief among its distinctive idioms and conventions are a dense visual style, song and dance sequences[1] and 'star power' – all of which are in full display in *Taare Zameen Par*. Though the lead in the film is played by an eleven-year-old newcomer, the film also features well-known actors from Bollywood and regional cinemas and stage.

Despite criticisms that allege a lack of nuance and subtlety regarding treatment of any social issue, the annals of Bollywood cinema are replete with narratives centered around casteism, ageism, the gulf between the rich and the poor, widow remarriage and sexism. Representations of disability, too, are found abundantly in Bollywood films. In fact, the portrayal of differently-abled people in Bollywood Cinema dates back to the earliest years of the industry when India was still under colonial rule. The 1925 film *Veer Kunal* (*Valiant Kunal*), for example, is set in the 3rd century BC. It tells the story of the blinding of Emperor Ashoka's son Kunal by a courtier and the emperor's slow realisation that the maiming could have been a punishment for his own sins. In other words, the film was a morality tale where the issue of disability served as a narrative device. This set the trend for decades in the film industry with physical and sensory handicap becoming a metaphor for sin and punishment. Bollywood films would henceforth often use the idea of service for the disabled as a means of penance for repentant sinners.

By and large, the trends and idioms found in Western fictional forms are also present in Bollywood texts.[2] However, as Joyjeet Pal (2013) explains, they are indigenised by grounding them in Hindu scriptures and social practices. Other scholars have found that Bollywood has also used people with physical disabilities as foils for the hero or heroine of the film, either to highlight the idealised body, to provide comic respites in an action or a suspense drama or to indicate their heroic status by 'rescuing' the disabled (see Andrade *et al.* 2010; Mohapatra 2012). Until very recently, psychological and psychiatric disabilities, too, have been used in similar ways or to heighten suspense in a narrative (see Bhugra 2006).

But as with representations of disability in Western television and cinema, in Bollywood, too, while images abound, the issue of disability gets shunted aside. Like portrayals in the West, disability in Bollywood cinema is used as a device to move the narrative forward or as an icon within a specific *mise-en-scène* to compress information about a character. Thus, as Paul Longmore (2006) states, images of disability have flourished in popular culture but it has not led to any real understanding about the disability. It is in this contextual framework that we must assess the pioneering contribution of *Taare Zameen Par* – for its examination of a non-corporeal disability, for its sustained critical focus on the lived experience of a differently-abled person and for its success in making visible a hitherto invisible disability.[3]

All Children Are Special

Taare Zameen Par marked the directorial debut of the immensely popular Bollywood star Aamir Khan. The film quickly became a huge commercial and critical success in India and was India's official entry for the 2008 Academy Awards. Subsequently, it was dubbed into several Indian and foreign languages. In 2009, it became the first Indian cinematic work to be bought by the Walt Disney company for global distribution (see IANS 2009).

The film explores the life of eight-year-old Ishaan Awasthi who lives in a middle-class neighborhood with his parents Nandkishore and Maya Awasthi and his older brother, Yohaan. Like many eight-year-olds, Ishaan has conversations with imaginary friends and foes, he sulks, he throws tantrums, he fights with neighborhood boys and he loves dogs. He has a vivid imagination and is a creative artist and painter. Unlike his older brother who excels in school and on tennis courts, Ishaan performs poorly both academically and in ballgames. His fellow classmates make fun of him and his teachers humiliate him. Unable to follow a classoom lesson or do well in any of his tests, he tunes out his teachers. But, while school life seems to bore and puzzle Ishaan, the world outside his classroom both fascinates him and feeds his imagination so much that one day he escapes from school and roams the city of Mumbai.

Frustrated by his continued poor academic performance and his school truancy, Ishaan's father determines that a boarding school will straighten out his child. At the new school, Ishaan experiences the same difficulties with his classes and gets the same treatment from his teachers; he gets lonely and depressed. A substitute art teacher, Ram Shankar Nikumbh, suspects that Ishaan may have dyslexia. He begins tutoring the little boy using remedial techniques especially developed for dyslexic children. Soon Ishaan's grades improve and so do his social skills. The film ends with both Ishaan and Nikhumb jointly winning the year-end community art competition hosted by the school.

Woven through this basic narrative of an individual overcoming immense hurdles to become successful, are many secondary themes – a fable about a father/son relationship, the story of a selfless teacher and his gifted student and an indictment of both the education system in India and its treatment of those with intellectual disabilities.

The Eugenicist Foundations of Disability

Several scholars in disability studies have shown that disability and normalcy are both concepts imbued with an eugenicist impetus used to define ourselves as distinct from others (see Garland-Thomson 1997, 2009; Barnes and Mercer 2003; Hayes and Black 2003). Arguing along the same lines, Harlan Hahn (1988) suggests that we seek to distinguish ourselves from disabled bodies because we understand the very real possibility that those bodies can become our own. At the most basic level, then, to shore up our own very temporal sense of able-bodiedness we 'Other' those with physical and mental disabilities. Furthermore, as Frantz Fanon argues 'othering occurs on the basis of physical and verbal differences' (1967: 154). Thus in an ableist culture, disability becomes a crucial vector that assists in the construction of ourselves as able-bodied, functional and ideal.

The 'othering' of Ishaan occurs time and again in the film in a myriad of ways, but chiefly through a binary opposition with his older brother Yohaan, who excels in both academics and athletics. Right at the start of the film, after he fails all his exams, Ishaan returns home from school and before he enters his home, he tosses his exams to the neighbourhood dogs who immediately shred them to pieces. When Yohaan comes home, he greets his mother by telling her that he has scored the highest points in his class in all but one academic area and in that area too, his score is merely a couple of points behind that of the lead student. He then asks his younger brother about his grades. At a parent/teacher meeting, Ishaan's teachers lament his poor performance, especially because his brother Yohaan is such an exemplary student. This comparison between Ishaan and Yohaan is taken to egregious lengths by their father who uses it to defend his decision to pack off his youngest child to a distant boarding school and to justify his continued disengagement with the child's problems.

Ishaan's 'othering' also happens when he is interacting with other kids either of his age or older, both at his old school and later in the new boarding school. Again and again he is shown fumbling at tasks that other children achieve with ease, be it reading from a textbook, tying his shoelaces or necktie that is part of his uniform or even throwing a ball. His peers, neighbourhood kids, his teachers and the supervisors at the boarding school repeatedly call him a 'dimwit', an 'idiot' and a 'duffer'. Ishaan's loneliness and alienation are mirrored by long shots and medium-range shots of him positioned at the far-side of the school's empty hallways, or sitting alone in an almost empty dining hall, or walking alone with his eyes cast downwards even as kids around him are chatting animatedly or playing with their peers. When Ishaan escapes from school and walks around Mumbai, the English/Hindi-language song lyrics, 'A little sweet, a little sour. A little close, not too far. All I need is to be free' are accompanied by quick shots of life in the chaotic city. The high camera angles position him as a speck against the big city's traffic, bustling markets and crowded streets. The dichotomy set up by the camera, the song lyrics and the narrative serve to signify Ishaan's internal state – his isolation from the rest of society and his slow descent into complete desolation and depression.

There is one area where Ishaan excels and is better than his brother and his peers, and that is art. Acknowledging this, in one scene, Yohaan watches his younger brother paint and praises his skills as 'Superb!' (in English). At the boarding school too, some students recognise Ishaan's creativity and call the teacher's attention to the intricate artistic work that the boy produces. However, most of the time Ishaan's vivid imagination and aesthetic competence go either unmarked or are criticised as 'useless' for the instrumental needs of a modern society. For such a culture, Ishaan's abilities become a disability and a burden and mark him as an outisder and a misfit from what is considered the 'norm'.

Disability as Cultural Work

The discovery of Ishaan's disability unfolds very gradually in the film. The word 'dyslexia' is mentioned for the first time almost three quarters of the way into the 2-hour and 24-minute film. However, there are oblique cues given right from the title scenes. As a teacher reads out the grades of her students' exams, letters dance around before falling into place as film crew credits. This jumble of letters refusing to take their place in an organised way that signifies 'correct spelling' is referenced later in a scene when, in his English class, Ishaan is asked by the teacher to read a passage from a specific page in his book. Unable to decipher the words, he tells the teacher that 'Yeh to naach raha hey' ('the letters are dancing'). When he is doing his homework at home, his mother reviews his work and is appalled to see that he has inverted characters, spelled the same word in three different ways, and substituted similar looking letters such as using a 'b' in place of a 'd'. At his new school, the camera adopts Ishaan's gaze and we see letters leaping out from the blackboard or his notebooks and reversing themselves.

One hour and 27 minutes into the film, Nikumbh systematically reviews Ishaan's work. As the camera adopts the teacher's gaze, we, as audience members, get to see the errors in detail for the first time – the confusion over similar-looking letters, the inversion of characters with similar orthography, the mixing up of words that use the same letters but in a different order. Nikumbh haltingly and hesistantly explains the details about dyslexia to the boy's parents, saying that Ishaan just has 'akshar hii nehi samajh mey aatey hongey' ('trouble in recognising letters').

Nikumbh also tells the parents that because their son has difficulty tying his shoes laces or buttoning his shirt, understanding the concept of numbers, following multiple instructions, or correlating size, distance and speed in ballgames, he has weak motor skills. This hints at the idea that in addition to dyslexia, Ishaan might also have dyscalculia and weak temporal-spatial skills, two additional intellectual disabilities. Given that these are not always prevalent in people with dyslexia (see Ramaa 2000; White 2002; Shaywitz *et al.* 1992, cited in Smith 2004), the filmmakers might have chosen to include them as important traits to enhance the pathos of the main character, to compress the varied difficulties children with learning disabilities face or perhaps simply to show a continuum among the myriad of intellectual disabilities.

Though dyslexia is not mentioned until late in the film, educators do hint that Ishaan's continued academic failure suggests that Ishaan may have a deeper problem. After the principal of the Mumbai school advises Ishaan's parents that they send him to a school that concentrates on special needs education, we see Nandkishore seething in anger at what he sees as an insult. He equates Ishaan needing special education as being a 'retard' and 'not normal'. In his Mumbai school, one teacher recognises the errors in Ishaan's work, but she fails to link it to an intellectual disability. Instead of seeing Ishaan's isolation, desolation and alienation from the world around him as a symptom of his dyslexia, she reads it metonymically as the cause of his poor scholastic achievement.

The art teacher tells Maya and Nandkishore that far from Ishaan being a 'retard', disobedient, rebellious, lazy or dumb, as they have decided, Ishaan realises his inadequacies and tries to overcome them by being openly disobedient and rebellious. With a shattered self-confidence, the teacher explains, Ishaan then adopts the position: 'Kyoon bataayoon duniya ko ki mujhe nahin aata? Nehin karna! Yeh kehekar baat taal do' ('Why admit to the world that I can't? Just say that I don't want to').

The trope of the 'good' student being the 'obedient' student cuts across many cultures. Unpacking the construction of students of colour from low-income households as 'troublesome' kids who are filling up special education courses, Tanya Titchkosky (2008) argues that reading disabilities are profoundly tied to identity politics. What constitutes 'literacy' and how young people are classified as learning disabled are very class specific. While America's class politics are not easily transferable to the Indian context, Titchkosky's core thesis – that modern 'literate' society only values one type of literacy, regards it as necessary and naturalises it – is applicable to both the Indian society in general and *Taare Zameen Par* in particular. It also correlates with another important theme taken up by the film – a critique of the Indian education system.

It is important to note that the film does not position Ishaan as a tragic victim. Rather than suffer his disabilities in silence, often the boy rebels against those who deem his behaviour a failure. In an English class, asked to read a passage and unable to do so, Ishaan starts speaking gibberish. When the teacher tells him to leave the room, he makes a furtive victory gesture to his classmates as if to say that this was his objective all along. When his father determines that he should be sent away to boarding school, he glares back at him in anger. That he is also very mischievous can be seen in the opening scenes of the film when he teases his mother by picking up a sandwich without washing his hands or his father by daring to eat strawberries that have not been washed.

Vestiges of Colonial Hangover

Though *Taare Zameen Par* is undoubtedly the story of one remarkable child, it is also the story of the limits and failure of the mainstream modern Indian education system. What is deemed as modern education in India owes much of its existence to colonialism. Education was a powerful tool in the arsenal of colonial administrations everywhere to both subordinate their subjects but also to 'liberate' them from their own cultures (see Said 1993). Thus, colonial education was intended to create hierarchical 'occident/orient' relationships. Initially, the British administration in India was tolerant of its indigenous systems of education (see Viswanathan 1998; Seth 2007; Rajivlochan 2008). However, as the administration evolved from overseeing trading to becoming a militarised presence and cementing its political hold on India, it became more coercive.

In 1835, Lord Thomas Macaulay's famous prescription on the kind of education to be imparted in India laid the groundwork for a system that still exists today in various incarnations. It essentially ended indigenous systems of science, medicine and literature at the charity-led Muslim educational institutions and the *Gurukuls* where students were expected to memorise extended excerpts of Hindu scriptures.[4] Under the guise of bringing equitable educational opportunities for all (and not just Brahmins), and introducing Enlightenment values and ideas from the Utilitarian movement, the brand called 'English education' was entrenched in India. For the rulers, and the comprador class alike, British education was the normative and civilising education as opposed to the indigenous forms of education. Colonial policy also created jobs that needed 'English education' thereby ensuring a continued demand for such education. In the mid-1950s, the post-independence nationalist policies of the country's first Prime Minister Jawaharlal Nehru articulated 'English' education as being consistant with Indian values. For Nehru, education, especially that which centred around science, engineering and mathematics, was central to the country's development and to the modernisation project. In this vision of modern India, art, literature and the social sciences played a secondary role. Decades later, the economic liberalisation policies of the late twentieth-century central governments, and the continued globalisation of the economy, further secured the place of English education in modern India.

The importance of arts and the creative imagination to Ishaan's wellbeing is shown in the way the boy is framed by the camera. Usually, we see Ishaan's gaze cast downwards and his shoulders slumped, as if in defeat. But when he paints we see him in medium close-ups with his face lit up. The camera is angled low setting his face against a backdrop that is often dark blue indicating the sky. The joy and wonderment in the boy's face are indicative of the integral role art plays in his life. Furthermore, often because the camera focuses on the child's face without actually showing him painting, the cinematography emphasises the human rather than the act. But the significance of the creative and fantasy world to Ishaan is not recognised by any of the adults in his life until his encounter with his new art teacher. It is through this tension between the child's artistic world which brings him pleasure and happiness

Fig. 1: Medium close-up of Ishaan with high-key lighting as he paints.

and the 'real' utilitarian world, that *Taare Zameer Par* enters the continuing debates about modern Indian education, an education that has been criticised both within the country and outside for being purely instrumental and reductionist. The child's impairment functions semiotically to question the extant education system.

At the very beginning of the film, we see a montage of quick shots of Ishaan's mother Maya preparing breakfasts for each member of the family and then seeing each off for the day. The chorus of the accompanying song goes 'Duniya Ka Naara Jame Raho / Manzil Ka Ishaara Jame Raho' ('It's the way of the world. Your goal beckons. Keep at it!'). The quick edits, the staccato rhythm of the camera shots and the iconography all work as a critique of the monotony of modern life that merely focuses on goals and successful results. A similar comment on modern capitalism is once again seen in another song and dance sequence we are introduced to the art teacher Nikumbh, he is dressed in a clown's costume and along with his third grade class launches into the song 'Bum bum boley, masti mey doley' ('Swing along, shake a leg, have lots of fun'). Through the song and his classroom interactions, the teacher tells his students to freely experiment with colours and shapes without any concern for the end product. He urges them, instead, to exercise their fantasy. This sets up the opposition between instrumental education that serves the capitalist world and an education that feeds the imagination and soul.

The instrumentalism of education, especially as opposed to art, is again re-emphasised towards the end of the film when Nikumbh goes to the principal's office to discuss Ishaan's dyslexia. At first, the principal is glad to hear Nikumbh's diagnosis – not because they can finally develop a programme to help the child but because, as he says, it would make it easier to tell Ishaan's father to withdraw him from his school and admit him in an institution for special needs children. Nikumbh reminds him that the Indian constitution mandates that every child has the right to an education at any school and that the school must make the necessary accommodations.[5] But, as he says, very few schools comply with this law. Sharing Ishaan's artwork with the principal, Nikumbh argues that the child is actually very bright and excels in conceptual thinking and that all he needs is some remedial tutoring. With help from his teachers, Nikumbh says, Ishaan would able to get passing grades in the usual subjects and concentrate on what is his 'true calling' – art. The principal retorts that Nikumbh seems to value art above science, mathematics, history, geography and languages – in other words, every academic area but his own. Yet when the teacher does get his principal's blessing to tutor the child, it is painting, drawing, clay art, computer games and hopscotch that help Ishaan improve motor spatial skills and finally learn to read, write and do arithmetic. In other words, it is art, and not utilitarian academic areas, that finally rehabilitates Ishaan. The message also is that when the skills of reading and writing are divorced from natural interactions, everyday communication (as opposed to highly stylised language found in literature) and play, children often are seen as, and even become, deficient in reading and writing.

At his boarding school, when a teacher in a Hindi literature class asks Ishaan to explain the meaning of a poem, he provides the conceptual meaning, which the teacher immediately rejects. The teacher then praises another student who gives an answer that is clearly memorised but perhaps not understood. Referring to that, Ishaan's only friend at the new school, a young boy who is physically disabled and uses crutches, assures him that his conceptual reading of the poem indicated that Ishaan was the one who had truly understood the literary work. However, he tells Ishaan that the teacher is very strict and always wants his pupils to simply regurgitate his own explanations. This practice of cramming, or 'mugging' in Indian vernacular English, is seen as a problematic practice. But as postcolonial historians point out, cramming was the result of deeply flawed colonial educational policies (see Seth 2007; Rajivlochan 2008). Under the garb of spreading education, the colonial administration opened numerous universities in the Indian subcontinent in quick succession. However, because it did not want to invest too heavily in them, these universities essentially became testing centres with little teaching or research undertaken. This created the tradition of Indian students committing information to memory rather than comprehending it and being personally transformed by it.

The signposts of colonial education can also be seen in the corporal punishment meted out by some of the teachers at the boarding school. As many historical accounts demonstrated, caning was standard procedure in most British schools and the practice came to India with colonialism. The language used by some of the teachers is also very regressive, reminiscent of colonial times. Nikumbh is only a substitute teacher at the boarding school. His full-time post is at a school for children with developmental disabilities. Some of Nikumbh's colleagues at the boarding school call Ishaan a 'retard' and tell him that his unorthodox teaching methods would only work at the school for 'retards'. Also contained in the film is a criticism of overcrowded schools with neither the will nor the imagination to make the resources work. Ishaan's father and the boarding school principal both complain about stuffing classes with students who do not get any individual attention.

Conclusion

Any discussion of *Taare Zameen Par* must be inserted within the larger context of disability studies in India and the disability movement. While disability studies have existed in India for decades (see Ramaa 2000; Anand 2013), critical disability studies is fairly new in the country. As Renu Addlakha points out in her landmark 2013 anthology, until recently, most research in the area was located within the disciplines of medicine, social work and pschology. Most of the empirical works were framed within a medical model which pathologises disabilities and frames deviations from ascribed bodily norms as 'abnormal'. As Shilpa Anand states, frequently these studies were based on Western epistemological models unapplicable or irrelevant in the Indian context (2013: 51). These studies also individualised the problem and assumed that the solution lay with the disabled person's acceptance of prescribed cures.

There is no doubt that *Taare Zameen Par* succeeds in eschewing the regressive medical model of disability which pathologises the impairment into an singular personality trait that the individual should keep hidden. The film shows us that naming the disability itself goes a long way to seeking ways to overcome the disability. However, the film never realises its truly revolutionary potential. It ultimately remains a narrative of individual triumph. It captures the story of a disabled protagonist who struggles with his impairment and overcomes his personal limitations at tremendous odds with the help of another extraordinary individual (see Mogk 2013: 5). In fact, in some sense, *Taare Zameen Par* becomes the story of a 'supercrip'. Ishaan's creative abilities make him an artistic savant. His success in the culminating art competition and his reintegration into his family and, by extension, the larger society become emblematic of a personal redemption.

Individualised narratives are instrumental as a storytelling mechanism; however, their message always ends up being a-political, reinforcing the very disabling difference that they construct. In such instances, unfortunately, disability ends up being symbolically used to disable people with impairments (see Ellis 2007: 2). The individualisation of impairment, its portrayal as a personal tragedy to be overcome, only serves to isolate disabled peoples. As Marja Evelyn Mogk (2013) suggests, such narratives, rather than indicting culture-specific practices, end up glorifying individuals. Rather than presenting a differently-abled mind as a continuum in the variablity of what is considered 'normal' and question how reading became a diagnostic category, the film ends up reifying the very system that created the stigmatised social status. After all, as Michel Foucault cautions us, the categories of disabilities are constructs and the exclusion of the disabled body are forms of social control.

For disability film politics to be truly transgressive and potentially revolutionary, impairment cannot be examined in isolation from the larger social system from which it emerges. As the social model of disability reminds us, the problems often do not lie in the damaged body or in the case of little Ishaan, in the mind, but in unfair social, political conditions and the neoliberal policies – things the film never addresses.

NOTES

1. So integral is song and music to Bollywood films, that the absence of them has spawned its own debate (see Garwood 2006).
2. See Colin Barnes' (2006) exhaustive typology of media images of the differently-abled; see also Gartner and Joe (1987).
3. In the Indian context, studies on dyslexia and dyslexic children date back almost thirty years. Yet, before the release of this film, there was little familiarity with this intellectual disability even among educators and education policy makers. In fact, in 2010 judges at the Delhi High Court advised a petitioner to watch *Taare Zameen Par* to clarify his understanding of dyslexia. They also severely criticised the Delhi government for being callous towards the needs of dyslexic children in schools when it was revealed that there were no trained doctors to identify or help such students (see Bhatnagar 2010).
4. Macaulay's 'Minute' categorically states that he wanted to make Indians 'Indians in skin colour but, English in taste' (in Rajivlochan 2008).
5. In fact, India is signatory to several United Nations Declarations and treaties that guarantee education as a human right and accommodations for youngsters who are differently abled. The 1995 Persons with Disabilities (Equal Opportunities, Protection of Rights and Full Participation) Act, in fact mandates training of educators to make necessary accommodations.

FILMOGRAPHY

Khan, Aamir (dir) (2007) *Taare Zameen Par* (*Like Stars on Earth*). 165 minutes. Aamir Khan Productions/PVR Pictures. India.

BIBLIOGRAPHY

Addlakha, Renu (2013) 'Introduction', in Renu Addlakha (ed.), *Disability Studies in India: Global Discourses, Local Realities*. New York: Routledge, 1-31.

Anand, Shilpa (2013) 'Historicising Disability in India: Questions of Subject and Method', in Renu Addlakha (ed.) *Disability Studies in India: Global Discourses, Local Realities*. New York, NY: Routledge, 35–60.

Andrade, Chittaranjan, Nilesh Shah and Basappa Venkatesh (2010) 'The Depiction of Electroconvulsive Therapy in Hindi Cinema', *Journal of Electroconvulsive Therapy*, 26, 1, 16–22.

Barnes, Colin (1992) 'Disabling Imagery And The Media: An Exploration Of The Principles For Media Representations Of Disabled People'. Krumlin: The British Council of Organisations of Disabled People/Ryburn Publishing. Available at http://disability-studies.leeds.ac.uk/files/library/Barnes-disabling-imagery.pdf (accessed 7 September 2015).

Barnes, Colin and Geof Mercer (2003) *Disability*. London: Polity Press.

Basu, Anustup (2010) *Bollywood in the Age of New Media*. Edinburgh: Edinburgh University Press.

Bhatnagar, Rakesh (2010) 'Watch *"Taare Zameen Par"* to Understand Dyslexia: Delhi HC', *DNAIndia*, 7 January. Available at http://www.dnaindia.com/india/report-watch-taare-zameen-par-to-understand-dyslexia-delhi-hc-1332163 (accessed 7 September 2015).

Bhugra, Dinesh (2006) *Mad Tales from Bollywood: Portrayal of Mental Illness in Conventional Hindi Cinema*. New York, NY: Psychology Press.

Bhugra, Dinesh and Gurvinder Kalra (2015) 'Applying Psychoanalysis to Hindi Cinema', in Lucy Huskinson, Terrie Waddell (eds), *Eavesdropping: The Psychotherapist in Film and Television*. New York: Routledge, 94-106.

Ellis, Katie (2007) 'Isolation and Companionship: Disability in Australian (Post) Colonial Cinema', *Wagadu*, special issue: 'Intersecting Gender and Disability Perspectives in Rethinking Postcolonial Identities', 4, 184–98. Available at http://journals.cortland.edu/wordpress/wagadu/files/2014/02/ellis.pdf (accessed 7 September 2015).

Fanon, Frantz (1967) *Black Skin, White Masks*. London: Grove Press.

Foucault, Michel (1988) *Madness and Civilization: A History of Insanity in the Age of Reason*. New York: Vintage Books.

Ganti, Tejaswini (2013) *Bollywood*. New York, NY: Routledge.

Garland-Thomson, Rosemarie (1997) *Extraordinary Bodies: Figuring Physical Disability in American Culture and Literature*. New York, NY: Columbia University Press.

____ (2009) *Staring: How We Look*. Oxford: Oxford University Press.

Gartner, Alan and Tom Joe (eds) (1987) *Images of the Disabled, Disabling Images*. New York, NY: Praeger.

Garwood, Ian (2006) 'The Songless Bollywood', *South Asian Popular Culture*, 4, 2, 169–83.

Gehlawat, Ajay (2013) *Reframing Bollywood: Theories of Popular Hindi Cinema*. New Delhi: Sage.

Gopal, Sangita and Moorti, Sujata (eds) (2008) *Global Bollywood: Travels of Hindi Song and Dance*. Minneapolis, MN: University of Minnesota Press.

Hahn, Harlan (1988) 'Can Disability Be Beautiful?', *Social Policy*, 18, 26–31.

Hayes, Michael and Rhonda Black (2003) 'Troubling Signs: Disability, Hollywood Movies and the Construction of a Discourse of Pity', *Disability Studies Quarterly*, 23, 2, 114–32.

IANS (2009) 'Disney Releasing "Taare Zameen Par" on DVD in US', *The Hindu*. Available at http://www.thehindu.com/features/cinema/disney-releasing-taare-zameen-par-on-dvd-in-us/article66773.ece?css=print (accessed 7 September 2015).

Longmore, Paul K. (2006) *Why I Burned My Book and Other Essays on Disability*. Philadelphia, PA: Temple University Press.

_____ (2013) '"Heaven's Special Child": The Making of Poster Children', in Lennard J. Davis (ed.), *The Disability Studies Reader*, 4th ed. New York: Routledge, 34-41.

Mishra, Vijay (2002) *Bollywood Cinema: Temples of Desire*. New York: Routledge.

_____ (2008) 'Towards a Theoretical Critique of Bombay Cinema', in Rajinder Dudrah and Jigna Desai (eds) *The Bollywood Reader*. Berkshire: Open University Press, 32–44.

Mogk, Marja Evelyn (2013) *Different Bodies: Essays on Disability in Film and Television*. Jefferson, NC: McFarland.

Mohapatra, Atanu (2012) 'Portrayal of Disability in Hindi Cinema: A Study of Emerging Trends of Differently-abled', *Asian Journal of Multidimensional Research*, 1, 7, 124–32.

Pal, Joyjeet (2013) 'Physical Disability and Indian Cinema', in Marja Evelyn Mogk (ed.) *Different Bodies: Essays on Disability in Film and Television*. Jefferson, NC: McFarland, 109–30.

Prasad, Madhava (2003) 'This Thing Called Bollywood', *Seminar*, 525, special issue on 'The Place of Cinema in India'. Available at http://www.india-seminar.com/2003/525/525%20madhava%20prasad.htm (accessed 7 September 2015).

Ramaa, S. (2000) 'Two Decades of Research on Learning Disabilities in India', *Dyslexia*, 6, 268–83.

Rajadhyaksha, Ashish (2003) 'The "Bollywoodization" of the Indian Cinema: Cultural Nationalism in a Global Arena', *Inter-Asia Cultural Studies*, 4, 1, 25–39.

Rajivlochan, M. (2008) 'Reforming Education for India, from England', in *Seminar* 587, special issue on 'Mortgaging the Future: a symposium on reforming India's higher education system'. Available at http://www.indiaseminar.com/2008/587/587_m_rajivlochan.htm (accessed 7 September 2015).

Said, Edward (1993) *Culture and Imperialism*. London: Chatto & Windus.

Seth, Sanjay (2007) *Subject Lessons: The Western Education of Colonial India*. Durham, NC: Duke University Press.

Smith, Frank (2004) *Understanding Reading: A Psycholinguistic Analysis of Reading and Learning To Read*. Mahwah, NJ: Lawrence Erlbaum.

Titchkosky, Tanya (2008) '"I Got Trouble With My Reading": An Emerging Literacy', in Susan Lynn Gabel, Scot Danforth (eds) *Disability & the Politics of Education: An International Reader*. New York: Peter Lang, 337-52.

Virdi, Jyotika and Corey K. Creekmur (2006) 'India: Bollywood's Global Coming of Age', in Anne Tereska Ciecko (ed.) *Contemporary Asian Cinema: Popular Culture in a Global Frame*. New York, NY: Bloomsbury, 133–43.

Viswanathan, Gauri (1988) 'Currying Favor: The Politics of British Educational and Cultural Policy in India, 1813-1854', *Social Text*, 19/20, 85-104.

_____ (1998) *Masks of Conquest: Literary Study and British Rule in India*. Oxford: Oxford University Press.

White, Linda Feldmeier (2002) 'Learning Disability: Pedagogies and Public Discourse', *College Composition and Communication*, 53, 4, 705–38.

Landscapes of Children

Picturing Disability in Buñuel's *Los olvidados* (1950)

Susan Antebi

In 1973, Luis Buñuel received a letter from Dr. Benjamin Viel, Chilean specialist in public health and family planning, and admirer of Buñuel's film *Los olvidados* (*The Young and the Damned*, 1950). The letter included the following statement:

> Hay una frase en *Los olvidados* que ha tenido profunda influencia en mi decisión de dedicar mi profesión de médico al control de nacimiento. La madre interrogada por un psicólogo, ante la acusación de 'usted no quiere a su hijo', contesta, '¿y por qué había de quererlo? Ni siquiera recuerda la cara de quien me violó cuando tenía 14 años'. Nunca he visto una acusación más clara al supuesto instinto maternal.
>
> (There is a phrase in *Los olvidados* that has had a profound influence on my decision to dedicate my medical career to birth control. The mother, questioned by a psychologist, faced with the accusation that 'you don't love your son', replies, 'and why should I love him? I don't even remember the face of the guy who raped me when I was fourteen'. I have never seen a clearer refutation of supposed maternal instinct.)
>
> (Viel, quoted in Sánchez Vidal 2004: 93)[1]

The explicit purpose of the letter was to ask Buñuel to direct a film on the topic of population control. As Viel notes, Buñuel had been cited by Carlos Fuentes earlier the same year as having said: 'Creo que la lucha de clases no es ya el problema central. El verdadero problema es el control de la natalidad y el equilibrio ecológico' ('I believe that class struggle is no longer the central problem. The real problem is birth control and ecological balance') (ibid.). Needless to say, the director did not take up Viel's suggestion, leaving us only to imagine the results of what such a film project might have entailed.

Perhaps not surprisingly, Viel did not choose to mention the famous line of the blind musician, don Carmelo, who shouts at the end of the film, '¡Ojalá los mataran a todos antes de nacer!' ('If only they killed them all before they were born!') in reference to the delinquent street children depicted in *Los olvidados*. This jarring conclusion and its gesture of retroactive violence must surely have caught the attention of the family planning physician. Moreover, it is a key instance of the complexity surrounding the film's depiction of disability, caught between the evocation of a grotesque corporeal aesthetics in which physical disability – in this case, blindness – corresponds to moral cruelty, and reference to societal ills, such as juvenile delinquency, which are inscribed on individual bodies and may inspire correctives, violent or otherwise.

The tension between these closely interrelated modes of disability representation in Buñuel's film is central to my analysis in the present chapter. I pay particular attention here to the juxtaposition of the work's capacity to trigger a visceral response, and its articulation of social problems that instead demand thought or action. These two aspects of the film, and the director's ability to contain them both in a single work, have in fact shaped the critical importance and reception of *Los olvidados*. The unique combination of visceral aesthetics and social critique has helped to determine the film's location at a turning point in Buñuel's career and in twentieth-century Mexican cultural production in general. As I argue, the film's use and depiction of disability are crucial to its ability to straddle and complicate the divide between aesthetics and critique. The roles and representations of disability in *Los olvidados* emerge, in turn, through the relationship between these competing but interlinked projects. The combined display of, on one hand, corporeal difference as moral cruelty, and on the other, violent action determined by conditions of socioeconomic inequality, reveals bodies at odds with their surroundings, and vice versa. In addition, through this juxtaposition Buñuel's film articulates a critical interweaving of violence and vulnerability as specific to Mexican revolutionary modernity.

In a sense, the imperfectly-defined opposition between aesthetics and critique reflects what Sebastiaan Faber has described as Buñuel's 'impure modernism' (2012: 63), shaped by a combination of aesthetic, political and commercial goals.[2] Many critics, including Faber, read *Los olvidados* as a key work in Buñuel's career, in part because of the film's effective merging of seemingly disparate cinematic projects. Buñuel's combined approach, or 'impurity', allowed the film to surprise and challenge audiences, breaking with expectations regarding Mexican society and cinema, social realism and the nature and intention of radical critique. Disability plays important roles in both Buñuel's broader trajectory as avant-garde writer and director – of which this film forms a part – and in *Los olvidados*'s discourse of social protest. For this reason, disability itself emerges at the centre of Buñuel's unique and often jarring combination of cinematic techniques. The uncertainty of this combination in turn helps to produce a work that is, as Ernesto Acevedo-Muñoz describes, 'amoral' in relation to Mexico as subject matter, and key to understanding 'Mexico's revolutionary crisis' (2003: 73, 61). The crisis here refers in part to ongoing socio-economic inequality, exacerbated by urbanisation and modernisation, as evidence of the Revolution's failure to deliver its promises. Such forms of injustice also contributed to an aesthetic crisis regarding what constituted Mexican cultural and national identity (2003: 77). Buñuel's film effectively situates disability within this crisis, through its depiction of bodies that do not and cannot fit seamlessly into the violent contexts they inhabit or create, and, perhaps most interestingly, through a refusal to finally judge the roles of such bodies in relation to Mexican moral or cinematic values.

Benjamin Viel's above-mentioned letter appears to have been inspired by elements of social critique present in *Los olvidados*, though it points towards a solution that is never addressed in the film itself. A fragment of the letter is reproduced in a monumental 2004 study of *Los olvidados*, published by Televisa and including the original screenplay as well as many film stills. Viel's writing might surprise the reader for its direct tone and rather literal ascription of a message to *Los olvidados*, as well as for its emphasis on a topic with no clear connection to Buñuel's interests as a filmmaker. The juxtaposition of a discourse of population control with the scenes and stories of the film also appears to suggest in a more general sense that *Los olvidados* offers the viewer the dynamic of a problem that corresponds to a specific solution. The problem, an urban scenario of violence and suffering, would from this perspective point towards a needed or proposed response, whether this might take the form of class revolution, social reform or, as Viel bluntly advocates, birth control.

Approaching Buñuel's classic film via the framework of problem and solution does in fact correspond to a history of some responses to the work. Julie Jones has argued that *Los olvidados* was, from Buñuel's own perspective a documentary film, but one that was never explicit in its proposal for change. Jones writes: 'The film itself presents no answer, and this absence left a number of reviewers, evidently accustomed to the problem-solution structure common in the documentary, at a loss' (2005: 23). The film's ambivalence in relation to the specificity of solutions to the problems it portrays in part reflects Buñuel's desire to let the spectators reach their own conclusions through contact with the work (ibid.). At the same time, the uncertain role of the problem-solution structure in *Los olvidados* points to the complexity of competing aesthetic and political projects in the film. The problem-solution dynamic shares the screen here with less programmatic gestures, guided in part by Buñuel's surrealist trajectory, and by Spanish literary influences, including the picaresque.[3]

Disability representation in *Los olvidados* might at first appear to be limited to the depiction of just two characters, the above-mentioned blind (and cruel) don Carmelo, and a more minor character, the legless man who is attacked and robbed by a group of street children near the beginning of the film. These figures are in fact only part of the story, but as Agustín Sánchez Vidal suggests, their juxtaposed presence in the film links this work to Buñuel's previous films such as *La edad de oro* (*The Golden Age*, 1930) and to Dalí's text, *Vida secreta* (*Secret Life*, 1942) thus revealing the importance of both surrealism and Sadean tendencies in *Los olvidados*.[4] From this perspective, the explicit violence surrounding the representation of these disabled characters becomes part of a distinctly surrealist moral universe. At the same time, when recreated in an urban, Mexican mid-century setting, the violence goes to work in new directions, in opposition to traditional Mexican filmic representations of local community values.[5] Viewers may read such scenes as part of an amoral universe, in Acevedo-Muñoz's terms, or as one aspect of a social critique of injustice. The representation of disability appears at the centre of the film's ambivalence here, whether the disabled character is a victim – as in the case of the attack on the legless man – or a perpetrator – as when don Carmelo inflicts physical or verbal abuse on children.

'Los cuerpos rotos son caros a Buñuel' ('Buñuel is fond of broken bodies') writes Julia Tuñón (2003: 138), with reference to the classic eye-cutting scene in *Un chien andalou* (1929) as well as to 'enfermedades y mutilaciones' ('illnesses and mutilations') throughout the rest of his work (2003: 139). Henri-Jacques Stiker, for his part, also notes the prevalence of 'boiteux, nains, sourds et surtout aveugles' ('cripples, dwarfs, deaf people, and especially blind people') in Buñuel's films (2007: 16). For Stiker, one of very few critics to address disability explicitly in Buñuel, disabled characters in films such as *La edad de oro*, *Viridiana* (1961) and *La voie lactée* (*The Milky Way*, 1969) as well as in *Los olvidados*, tend to represent social ills. But in addition, in Stiker's view, the films suggest that such ills, like the disabilities offered as their metaphors, have no solution; rehabilitation thus does not figure in Buñuel's cinema of disability.[6] This second observation regarding the absence of a solution aligns with the above-mentioned link between disability representation and the director's surrealist tendencies.

A more complete picture of the role of disability in *Los olvidados* emerges, however, when one extends beyond explicit corporeal impairments to consider the overall social field represented in the film. The 'forgotten ones' who define this field as modern, urban, poor and marginalised, are themselves victims of social inequality, and perhaps strangely, of the fact of being young. In this precarious setting, youth and childhood become markers of ongoing potential social ill, as representative of the growth of a poor, hence undesirable, population sector. Classic disability studies criticism has argued that, as in the case of explicitly represented physical disability, social ill in narrative is frequently destined for rehabilitation or erasure (see Davis 2002; Stiker 2007). It may also be explained in terms of a corporeal or genetic abnormality affecting a family or community lineage and emerging on and through the bodies of offspring.[7] In this way, social problems such as poverty, crime and domestic violence come to denote a temporal trajectory of disability as collective history and potential reproductive future, hence requiring intervention. While Buñuel's depictions of physical disability, as suggested, generally avoid such a discourse of rehabilitation, a different pattern appears when the field of disability is broadened to include the context of social ill and social reform.

In the film's opening credits, Buñuel includes thanks to several heads of state-sponsored agencies, including Dr. José Luis Patiño Rojas, psychiatrist and Director of the Clínica de la Conducta, founded in 1948 at the request of President Miguel Alemán (see Villaseñor Bayardo 2004: 335). In Sergio Javier Villaseñor Bayardo's account, Patiño Rojas briefly describes his work with 'problem children' or those who had difficulty studying, and his collaboration with Buñuel. Buñuel himself emphasises the various sources he researched for the film, including, 'Juvenile Court … reports of … social workers … clinics for the retarded … reports on individual beggars'.[8] This seemingly eclectic combination of sources from which Buñuel drew his material offers useful perspective on varied categories of deviance or abnormality in mid-century Mexico, as well as the potential conflation of these categories. Buñuel's interest in Patiño Rojas's work at the Clínica de la Conducta, and in 'problem children' also points to a key link between *Los olvidados* and the combined roles of healthcare and education in Mexico's post-revolutionary period, particularly within the discipline of so-called psychopedagogy, a topic by which Buñuel actually claimed to be 'inspired' (Jones 2005: 22). The history of psychopedagogy in this period reveals complex interdependencies between notions of education, physical and mental health and hygiene, contributing to state-sponsored initiatives to classify and correct abnormality towards the goal of collective social improvement. Whether the thanks to Patiño Rojas may be read as a direct advocacy of state-sponsored social reform is a debatable point. Nonetheless, the connection does suggest that the social marginalisation of the young characters represented in *Los olvidados* derives meaning from the concept of abnormality in circulation at the time. Such so-called abnormality was defined through a range of intersecting factors, including physical and psychological characteristics, academic performance, markers of ethnicity and economic status and histories of family illness, alcoholism and criminal records.

A 1954 text co-authored by Drs Alfonso Campos Artigas and Patiño Rojas documenting the work of the Clínica de la Conducta since its opening in 1948 provides relevant background on the notion of 'problem children' at the time, as well as insight into the role of psychopedagogy in defining the biological and social causes of categories of abnormality among the young Mexicans diagnosed at the clinic. The text describes the children according to classifications such as 'débiles mentales' ('mental weaklings'), 'psicóticos' ('psychotics'), 'epilépticos' ('epileptics'), 'neuróticos' ('neurotics') and 'sujetos que atraviesan etapas críticas transitorias, en quienes las variaciones psico-biológicas explican, en cierta forma, su pasajero desajuste con el medio ambiente que los circunda' ('subjects going through critical transitory stages, in whom psycho-biological variation explains, in a way, their temporary imbalance in relation to their surrounding environment') (1954: 30). The authors return throughout the text to the role of the environment, noting, for example, 'Conviene enfatizar que, aunque la debilidad mental es siempre orgánica, de origen, en alto número de casos la inadaptación infantil no es dada por ella misma, sino por el mal manejo psicopedagógico de tales menores' ('It is worth emphasising that although mental weakness is always organic in origin, in a large number of cases, the schoolchild's maladjustment does not arise on its own, but because of the psychopedagogical mismanagement of such youth') (Campos Artigas and Patiño Rojas 1954: 79). Buñuel would certainly have come across such theories in his research for the film; moreover, the medical specialists' repeated insistence on a dynamic but uncertain relationship between 'organic' (or congenital) factors and environmental influence finds a clear echo in *Los olvidados*, and in particular in the film's multiple and ambivalent depictions of disability.

The Clínica de la Conducta was not the first of its kind, nor were the theories represented in the 1954 study new ones. The clinical work documented by Campos Artigas and Patiño Rojas appears within a post-revolutionary trajectory of national emphasis on the need to both measure and improve the characteristics of the Mexican population, especially through attention to children and youth. In this sense, Patiño Rojas's clinic and the inspiration it provided for the creation of *Los olvidados* could be read as a critical culmination of decades of work, centred on the figure of the child as key to the definition, diagnosis and correction of individual and collective abnormality.

As an earlier example, one might consider Dr. Rafael Santamarina's 1927 conference, presented at the second annual meeting of the International Association for the Protection of Infancy, in which the author discusses the concept of 'educability', and presents a graphic suggesting that a large percentage of Mexican school children fall outside its parameters. Santamarina's notion of educability borrows from the work of Eugénie Monchamps and that of Georges Paul-Boncour, and is described as the tendency of the child to gradually begin to perform adult activities (1927a: 2). Santamarina's graphic shows a scale of different groups of children in the Mexican context, based on their levels of educability. The vast majority are classified as 'irregular', though only a small group of these, tagged as 'idiotas' ('idiots') and some classes of 'imbéciles' ('imbeciles') are completely 'ineducables' ('uneducable'). Levels of educability are further classified by causes, including psychic, physical, hereditary and social, and correspond to outcomes including apathy, maladjustment, weakness, blindness, deafness, lameness and poor life conditions, all of which negatively impact educability in varying degrees (1927b: n.p.). Curiously then, in this interpretation the less a child resembles an adult by beginning to behave like one, the more closely he corresponds to the overarching category of irregularity, which encompasses a range of disabilities and conditions, including poverty, and which in turn limit his ability to succeed in school. Inverting the analysis, one could also conclude that all of the disabilities and conditions included prevent the child from becoming like an adult, and hence from effectively reaching adulthood. In either case, the irregularity to which Santamarina refers is essential to childhood and childishness, and helps to define a separation between children and adults.

Insistence on the measurement and testing of children and on dissemination of statistical data was linked to goals of social reform and improvement of the population that would continue into the 1940s and beyond.[9] In this context the state – via the Ministry of Public Education – was mandated to address and remedy individual and collective pathology for the public good; and the public, in turn, was impelled to collaborate in the task, through hygiene and reproductive practices. The concept of mental hygiene, as well as theories of continuity and causality between physical and psychological abnormalities, perversion and immorality, also played an important role in the areas of public health and education, as evidenced in the 1937 formation of the National Institute of Psychopedagogy, which included a combined Servicio de Higiene Mental Escolar and Clínica de la Conducta. As Beatriz Urías Horcasitas notes, the same theories were brought to bear on the problem of crime, a connection of clear significance in considering Buñuel's research for his film. Theories of criminal sociology in the early 1950s, for example, emphasised the importance of understanding the biological and psychological bases of criminal behaviour, the impact of the social environment in combination with inherited characteristics and the need to distinguish between combined and isolated categories of delinquency, laziness, mental illness and social parasitism (2007: 164–8).

The young characters at the centre of *Los olvidados* do not display, strictly speaking, the 'broken bodies' to which critics tend to refer when noticing the prevalence of visibly disabled people in so many of Buñuel's films. Yet these characters depict disability in several other interrelated ways. They appear through interaction and symbolic association with the explicitly disabled don Carmelo, and with the unnamed, legless man, both of whom are victims of the youths' assault in different scenes. In addition, their potential or realised criminal activities, including theft, assault and murder, link them to the previously mentioned sociological theories of degeneracy, mental illness and biopsychological disorder, available to Buñuel in his research into 'problem children' of the time. The leading figure and most violent member of the group is el Jaibo, who in one scene makes a brief reference to his childhood shaking attacks ('temblores'), a probable allusion to epilepsy.

According to theories of eugenics, psychopedagogy and hygiene of the period, epilepsy was directly associated with delinquency. For example, a reference to epilepsy as cause of murder in a 1935 school hygiene text describes the condition as follows:

> Aquel que tiene algo en su interior que quiere contener y no puede, aquel que no puede inhibirse, que cuando sufre algún choque no puede contener sus brazos y se va sobre el contrario y lo golpea, o aquel que en

un momento dado o en un arranque de pasión no detiene sus brazos y da una puñalada no son otra cosa que grados diferentes.

(He who has something inside him that he wants to contain but can't, he who cannot be inhibited, so that when he suffers some shock he can't control his arms and hits his opponent, or he who at some point or in a sudden passion doesn't restrain his arms and stabs someone, these are nothing but different degrees of the same thing.)

(Solís Quiroga 1935: 37)[10]

Along the same lines, and within the logic of the film, el Jaibo's violent actions and lack of moral constraint may therefore be interpreted as a direct result of this condition.

In two key scenes, the film connects disability to youth through violent interactions between the blind and aged don Carmelo and the marginalised children. The first case concerns Ojitos, a rural indigenous boy, abandoned by his father in the city, who comes to work as guide and assistant to don Carmelo, in exchange for limited and precarious food and housing, as well as frequent physical abuse. In the scene in question, after don Carmelo has punished Ojitos by pulling him off the ground by one ear, Ojitos picks up a concrete block and holds it in the air, as if about to hit the old man over the head with it. The boy resists his initial impulse and tosses the block to the ground. The effect of the sequence is heightened, inevitably, by don Carmelo's blindness. The threat of the block in Ojitos's raised hands suggests a visual pact between the younger character and the viewer, since don Carmelo is apparently not aware of the danger. This technique plays into the voyeuristic tendencies of the film, in letting the audience secretly witness both a potential, violent action before it unfolds, and the old man's ignorance of what is about to take place. Yet when the block hits the ground, don Carmelo immediately responds to the sound by questioning what it was. His sarcastic repetition of Ojitos' reply – 'a rock that fell' – informs the viewer that he is not so easily fooled. At the same moment, the camera shifts to focus on the knife in don Carmelo's hands as he slices potatoes, thus transferring the violent potential from the heavy rock to an alternative and equally lethal instrument.

In a second instance, later in the film, Meche, a young girl and friend of Ojitos delivers donkey's milk to don Carmelo, who pulls her onto his lap and comments on the nice smell of her hair. In reaction to this molestation, Meche lifts her skirt to retrieve a pair of scissors, which she holds as if about to stab the old man. She and Ojitos exchange glances and he gestures emphatically in

Fig. 1: The blind don Carmelo is unaware of Ojitos's threat to hit him with a concrete block. This scene underscores the reciprocally determined vulnerability of childhood and disability, as well as the instrumental relationship between disability and violence in the film.

favour of her obvious intention. As in the earlier sequence, blindness allows for a heightened intensity in the exchange; this time, the two children plot together silently, unbeknownst to don Carmelo, yet in addition, the viewer gains access to Meche's sexualised body as she reveals her upper thighs while taking the scissors from the inner pocket of her skirt. At the same moment, don Carmelo laments his lack of eyesight which prevents him from seeing Meche. The scene thus repeats the voyeurism of the earlier one, though in this case positioning the viewer – via the camera – as both witness and substitute for don Carmelo's paedophilic 'gaze'.

Both scenes emphasise the mutual dependence of the blind man and the children, as well as their vulnerability to one another's violent intentions. Unlike in the scenes of brutal assault and murder carried out by el Jaibo at other points in the film, here violence remains primarily at the level of gestured possibility, a threatening potential that may or may not be realised and therefore exerts ongoing control over its victims. The association between don Carmelo's blindness, the specificity of which is crucial to the logic of the two scenes, and Ojitos's and Meche's youth, does suggest a metaphorical link between disability and childhood. Yet interactions in these scenes reveal a relationship that might be better described as metonymic, based not simply on one form of bodily vulnerability as symbolic substitute for another, but also on physical proximity that produces an ongoing displacement of intention and meaning between bodies. The violent gestures displayed by both don Carmelo and the children necessarily build on one another, through a web of vulnerability and defence of personal interests, in which it becomes difficult to distinguish clearly between cause and effect, perpetrator and victim, and perhaps ultimately between violence produced through physical difference and through social conditions.

In the first scene, don Carmelo lifts Ojitos by the ear because he has just overheard him talking to someone, and wants to find out who it was. The passerby in question was el Jaibo, who moments earlier had threatened to kill Ojitos if he told anyone he had seen him. Earlier in the film, el Jaibo had beaten another boy (Julian) to death after hitting his head from behind with a rock. The image of Ojitos with the concrete block raised as a weapon thus links a prior scene of violence to the present one, not only by suggesting that one act of violence tends to lead to another, but also by extending a sense of physical continuity between the characters and objects featured in these

Fig. 2: El Jaibo uses a sling on his arm both to feign an injury and to conceal the rock with which he plans to attack Julian. As in figure 1, invisibility is the key feature of the weapon. Disability, a false injury in this case, again becomes inseparable from the gesture of violence.

scenes. In the earlier scene, el Jaibo conceals the rock that he plans to use as a weapon by placing it in a sling that he wraps around his arm, feigning an injury. This false temporary impairment creates an effective hiding place for a weapon, while at once effectively disarming el Jaibo's victim, who refuses to initiate a fight with a seemingly injured person. The false injury thus occupies the site of the weapon it hides, but in the process also becomes a weapon itself. Interestingly, el Jaibo 'borrows' the cloth for his sling from another boy, who had been wearing it around his neck because of a cough. In this way, the cloth as object creates continuity between scenes, marking physical vulnerability through a clever shift between the functions of protection and violent deception.

When Ojitos raises the concrete block as if to strike don Carmelo, the old man's blindness serves the same purpose as el Jaibo's sling from the earlier scene, for in each case the potential victim cannot see the weapon held by the aggressor. Violence, whether proposed as a gesture or consummated through an attack, serves to create an associative link between bodies, and between violent action and impairments or vulnerabilities. This is not only because, in an obvious sense, violence damages bodies, but more importantly because such actions depend on a fluid and repeating continuity between violence and corporeal difference.

These scenes of metonymic association between youth as a social problem and explicit physical disability thus demonstrate the film's insistence on the complex intertwining of a discourse of social reform and a surrealism-inflected aesthetics of corporeal difference as violence. Youth is figured here as delinquency or vulnerability, through characters such as el Jaibo, Ojitos and Meche, while the blind and cruel don Carmelo is the primary representative of explicit physical disability. The visual continuity between these characters in their violent interactions suggests a language of disability that cannot be restricted to an individual body or ideology, but instead circulates and reveals itself as central to both Buñuel's larger cinematic project and to the Mexican crisis of revolutionary modernity that the director encountered and fundamentally shaped.

NOTES

1 All translations are mine.
2 Faber also refers to Agustín Sánchez Vidal's work on this point.
3 Agustín Sánchez Vidal notes that for Octavio Paz, *Los olvidados* can be read in the context of the picaresque, and in relation to the work of Galdós and Valle-Inclán (2004: 13).

4 Sánchez Vidal writes that the blind don Carmelo and the legless man from *Los olvidados* are in fact based on Dalí's character of a blind, legless beggar in *Vida secreta*, whom the narrator violently pushes across the street on his cart. In the context of Dalí's writing, according to Sánchez Vidal, this scene was meant as a 'programa de aprendizaje de la moral surrealista, de signo opuesto a la burguesa' ('learning programme in surrealist morals, in opposition to bourgeois morals') (2004: 77).
5 For Ernesto Acevedo-Muñoz, *Los olvidados* breaks with Mexican cinema of the period by presenting a simultaneously violent and modernising Mexico (2003: 73).
6 Note that Martin F. Norden (1994) also makes reference to *Los olvidados* and to Buñuel more generally, in relation to disability in film.
7 In *Nadie me verá llorar* (*No One Will See Me Cry*, 2003), Cristina Rivera Garza provides both a fictional representation and a critical view of this early twentieth-century eugenicist thinking in Mexico. The discourse of social ill in relation to corporeal difference and reproductive future is fundamental to theories of eugenics and related concepts that would impact Mexican public health and education through the 1940s.
8 Julie Jones cites several archival sources and interviews with Buñuel on this material (2005: 22).
9 By the late 1930s, the notion of biological improvement of the population had shifted, thanks in part to the discrediting of the neo-Lamarckian concept of the inheritance of acquired characteristics, and the rise of biotypology in Mexico. As Stern notes, José Gómez Robleda's 1937 study of proletariat school children found that their characteristics were 'prácticamente imposibles de modificar' ('practically impossible to modify') (quoted in Stern 2000: 87). Yet official discourses of social reform and hygiene continued to have a strong impact; see Urías Horcasitas (2007: 141).
10 On the relationship between disabilities, including epilepsy, and behaviour, Campos Artigas and Patiño Rojas write: 'Entre los factores patológicos que por si mismos y en forma directa son responsables de alteraciones de la conducta, pueden citarse en los casos estudiados, los siguientes: Encefalítis diversas de la más variada etiología, disendocrinias, epilepsia, corea, déficit de los sentidos visual y auditivo' ('Among the pathological factors that by themselves are directly responsible for behavioral alterations, one may cite the following of the studied cases: Encephalitis of varied etiology, endocrinosis, epilepsy, chorea, visual and auditory impairments') (1954: 40). Note that both Faber and Medina Jiménez also refer to el Jaibo's epilepsy in the film.

FILMOGRAPHY

Buñuel, Luis (dir) (1950) *Los olvidados* (*The Young and the Damned*). 80 minutes. Ultramar Films. Mexico.

BIBLIOGRAPHY

Acevedo-Muñoz, Ernesto (2003) *Buñuel and Mexico: The Crisis of National Cinema*. Berkeley, CA: University of California Press.

Campos Artigas, Alfonso and José Luis Patiño Rojas (1954) *La clínica de conducta y el niño problema*. Mexico: Secretaría de Educación Pública.

Davis, Lennard J. (2002) *Bending Over Backwards: Disability, Dismodernism and Other Difficult Positions*. New York, NY: New York University Press.

Faber, Sebastiaan (2003) 'Between Cernuda's Paradise and Buñuel's Hell: Mexico through Spanish Exiles' Eyes', *Bulletin of Spanish Studies*, 80, 2, 219-51. Web. http://www.tandfonline.com/doi/abs/10.1080/14753820302026 (accessed 12 May 2015).

——— (2012) 'Buñuel's Impure Modernism (1929–1950)', *Modernist Cultures*, 7, 1, 56–76. Available at http://www.euppublishing.com/doi/abs/10.3366/mod.2012.0028 (accessed 12 May 2015).

Jones, Julie (2005) 'Interpreting Reality: *Los olvidados* and the Documentary Mode', *Journal of Film and Video*, 57, 4, 18–31. Available at http://www.jstor.org/stable/20688502?seq=1#page_scan_tab_contents (accessed 14 May 2015).

Medina Jiménez, Hernán (2014) 'Pedagogía, subalternidad y *fatum* en *Los olvidados* (1950) de Luis Buñuel: ambivalencias entre la diáspora repúblicana en México y la 'Época de oro' como cine nacional', *A contracorriente: A Journal on Social History and Literature in Latin America*, 11, 2, 221-56. Web. http://acontracorriente.chass.ncsu.edu/index.php/acontracorriente/article/view/763 (accessed 14 May 2015).

Norden, Martin F. (1994) *The Cinema of Isolation: A History of Physical Disability in the Movies*. New Brunswick, NJ: Rutgers University Press.

Rivera Garza, Cristina (2006) *Nadie me verá llorar*. Mexico: Tusquets.

Sánchez Vidal, Agustín (2004) *Los olvidados: una película de Luis Buñuel*. Mexico, D.F.: Fundación Televisa.

Santamarina, Rafael (1927a) 'La cuestión de los anormales'. MS. Fondo Secretaría de Educación Pública, Departamento de Psicopedagogía e Higiene. Archivo General de la Nación. Mexico, D.F.

——— (1927b) 'Clasificación del Dr. Santamarina'. MS. Fondo Secretaría de Educación Pública, Departamento de Psicopedagogía e Higiene. Archivo General de la Nación. Mexico, D.F.

Solís Quiroga, Roberto (1935) 'El alcoholismo como causa de deficiencia mental. Especial para el nacional'. MS. Fondo Secretaría de Educación Pública, Departamento de Psicopedagogía e Higiene. Archivo General de la Nación. Mexico, D.F.

Stern, Alexandra (2000) 'Mestizofilia, biotipología y eugenesia en el México posrevolucionario: hacia una historia de la ciencia y el estado (1920-1960)', *Relaciones*, 81, 21, 58-91. Available at http://www.colmich.edu.mx/relaciones25/files/revistas/081/pdf/Alexandra_Stern.pdf (accessed 15 May 2015).

Stiker, Henri-Jacques (2007) 'Approche anthropologique des images du handicap. Le schème du retournement', *ALTER, Revue européenne de recherche sur le handicap*, 1, 10–22. Available at http://www.em-consulte.com/article/150613/approche-anthropologique-des-images-du-handicap-le (accessed 15 May 2015).

Tuñón, Julia (2003) 'El espacio del desamparo. La ciudad de México en el cine institucional de la edad de oro y en *Los olvidados* de Buñuel', *Iberoamericana*, 3, 11, 129–44. Available at http://journals.iai.spk-berlin.de/index.php/iberoamericana/article/view/620 (accessed 24 April 2015).

Urías Horcasitas, Beatriz (2007) *Historias secretas del racismo en México (1920–1950)*. Mexico: Tusquets.

Villaseñor Bayardo, Sergio Javier (2004) *Voces de la psiquiatría. Los precursores*. Guadalajara: Universidad de Guadalajara/Centro Universitario de Ciencias de la Salud.

Fearful Reflections

Representations of Disability in Post-war Dutch Cinema (1973–2011)

Mitzi Waltz

One can tell a great deal about a culture's concerns by examining the content of its insults (see Bourdieu 1991). A range of popular Dutch epithets employ mental illness, developmental disability, physical disability and, particularly, cancer (see Natrop 2014; *De Telegraaf* 2015). This fear of illness and disability is frequently mirrored in the context of Dutch-language film culture, informing and being strengthened by portrayals of disabled characters that emphasise dependency, lack, abjection and dread.

This chapter provides an overview of post-war representations of disabled people and their lives in Dutch cinema. It references a variety of films and performances that have had great artistic or commercial impact, and films that provide potential counter-narratives to these representations. Rather than restricting this study to national boundaries, films in the Dutch language (Nederlands or Vlaams/Flemish) are included regardless of whether they were made in the Netherlands or Belgium, as well as one Belgian film in the French language. Co-production is common in the lowlands due to the small market for films in a language spoken by so few people outside of the region, and national borders that have shifted historically mean that language rather than political formations takes on predominant cultural importance. American films tend to dominate the screen space in the Netherlands, while both English and French films find mainstream release in Belgium. However, Dutch-language films are to some extent subsidised via preferential tax arrangements for investors.

In this chapter I first discuss the ways in which disability came to prominence in Dutch film, and the cultural background of these initial portrayals. This section focuses in particular on the early Dutch work of director Paul Verhoeven, among others. Next, I consider more recent films that feature representations of young male wheelchair users, and provide an overview of other types of disability portrayals that have been presented to audiences more recently. Following this, I consider how disability is deployed in the arthouse cinema of Alex van Warmerdam, and then discuss two films that have central characters on the autism spectrum. The chapter concludes with an analysis of disability representation in Dutch film as a whole, considering a range of somewhat troubling dominant narratives but also other narratives that may deviate from or challenge these.

The Post-war Turn in Dutch Cinema

As Piet Calis (2010) has noted, Dutch-language literature and film changed drastically in the post-war era. Sexual themes met strong resistance from officialdom and the mainstream media, particularly in the dourly Calvinist Netherlands, but by the early 1970s they had nonetheless become commonplace. It is in this environment of social change and exploration that disability first becomes fore-grounded in Dutch film, as one of several topics that filmmakers felt they had permission to explore in a more permissive era.

This occurred in Paul Verhoeven's *Turks Fruit* (*Turkish Delight*, 1973), which remains the most-seen Dutch film of all time (see Vollmer 2006). *Turks Fruit* was based on a popular 1969 novel by Jan Wolkers, and is now one of the sixteen films listed in the official Dutch Film Canon (see Nederlands Film Festival 2012). At its heart is a love story between a turbulent, emotionally damaged sculptor, Eric (Rutger Hauer), and a free-spirited young woman, Olga (an iconic performance by ingénue Monique van de Ven). Between these characters stands Olga's family, although she is encouraged to fly by her understanding father. The struggle of rural, poor or non-conformist people against barriers such as mainstream culture or fate is an enduring theme throughout modern Dutch film, although disability is rarely placed within screenplays as one of these barriers.

Both Olga and her father succumb to cancer during the course of the film; her mother has also had cancer, although this is only mentioned in passing. Cancer is depicted in visual set-pieces reminiscent of Cronenbergian body horror, including a particularly arresting chiaroscuro tableau in which the camera pulls back from the disease-wracked body of the dying father to show that he is literally leaking bodily fluids through his sickbed onto the floor. Xavier Mendik (2004: 109–18) has also noted the equation through cancer of abjection and disgust with femininity and desire in Verhoeven's work.

Olga's sexual disinhibition, it is hinted, may be due to the brain tumour that later kills her. Her lover is the first to discern that she has cancer (deduced through his discovery of bloody faeces in the toilet bowl) but he disregards the evidence. Although van de Ven's vivacious beauty and rampant sexuality present a strong image, they are expressed in relation to men, in the role of an artist's muse. At the end of the film, as her physicality is confined to a hospital bed, Olga can only gratify her appetite for sweets. The film can be read as showing that that choosing to break social convention has deadly consequences for women, while for men similar iconoclasm brings strength, independence and creativity.

As in England, much post-war Dutch film moved from the historical or romantic themes that once predominated towards documentaries and New Wave-influenced crime dramas (see Blom and van Yperen 2004). The documentary genre often touched on disability-related topics, as in the well-known short documentary *Blind Kind* (*Blind Child*, 1964) directed by Johan Van der Keuken. These tended to approach disability in an anthropological fashion, emphasising the 'otherness' of disabled people and their lives.

Another strong post-war cinematic theme involved plotlines that purported to celebrate or represent working-class realities, such as Gerard Rutten's *Het Wonderlijk Leven van Willem Parel* (*The Wonderful Life of Willem Parel*, 1955), Wolfgang Staudte's *Ciske de Rat* (*Ciske the Rat*, 1955) and *Keetje Tippel* (*Katie Tippel*, 1975), directed by Paul Verhoeven. Any disabled characters in such films usually played a peripheral role. *Ciske de Rat*, provides a typical example: the titular character, an Amsterdam street urchin, is bullied for befriending a child with polio. The figure of the crippled child appears primarily to create the desired image of Ciske as a naughty boy who nonetheless has a heart of gold, and soon disappears from the storyline.

Reflecting this trend towards gritty realism, the Verhoeven film *Spetters* (*Splatters*, 1980) centres on the exploits of a group of young Dutch men involved in motocross racing, and is unusual in that disability features as a major plot point. One of the main characters, Rien (Hans van Tongeren), becomes paraplegic following a motorcycle accident. Afterwards he is dumped by his gold-digging girlfriend, whom rehabilitation staff and Rien himself discourage from visiting him during his recovery. Despite being welcomed home by a brass-band parade (and another former girlfriend), and finding that his family have adapted their car, home and business for wheelchair

Fig. 1: In Paul Verhoeven's *Spetters* (1980), disability is portrayed as the antithesis of masculinity. Rien chooses suicide when a motorcycle accident ends his dream of becoming a motocross racing champion.

access, Rien soon commits suicide by rolling his chair in front of an oncoming truck.

Verhoeven's portrayal of paraplegia as the end of hope fits the overall narrative of the film, which depicts the struggle of young, working-class adults against economic and cultural odds. For Rien, whose identity is wrapped up in hypermasculine physical prowess, bitterness is perhaps inevitable: his dreams of escape from working behind the bar in the family pub via motocross championship are clearly over. At his homecoming party he tries to put on a brave face: presented with an electric wheelchair by his gathered friends and neighbours, Rien jokes that perhaps now he'll become a wheelchair racer. But unlike the similarly situated young male paraplegics featured in Henry Rubin and Dana Shapiro's documentary *Murderball* (2005), in the 1980s wheelchair sport did not offer a real alternative arena for performance of masculinity.

Each of the three main male characters in *Spetters* is in some way fighting this identity battle, depicted through their contest for the attention of the same young woman. Hans is handsome and well-built, but inept as a racer; Eef is physically fit and rivals Rien as a racer, but is secretly homosexual and further oppressed by a fundamentalist family. These obstacles seem no barrier to the creation of alternative masculinities – but physical disability is.

Young male wheelchair users in Dutch films since *Spetters* have frequently been depicted as tragic and bitter, in keeping with the negative disability imagery traditionally found in Western literature (see Longmore 1997; Albrecht *et al.* 2001). In these representations, filmmakers use physical disability as a way to visualise themes like isolation, individual struggle or loss of masculine prowess. Screenwriters' storylines simply reflect a larger cultural narrative that associates personal independence, efficacy and success with inhabiting an idealised body. As David Mitchell and Sharon Snyder write, 'the disabled experience is never imagined to offer its own unique and valuable perspective' (1997: 2) – and the power of these media images affects not only general social perceptions of what disabled lives contain, but how individuals interact with their own disabled status.

Aaltra (Benoit Deléfine and Gustave Kerverne, 2004) is a Belgian film that places the figure of the angry, bitter wheelchair user within a more confrontational narrative.[1] It diverts from the typical by making it clear that its two protagonists were hapless and vindictive before the inter-neighbour feud and subsequent accident that has caused them both to end up in wheelchairs. The film follows the duo as they make an absurd journey to Finland (without the travel documents they need, and therefore are dependent on the dubious kindness of others or their own wiles), where they intend to demand compensation from Aaltra, the company that made the farm machinery involved in their disabling accident.

Directors Deléfine and Kerverne themselves play the lead roles, placing their characters in situations that show up the motives of would-be helpers, and portraying the physical and attitudinal obstacles that their protagonists face. It is clear that these two men also face inner obstacles, but these are related less to their newly disabled status than to ingrained character traits. *Aaltra* received positive reviews in the Dutch press, with publications like the *Film Krant* making references to its Jacques Tati-like irreverence, excellent cinematography and the 'cantankerous wheelchair passengers' (Herder 2004) around whom the story revolves.

The Belgian comedy *Hasta la Vista* (*Come As You Are*, 2011), directed by Geoffrey Enthoven, provides another nuanced vision. In this film, three young disabled men (two wheelchair users, one blind man) escape the confines of infantilising 'care' to travel to a Spanish brothel. However, in a plot element reminiscent of Damien O'Donnell's *Inside I'm Dancing* (2004), one of the lead characters dies during the night after achieving his first sexual experience, having played out his role as an inspirational figure to the others.

Disability is presented as necessarily creating a barrier to sexuality and romance, as played out in a plot line in which young disabled men feel that their only option is to pay for sex. However, like Aaltra, this 'rollstoel-roadmovie' ('wheelchair road movie') goes where some filmmakers fear to tread, allowing elements of everyday life with a disability to be used as comic material. The characters express the exuberance of youth via male banter that encompasses all elements of their lives, including parental overprotection and access barriers. However, this otherwise normalised disability discourse is bracketed between the film's ableist premise and its unexpectedly tragic ending.

Audience reception studies are not available for these two films, but it is likely that wheelchair-using and non-wheelchair-using audiences might view them quite differently. Lotte Werkema, a disability studies scholar with a physical impairment, has written about *Aaltra* that it compares favorably to other 'disability themed' films in that its protagonists are active rather than passive, and do not live the isolated lives shown for other disabled characters. Indeed, she makes a general observation that 'Opvallend is dat de gehandicapten in de Nederlandse films passief zijn en dat we medelijden met ze voelen. In de Waalse films zijn de personages actiever en niet alleen maar slachtoffer, hoewel we soms wel medelijden met hen hebben' ('It is striking that disabled people in Dutch films are passive and pitiful. In the Walloon [French-language Belgian] films the characters are active, not just a victim, although we sometimes still pity them') (2011: 43).

Werkema's comments echo the analysis of Paul Darke (1999), who has noted that depictions of disability that non-disabled people may view as 'positive' can be read otherwise by people who themselves have a disability. 'Positive' depictions may actually serve to 'other' disabled people, or may retail potentially harmful stereotypes, such as that of the 'supercrip' (see Pointon and Davies 2008). Such representations tend to use disabled people as fodder for the inspiration or motivation of non-disabled people. Conversely, portrayals that include 'negative' elements (as in the case of *Aaltra*), can serve to show disabled individuals as whole, complex people with the full range of human character traits, and as active participants in life rather than passive, impotent recipients of care and control.

Rue des Invalides (Mari Sanders, 2012) also presents a young wheelchair-using male protagonist, Nathan, in search of romance. When Nathan meets a potential girlfriend in Paris, her current boyfriend berates her in English – 'the guy's in a wheelchair, you're gonna have to nurse him and wipe his ass all day long – this is what you want?' The result is a bittersweet coming-of-age tale. This film presents an interesting departure in the form of a social-model critique: Nathan is intelligent, independent, curious and mobile, but faces a series of external barriers, ranging from low expectations at home to the lack of curb-cuts and elevators that makes Paris difficult to access. It is perhaps not a coincidence that the writer and director, Mari Sanders, is himself a wheelchair user and incorporated autobiographical elements in the scenario.

The use of disabled actors is as rare in Dutch and Belgian films as it is in Hollywood, with the notable exception of Pascal Duquenne, an actor with Down syndrome who plays the lead role in Jaco van Dormael's *Le huitième jour* (*The Eighth Day*, 1996) and who has appeared in a few other films in minor roles. None of the wheelchair users in *Aaltra*, *Hasta la Vista* or *Rue des Invalides* are played by physically disabled actors. Film directors and producers need to take multiple considerations into account when casting, including audience familiarity with the actors in lead roles, acting ability and 'chemistry' with other cast members. However, it would appear that there are very few possibilities for disabled actors in Dutch film, as they rarely appear in secondary or walk-on parts either. Linus Hesselink and Petra Jorissen (1999) have noted that disabled artists and actors face many career barriers in the Netherlands, and generally find their work confined to 'special' productions or billed as a form of therapy. Segregation at the level of training, plus a lack of attention to the issue in the curricula of the film academies that produce most Dutch directors, creates a working atmosphere in which directors are unlikely to consider or even encounter disabled actors, and in which disabled actors may not have access to the training and networks they need to compete. As of yet, there has been no national conversation on the issue of casting non-disabled actors in disabled roles.

Casting decisions also have a financial aspect, and it is interesting to note that two of the films that present the most well-rounded representations of disabled people were also financed outside the mainstream system. The team behind *Rue des Invalides* was essentially a very high-quality student project completed via crowdfunding (see Knol and Sanders 2012), and *Aaltra*'s makers borrowed their funding (€150,000 – a tiny sum for a full-length film with high production values) by promising a notary a minor role (see de Foer 2004).

One outcome of non-disabled people imagining the lives of disabled people and then presenting this on screen is that disabled people tend in these depictions to play a secondary, supporting or incidental role in relation to other characters. For example, *Pauline and Paulette* (2001) concerns an intellectually disabled woman whose sisters are tasked with her care. Director Lieven Debrauwer has stated that she added the intellectually disabled character to a story that is essentially about sisterhood to introduce an element of conflict (see Moroni 2001). Actress Dora van der Groen presents a well-studied portrayal of an older woman with limited intellectual ability, but this functions in the plot in stereotypical ways. First, she is always in a position of requiring care and confinement – as is typical of disabled characters in film generally (see Hayes and Black 2003) – and is discussed in the film and its promotional materials as 'a 66-year-old child'. Second, her fragile steps towards increased independence following the death of her caretaking sister are eventually thwarted, another typical plot point in which, as Michael Hayes and Rhonda Black write, 'the focus of the plot instantaneously shifts and the struggle for independence is replaced by an acceptance of benevolent confinement [...]. The end point of the movie typically has the character with a disability, and most importantly the viewer, accepting the disabled character's life lived within the parameters of confinement' (2003: 124). In *Pauline and Paulette* – and *Le huitième jour* – although a central character is a person with an intellectual disability it can be seen that their main function in the plot is to improve the lives of 'normal' people. In each of these films, non-disabled characters experience personal growth through their relationship with an intellectually disabled character.

Disability in the Films of Alex van Warmerdam

Linguistic issues mean that most Dutch films have a relatively small audience potential, which for production companies in an era of limited state subsidy tends to dictate in favour of childrens' films or movies with broad appeal. That places art-house fare in an even more precarious position. In the Netherlands, one exception to this rule is the auteur Alex van Warmerdam, who comes from a theatrical background and frequently works with the same ensemble of actors and crew.

In van Warmerdam's darkly comic films, disability and illness, whether real, feigned or exaggerated, are used to control, and often portrayed as dangerous. In *Abel* (1986), an 'imbecile' son (who appears to be exaggerating his intellectual disability to at least some extent) uses his condition to control his family. Abel is shown deliberately 'failing' a psychiatric examination. He also employs his seeming vulnerability to provoke pity, favours and sexual interest. Abel is portrayed as quite aware of the impact of his status, capable of acting in his own self-interest and, indeed, capable of conniving to get what he wants from others. His mother is depicted as encouraging this behaviour as she desires his company, and they have a vaguely incestuous relationship.

In *Kleine Teun* (*Little Teun*, 1998), infertility is again the medical issue that leads to insanity, turning a rural wife into a would-be kidnapper and murderer. Meanwhile, her 'simple' and illiterate husband Teun uses his status to avoid work and launch an affair. Both characters manipulate a pretty young tutor to achieve their own ends.

In a final attempt to gain power within her family and community, a religion-obsessed wife in *De Noordelingen* (*The Northerners*, 1992) decides to refuse food and die in a sort of ecstatic pseudo-anorexia. A male character driven mad (again seemingly by infertility) is blinded by a man he attacks, and freezes to death in the forest. Theo van Gogh plays a cameo role as their malicious, apparently intellectually disabled scooter-riding neighbour, Dikke (Fat) Willy. It too is included in the official Dutch Film Canon (see Nederlands Film Festival 2012).

The theme of the manipulative sick person is particularly strong in van Warmerdam's *Grimm* (2003). Loosely based on the fairy tale 'Hansel and Gretel', a brother and sister are befriended by a Spanish doctor. It emerges that he has lured them in to provide his sister with an (involuntary) kidney donor. Although she seems to be a pious and sympathetic person, her ill health is shown as having twisted her morally to the extent that she is willing to murder someone to benefit herself.

Van Warmerdam often acts in his own productions, as in his lead role as a luckless waiter in *Ober* (*Waiter*, 2006). The postmodern plot of this film sees its characters interacting with the screenwriter. Van Warmerdam's character originally has an ill, bedridden, nagging wife, behind whose back he is conducting affairs. He successfully begs the screenwriter to kill her off because having a sick wife is 'sad'. Only with the wife out of the way can he act freely, although fate (in the form of the screenwriter) insists on intervening.

The lead character in *De Laaste Dagen van Emma Blank* (*The Last Days of Emma Blank*, 2009) uses being 'fatally ill' to control her entire family and

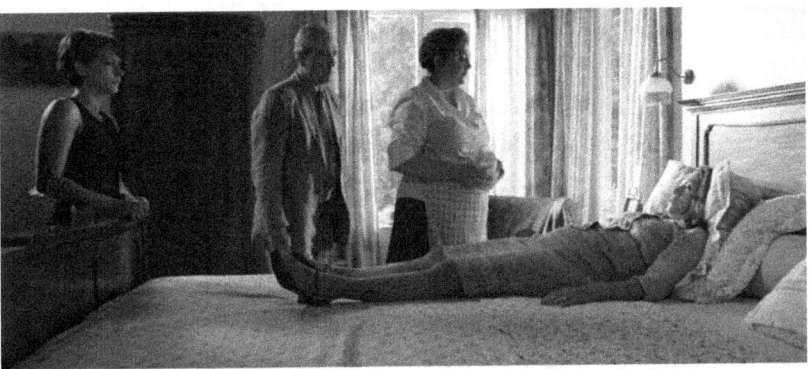

Fig. 2: In *De Laatste Dagen van Emma Blank*, Emma Blank, suffering from an unnamed terminal condition, coerces her daughter Gonnie, husband Haneveld and her husband's lover Bella to wait on her as servants.

her husband's lover, convincing them to act as her servants in a bid for a non-existent inheritance. When her deception is revealed, they turn on their former tormentor. At the end of the film, Emma's daughter Gonnie walks away following her mother's death, having dropped hints throughout the film that she is likely to use similar behaviour to control others in future.

Although van Warmerdam always sets his films in a sort of unique alternative reality, this reality is of course a skewed mirror image of the Netherlands that permits him free reign for comment. Despite expressing disdain for 'social themes' (see Linssen 2015), he typically skewers middle-class behaviours and mores with pointed venom. However, the continual appearance of disabled characters in manipulative roles is a paradoxical element within his iconoclastic vision, reflecting a common Dutch social belief that many disabled people are parasitic shirkers who should be forced to *op eigen benen staan* (stand on their own two feet).

Stigma and Marking

The deployment of disability in van Warmerdam's films is significant, and fits within a longstanding tradition. Paul Darke (1998) has noted that disability is frequently used to literally stigmatise film villains, giving audiences an instant clue about who to fear, in a practice that mirrors ancient cultural tropes (see Pointon and Davies 2008).

As in typical Hollywood fare, this trope persists in the Dutch thriller and horror genres. For example, the scuba-diving murderer in Maas Dick's *Amsterdamned* (1988) has severe facial scarring. His psychopathic desire to kill is said to derive from his disfigurement. For Maarten Treurniet's costume drama *Kenau* (2014), about the Spanish siege of Haarlem, villainous Spanish commander Don Faderico de Toledo is marked with a prominent facial scar to underline his status.

The Belgian film *Ex Drummer* (Koen Mortier, 2007) also uses disability to mark and accentuate the uselessness of its punk-musician protagonists. Having recruited a famous writer whose only 'disability' is his inability to play the drums as their drummer, the three disabled musicians aim to win a battle of the bands with their rendition of Devo's 'Mongoloid'. Disability in this film is used to draw attention to the characters as deficient, even within a youth subculture (punk) that supposedly celebrates difference and deviance. The plot revolves around the writer's ability to manipulate them, and their own sordid lifestyles.

Disability and Looping Effects

Ian Hacking (1996) has suggested that ways of experiencing and performing difference as disability are created through both medical and popular media representations. People seen as disabled absorb these definitions and depictions, and often reproduce them in their own embodied discourses. Hannah Ebben (2015) has considered these looping effects in the lives of people who identify with the label of autism or Asperger syndrome and interact with media representations of autism.

Two Dutch-language films that deal with autism, Diedrik van Rooijen's *Daglicht* (*Daylight*, 2013) and *Ben X* (2007), directed by Nic Balthazar, are interesting to consider in this context. Conceptions of autism have been heavily mediated, from Bruno Bettelheim's popular-science books and articles to Dustin Hoffman's turn as an autistic adult in *Rain Man* (Barry Levinson, 1988). Often, as in the case of *Rain Man*, medical professionals and/or parents' organisations have been intimately involved in ensuring that specific depictions of autism are put forward on film. Far more rarely, people with autism themselves have had unmediated input (see Waltz 2013).

In *Daglicht* (based on the 2008 novel by Marion Pauw), the depiction of autism in two characters is relatively stereotypical, and forms a key part of the plot. Iris, a lawyer and the mother of a mildly autistic child, inadvertently learns that she also has an autistic brother, Ray, who was placed in an institution for the criminally insane when she was an infant. Played by Fedja van Huêt, Ray is portrayed as almost a carbon copy of Dustin Hoffman's character Raymond in *Rain Man*: a savant with behaviours deemed characteristic of autistic people with intellectual disabilities. He is shown as morally and sexually 'innocent', and provides the missing puzzle pieces (in the form of drawings that are assembled by Iris's autistic child) that can solve the central mystery. The association of autism with puzzle images and metaphors is a longstanding practice that serves to mystify autism and portray individuals with the condition as incomplete (see Waltz 2003). Iris uses her skills to prove that Ray was incapable of committing the murders he was convicted of, and helps to gain his release, learning in the end that (in true soap-opera style) Ray is actually her father.

Pauw has stated in interviews that she consulted professionals about the portrayal of autistic characters; she is also the mother of a child with Asperger syndrome, a form of autism (see de Bree 2008). The presentation of autism in the film includes a retread of the old 'refrigerator mother' stereotype in the person of Iris's (grand-)mother, who turns out to be one of the actual murderers. Despite their intelligence, Ray and Iris's son are both shown as requiring special education and support.

Based on a novel by its director, Nic Balthazar, *Ben X* is one of the few recent Dutch films to make an impact outside of linguistic barriers, perhaps because it depicts gamer culture, still a relatively unexplored area of youth culture for filmmakers. It has been widely dubbed and/or subtitled. Its autism narrative also fits into the current zeitgeist. Ben, played by Greg Timmermann, is a young autistic man trying to cope with extreme bullying at a technical college. He finds his escape, and eventually an ally, in the videogame world that forms his alternate reality. As a game player he achieves not just equality but prowess, and is able to communicate with others through text and play.

Ben's difficulties with communication, and the negative impact of bullying and cyberbullying, are key plot points. He is a passive character through most of the film, only taking action at the end, and then only with support from his family and a friend. His successful effort to show up the bullies, however, is not an unmitigated triumph – in the final scene, Ben is revealed to be more 'in his own world' than ever, despite appearing to have left the world of gaming for therapeutic horse-riding. What appeared to be a developing romantic relationship seems now to remain only in his mind. One could read this narrative as saying that people with autism are better off when captured within a separate therapeutic milieu rather than thinking or acting independently in an inclusive sphere. The filmmakers credit the receipt of official advice from the Belgian state education agency and from Autisme Centraal, a Belgian charity.

In both films, visual elements such as lighting, posture and hairstyle are used to denote that a character has autism. In *Ben X*, Ben hides his face behind his hair and keeps his face down when speaking; light and shadow are used to create a sense of his being closed off from other characters. In *Daglicht*, Iris's autistic son hides his eyes behind a similar hairstyle and again, heavy shadow generally features in scenes where autistic characters are central; in other scenes characters are obscured by water or stand behind non-autistic characters. These motifs create an impression of 'otherness' and isolation that separates autistic characters from the rest, in keeping with common (mis-) conceptions about autism (see Broderick and Ne'Emen 2008).

Publicity materials for these films played up the autism angle, and both have featured in mediated discussions about autism (for example, see 'Marjolein' 2013). Parents, people with autism and professionals have used these and similar films about disability in a variety of ways to construct 'disability identities' – what Hacking (1996) calls 'kinds of people' – for themselves or others.

Characteristics presented visually via film may be used to define what it means to have a particular difference or condition, and also what the appropriate role of those around a disabled person is in relation to him or her. Films that valorise the roles of parents and professionals, as both *Ben X* and *Daglicht* do, have a strong appeal to non-disabled individuals who are constructing their personal or professional identities. Unfortunately, this process of parental or professional role valorisation can have negative effects for disabled people, who are constructed as passive recipients of external help and control.

Fearful Representations and Everyday Realities

The influence of culture through historical and literary references, linguistic formations and stock characters is always visible in film, but may be balanced by the personal creative input of writers, directors and actors. As in the case of the films about autism discussed in this chapter, outside influences in the form of medical, parental and disabled peoples own discourses may also play a role. The depiction of disability in Dutch film does not depart markedly from the norm in this respect. With notable exceptions, disability is typically used as a dramatic and often tragic plot point, or as shorthand for a character flaw. The past deployment of disability on screen in this way induces mimesis (see Bourdieu 1990), as producers look to tropes that have had success for others in the past.

It is also notable that while some young male disabled characters in coming-of-age narratives are portrayed as actively trying to engage with life (for example, the protagonists of *Hasta la Vista* and *Rue des Invalides*), disabled female characters are fewer in number, tend to be older, and often exhibit either passivity or a disturbingly passive-aggressive stance in which ill health is deployed as a weapon.

Jenny Slater (2015) has discussed ways in which dominant youth-culture narratives actively exclude people with disabilities, and particularly disabled females. She writes that youth is a liminal space between childhood and adulthood that is often characterised as a time for risky, unreasonable (but character-forming) behaviour. For disabled characters, as with actual disabled young people, behaviour that for typical young people would be unremarkable is characterised as 'unreasonable' enough to form the basis of a dramatic film plot. Young disabled people, in film and in real life, have to contend with paternalism, overprotection and near-constant adult supervision (in addition to any actual support needs, which are necessarily usually performed by adults) in their quest for adult independence. In the case of

Dutch cinema, this tendency to paint typical youth behaviour by disabled characters as 'unreasonable' is frequently paired with a rather conservative narrative about appropriate male and female roles that foregrounds ableist narratives of athletic masculinity, increasing the dramatic effect of disability within film narratives.

As Tanya Titchkosky (2011) has asserted, the figure of the disabled person acts to define an opposing figure, that of the 'normal' person. Disabled characters in film are rarely drawn from real life, but constructed from and within pre-existing cultural narratives. Of course, directors and actors may seek out information about disabled bodies in order to 'get it right', resulting in the kind of skilled performance that when successful is sometimes described or derided as deliberate 'Oscar bait'. Indeed, Gabriel Rossman and Oliver Schilke (2014) have carried out an extensive keyword analysis on films most likely to be nominated for an Academy Award, developing an algorithm that reveals how disability-linked themes such as 'stigmatized minority', 'physical therapy' and 'family tragedy' push up a film's appeal to the judges (see, also, Keating 2014). However, a realistic-looking physical performance, while impressive as evidence of an actor's craft, reproduces exterior form rather than the far more nuanced, messy and surprising everyday realities of disabled lives – which, as Mari Sanders shows in *Rue des Invalides*, have great dramatic potential in of themselves. Integration and participation of people with disabilities in Dutch cinema as critics, screenwriters, actors and directors could serve to produce fuller and more realistic representations, including accurate representation of disabled people across age, gender, race and class lines. However, non-disabled Dutch screenwriters and directors also need to consider how the use of disability in stereotypical and stigmatising ways may actually confuse and dilute the impact of their work.

NOTE

1 Unlike the other Dutch and Belgian films considered in this chapter, *Aaltra* is primarily in the French language.

FILMOGRAPHY

Balthazar, Nic (dir) (2007) *Ben X*. 93 minutes. MMG Film & TV Production. Belgium/Netherlands.

Debrauwer, Lieven (dir) (2001) *Pauline and Paulette*. 78 minutes. Canal+/K-Star. Belgium/France/Netherlands.

Deléphine, Benoît and Gustave Kervern (dirs) (1996) *Aaltra*. 92 minutes. La Parti Production/Lumière. Belgium/France.
Enthoven, Geoffrey (dir) (2011) *Hasta La Vista* (Come as You Are). 115 minutes. Fobic Films/K2. Belgium.
Levinson, Barry (dir) (1988) *Rain Man*. 133 minutes. Beverly Hills: United Artists. USA.
Maas, Dick (dir) (1988) *Amsterdamned*. 114 minutes. First Floor Features. Netherlands.
Mortier, Koen (dir) (2007) *Ex Drummer*. 100 minutes. CCCP/Czar. Belgium/France/Italy.
O'Donnell, Damien (dir) (2004) *Inside I'm Dancing* (a.k.a. *Rory O'Shea Was Here*). 104 minutes. WT2 Productions/Focus Features. UK/Ireland/France.
Rubin, Henry and Dana Shapiro (2005) *Murderball*. Hollywood: Paramount Pictures.
Rutten, Gerard (dir) (1955) *Het Wonderlijk Leven van Willem Parel* (The Amazing Life of Willem Parel). 91 minutes. Joop Geesink Producties. Netherlands.
Sanders, Mari (dir) (2012) *Rue des Invalides*. 22 minutes. Jasper Knol Producties. France/Netherlands.
Staudte, Wolfgang (dir) (1955) *Ciske de Rat* (Ciske the Rat). 88 minutes. Filmproductie Maatschaapij Amsterdam. Netherlands/West Germany.
Treurniet, Maarten (dir) (2014) *Kenau*. 113 minutes. Fu Works/I'm Film. Netherlands/Hungary/Belgium.
Van der Keuken, Johan (dir) (1964) *Blind Kind* (Blind Child). 25 minutes. VPRO. Netherlands.
van Dormael, Jaco (dir) (1996) *Le huitième jour* (The Eighth Day). 118 minutes. Canal+/Center for Film and Audiovisual Arts of the French Community of Belgium. Belgium/France.
van Rooijen, Diedrik (dir) (2013) *Daglicht* (Daylight). 114 minutes. Eyeworks Film & TV Drama. Netherlands.
van Warmerdam, Alex (dir) (2009) *De Laatste Dagen van Emma Blank* (The Last Days of Emma Blank). 89 minutes. Fortissimo Films/A-Film. Netherlands.
____ (2006) *Ober* (Waiter). 97 minutes. Graniet Film BV/A-Film. Netherlands/Belgium.
____ (2003) *Grimm*. 103 minutes. Graniet Film BV/A-Film. Netherlands.
____ (1998) *Kleine Teun* (Little Teun). 95 minutes. Graniet Film BV/A-Film. Netherlands.
____ (1992) *De Noorderlingen* (The Northerners). 108 minutes. First Floor Features. Netherlands.
____ (1986) *Abel*. 100 minutes. First Floor Features. Netherlands.
Verhoeven, Paul (dir) (1980) *Spetters* (Splatters). 120 minutes. Endemol Entertainment/VSE Film BV. Netherlands.
____ (1975) *Keetje Tippel* (Katie Tippel). 100 minutes. Rob Houwer Productions. Netherlands.
____ (1973) *Turks Fruit* (Turkish Delight). 108 minutes. Verenigde Nederlandsche Filmcompagnie. Netherlands.

BIBLIOGRAPHY

Albrecht, Gary L., Katherine D. Seelman and Michael Bury (2001) *Handbook of Disability Studies*. London: Sage.

Blom, Ivo and Paul van Yperen (2004) 'Netherlands: Post-war cinema'. Available at http://www.filmreference.com/encyclopedia/Independent-Film-Road-Movies/Netherlands-POST-WAR-CINEMA.html (accessed 21 May 2015).

Bourdieu, Pierre (1990) *The Logic of Practice*. Cambridge: Polity Press.

___ (1991) *Language and Symbolic Power*. Cambridge, MA: Harvard University Press.

Broderick, Alicia A. and Ari Ne'Emen (2008) 'Autism as Metaphor: Narrative and Counter-narrative', *International Journal of Inclusive Education*, 12, 5, 459–76.

Calis, Piet (2010) *Venus in Minirok: Seks in de Literatuur na 1945*. Amsterdam: Meulenhoff.

Darke, Paul (1998) 'Cinematic representations of disability', in Tom Shakespeare (ed.) *The Disability Reader*. London and New York: Cassell, 181–98.

___ (1999) *The Cinematic Construction of Physical Disability as Identified Through the Application of the Social Model of Disability* [PhD Thesis]. University of Warwick. Available at http://wrap.warwick.ac.uk/36342/1/WRAP_THESIS_Darke_1999.pdf (accessed 29 May 2015).

De Bree, Kees (2008) 'Interview: Marion Pauw', *Hebban*, 22 August. Available at http://www.hebban.nl/artikelen/interview-marion-pauw (accessed 26 May 2015).

De Foer, Steven (2004) 'Aaltra: Met de rolstoel naar Finland', *De Standaard*, 23 June. Available at http://www.standaard.be/cnt/gmi6s36h (accessed 28 May 2015).

De Telegraaf (2015) '"Kanker" meest kwensende scheldwoord', 27 March. Available at http://www.telegraaf.nl/binnenland/23854939/___Kanker__meest_kwetsend__.html (accessed 21 May 2015).

Ebben, Hannah (2015) 'Traversing the Empty Fortress: The Possibility of Counter-Metaphors in Representations of Space in Filmic Personal Accounts on Autism' [presentation], Rethinking Disability On Screen symposium, 14 May, York University. Available at https://www.academia.edu/12452003/Traversing_the_Empty_Fortress_The_Possibility_of_Counter-Metaphors_in_Representations_of_Space_in_Filmic_Personal_Accounts_on_Autism (accessed 27 May 2015).

Ellis, Katie (2008) *Disabling Diversity: The Social Construction of Disability in 1990s Australian National Cinema*. Saarbrücken: VDM Verlag.

Hayes, Michael T. and Rhonda S. Black (2003) 'Troubling Signs: Disability, Hollywood Movies, and the Construction of a Discourse of Pity', *Disability Studies Quarterly*, 23, 2, 114–32.

Hacking, Ian (1996) 'Kinds of People: Moving Targets', *Proceedings of the British Academy*, 151, 285–318.

Herder, Rik (2004) 'Bloedmooi venijn: *Aaltra*', *Film Krant*, September. Available at http://www.filmkrant.nl/_titelindex_A/516 (accessed 28 May 2015).

Hesselink, Linus and Petra Jorissen (1999) *Kunst en Handicap in Nederland*. Amsterdam: Boekmanstudies.

Keating, Joshua (2014) 'The Most (and Least) Oscar-bait-y Movies Ever, According to Science', *Slate*, 15 January. Available at http://www.slate.com/blogs/browbeat/2014/01/15/oscar_bait_study_ucla_social_scientist_study_keywords_and_other_factors.html (accessed 29 May 2015).

Knol, Jasper and Mari Sanders (2012) 'Voordekunst: *Rue des Invalides*, de film'. Available at https://www.voordekunst.nl/projecten/304-rue-des-invalides (accessed 29 May 2015).

Linnson, Dana (2015) 'Alex van Warmerdam over Schneider vs. Bax', *Film Krant*, May. Available at http://www.filmkrant.nl/TS_mei_2015/12052 (accessed 29 May 2015).

Longmore, Paul (1997) 'Screening Stereotypes: Images of Disabled People in Television and Motion Pictures', in Alan Gartner and Tom Joe (eds) *Images of the Disabled, Disabling Images*. New York, NY: Preager, 65–78.

'Marjolein' (2013) '*Daglicht*, de film', *Autisme in ons Gezin* blog, 26 May. Available at http://autismeinonsgezin.blogspot.nl/2013/05/daglicht-de-film.html (accessed 27 May 2015).

Mendik, Xavier (2004) 'Turks Fruit/Turkish Delight (Paul Verhoeven, The Netherlands, 1973)', in Ernest Mathijs (ed.) *The Cinema of the Low Countries*, London and New York, NY: Wallflower Press, 109-18.

Mitchell, David T. and Sharon L. Snyder (1997) *The Body and Physical Difference: Discourses of Disability*. Ann Arbor, MI: University of Michigan Press.

Moroni, Simona (2001) 'Lieven Debrauwer: Tuinkabouters en gratis bloemen', *Film Krant*, November. Available at http://www.filmkrant.nl/av/org/filmkran/archief/fk227/debrauwe.html (accessed 22 May 2015).

Natrop, Maartje (2014) *Scheiten & Schelden: Scheldgedrag van gamers tijdens FPS* [MA thesis]. Utrecht University. Available at http://dspace.library.uu.nl/handle/1874/288907 (accessed 21 May 2015).

Nederlands Film Festival (2012) 'FilmCanon.nl'. Available at http://www.filmfestival.nl/publiek/nff-school/filmcanon/ (accessed 21 May 2015).

Pointon, Anne and Chris Davies (eds) (2008) *Framed: Interrogating Disability in the Media*. London: British Film Institute.

Rossman, Gabriel and Oliver Schilke (2014) 'Close, but No Cigar: The Bimodal Rewards to Prize-seeking', *American Sociological Review*, 79, 1, 86–108.

Slater, Jenny (2015) *Youth and Disability: A Challenge to Mr Reasonable*. Farnham: Ashgate.

Titchkosky, Tanya (2011) *The Question of Access: Disability, Space, Meaning*. Toronto: University of Toronto Press.

Vollmer, Sideny (2006) *Haaien, Hollande Haring en de overheid: Onderzoek naar de invloed van de blockbuster en de overheid op het Nederlandse filmklimaat* [MA thesis]. University of Utrecht. Available at http://dspace.library.uu.nl/handle/1874/20565 (accessed 21 May 2015).

Waltz, Mitzi (2003) 'Metaphors of Autism, and Autism as Metaphor: An Exploration of Representation' [presentation]. Making Sense of: Health, Illness, and Disease Global Conference, Oxford University. Available at https://www.inter-disciplinary.net/ptb/mso/hid/hid2/waltz%20paper.pdf (accessed 26 May 2015).

____ (2013) *Autism: A Social and Medical History*. London: Palgrave Macmillan.

Werkema, Lotte (2011) *(In)valide representatie: Een aanzet tot onderzoek van disability in de Nederlandse en Belgische film* [MA thesis]. University of Amsterdam.

'People Endure'

The Function of Autism in *Anton's Right Here* (2012)

José Alaniz

People with disabilities usually realize that they must learn to live with their disability, if they are to live life as a human being. The challenge is not to adapt their disability into an extraordinary power or an alternative image of ability. *The challenge is to function.* I use this word advisedly and am prepared to find another if it offends. People with disabilities want to be able to function: to live with their disability, to come to know their body, to accept what it can do, and to keep doing what they can for as long as they can. They do not want to feel dominated by the people on whom they depend for help, and they want to be able to imagine themselves in the world without feeling ashamed.

(Siebers 2010: 69; emphasis added)

The Russian documentary *Anton tut riadom* (*Anton's Right Here*, 2012) by Liubov Arkus, opens with a hand-held close-up of an enigmatic young man on a mist-covered dock. His gaze avoids the camera, which remains tight on his face as he lopes with vague alarm. Suddenly he starts to emit a deep-throated keening noise. In his review, Greg Dolgopolov describes these odd sounds as 'yelping incoherently in the grey light of destitution' (2013: n.p.), but they seem more guttural, even primal – an ape-like '*Ahhhhhh...*'. Along with the twilight conditions, the boy's inscrutable expression and almost total lack of context (these are the very first few seconds of the film), his eerie non-language disorients profoundly – as I have noted while watching with different audiences. The mood it creates is nightmarish, apocalyptic. But perhaps its most disturbing aspect (as elaborated below) is that this ambiguous proto-speech, signifying nothing, *fails to function.*

We soon come to know the entrancing figure onscreen as Anton Kharitonov, a St. Petersburg adolescent with autism. We come to know him well. *Anton's Right Here*, a 'first-person' account of the director's close involvement with the boy over four years, represents a breakthrough in non-fiction depictions of the disabled in Russia. This owes largely to its unflinching intimacy, an insistence on its subject's uniqueness and the director's determination to understand him as much as possible on his own terms. We might say Arkus sets herself the task of inverting the audience's discomfited presumptions at that opening scene's portrait of Anton: menacing, quasi-human, yowling.[1] She in fact repeats that same footage some fifteen minutes later, only now the backstory more fully explains Anton's anxiety. Disquiet turns to empathy.[2] Context matters.

For all that, though – and to take nothing away from its achievement – *Anton's Right Here* operates too under the influence of other, very different contexts (which it only partially resists): the long tradition of representing mental disability in Russia, and the current Putin era of 'healthy-minded' efficiency, competition and personal advancement. Taking such frames into account, this chapter first examines the documentary in light of its cinematic predecessors, before interrogating the film through Stuart Murray's concept of 'function' in contemporary discourses of autism. In doing so, we will weigh the ethical stakes in Arkus's very personal vision of the autistic subject amid a changing landscape for disability rights in post-Soviet Russia.

Anton's Right Here

Divided into five chapters, the documentary details Arkus's relationship with Anton, whom she finds in the course of researching another project. As a child, he had written a poem-essay, 'Liudi' ('People'), which had achieved notoriety on the internet in the early 2000s. In the ensuing years, Anton's condition has worsened; she finds him living with his mother Rinata (his father had long since left the family). Arkus and her cinematographer, Alisher Khamidkhodzhayev, follow the young man to Onega, a camp for autistic children on Lake Onega, and a poignant bond develops on camera. When Rinata, stricken with terminal cancer, grows increasingly ill, Arkus decides to somehow rescue Anton from life in an orphanage or mental institution – his assured fate upon his mother's death (as a montage of quick interviews with various experts confirms).[3] In the work's most dramatic scene, the filmmaker shows how far she will go to save Anton: she and her crew *kidnap* him from a hospital (again, live on camera). Arkus's daring act of 'enter[ing] the frame'[4] – arguably wresting Anton's story away from him – transgresses conventional limits on the subject/author relationship, to say nothing of the law.

What emerges more prominently over the course of the film, however, is a subtle, achingly intimate portrait of Anton: his charming boyishness and vulnerability; his unknowable gaze and language (consisting of echolalia or repetitive speech, and other verbal tics); unpredictable bodily movements (e.g. he tent-poles his blanket over himself at odd angles); and, at times, heart-wrenching emotion, as when tears stream down his face on his way back to the hospital after a brief furlough.[5]

Furthermore, Arkus – a long-time film critic and occasional actress, but first-time director – finds brilliant devices to visualise Anton's plight.[6] A wintertime long shot early in the movie shows the boy walking in snow as voice-overs from different people seem to bicker over what he needs: 'On ishchet cheloveka, kotoriy ego poimet. ... Dlia nego samoe glavnoe, to, chto ty chuvstvuesh'. ... A chto dlia nikh samaia bol'shaia travma? Predatel'stvo, konechno, kak i dlia vsekh ... On ne mozhet byt' bez cheloveka riadom' ('He's looking for someone who will understand him. ... What's most important for him is what you feel. ... What's the biggest trauma for them? Betrayal, of course, like for all of us. ... He can't be without someone by him').

Other sequences verge on the lyrical. We see close-ups of Anton through reflections, branches and plants, recalling Andrei Tarkovsky's opening for *Ivanovo detsvo* (*Ivan's Childhood*, 1962). These shots of the blank-faced boy evoke what Stuart Murray calls the popular conception of autistics' faces as 'masks' or 'curtains' which foreground their social withdrawal (2008: 113). Likewise they contrast sharply with photos of Anton as an infant, smiling happily.

As if to defuse viewer presumptions about the 'sordidness' of her subject matter, Arkus sprinkles high-culture markers throughout: at one point Anton reads aloud from Mikhail Lermontov's 1832 poem *Parus* (*The Sail*), while his stepmother Nina sings 'V lunnom siannii' ('In the Moonlight'), a turn-of-the-twentieth-century lyrical song by Yevgeny Yuriev (1882–1911). The lyrical song (romans), a genre initially denounced as a bourgeois holdover by the Soviets, resonates with Arkus's anti-authoritarianism elsewhere in the film. Nina sings it near the end, when she, Vladimir and Anton have all settled at an idyllic dacha, to heal as a family. But the song's more immediate relevance is intertextual, involving a different 'rehabilitation'. For precisely this piece is heard in Alexei Balabanov's notoriously grotesque *Pro urodov i liudei* (*On*

Freaks and People, 1998), in which it is performed more than once by enslaved conjoined twins. Arkus's inclusion of 'In the Moonlight' thus 'overwrites' its dehumanising, ableist association with the earlier film. Through these and other means, the documentary seeks to re-centre long-marginalised others in Russian society.

Birth imagery, too, makes conspicuous appearances. We repeatedly see Anton completely under covers, as if in a cocoon, pupating. (This seems a way of blocking out unpleasant stimulation.) In footage of him disembarking from the watercraft (which in terms of chronology immediately precedes the film's 'mysterious' opening), not only do we come to understand why Anton feels so distraught as to yowl – 'izvestie o tom, chto uezhaem, Anton vstretil s otchaianiem' ('Anton reacted to news that we were leaving [from Onega] with despair'), Arkus notes – but his uncertain movements, ambling off the boat, then back on, then off again, signal a sort of stillbirth. Many details of this key long shot seem ripe for a psychoanalytic reading (complete with a raised-voice law of the father): the water, the red of the boat and of Anton's clothes, Arkus entering from offscreen to help, and Khamidkhodzhayev angrily yelling at her, 'Lyuba, iz kadra!' ('Lyuba, out of the shot!'). Odder still, the ship is brightly labeled 'Comet-9', evoking the neurotypical stereotypes of autistics as 'alien' beings; Anton has landed on Earth. If nothing else, such shots attest to the volatility of autism as a cinematic subject.

The scene – one of several in which the director increasingly violates the injunction to stay off-frame – also represents a re-birth. For ultimately, the filmmaker's directness and self-examination leads us to the realisation that *Anton's Right Here* is also a self-portrait; Arkus's own needs and personal trauma play a shaping role in her sense of mission (family members, including her father, were repressed by the Soviets). As she puts it: 'Istoriia ne pro to, kak odin chelovek pomog drugomu, a pro to, kak odin chelovek uznal sebia v drugom. ... Anton, kotoryi ponimaet tol'ko iazik liubvi, i na men'shee ne soglasen, eto ia. Eto tot samiy drugoi chelovek vo mne, kotoryi vo vsiu zhizn' nuzhno bylo ubivat' sebia, chtoby vyzhit' ('This is not a story about how one person helped another, but about how one person found herself in another. ... Anton, who understands only the language of love and will agree to no less, is me. This is that other person in me, who all my life I've had to kill over and over so I could survive').

Audiences responded; in 2013 *Anton's Right Here* won two of the Russian film industry's most significant prizes – a Nika and a Golden Eagle, for Best Documentary – and earned above averagely in limited release. The page devoted to the film on the *Seans* website features glowing accolades from leading auteurs, scholars and critics. Alexander Sokurov's comment there is representative: 'Zdes' vyrazitel'nye sredstva kino napravleny na to, chtoby doyti do samoi suti, razobrat'sia v prirode cheloveka, pred'iavit' nam to, shto my o sebe ne znaem' ('Here the expressive powers of cinema are directed towards reaching to the very essence, to grapple with the nature of man, to show us that which we don't know about ourselves') (quoted in Anon. 2012). The questions remain, however: How do 'the expressive powers of cinema' accomplish this? And what role does Anton's autism play in the process?

The Function of Function

In an important essay, 'Autism Functions/The Functions of Autism' (2010), Murray argues that 'An idea of "function" and "functioning" is central to contemporary discussions of autism'. He cites such common descriptors for spectrum disorders as 'low-' and 'high-functioning', as well as the insistence with which discussions of these conditions center on notions of 'too much' (i.e. savantism) or 'too little' function (2010: n.p.). Too much or too little for what? As Murray writes:

> [T]he worrying aspect is that an idea of autistic *functioning* equates with an idea of disabled human *value*, that the shorthand that 'function' has become allows for processes of assessment and judgment that fix those with autism into inflexible ontological categories, and that these categories themselves then pass for the norm. Equally, there is a very real sense that this idea of function dangerously misrepresents the actual nature of ability and intelligence in those with autism, that it creates the presumption of a link between the condition and the 'deficit' in a manner which misreads what autistic intelligence actually is. (Ibid.)

Media depictions of autism, both fictional and non-, have internalised the 'blanket term' of function, which allows for 'a series of interconnected moments between the cognitive, linguistic and the social' (ibid.). In a vicious loop, these unexamined biases yield highly-flawed representations which themselves influence presumptions about and relations with real autistic people, as well as state policies directed toward them. This was clearly the case in the Soviet Union.[7]

More worrying still: the ways in which the function frame dovetails too with the demands of late capitalism, which has so profoundly reshaped Russia since the collapse of the USSR. While focused on autists assimilated into the labour force in the neoliberal West, Murray's thesis applies just as well to conditions in Anton's home country:

> [T]he working individual with autism is also the individual who behaves in an *orthodox* manner, whether that behavior is deemed 'acceptable' by society at large or is consistent with the stereotypes that come with perceived 'extraordinary ability'. Such individuals, in this emerging terminology of assessment, can be understood to be useful and valuable. The language of function and the functional here carries overtones of management systems and the rhetoric of supply-side macroeconomics, vocabularies that are themselves increasingly part and parcel of the languages utilized by the major autism charities and foundations in their fundraising activities. (Ibid.)

The ubiquity of the function imperative in twenty-first-century discourses about disability (including mental disability) compels the question: to what extent does it participate in even an expressly 'spiritual' film, whose supporters call 'chudo na ekrane, zadokumentirovannoe rozhdenie dushi v nash mir' ('a miracle on screen, the documented birth of a soul into our world')?[8] What is the function of the function of autism in *Anton's Right Here*? To begin to answer, I want to look at a number of scenes, shots and cuts which relate to the film's primary themes of love, national critique and the 'miracle' of cinema. At the centre of them all lies Anton's autism – and, to one degree or another, this question of function.

The Beach

'Pervoe vremia' ('At first'), says Arkus in voice-over, 'Anton boialsia kamery, a ia boialas' Antona. Ia boialas' prichinit' emu vred ili bol' kakim-nibud' neostorozhnym slovom. Boialas', chto on ubezhit' ('Anton was afraid of the camera, and I was afraid of Anton. I was afraid of inflicting harm or pain on him through some careless words or other. I was afraid he would run away'). We hear these words over a series of shots in which Anton walks off, avoids the apparatus's gaze, fleeing along the trails and woods of the Onega camps. Eventually he grows 'to love the camera' and even enters shots he should not.

The breakthrough happens on a lake beach at dusk. A baseball-capped Anton, in his characteristic back-and-forth motion, approaches the off-screen Arkus (the camera pans to follow) before retreating to the water's edge, twice. Arkus asks if he wants to write on the sand. We then see a closer medium shot of Anton, his back to us, framed against the water. The implication: something about writing, sociality, water and the camera are about to effect a change. Indeed, we return to the longer shot as Anton shuffles back up the bank. Then, a jump cut: Anton is 'helped' to close the distance to Arkus again. He hugs her, over and over, caresses her hair, smiling radiantly. A miracle.

Everything about the action in this sequence speaks of spontaneity; Arkus and Khamidkhodzhayev, after patiently following their subject, have captured a crucial moment in June 2008: 'the birth of a soul'. And it does take a heart of stone to remain unmoved by the scene. Yet notice too the extravagant artificiality of its construction: the steady camera, which is not hand-held but rather seems to sit on a tripod (hence the smooth pans); the 'catalytic' effect of Arkus's suggestion to write (which we can link with the poem that first brought them together, as well as with Anton's apartment walls covered in his scrawl – biblical associations and all); the water imagery and soundscape betokening birth; and, last but not least, the 'assistive' jump cut, which literally brings our two protagonists into physical contact. It all points to i) a staged quality on location and ii) meticulous editing to achieve maximum emotional impact.

The beach 'birth' scene, eight minutes into the film, serves both as lynchpin to the film's narrative and as a marker of authenticity – the rest of the story, as well as our emotional commitment to it, flows from its sands. Yet even here the chicanery of montage – to put it bluntly – remakes the pro-filmic event to manipulate viewers' perceptions (to say nothing of their heartstrings). While such orchestration is inherent to all cinema, including documentaries, the stakes here seem transformed by the presence of an autist, whose way of thinking defies conventional ableist categories. Is our cognitively disabled subject made to 'function' onscreen in ways to which a more presumably autonomous neurotypical might object? Do metaphor, ideology, the language of souls and rebirths and Final Cut Pro swoop-in to speak for Anton where other figures might verbalise more directly for themselves? The question, once raised, practically answers itself. Dolgopolov seems to worry along similar lines when he writes: 'There is something in the fine line between Arkus's seemingly tacit cooperation with Anton that stops the documentary from becoming an act of exploitation, but it does walk a fine line' (2013: n.p.).

The Portrait

Throughout the film Anton mostly utters such repeated phrases as 'Anton tut riadom' (e.g. 'OK, eat pea soup', 'Will sleep on bed on yellow bed here', as well as 'OK, Anton's right here'). But, as the 'walking in the snow' scene suggests, there is no shortage of people in the film who speak about Anton, for Anton, against Anton – though they rarely do so in deference to Anton.

Among the most egregious instances: a scene in which Arkus objects to the boy's removal after only nineteen days from a so-called 'elite children's home' (internat) with that institution's staff. He has been acting disruptive and does not get along with the other kids. In an extended take, a medium close-up, we see an unnamed woman in glasses lit by fluorescents that seem to drain human warmth from the image. Most striking, though, is a portrait of then-Prime Minister Vladimir Putin on a wall behind her (you really can't not see it), which seems to authorise and reinforce the staff member's opinions as the scene unfolds. The key exchange, all in the aforementioned shot, is this one:

Woman: 'Anton, k sozhaleniiu, interesa k rabote i zaniatiiam ne proiavlial. Razve ego mozhno v masterskuiu otpravit'? A libo v shveinuiu, libo v tsekh po sboru ruchek?'
('Unfortunately, Anton didn't demonstrate any interest in work or classes. Can he really be sent to a workshop? Or to a sewing shop, or a pen assembly shop?')

Arkus (off-screen): 'A on mozhet pisat' chasami...'
('But he can write for hours at a time...')

Woman: 'Nu, khorosho, on mozhet pisat' chasami. Skazhite mne, pozhalujsta, kakaia pol'za, esli chelovek pishet chasami? My staraemsia privivat' i vospitat' im prakticheskoe znanie, da? I vot oni obuchaiutsia po professii tsvetovod. Eto praktichno. Oni potom, esli khorosho zakonchat, osvoiat, oni mogut trudoustroit'sia. Eto daet vozmozhnost' zarabotka, da?, v zhizni, eshche tam chego-to. Byt' poleznym obshchestvu. A pisat' chasami, nu a tsel', skazhite mne. Dolzhen by byt' konechnyi resul'tat, konechnyi itog.'
('Well, great, he can write for hours at a time. So, tell me, please, what use can a person get out of writing for hours at a time? We're trying to train our children in practical skills, aren't we? So they learn, for example, how to be a florist. This is practical. Then, if they master that well, they'll be able to find a job. This gives them a chance to earn money to live and so on. Be useful to society. But writing for hours at a time – well, what's the point in that, tell me. There would have to be a result, a final product').

The scene comes off as a condemnation of Putinism, whose 'practical' economics-driven values sap the life out of human relations the way the fluorescents 'deaden' the woman's image. In a world where what matters is only 'a result, a final product' – in short, function – people like Anton have no place. (Arkus, in addition, seems to attack dodgy patriarchal figures: here Putin and, in the scene which immediately follows, Anton's father Vladimir, who meets him for an extremely awkward session of tea-drinking.) This treatment of defenceless autistic boys simply fulfills the prerogative of a compassionless society produced by power, personified by one man. Yet here, too, we have a bit of 'functional' editing. For in the gap between the woman saying 'But writing for hours at a time' and 'well, what's the point in that, tell me', Arkus inserts a jump cut. Who is speaking for whom, again?

Putin's image also appears on a television at another institution, the Petergof Neuropsychiatric Hospital, where doctors tell Rinata autism is not a diagnosis in their country, where neglected disabled children live in overcrowded conditions with overworked staff – in other words, a vision of hell (or so the film presents it).[9] The triad of Putin, a soulless healthcare system and human suffering is once more cinematically reinforced.

Much of the rest of the film depicts Anton as victim of that convergence, as he repeatedly fails to conform, even at Camphill Village Svetlana, a seemingly ideal charity-funded community for mentally disabled people on Lake Ladoga – very much the anti-Petergof – where he does well for a time. Everyone wants Anton to function; he never does. His father, in the excruciating tea scene, tells him over and over to speak louder. Other residents at Svetlana object when Anton shirks his work duties and disrupts evening dinner.[10] Later he manages to perform chores well while accompanied by David, a Svetlana volunteer – but when David leaves, Anton reverts to his old impractical habits. He runs away several times, eventually getting hit by a car. When Anton winds up in an institution (from which he is 'rescued' by Arkus), he cannot live on set schedules and appears drugged, slowly wasting away on his bed. Even the saint-like Sarah Hagnauer, the director of Svetlana, comes to speak in terms of function in reference to Anton's, antics, which have driven her staff to the verge.

Such scenes affirm the link between autism and isolation; Anton can never fit in, neither with other mentally ill people nor with a competitive society that privileges pragmatism over uniqueness. Yet Anton – and this seems very much the point of the film – is the most 'functional' of all. As Arkus puts it, the whole story began with his writing 'People' and posting it on the internet. It put everything in motion, from the comfort of his dying mother to his escape from institutionalisation to the reunion with his father to Arkus's self-realisation to the very film we watch today, and beyond. The climax of the film, in which Anton's recitation of his poem-essay 'People' plays over a montage of anonymous crowds as well as the men and women we have come to know, is nothing if not functional – dramatically, emotionally, powerfully so: 'Liudi terpiat. Liudi ne terpiat. Liudi poterpiat. ... Liudi konechnye. Liudi letaiut' ('People endure. People can't endure. People will endure ... People are finite. People fly').

The Camera

The cinema scholar Yurii Tsivian has praised *Anton's Right Here*:

> V etom fil'me sbylas' mechta Dzigi Vertova – mechta o tom, chto kamera izmenit mir, gradus chelovecheskikh otnoshenii; mechta o tom, chto geroi sam voz'met kameru i stanet soavtorom. Imenno eta vertovskaia ideia i est' vnutrenniy siuzhet Liubinogo fil'ma. Anton – chelovek, kotoryi, vo-pervykh, otkryvaet poeziiu, vo-vtorykh, otkryvaet kino. ('In this film the dream of Dziga Vertov has been realised, a dream of the camera changing the world and the degree of human relations; a dream of the subject himself taking the camera and becoming the co-author. Precisely this Vertovian idea is the embedded storyline of Lyuba's film. Anton is a person who first discovers poetry and then discovers cinema'). (Quoted in Anon. 2012)

It is true that Anton at one point gains access to the camera at Svetlana, and shoots in his own 'cine-eye' style. As Dolgopolov describes it: 'He instantly goes against the grain of filmmaking – shooting the sky and the clouds, which fill the screen. He sees the clouds in close-up and revels in the pleasure of his handiwork' (2013: n.p.). 'Letaiu!' ('I'm flying!'), we hear Anton exclaim as he zooms in. 'Letaiu!' ('I'm flying!'). This footage closes the film.

On the other hand, a more fully-realised Vertovian revolutionary vision would have Anton in charge of editing his own footage, not being subject to Arkus retaining control and choosing to include it through the power of the final cut. More central, I would argue, is how Arkus deploys that power not only to alter the order of events, repeat sequences, add syrupy background music and otherwise reconfigure reality, but also to exclude whole swathes of Anton's ontology. (Again, such exclusions happen in all documentaries; this is what makes the director's choices about what to leave in and out, as well as their motivations, so consequential.)

For one thing, Anton – a healthy teenage male – exhibits no sex drive, in a cultural context that has traditionally infantilised and asexualised the disabled, especially the cognitively disabled. Secondly, as Arkus told an interviewer: 'In the whole movie, I only included one episode in which Anton is actually screaming out loud. … There are certain things that you should not overdo. People will ask why there is so little of that, because it is the reality of their lives. But the camera can only do so much' (quoted in Nelson 2013: n.p.). The director clearly treads a fine line between engaging her audience with the real life struggle of her subject, and alienating it with 'too much' naturalism (tantrums, self-harm).[11] This trade-off, however, means an even greater distortion of who Anton is – and as a person with autism, he finds himself in a very disadvantaged position to object.

Instead, to a considerable degree we get not the dream of Dziga Vertov or the discovery of cinema, but the dream and self-discovery of Liubov Arkus. The film, in fact, is cut, its narrative arc structured and events arranged to arrive at the critical lesson that Anton 'is that other person in me, who all my life I've had to kill over and over so I could survive'. Yet, as Murray reminds us, 'the "we-learn-from-them" story is a staple of both film and literature … promoting the disabled figure either as a figure worthy of pity, or, conversely, of heroic perseverance and achievement' (2012: 68).

Anton's Right Here is not *Rain Man,* of course, but Arkus continues to speak of her own personal transformation, with Anton as its stimulus, in very similar terms (see Nelson 2013). If for her Anton served as the stimulus, then for Anton that role was played by the camera, she maintains. Indeed, the power of cinema to effect change offscreen attains a utopian religious stature in the film. 'Ia davno poniala, chto kamera glavnoe deistvuiushchee litso etoi istorii' ('I had long realised that the camera was the main character in this story'), Arkus says in voice-over, as the people mentioned flash by. 'Kamera pomogla pape priniat' reshenie. Kamera prodlila Rinate zhizn'. Ona umerla, kogda kamera byla vykliuchena. Kamera izmenila Antona. Kamera izmenila menia' ('The camera had helped his dad make the decision. The camera extended Rinata's life; she died when the camera was off. The camera transformed Anton. The camera transformed me').

The film's climax occurs when Vladimir and his second wife Nina watch footage of Anton on computer monitors, which precipitates tears and the final decision to move to a summer home that Arkus has procured, if they will take Anton with them: '[I]menno etot prosmotr i vse pridedushchie s'emki reshili delo' ('[It was] precisely this viewing and all the previous filming we did that settled the matter'), Arkus's voice-over insists.[12]

We last see Anton docilely doing chores at the dacha with his father and step-mother. By then his transfiguration into a 'functioning' adult – realised first and foremost through the camera's power to penetrate to the essence of things – seems complete. Complacently gathering firewood, hauling buckets of water, peeling potatoes, he appears as happy as anyone in such circumstances – perhaps more so. Over a long shot of Arkus and Anton strolling the woods, her voice on the soundtrack declares:

> Za eto vremia Anton mnogomu nauchilsia: plakat', gotovit', myt' posudu, govorit' po telefonu, ne boiat'sia sobak, razgovarivat' s liudmi. Nauchilsia ne ubegat', ne kusat' ruki, ne rvat' odezhdu ... U nego teper' bol'she spokoistva, i menshe sveta. Anton nauchilsia terpet'. I ia nauchilas' terpet'. Nu, vozmozhno, eto priuvelicheniie. Vo vsiakom sluchae my umeem eto luchshe, chem prezhde. Terpet'-to, chto chelovek vsegda odin, dazhe kogda seichas kto-to tut riadom ('Over this time Anton learned a lot: how to cry, how to cook, to wash dishes, talk on the phone, not be afraid of dogs, how to talk to people. He has learned not to run away, not to bite his arms, not to tear up his clothes. ... He is calmer now, and less radiant with light. Anton has learned to endure. And I have too. That may be an exaggeration, though. In any case, we can do it more easily than before. To endure the fact that human beings are always alone, even when someone is right here').

One irony of this resolution: Anton has become someone closer to the sort of person lionised by the staff member at the 'elite' children's home (with the portrait of Putin): a 'practical' worker with real skills, who follows orders well. Another irony: the change is effectuated not only through 'the expressive powers of cinema', or the state, or bonds of blood, but by an outsider to the family with the resources to make it happen, to engineer the happy ending.

Bakuradze lauds the film because 'on ne dokumentoval real'nost' v chistom vide. On korrektiroval real'nost', menial ee v korne i zatem sozdaval dokument. *Anton tut riadom* – eto kakoi-to novyi, tretiy vid kinematografa' ('it didn't document reality in its pure form. It corrected reality, changed it at its roots and then created the document. *Anton's Right Here* is some kind of new, third species of cinema') (quoted in Anon. 2012). A functional cinema, in which 'people endure'. But is a conventionally functional cinema at odds with the experience of autism?

Conclusion: Anton's Not Here?

Through an examination of the Russian documentary *Anton's Right Here*, this chapter has argued i) that films devoted to the autistic must contend with the unique complexities of this population, and ii) the strategies filmmakers use to try to negotiate that complexity can easily work at cross-purposes to each other. In seeking to 'humanise', they may in fact achieve something closer to the opposite (or in any case, some very mixed messages), not in spite of but because of the satisfying dramatic payoffs involved.

In Russia, a nation with a nascent disability rights movement and an ancient tradition of marginalising physical/cognitive difference, the odds would seem even longer for producing respectful, dignified, complex cinema on such subjects. Therefore Arkus's remarkable film, with all its pitfalls and unexamined presumptions, its transgressions and mysticism, deserves great praise for a portrayal of autism that comes, before anything else, from a place of real love. Its mission lives on: after the movie's release, Arkus headed the St. Petersburg branch of Vykhod (Coming Out), a foundation for autistic children, and in late 2013 founded the Anton's Right Here Centre, the first institution in Russia to provide job training and other support to adults with autism. It initially served some forty autistic adults and twenty people with different psychological issues (see Stolyarova 2013).

But putting forth Anton as a living alternative to an intolerable status quo, in which human beings are warped by a soulless function ultimatum and work ethic, poses its own problems. To say the least, it seems too heavy a metaphorical burden for Anton or anyone to justly bear. The hardest thing, as we have seen, is to resist the impulse to remake autistic people into symbols, over which they have precious little say; i.e. to make Anton 'not here'. One way to avoid this, Murray contends, is to make 'the presence of the person with autism, rather than an abstracted idea of the condition itself … the starting point of any enquiry' (2008: 28). Due to the especially potent spell it casts over our perceptions, perhaps cinema should heed that counsel even more closely than other media.

I want to close with a minor but exemplary manifestation of that spell from *Anton's Right Here*. Some fifteen minutes in, our young autistic sits apparently despondently in the passenger seat of a car, as someone shuts the door on him. We see him in a tight close-up, through the glass. It's sunny. He's waiting to start the journey home from Onega. We know he does not want to go, because Arkus has told us. The camera dwells on him for a few seconds. Then, after a jump cut (considerable time has passed because the light changes), Anton gazes up, apparently at something in the distance. An eyeline match cut 'shows' what our subject 'sees': tree leaves rippling in the wind, the woods beyond. On the soundtrack, a car engine starts up. In short, we witness an autistic experience fabricated through Eisensteinian montage.

I have no inkling what really caught Anton's attention, what if anything actually made him look out the window at that moment. For all I know those trees could have been filmed somewhere a hundred miles away, twenty years earlier. But the sequence is well edited. It brilliantly and subtly captures a boy's disappointment at leaving a cherished spot; his sadness seems to suffuse the leaves, all aflutter. I know those shots of Anton and the trees 'feel' right. Art overlaying life often does.

I love that sequence, but I prefer to think Anton was not just looking at trees. Or perhaps glimpsing something in trees that I never will. He may have seen lots of other things, too, things I can't imagine. All the while, he might have been thinking thoughts far beyond my comprehension – but no more or less human.

'People are finite. People fly.'

NOTES

1. Today, reports Galina Stolyarova, autism figures as 'a socially-charged illness in Russia in the sense that it provokes fear rather than compassion and leads to social isolation' (2013: n.p.).
2. Dolgopolov seems to read the audience's journey this way when he writes: 'From the first shot of Anton running around, yelping incoherently in the grey light of destitution, there is a realization that this is going to be difficult viewing: the lead character will repulse, he will be exploited and tragedy will befall him. But gradually we warm to Anton' (2013: n.p.).
3. In large measure, this has proven indistinguishable from imprisonment and criminal mistreatment. A 2013 Human Rights Watch report, *Abandoned by the State: Violence, Neglect, and Isolation for Children with Disabilities in Russian Orphanages*, reports on a devil's brew of abuses, including the case of Nastya, a nineteen-year-old girl with a developmental disability who described her torment in a Pskov orphanage from 1998 to 2011: 'The staff used to hit me and drag me by the hair. They gave me pills to calm me down' (Mazzarino and Human Rights Watch 2013: 3).
4. As Arkus herself describes it in the film.
5. Based on his representation, Anton seems to belong to the fourth ('mildest') category for autistic children as determined by Russian healthcare workers (see Lebedinskaya and Nikolskaya 1993: 677).
6. Arkus co-founded the important film journal *Seans* in 1989, and continues to serve as editor-in-chief. The journal has championed many important auteurs, including

Alexander Sokurov. She has also acted in such films as *Fontan* (*The Fountain,* 1989) and *Kokoko* (2012).

7   Sarah Phillips reminds us: 'The Soviet state employed a functional model of disability, based on a person's perceived "usefulness" to society' (2009: n.p.).
8   The Georgian director Bakur Bakuradze's encomium, from the *Seans* accolades page.
9   According to Dobro, one of the few organisations serving this population, autism is too often still not recognised as a developmental disorder, nor included in legislation, and continues to be lumped with schizophrenia. The number of autistics is in dispute, due to Russian doctors' reluctance to diagnose the disorder. In any case, resources for them are few, and chiefly involve institutionalisation (see Golubovsky and Reiter 2011).
10 These antics carry more than a whiff of Ivan Durachok, the beloved fool of Russian folk tales, and make for some of the funnier material in the film.
11 In this, the film seems very much informed both by Orthodox Christianity's views on suffering (Arkus titles one of the chapters 'Mytarstva' ['Tribulations']) as well as the Russian documentarian Alexander Rastorguev's 'Natural'noe kino' ('Natural Cinema') manifesto (2008), which privileges the human experience of pain as a marker of authenticity; see Vivaldi.
12 As indicated to an interviewer, Arkus has a mystical, almost pre-modern belief in the capacities of cinema, comparable to an Orthodox believer's veneration of icons: 'Right now, I think cinema is in a deep crisis. For many people the cinema is more like a video game than art. The camera is not a secret [sic] machine any more. Everybody can shoot little clips with a cell phone. It is part of the mass media. I want to underline this sacred meaning of the camera, what it can actually do and what it *has* done for Anton' (quoted in Nelson 2013; emphasis in original).

FILMOGRAPHY

Arkus, Liubov (dir) (2012) *Anton tut riadom*. 110 minutes. CTB Film Company/Masterskaya Seance. Russia.

BIBLIOGRAPHY

Anon. (2012) 'Anton tut riadom', *SEANS*. Available at http://seance.ru/blog/festivali/anton-tut-ryadom/ (accessed 13 July 2015).

Dolgopolov, Greg (2013) 'Anton's Right Here', *KinoKultura*, 40. Available at http://www.kinokultura.com/2013/40r-anton-ryadom.shtml (accessed 13 July 2015).

Golubovsky, Dmitry and Svetlana Reiter (2011) 'Concealed Lives: Autism in Russia', *ODR: Russia and Beyond*. Available at https://www.opendemocracy.net/od-russia/dmitry-golubovsky-svetlana-reiter/everyones-different-living-with-autism-in-russia (accessed 13 July 2015).

Lebedinskaya, Klara S. and Olga S. Nikolskaya (1993) 'Brief Report: Analysis of Autism and its Treatment in Modern Russian Defectology', *Journal of Autism and Developmental Disorders*, 23, 4, 675–79.

Mazzarino, A. and Human Rights Watch (2013) *Abandoned by the State: Violence, neglect, and isolation for children with disabilities in Russian orphanages*. https://www.hrw.org/report/2014/09/15/abandoned-state/violence-neglect-and-isolation-children-disabilities-russian (accessed 15 July 2015).

Murray, Stuart (2008) *Representing Autism: Culture, Narrative, Fascination*. Liverpool: Liverpool University Press.

____ (2010) 'Autism Functions/The Functions of Autism', *Disability Studies Quarterly*, 30, 10. Available at http://dsq-sds.org/article/view/1048/1229 (accessed July 13, 2015).

____ (2012) *Autism*. New York, NY: Routledge.

Nelson, Max (2013) 'Interview: Lyubov Arkus', *Film Comment*. Available at http://www.filmcomment.com/entry/interview-arkus-lyubov-antons-right-here (accessed 13 July 2015).

Phillips, Sarah (2009) '"There Are No Invalids in the USSR!": A Missing Soviet Chapter in the New Disability History', *Disability Studies Quarterly*, 29, 3. Available at http://dsq-sds.org/article/view/936/1111 (accessed 13 July 2015).

Siebers, Tobin (2010) *Disability Theory*. Ann Arbor, MI: University of Michigan Press.

Stolyarova, Galina (2013) 'City Opens Center for Autistic Adults', *St. Petersburg Times*, 1791, 50. Available at http://sptimes.ru/index.php?_id=100&storyid=38726 (accessed 15 November 2014).

Vivaldi, Giuliano (2013) 'New Objective: Autism Documentary *Anton's Right Here* Rewrites the Rules', *The Calvert Journal*. Available at http://calvertjournal.com/comment/show/833/antons-right-here-documentary (accessed 13 July 2015).

Displaying Autism

The Thinking and Images of *Temple Grandin* (2010)

Katherine Lashley

The film *Temple Grandin* (2010), directed by Mick Jackson and starring Claire Danes, is based on its title character's life. Increasingly, Grandin is internationally known as a woman who has autism, an autism advocate, a designer of humane cattle slaughter systems and an animal science professor. It portrays a good portion of her life: focusing mostly on her high school, college and early career years, it also provides flashbacks from her childhood. In many respects, the film is a realistic presentation of Grandin's life – many scenes are directly inspired by events that she herself describes in books such as *Emergence* (Grandin and Scariano 1986) and *Thinking in Pictures* (Grandin 1995). The value of such scenes, some of which are discussed in this chapter, is that these scenes introduce viewers to autism and may even encourage viewers to recognise their own neurotypical bias. And yet other aspects of the film are more problematic: the portrayal of Grandin by a neurotypical actor – what Tobin Siebers refers to as 'disability drag' (2008: 115) – has been rightly criticised, and there is a risk that introducing autism through Grandin in particular merely serves to reinforce what disability studies scholars have identified as the supercrip narrative in media representations of disability.

I see *Temple Grandin* as a complex film that is neither easily dismissed nor unproblematic. It is important to remember that it breaks some boundaries in disability film by putting Grandin's character in the spotlight, drawing on her own narratives of autism, allowing viewers to visualise her method of 'thinking in pictures' and her original door metaphor, and in the end presenting her experience through her perspective – an autistic perspective – and not that of the neurotypical mind. Grandin herself asserts that the film is an accurate representation of her life and how she sees the world. She explains that one of the reasons why the film is so accurate is that the director Mick Jackson also has autism and also thinks in pictures: they both see images in their mind and they can remember images more easily than words (see Grandin and Panek 2013: 197). Since he thinks in a similar way to Grandin, he could also use his own experiences with picture thinking in order to effectively portray her thought processes.

At the same time, however, *Temple Grandin* becomes one of the many films that, as Alexandria Prochnow notes, depict high-functioning autism, 'which simply is not the norm in the autism community' (2014: 136). This film, and a number of authors and public speakers, tend to emphasise and focus on those with high-functioning autism, which is a disservice to those in the autism community who are working with severe autism. The film's overall uplifting image of autism can provide encouragement for those dealing with autism, but it can also give viewers false expectations and parents false hope, especially if their child has severe autism and is not progressing well. That is, in a sense, Grandin is far from being representative of all autistic people.

In what follows, I outline how Grandin is portrayed as a supercrip in the film, and how this supercrip motif encourages people in the autism community, educates a general audience on autism, yet also neglects another reality of autism which includes those who are not supercrips, savants and not high-functioning. I then argue that the actress Claire Danes engages in disability drag as she is not disabled, though she portrays autism. The use of disability drag in filming the work also contributes to the supercrip motif and the image that autism is not a severe disability. In the last section, I argue that the film emphasises the common metaphor of the door, which illustrates Grandin's separation in the autistic world from the neurotypical world. The door metaphor also extends to the viewers as the film becomes the door (or window) through which neurotypicals can learn about autism and hopefully become more understanding of the autism community.

On-Screen: Grandin as Savant/Supercrip

In his book *Representing Autism: Culture, Narrative, Fascination*, Stuart Murray notes that 'with autism, it is especially the imagined place of savantism that appears to exercise public imagination' (2008: 13). When it comes to savantism, probably the most iconic image is Raymond in *Rain Man* (1988), who can calculate objects and number instantly – a human calculator. It is interesting that Prochnow does not see savantism as playing a role in Jackson's film:

> *Temple Grandin* is a unique case of a realistic depiction that just happens to be a high-functioning, super intelligent, autistic person; Temple is not a savant nor is she portrayed as one. She is not just a quirky person, and she is certainly not undiagnosed. This HBO film realistically shows the struggles and achievements of a real-life autistic person, though it certainly cannot be generalized as representing all people with ASD. (2014: 145)

That Grandin is not a savant and is not portrayed as one is an assertion I do not find to be wholly satisfying. The fact that Grandin discovered that she could more easily understand animals and communicate between them and humans greatly enhanced her value as a student and employee: she was able to give her professors and employers material that other people could not provide for them. The level of education she has attained and the recognition that has been directed at her professional achievements are both highly unusual. As the film makes clear, Grandin graduated from high school, college, earned her PhD and redesigned livestock facilities; in fact, as she writes in *Animals in Translation*, 'Half the cattle in the United States and Canada are handled in humane slaughter systems I've designed' (Grandin and Johnson 2005: 7).

While Grandin is not a savant in the way that other savants can calculate complex numbers or hear a piece of music once and play it on an instrument, some would say she is a savant in her communication and intellectual abilities – in fact, a number of people in the autism community consider her to be one because of her achievements. Prochnow's most compelling statement is her observation that Grandin's life cannot 'be generalized as representing all people with ASD'. A number of parents and specialists of autism have recognised that Grandin's experiences, especially those in her later years after she graduated high school, cannot be applied to all autistics because a number of autistics have trouble graduating from high school, attending college and gaining employment. An article entitled 'Postsecondary Education and Employment Among Youth With an Autism Spectrum Disorder' by Paul T. Shattuck *et al.* (2012) analyses the education and employment of those with ASD between the ages of 19 and 23:

> The overall rate of paid employment since high school among youth with an ASD was 55.1%. Twenty-eight percent had attended a 2-year

college, 12.1% had attended a 4-year college, the combined rate of attendance at either a 2- or 4-year college was 34.7%, and 9.3% had attended a vocational or technical education program. Approximately one third (34.9%) had not participated in any postsecondary employment or school. (2012: 1046)

These recent statistics illustrate how difficult it is for those with ASD to attend and graduate college, and to gain and keep a job. Most important, Grandin herself recognises that she is not a representative example of an adult with autism.

A number of disability studies scholars recognise the image and stereotype of the supercrip as a staple of media representation of people with disabilities. The supercrip is someone with a disability (whether physical or mental) who does not succumb to the disability, but rather overcomes the disability by having a good attitude, working hard in life and at their education and career and finding what typical people would consider to be a fulfilling life. Supercrips accomplish their dreams and succeed in life despite their disability. The supercrip is popular in media because it sends an uplifting message to the nondisabled, who may think: 'If they can achieve this with a disability, then so can I, since I don't have a disability.' Nevertheless, a number of disability studies critics recognise the negative impact of the supercrip on those with disabilities who have not achieved great success and also on those with more severe disabilities, especially for those people who are so severely disabled that the disability (not the person) does hinder the individual from achieving more (see Longmore 2001; Black 2007; Gregory 2013; Haller and Zhang 2013).

Rhonda Black writes that the supercrip 'portray[s] the individual with a disability as exhibiting great courage, stamina, and determination to overcome his or her disability. This individual then serves as a motivational role model for others but may lead individuals with disabilities into feeling like failures if they have not accomplished something extraordinary' (2007: 67). The film portrays Grandin as a supercrip because it shows her courage, stamina and determination to prove herself and to do the work that she wants to do. To be fair, these qualities are evident in Grandin's own narratives of her life – which rightly emphasise perseverance in the face of challenges – as well as in her on-screen portrayal. For example, when Grandin is in high school, she discovers that when she gets into the cattle chute, which squeezes her sides, she feels calm. Therefore, she creates her own version of the cattle chute, called a squeeze machine that is built for a person and kept in her dorm room.

When it comes to the challenge of the squeeze machine, she carried out a social experiment, and then wrote a report to prove to the school board that other people also find the squeeze machine soothing. When her math teacher challenged her to discover how the visual room was distorted, she persisted in finding the solution. When ranchers and cattle hands told her that cattle moo anyway and that the moos do not have a meaning, she completed her observations and research to prove that cattle moo and act in certain ways for a reason. But the risk is that general viewers unfamiliar with autism may believe that this is an accurate representation of autism – that all or most autistics are like Grandin, which would encourage viewers to ignore people on other areas of the spectrum, especially those who are not savants and those who are not as high-functioning as Grandin. Yet because of the history and proliferation of the supercrip in films in television shows – not only with autism but supercrips with other disabilities as well – viewers are primed for the supercrip autistic and are therefore not expecting (in some ways) a view of autism that comes across to many in the autism community as more realistic or honest.

Black addresses the connection between the supercrip and the inspiration provided: 'While it may be argued that a true story does not perpetuate stereotypes, we believe that the focus of the characters' lives as "inspiration" and "full of great accomplishments" perpetuates the images of the "supercrip"' (2007: 79). Rochelle Gregory asserts that 'HBO's portrayal of Grandin does occasionally slide into a supercrip narrative', and I agree with her. Grandin's inspiration and accomplishments shown in the film contribute to her image as a supercrip. Terri Thrower also asserts that it uses the supercrip and overcoming narratives (2013: 208). Gregory further explains of the scenes that show Grandin's mind: 'Ultimately, these scenes spectacularize Grandin by setting her apart, both intellectually and socially, from the world around her' (2007: 79). While Grandin as supercrip is distinguished from both autistics and typicals, the film also attempts to join these worlds together through her portrayal. Earning a PhD, becoming a professor and creating one's own livestock consulting business are impressive achievements, whether one is neurotypical or autistic. Of course, Grandin's success translates easily to the neurotypical world because neurotypicals are more familiar with higher education, developing a career (especially in teaching) and building a business.

Beth Haller and Lingling Zhang state: 'The role [of the supercrip] reinforces the idea that disabled people are deviant – that the person's accomplishments are "amazing" for someone who is less than complete' (2013: 20). Grandin's autism is portrayed as deviant at first as it leads her to the squeeze machine and cattle, yet her accomplishments – college degrees, books published, public speaking, teaching – are seen as amazing because she has autism, and previously the research on autism had asserted that autistics could not achieve very much. Also related to the supercrip theme is the idea of compensation: the disabled person is compensated with a gift or talent to make up for being disabled in some way. Paul Longmore writes: 'A recurring explicit or implicit secondary theme of many stories of adjustment is the idea of compensation. God or nature or life compensates handicapped people for their loss, and the compensation is spiritual, moral, mental, and emotional' (2001: 8). Grandin appears to be compensated when it comes to cattle because she notices patterns about cows' behaviour that others do not. Thus, her compensation is mental because she can see things that others cannot and she devises solutions that others have not thought of or implemented. She is also compensated morally as she is inspired to produce more humane ways to give cattle injections and to slaughter them. This moral compensation is pertinent because in the past, a misconception about autism was that autistics are unable to understand what another being thinks or feels and cannot sympathise. Yet Grandin demonstrates that she can sympathise, especially with cattle (moral compensation) and that she has the intelligence to do something about it (mental compensation).

A motif in disability narratives that appears to be related to the supercrip narrative is the story of adjustment. Longmore describes the story of adjustment: 'the dramas of adjustment say that disability does not inherently prevent … handicapped people from living meaningfully and productively and from having normal friendships and romantic relationships but these stories put the responsibility for any problems squarely and almost exclusively on the disabled person' (ibid.). Haller and Zhang have recognised that 'disabled people receive messages about society's expectations of them through mass media representations such [as] the Supercrip narrative, which tells them to "overcome" a disabling condition, or to seek "cures" as in the Medical Model' (2013: 19). Indeed, Grandin's story is one of adjustment to problems linked to the social negotiation of and reaction to autism. As Grandin herself suggests in her various books, she has adjusted to society and the strictures set by typical people. In this sense, because she has overcome and adjusted, she becomes a supercrip.

Connected to the image of the supercrip is the message sent by the media when nondisabled actors portray those with disabilities and portray the supercrip: the disability in 'disability drag' can be viewed as not as disabling as the disability really is, simply because the actor is not disabled and the actor is playing a supercrip. Thus, the image of the supercrip and the disabled person who can easily be healed is proliferated, causing even more issues with the accurate representation of autism.

Beyond the Screen: Disability Drag and Issues of Performance

Claire Danes' performance as Temple Grandin brings up the issue of disability drag, as termed by Tobin Siebers, where an able-bodied actor portrays a disabled character on screen. Such a performance makes the audience aware of disability, and potentially even accepting of disability, though the audience is aware that the actor will return to being able-bodied (2008: 114–16). In one sense, the performance of disability drag actually reinforces the preference for able-bodiedness. However, Siebers goes deeper to understand how disability drag functions: 'it also exposes and resists the prejudices of society. The masquerade fulfills the desires to tell a story seeped in disability, often the very story that society does not want to hear, by refusing to obey the ideology of ability' (2008: 118). In this sense – although it is an imitation that highlights the able body and ability of the actor – disability drag also makes disability present and sometimes more visible, encouraging audiences to confront disability rather than to hide it. In this way, more able-bodied people can learn more about disability; through performance disability can be brought into cultural discourse. Instead of hiding the disability, it is brought to the forefront (2008: 119).

That Siebers' understanding of disability drag is nuanced, however, does not mean that he sees such performances as unproblematic. Prochnow writes:

> One problem that would be hard to fix is that there are no autistic actors playing characters with autism; obviously, acting is not a career choice conducive to most symptoms of autism, but at the same time it can be inappropriate to have actors play roles that they have not experienced themselves. (2014: 147)

Prochnow aptly points out that many autistic people are played by neurotypical actors and that there are few, if any, actors who actually do have autism. While it can be inappropriate to have typical actors portraying autistics, there is also a need for representations of autism that are as accurate and realistic as possible. Although the director, Mick Jackson, has autism and brought his own autistic experiences to the film, many – if not all – of the actors are typical. That is, even though Danes is typical, she is being directed by Jackson, which returns disability to the performance in a way. Viewers should determine which may be more problematic in a presentation of a disability, particularly autism: a non-disabled actor directed by an autistic director, or an autistic actor directed by a neurotypical. In the case of film – which is, after all, an artistic form largely driven by speculation and judged based on its investment return – one must wonder whether the use of big-name stars can be effective at rendering disabilities visible. A number of scholars, including Haller and Zhang, Black and Prochnow assert that more people with disabilities should be playing characters with disabilities. In particular, Black writes about the relative benefits and risks of casting decisions relating to disability:

> The films we reviewed employed famous actors and actresses, an obvious box office draw. In one sense, if the movie has a positive portrayal of a character with a disability, the increased viewing audience provided by a big-name star could help increase public awareness. On the other hand, what message is being sent if audiences never see actors with disabilities? (2007: 82).

The influence of the big-name star can be seen clearly in the marketing for *Temple Grandin*. The DVD case and film poster show a close-up of Grandin's character (with Danes' face, although quite changed due to make-up and costume) and large letters at the top-centre announce 'Claire Danes', while the name and title of the film is placed in large letters at the image's bottom-centre. The announcement that Danes portrays Grandin helps to attract audiences to a film about autism and Temple Grandin that they might not have seen if it were not for the popular actress.

In addition to noting the difference that a famous actor makes in a film about disability, Black also focuses on the plot lines and issues dealt with in disability films:

> And finally, more films should portray individuals with disabilities as having 'typical' emotions, routines, interpersonal conflicts, and in general have plot lines more similar to those in films featuring main characters without disabilities. Films including a character with a disability should not focus on the valiant struggle against the odds, where the disability is the central focus of a person's life. Instead, we would recommend that feature films portray a person with a disability living

> a full and rich life where the disability is incidental to the character's role. (2007: 82)

The goals of having a character or disabled character engage in a plot that does not centre around the disability is commendable. Can this be done for films on autism? For *Temple Grandin*, I am not so sure the film could have focused on much else other than her autism, despite the fact that it devotes much time to Grandin developing her career at the ranch. While her story includes being a woman and being a minority in a male-dominated business, her education and career are driven by her autism. Her autism – her perseverance – leads her to pursue her desire, which is to work with cattle, despite the sexism she experiences on the ranch. If anything, the sexism engages her autism – her perseveration and fixation – in order to help her become successful. All the while, autism is in the background, influencing everything she does.

As *Temple Grandin* follows the supercrip narrative and uses non-autistic actors, it is also of importance to analyse how this positions the audience. Martin Norden notes that many disability films place the audience in the able-bodied perspective, not the perspective of the disabled character, and that this makes the disability into a 'spectacle' (2001: 21–2). The film, however, presents everything from Grandin's perspective. Audience members do not view through an able-bodied perspective or character, but rather through an autistic perspective. As the film follows the supercrip narrative, the story of adjustment, and engages in disability drag, it does break away from the need to present disability narrative through an able-bodied perspective.

The most pertinent part of *Temple Grandin* includes the presentation of Grandin's term and description of her thought processes that she calls 'thinking in pictures'. In her books, she explains that images, not words, flash through her mind, which tends to operate visually (1995: 19). She also explains that language does not come easily to her, so much so that it is almost like a second language that she has had to learn. She has to translate the images in her mind into words in order to communicate with others, something Grandin explains multiple times throughout her books so that readers can understand her thought process of images. Similarly, the film illustrates this – taking the 'thinking in pictures' description back to images and away from language. When someone asks Grandin about a church steeple, images of different steeples appear quickly on the screen. The film shows the fragmentation of her thinking by displaying the images so rapidly. It also shows how Grandin has often translated language into pictures in her mind using specific examples and exploiting the visual nature of film. In one scene depicting graduate school, Grandin wants to study the meaning of cows' mooing for her thesis. In order to do so, she must have a form signed by the feedlot owner. After getting that signature, Grandin runs to her professor's office and hands him the graduate study form, which is dirty and wrinkled. The professor comments: 'It smells like half the cows signed it.' In her mind, she pictures a cow sitting at a desk and signing the form, after which she says, 'No. Cows can't write.' This exchange also shows that she is a literal thinker: she takes the words literally and therefore envisions a cow signing a piece of paper.

Another example of Grandin thinking in pictures is shown when she is a teenager and temporarily living with her aunt at her ranch. Her aunt tells her, 'We get up with the roosters', and Grandin then imagines her aunt sitting atop a roof with the rooster, also doing the 'cock-a-doodle-doo'. It is a funny image – even Grandin smiles and laughs, recognising how silly it is. Once again, viewers visualise the literalness of her mindset, and they see that Grandin seems to realise that she is literal, though she cannot entirely help it because that is how her mind works – routinely transforming language into images so she can remember and understand. The film allows neurotypical viewers visual access to how Grandin sees her world, how she thinks and how she interprets language through the use of images. It automatically turns Grandin's experiences into a visual representation, creating a valuable connection between the film, the mind of its title character and the audience.

The Metaphor of the Door

This metaphor of the door – appearing both in her books and in the film – is one that she enjoys using because it has helped her to understand complex situations. She has used it in order to help herself transition from one stage of life to another: graduating high school, graduating college, embarking on a new career and even when overcoming her fears of going through transitions. Joseph Straus has observed that the metaphor of the door is popular in a number of autistics' writings: 'Much more commonly, we find a metaphors [sic] of doors ... and glass. Both involve an idea of separation – the autistic world and the normate world are distinct – but the boundary between them permits people on both sides to see through ... and possibly move through as well' (2013: 471). Grandin recognises the meanings of the door metaphors she uses as well. She sees the doors as the path that will transition her from one period of her life into another. She would find physical doors that she would look at, draw, write about and eventually even walk through, physically signaling to herself that she is transitioning in her life. While Grandin discusses several doors in her books, the film covers two sliding glass doors: one in the cafeteria at her school and the other at the supermarket.

When Grandin is getting lunch at school, the sounds and sights overwhelm her so much that she rushes to leave the cafeteria. However, when she arrives at a sliding glass door, it opens and closes in front of her, scaring her and stopping her. The film connects the swift open and close motion of the sliding glass door to an image that Grandin has stored in her memory from a black-and-white film of the blade coming down in a guillotine. She also connects the sliding glass door to a butcher knife chopping salami, again envisioned in black and white. She tries a second time to rush through the door. The third time the door opens, she drops her tray and finally runs through the sliding glass door when it is open.

When Grandin was in her early twenties, after she had graduated from college and was working at the feedlot, she lived by herself and had to do her own grocery shopping. The supermarket has a sliding glass door, and she is afraid at first to enter. The door opens the first time, but she does not walk through. It closes and then opens again when a couple walk past her into the supermarket. She rushes in after them, as if using them for protection against the sliding door closing upon her. Upon leaving the supermarket, she again feels fright at the automatic sliding glass door. She reminded herself that it was a door and that she could see through it and walk through it – that a door would not keep her from living as 'normal' a life as possible. The automatic sliding glass door that Grandin encounters in the film echoes her experience that she recounts in *Thinking in Pictures*: she had to clean a series of three sliding windows, and one day she became stuck between two of the windows. 'While I was trapped between the windows, it was almost impossible to communicate through the glass. Being autistic is like being trapped like this. The windows symbolized my feelings of disconnection from other people and helped me cope with the isolation' (1995: 63).

The film shows some of the discrimination that Grandin experiences at the cattle yards and what she viewed as yet another door keeping her from her work: the men would not allow her into the ranch and past the gate because she is a woman. Since she knows that they are discriminating against her based on her gender and not on her autism, she decides to imitate them: she trades in her car and buys a big, old, beat-up pick-up truck. She buys jeans and a cowboy shirt, then proceeds to roll in the mud to dirty up her appearance and even smears mud on the truck. Once she manages to get inside the ranch and is working alongside the men, the men further antagonise her by placing bloody guts and entrails on the front window and on the top of the

Fig. 1: Temple Grandin's door metaphor is rendered visually for audiences.

truck. Offended and enraged, with her bare hands she wipes and throws the guts on the ground and yells at the men who are laughing at her, 'I've eaten bulls' testicles. Ate 'em at my aunt's ranch. Regularly! This is a waste!' Viewers then see the men appearing contrite as they have stopped laughing and watch her drive off. Although the film does not connect the bloody entrails on the truck window with the other images of windows and doors, this, too, holds the same meaning. She has faced discrimination and ostracism at the ranch from the men, and this is literally and physically represented by the blood and guts on her truck's front window. This bullying is an obstacle or window that keeps Grandin from fully working at the ranch and being accepted by the men there. Like the other windows and doors she has encountered, though, she does not allow this to stop her from pursuing what she wants to do (see 1995: 110).

Another metaphor of the door appears at the end of the movie. Grandin is with her mother at an autism meeting. The presenters invite her to speak at the podium. As she walks up the centre isle from her place in the back, the film shows the image of the door on the screen, and she imagines herself walking through it. She tells herself: 'It's a door', meaning that speaking about autism in front of all these people is a door that she is passing through: she is transitioning from being an autistic herself to being an autistic who can explain autism and in the process become one of the best and strongest autism advocates there is.

An interesting point about the door metaphor is the fact that it *is* a metaphor. A number of people have argued that autistics have trouble with metaphors and abstract thinking. Even Grandin asserts that she has trouble with abstract thinking, yet she explains that she can use and think in metaphors. She turned the metaphor into a real door several times throughout her life in order to make the metaphor tangible. She has written that as she has grown older and has had more experiences, she no longer needs the tangible door, but that she may still use the door metaphor in her mind. She has proven that her mind can grasp the intangible through images. A metaphor, in this case, and in many cases, is visual after all.

Temple Grandin accurately reflects one experience of autism, providing typical viewers the opportunity to see Grandin's story of autism and how sensory issues have affected her. When it comes to considering just how many television shows and films portray autism and whether or not they are true in their presentations, *Temple Grandin* stands out. The film was not made to show other autistics how to navigate the outside world; rather, it shows neuro-typicals what the world can seem like to an autistic person: sights, sounds and other sensory issues are illustrated to inform the viewer that little things that they might take for granted can often cause problems for the person with autism. The film attempts to do what Grandin does in her books, and that is to make the experience of autism open and available to neurotypicals so that they may better understand autism. To this end, the film is successful. In keeping with Grandin's metaphor of the door: this film is itself a door, available for neurotypicals and autistics to view in order to understand another aspect of autism. One need only open the door and enter in order to be fully immersed in Grandin's life.

Conclusion

What is clear is that *Temple Grandin* can open more doors to discussion and knowledge of autism. For instance, in the spring semester of 2015, my first-year writing class read Grandin's book *The Autistic Brain* (with Richard Panek, 2013), watched *Temple Grandin* and wrote an essay about autism in connection to something in society, such as school or career. Many of my students said that before reading and watching about Grandin that they did not know what autism was, or that they had misconceptions about autism. A discussion about the role of autism in society can also lead into a discussion of the disability and disabled in society. Students looked more critically at the education system – what was good and what could be done to improve it. Students examined the workplace and social acceptance, recognising that there needs to be more acceptance, education and understanding. Through the perspective of Grandin's autism, students (and by extension, viewers) can experience one version of autism and learn a little more about the developmental disability that affects at least one in eighty people.

Indeed, as a viewer I have experienced the ambivalence of watching the uplifting story of Grandin and then reflecting on my sister, who is not a supercrip, but an adult with autism who works a part-time job, cannot keep up with college work, and who may never be able to live on her own. I have just felt uplifted by the supercrip narrative applied to autism – if Grandin can do this, then so can other autistics! And I have just felt let down, because I recognise that my sister is not that kind of supercrip, even though she is very advanced in her autism and has improved so much from being labelled as severely autistic and nonverbal to talking and working part-time.

The supercrip narrative, though a common motif and often unrealistic, may provide hope for parents whose child has recently been diagnosed as on the spectrum. For those with high-functioning autism and Asperger syndrome, this film can be more of an accurate representation, especially for Aspergians, as they themselves may also be a supercrip having achieved higher education and/or a promising career. While this film follows many of the conventions seen in disability film, it is one of the few films of autism, and it is paving the way for more in the future that will hopefully provide more realistic representations that are more applicable to others on the spectrum. Thus, more doors between autistics and neurotypicals are being opened, not only by scholars, but also by those in the autistic community and potentially by neurotypical audiences.

FILMOGRAPHY

Jackson, Mick (dir) (2010) *Temple Grandin*. 107 minutes. HBO Films. USA.

BIBLIOGRAPHY

Black, Rhonda S. (2007) 'Victims and Victors: Representations of Physical Disability on the Silver Screen', *Research & Practice for Persons with Severe Disabilities*, 32, 1, 66–83.
Grandin, Temple (1995) *Thinking in Pictures: And Other Reports from My Life with Autism*. New York, NY: Doubleday.
____ (2011) *The Way I See It: A Personal Look at Autism & Asperger's*, 2nd. ed. Arlington, VA: Future Horizons.
____ (2012) *Different…Not Less: Inspiring Stories of Achievement and Successful Employment from Adults with Autism, Asperger's, and ADHD*. Arlington, VA: Future Horizons.
Grandin, Temple and Catherine Johnson (2005) *Animals in Translation: Using the Mysteries of Autism to Decode Animal Behavior*. New York, NY: Harcourt.

Grandin, Temple and Richard Panek (2013) *The Autistic Brain: Helping Different Kinds of Mind Succeed*. Boston: Mariner.

Grandin, Temple and Margaret M. Scariano (1986) *Emergence: Labeled Autistic*. Novato, CA: Arena Press.

Gregory, Rochelle (2013) 'Beyond the Spectacle of the Autistic Adult', *Disability Studies Quarterly*, 31, 3. Available at http://dsq-sds.org/article/view/1659/1610 (accessed 6 August 2015).

Haller, Beth and Lingling Zhang (2013) 'Stigma or Empowerment? What Do Disabled People Say About Their Representation in News and Entertainment Media?', *Review of Disability Studies: An International Journal*, 9, 4, 19–33.

Longmore, Paul K. (2001) 'Screening Stereotypes: Images of Disabled People', in Anthony W. Enns and Christopher R. Smit (eds) *Screening Disability: Essays on Cinema and Disability*. New York, NY: University Press of America, 1–17.

Murray, Stuart (2008) *Representing Autism: Culture, Narrative, Fascination*. Liverpool: Liverpool University Press.

Norden, Martin F. (2001) 'The Hollywood Discourse on Disability: Some Personal Reflections', in Anthony W. Enns and Christopher R. Smit (eds) *Screening Disability: Essays on Cinema and Disability*. New York, NY: University Press of America, 19–31.

Prochnow, Alexandria (2014) 'An Analysis of Autism Through Media Representation', *ETC: A Review of General Semantics*, 71, 2, 133–49.

Shattuck, Paul T., Sarah Carter Narendorf, Benjamin Cooper, Paul R. Sterzing, Mary Wagner and Julie Lounds Taylor (2012) 'Postsecondary Education and Employment Among Youth With an Autism Spectrum Disorder', *Pediatrics*, 129, 6, 1042–9. Available at http://pediatrics.aappublications.org/content/129/6/1042 (accessed 6 August 2015).

Siebers, Tobin (2008) *Disability Theory*. Ann Arbor, MI: University of Michigan Press.

Straus, Joseph N. (2013) 'Autism as Culture', in Lennard J. Davis (ed.) *The Disability Studies Reader*, 4th ed. New York: Routledge, 460–84.

Thrower, Terri (2013) 'Overcoming the Need to 'Overcome': Challenging Disability Narratives in The Miracle', in Marja Evelyn Mogk (ed.) *Different Bodies: Essays on Disability in Film and Television*. Jefferson, NC: McFarland, 205–18.

More than the 'Other'?

On Four Tendencies Regarding the Representation of Disability in Contemporary German Film (2005–2010)

Petra Anders

This overview identifies four tendencies regarding contemporary German film on disability that suggest close ties between disability and norm(ality). These ties exist in recent German films no matter whether they tend to reinforce the separation of disabled character(s) from 'normality', a trend that is criticised by most disability studies scholars, or whether they aim to bridge this gap. In this context it becomes important to investigate the stereotypes, myths and metaphors surrounding disability that the selected German films perpetuate or challenge, and to reflect on the consequences of representing disability in terms of the disabled or the able-bodied self/Other. As some of the films selected may not be familiar to the Anglophone word, some basic details about the plots of each film are provided. In the sections that follow representations of 'The Disabled Evildoer', 'Institutionisation and (Self-)Improvement', 'Disability in Everyday Life' and 'Introducing Sexuality' are explored as a way of chronicling the state of disability in contemporary German film.

The Disabled Evildoer

Reinforcing problematic perspectives, Christian Alvart's thriller *Antikörper* (*Antibodies,* 2005) portrays a paedophiliac killer named Gabriel Engel and employs disability as outer sign and punishment for a mentally disordered soul. British academic and journalist Paul Darke states: 'Formula films, or genre movies, seem to have played a key part in perpetuating disability's image as one-dimensionally bad' (1997: 12). Accordingly, Engel's very first sentence in *Antikörper* indicates that he is not only an evildoer, but a criminal, a narcissistic parasite, an immoral person, a monster, a freak/murdering lunatic, a hater and a sinister and sexually abnormal person as well:

> Die Welt ist ungerecht, sogar zu Leuten wie uns. Pedro Alonso López, das Monster der Anden, hat 300 Sexualmorde begangen. Und wer kennt ihn heute noch? Kein Schwein. Jack the Ripper ist noch nach 120 Jahren weltberühmt. Und weswegen? Wegen fünf Nutten, fünf. Und Charlie Manson, dieser Hippie, hat es fertig gebracht, unser Kaiser genannt zu werden, und dabei nicht mal einen einzigen Scheiß-Mord selbst begangen.
>
> (The world is unfair, even to people like us. Pedro Alonso Lopez, the monster of the Andes, committed 300 sex killings. And who remembers him nowadays? No one. Jack the Ripper is still world-famous 120 years later. And for what? Because of five whores, five. And that hippie, named Charlie Manson, managed to be called our emperor, even if he himself did not even commit a single fucking murder.)[1]

This first-person narrator's characteristics are one-dimensional, too: he is mad, distant, brutal, demanding, mean, selfish, impatient, determined, jealous, talkative or stubborn. His actions are unpredictable. Moreover, Engel takes pleasure in scaring, terrorising and manipulating people around him, especially his antagonist, the policeman Michael Martens. In short, this character is a personification of all evil. Although he speaks of 'us' and 'our', it is clear that (most of) the audience will not want to identify with Engel but make sure he is the 'Other'.

Susan Wendell explains the mechanism of othering in connection with disability: 'When we make people "other", we group them together as the objects of our experience instead of regarding them as fellow subjects of experience with whom we might identify' (2006: 251). The asymmetrical consequences of this are dramatic:

> If you are 'other' to me, I see you primarily as symbolic of something else – usually, but not always, something I reject and fear and that I project onto you. We can all do this to each other, but very often the process is not symmetrical, because one group of people may have more power to call itself the paradigm of humanity and to make the world suit its

own needs and validate its own experiences. Disabled people are 'other' to able-bodied people, and ... the consequences are socially, economically and psychologically oppressive to the disabled and psychologically oppressive to the able-bodied. (Ibid.)

This also means that: 'Able-bodied people may be "other" to disabled people, but the consequences of this for the able-bodied are minor (most able-bodied people can afford not to notice it)' (ibid.). In Alvart's film, the last name of the main character, Engel – which means 'angel' – brings up the binaries of good/evil; as does his first name, Gabriel, which suggests religious connotations in its connection to the archangel of the same name. He is further presented as other through suggested mental illness, immoral attitudes and criminal behaviour – a portrayal that intersects with physical disability. The paedophiliac becomes a wheelchair user after he has tried to escape the police by jumping out of a window. Within the genre conventions of the horror film, this physical disability serves as atmosphere of 'menace, mystery or deprivation' (Barnes 1992: n.p.) and as punishment for the crimes Engel commits. In this case, disability symbolises danger, too: a threat to characters in the film as well as to able-bodied norms. This becomes even more obvious when considering the policeman Martens, whose identity is deeply rooted in Christianity. That Martens becomes increasingly involved in Engel's manipulations, unable to resist them until the very last chance, makes the film a prime example of a story in which the good able-bodied normality wins the fight (see Darke 1997: 13).

Accordingly, it is no wonder that this disabled character, who is far from 'normal', makes fun of norms. Regarding performing arts and cinematic representations, both Darke and Markus Dederich, a German professor working on disability studies, agree that normality is the key to understanding representations of disability (see Darke n.d.; Dederich 2007: 127, 139). Although 'normality' and 'disability' are both imprecise terms, disability is often codified as a medical and legal category.[2] As a consequence, (German) medical or legal standards decide whether people are considered disabled or not, and self-definition and individual agency become less significant than wider social structures that are conditioned by able-bodied norms. Anne Waldschmidt, head of the Internationale Forschungsstelle Disability Studies (International Research Unit Disability Studies) at the University of Cologne, for example, emphasises that normality serves to assure able-bodied people of their reasonability and, in this way, legitimises their participation in civil liberties (2003: 20).

Fig. 1: Prison cell bars separating the disabled evil from 'normality'.

The power struggle between the bad (disabled) and the good (able-bodied) in *Antikörper* reaches its visual peak in the way the bars of Engel's prison cell are depicted. In the relevant scenes, the disabled 'evil with a human face' is put behind bars, most clearly separated from 'normality'. In one of these scenes, Martens decides to sit down while questioning Engel. He is (figuratively as well as physically) willing to get down to Engel's level in order to get the information he needs to convict him. Martens' decision is telling because he trusts in his own moral superiority.

Engel's acts and their consequences – first disability and jail, then suicide (but not out of guilt) – contribute to a narrative in which the bad is needed to identify the good. Martens and Engels are, in this way, presented as characters that symbolise opposite ends of a moral spectrum.

The disabled Karl Winter in Margarethe von Trotta's *Ich bin die Andere* (*I am the Other Woman*, 2005) can also be considered a disabled evildoer. Winter is the patriarch of a family that he believes is there to serve him, and his wheelchair serves as an outer sign for his moral wickedness. He even uses his hydraulic lift, which is supposed to help him overcome obstacles, as a murder weapon. The fact that he takes pleasure in exerting pressure on people, especially on his mentally ill daughter, Carolin, who obeys him, shows the pervasiveness of the mechanism that Martin Norden calls 'the age-old practice of linking evil or innocence with disability' (2002: n.p.). Interestingly, *Ich bin die Andere* does without point-of-view shots which could help the audience to either empathise with the mentally ill daughter or to maybe get a better understanding of why Winter behaves the way he does. This makes it very easy for viewers to uncritically accept the stereotypes and the portrayal of disability as synonymous with evil as well as 'the stigma attached to psychiatric disability' (López Levers 2001: n.p.). Lisa Lopez Levers' statement regarding the film sample for her analysis of Hollywood film is to some extent applicable to the characters of Winter and his daughter and fully applicable to the disabled evildoer in *Antiköper*: 'These portrayals of "madness" are not necessarily or even usually reflective of the reality of psychiatric impairment' (ibid.). She further underscores the significant and 'powerful impact which such stereotypical filmic images may have upon the viewer' (ibid.). Accordingly, von Trotta's film aims at evoking a distanced fascination and growing disgust for the wheelchair user Winter, thus reducing him to an example of what Colin Barnes, founder of the Centre for Disability Studies at the University of Leeds, calls 'objects of curiosity' (1992: n.p.).

Making Winter an object instead of a fellow subject leads to solidarity with the (able-bodied) character of Fabry, who wants to marry Winter's daughter. Winter explains: 'Kein Mensch beruhrt gern einen Kruppel. [...] Die Einzige, die mich gern beruhrt, ist meine Tochter' ('No one likes to touch a cripple. [...] The only one who enjoys touching me is my daughter)'. Talking to Fabry he says: 'Sie mag Ihre Frau werden, aber sie wird Sie nie lieben konnen, weil sie schon einen anderen liebt. [...] Mich liebt sie' ('She may become your wife but she will not be able to love you because she loves someone else. [...] She loves me'). He becomes even more precise later: 'Sie kriegen ihren Korper, ich behalte ihre Liebe. [...] Ohne mich wird sie leblos sein. Ohne mich wird sie ein Nichts sein. [...] Ich werde auch leblos sein. Ich werde auch ein Nichts sein' ('You will get her body, I will keep her love. She will be lifeless [...] without me. Without me she will be nothing. I will [...] be lifeless as well. I will be nothing, too'). In order to suit the action to the word, Winter manipulates the hydraulic lift that should bring him and his daughter up the hills, right into his vineyard, where Carolin's groom and the whole wedding party wait for them. But instead of arriving at the top of the hill, Winter, wearing a white suit, and his daughter, dressed in red instead of a traditional white wedding dress, plunge into the depths below them – thus solidifying the film's links between disability and evil/criminal behaviour.

Institutionalisation and (Self-)Improvement

Til Schweiger's *Barfuss* (*Barefoot*, 2005) portrays a young woman with mental health problems who is supposed to live in a psychiatric ward after her mother has died. The most striking point about this film is neither the extremely stereotypical characterisation of Leila, nor her escape from the ward, but the idea that living in the ward for some time can even be 'healthy' for so-called healthy people. Thus, Nick, the main character of the film, benefits from 'moving in' with Leila – something he is allowed to do despite the fact that Leila's doctor knows that there is no medical reason for him being there. In this case, Leila serves as a saviour of sorts who initiates emotional healing. By spending time with sweet, kind, innocent, childish and anxious Leila, Nick becomes a better person. This is an example of how (psychiatric) disability is exploited as trigger for the improvement of an able-bodied person. Therefore, this film does not imply that 'we are all the same', or that 'we are all more or less disabled (or mentally ill)'. It once again clearly separates 'normal' people from 'the weird' in the ward. This can, for example, be proven by the fact that the film concentrates on Leila's escape from the institution. Once she is officially allowed to leave the clinic she dresses like everyone else. All that is left of the rebellious free thinker are her bare feet.

Vincent will Meer (*Vincent Wants to Sea*, 2010) by Ralf Huettner tells quite a similar story. This time three outsiders – Vincent with Tourette syndrome,

Fig. 2: Extreme close-up on Leila's bare feet in the last scene of *Barfuss*. The film's title means 'barefooted'.

Fig. 3: From the same scene, apart from not wearing shoes Leila now wears 'normal' clothes. The person in front is Nick who is waiting for her.

Alexander with a obsessive-compulsive disorder and Marie with anorexia – escape from a clinic. Just like Leila in *Barfuss*, Vincent is traumatised after his mother's death. But why does this film try to make viewers believe a person with Tourette syndrome needs to be institutionalised at all? It seems as if this clinical picture fulfils the '"quick fix" syndrome' (Klobas 1988: xv). This is also indicated by the fact that institutionalisation does not seem to be an appropriate way to cure a possible agoraphobia. It is mentioned several times that Vincent has had difficulties leaving his mother's house. Nevertheless, he is fine with a little spontaneous 'road trip' to Italy with Alex and Marie. It seems that he simply felt obliged not to leave his alcohol-addicted mother alone until she died. In Vincent's case the disability is needed to tell the narration of two outsiders, Vincent and Marie, who fall in love with each other. This enables at least one of them, Vincent, to develop a more mature and also more normalised self in the end. Meanwhile, Vincent's selfish father slowly but surely becomes a better person, too, while trying to find his son. Both 'improvements' need to be criticised: in the first case because Marie, who cannot simply shake off her anorexia in order to behave more 'normal' or at least more 'healthy', is left behind.

For Barnes the 'normalisation' of disability 'does not really challenge or undermine its meaning to non-disabled people' (1992: n.p.):

> Like all media portrayals of disabled people they do not reflect the racial, gender and cultural divisions within the disabled community as a whole – disabled people do not fit neatly into able-bodied perceptions of normality. Also the emphasis on normality tends to obscure the need for change. Logic dictates that if disabled people are perceived as 'normal' then there is little need for policies to bring about a society free from disablism. (Ibid.)

Vincent's disability is exploited as a trigger not only for the transformation of his able-bodied father but also for the disabled son himself. In the most important dialogue of the film, Vincent's father wants the doctor to call the police because his disabled son has escaped from the clinic, together with two other patients whom he refers to as 'disabled' as well. It is the doctor that reminds him that his son is 27 years old and therefore does not have to ask anyone for permission to leave the clinic.

Although this doctor is strict with Marie and Alex, she differs very much from the intrusive institution's administration in Anno Saul's *Wo ist Fred?* (*Where is Fred?*, 2005). Given that this film is a comedy whose humour arises from able-bodied perspectives on disability, what Barnes says about 'The Disabled Person as an Object of Ridicule' is important to keep in mind:

> While such thoughtless behaviour might be expected in earlier less enlightened times making fun of disabled people is as prevalent now as it was then. It is especially common among professional non-disabled comedians. Several of the comedy 'greats' who influenced today's 'funny' men and women built their careers around disablist humour. [...] Today the mockery of disabled people is a major feature of many comedy films and TV shows. [...] Those who exploit this kind of material are not confined to one specific brand of comedy – they are common to them all. (Ibid.)

In the film, Fred is an able-bodied construction worker who pretends to be a wheelchair user and to be unable to speak so that he can get a signed basketball, which is given only to disabled fans of a certain basketball team. Fred's 'disabled' self, named 'Fred Krüppelmann', which means 'Fred Cripplemann', represents the opposite of the able-bodied, rude, extroverted redneck Fred usually is. All of the sudden, he turns into a modest, empathetic, withdrawn, adorable, shy do-gooder who realises what really counts in life. At the same time, the (allegedly) disabled Fred becomes a stereotypical helpless victim of the nursing staff at the institution that he has been brought to. Whenever he pretends to be a wheelchair user, Fred becomes an object rather than a subject and can be ridiculed (in the film as well as by the audience watching the film). This short description already shows that the rude and blunt humour used here does not aim at bridging the gap between able-bodied and disabled people at all. In each of the cases above, the narrative of (self-)improvement hinges on somewhat superficial and stereotypical representations of disability.

Disability in Everyday Life

In contrast, Andreas Dresen's *Sommer vorm Balkon* (*Summer in Berlin*, 2005) integrates disability into the everyday urban life of its able-bodied protagonists. One of them, Nike, works for a nursing service and competently deals with her disabled clients. Using a Berlin dialect, she interacts with them in a respectful manner, provides assistance in everyday tasks such as getting washed, getting dressed, reading books and eating meals. In contrast to the films mentioned before, *Sommer vorm Balkon* gives a rare example of a character working with and for disabled persons that does without the stereotype of the good carer who benefits from helping by becoming a better person. Instead, Nike wants to make her clients' lives a little easier and more self-determined.

While clients such as Oskar and Mr. Neumann have dementia, Helene has physical disabilities. Significantly, all three of these fully developed characters are portrayed as having various character traits: they can be friendly, well tempered, generous, adorable, humorous or happy but also pessimistic, desperate, fearful or jealous. They are talkative and caring as well as shy, insecure or childish. This proves that filmmakers can tell narrations and create representations that go beyond one-dimensional disabled characters or able-bodied carers. Thus, Dresen's disabled characters make less use of stereotypes, myths and metaphors. In *Sommer vorm Balkon* disability serves at best as a metaphor for dependency or vulnerability, but foremost it is simply a part of Nike's job at the nursing service.

Camera and editing contribute to this impression by making the audience eye-witnesses of disability seen as an everyday reality. This means that the camera precisely observes how Nike changes Mr. Neumann's incontinence pads or feeds him, using close-up or extreme close-up views. Instead of cutting these scenes out, which would be quite common in other films, Dresen makes the decision to use the camera as a way of having viewers co-exist with the characters they see. When the camera gets quite close to the film's characters, the lightning is restrained and contributes to the impression that the camera is actually another human being present at the scene. It is important that Dresen uses this same close but respectful method to observe Nike spending time with her friend Katrin or her boyfriend, who are not disabled. Thus, the camera uses the same representational strategies whether at Nike's work or in her private life.

The emotions evoked by Dresen's disabled characters are much more complex than we have seen in the other films above. His approach induces a cautious empathy in viewers of the film. For example, able-bodied viewers may wonder what it would mean to need help to wash oneself, to be as disoriented as Oskar who sees and talks to his deceased mother although he is alone in the room or puts the coffee in the bathroom instead of the kitchen, or Mr. Neumann, who is convinced that he is a young pupil who needs to go to school. Who would want to rely on help in order to change incontinence pads?

As all of Nike's clients live their own flats and not in a retirement home, *Sommer vorm Balkon* moves away from a culture of caring that relies on the

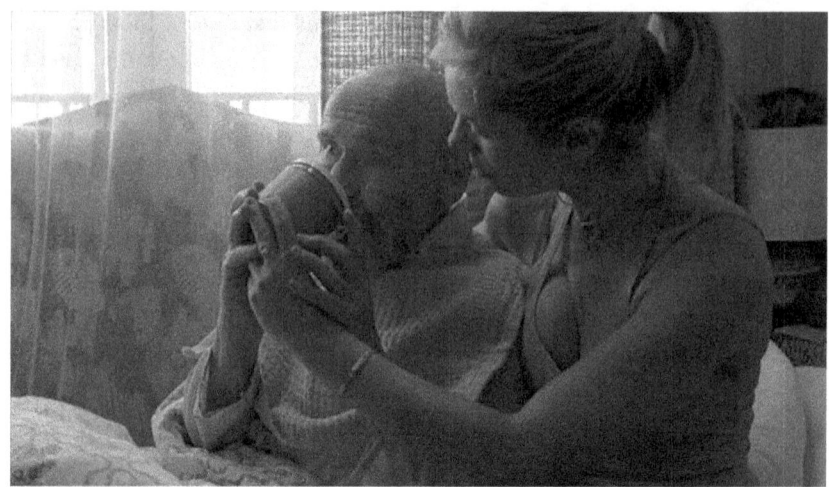

Fig. 4: Nike feeding one her clients is shown in close-up just like...

Fig. 5: ....Nike and her boyfriend

spatial separation of disabled from able-bodied characters, and toward an everyday realism that is significant among other recent German films.

Introducing Sexuality

Noting how disability falls outside of social expectations, attention can be drawn to the way the concept of 'survival of the fittest' lies close at hand, dividing disabled people into ill-fitting 'bad cripple[s]' on the one hand, and 'good cripple[s]' whose bodies can be 'normalised' on the other (Darke n.d.). In this context, the sexuality of disabled characters has often been erased, ignored or even vilified. As Barnes notes, 'The Disabled Person as Sexually Abnormal' is an extremely old stereotype (ibid.). Both *Renn, wenn Du kannst* (*Run if You Can*, 2010) by Dietrich Brüggemann and *Phantomschmerz* (*Phantom Pain*, 2009) by Matthias Emcke deal with disability and matters of physical attraction/sexuality in a way that other German films have avoided.

Importantly, *Renn, wenn Du kannst* quite explicitly deals with the disabled person's sexual appetite and opts not to link disability with either sexual abnormality or asexuality but instead to pursue its resonance with the notion of autonomy. It tells the story of the paraplegic Ben who can live in his own flat thanks to his mother and his helper Christian. Ben and Christian both make advances to Annika, a beautiful young musician, who is attracted to both of them. In the context of the representation of disability in other German films, it is astonishing not only that Ben and Annika want to have sex but also that they talk about Ben's bladder bag, Viagra and the penis pump. This scene shows how uneasy Annika feels about these things, but Ben utters: 'Wir müssen drüber reden. Einfach machen geht nicht' ('We have to talk about it. Simply having sex won't work'). Although they stop having sex at that moment, Annika is still attracted to Ben, who remains the rival to the able-bodied Christian.

This love triangle is unconventional for German film, as yet another dialogue between the characters shows. When Annika wants to know why Ben separated from a young woman he had met after the accident that caused his disability he remarks:

> Ben: 'Sie war behindert. Und zwar von Geburt an. Und mit Behinderten kann ich einfach nichts anfangen. Ich wünschte es wäre anders, aber es ist so' ('She was disabled. Disabled since she was born. And disabled [women] don't mean anything to me. I wish that wasn't the case but it is').
> Annika: 'Heißt das, wenn ich jetzt im Rollstuhl landen würde, würdest du michts mehr wollen?' ('Does that mean that if I would need a wheelchair you would not want to be with me anymore?').
> Ben: 'Ja' ('Yes').
> Annika: 'Weißt du, was du da sagst?' ('Do you know what that means?').
> Ben: 'Weißt du, man muss bei seinem Marktwert bleiben. Schöne Menschen haben die Auswahl. Durchnittsmenschen müssen Kompromisse machen und Behinderte halten miteinander Händchen'

('You know, you need to stick with your market value. Beautiful people can choose. Average people have to make compromises. And disabled [people] hold hands').

Annika: 'Das ist Müll' ('That's rubbish').

Ben: 'Das ist kein Müll' ('No, it's not').

Annika: 'Doch! Wenn man jemanden kennenlernt, der im Rollstuhl sitzt, ja, dann denkt man nicht sofort daran, mit dem was anzufangen, aber wenn derjenige interessant ist, dann... Es gibt doch Partnerschaften zwischen Behinderten und Nichtbehinderten' ('Yes, it is! If you meet someone in a wheelchair, you don't necessarily think: "He means a lot to me". But if he is interesting... There are relationships between disabled and able-bodied people').

Ben: 'Ich will aber keine Partnerschaft...' ('I don't want a relationship...').

Annika: 'Wieso? Was willst du dann?' ('Why? What do you want?').

Ben: 'Liebe' ('Love').

Annika: 'Aber das kann es doch auch geben' ('But that's possible, too').

Ben: 'Soweit ich weiß, nein. Es gibt nur das Modell resolute Pflegefrau bemuttert Invaliden oder zwei Behinderte machen sich gegenseitig ihr Los ein bisschen lustiger. Beide Modelle kotzen mich an' ('As far as I know, no. There's only the model of a resolute female nurse who chaperones an invalid or two disabled persons who try to put up with their fate. Both models are disgusting').

Annika: 'Weißt du, was mich anekelt?' ('You know what sickens me?').

Ben (interrupting her): 'Ach, was soll's. Es laufen eh lauter Kompromisse rum und haben Liebesbeziehungen miteinander' ('Well, who cares, the world is full of walking compromises who are in relationships').

Annika: 'Mich ekelt deine Vorstellung von Liebe an' ('Your idea of love is disgusting').

In the end, Ben's desire for love does not seem to fit the role he is meant to play in society. Social convention would dictate that he should either be happy with a carer who likes him or find someone of his own kind: a disabled person.

Emcke's *Phantomschmerz* is based on a true story. Therefore, it is in some respects more realistic than other dramas or thrillers and crime stories that use disability to separate the 'Other' from the able-bodied majority. Still, the basic plot is that of a disabled man who triumphs over his fate and becomes a better person. In a sense, the film plays on the 'supercrip' dichotomy:

> By emphasising the extra-ordinary achievements of disabled [people] ... the media implies that the experiences of 'ordinary' people – disabled or otherwise – are unimportant and irrelevant. Hence non-disabled people view super cripples as unrepresentative of the disabled community as a whole and the gulf between the two groups remains as wide as ever. (Barnes 1992: n.p.)

In this case, the man who had once been a loving, but not necessarily reliable, father finds out what really counts in life after he loses a leg in an accident. Marc, who used to have a lot of one-night stands, was forced to earn his living with odd jobs, but he soon realises that Nika is his true love and makes peace with his deceased father. This moral improvement is directly linked to the 'new and better' self as disabled person while the character of Vincent has lived with Tourette syndrome for a long time. Marc's 'triumph over his fate' is most observable in that by the end of the film, this man who used to be a passionate hobby athlete prior to his accident now rides his bike as an amputee thanks to a high-tech artificial limb.

Marc's stump is shown in an extreme close-up focusing on the ugly stump's large scar. It is the stigma on the perfect body that I will refer to below. The ugly scar is the symbol for the trauma that the loss of a body part means. At the same time it symbolises the healing and 'normalisation' process. At the beginning of this process, Marc needs a wheelchair; a little later he can already walk on crutches. Once Nika helps him to get rid of them (both figuratively and literally), Marc can walk on his artificial limp. At the end of the film, he can conquer a mountain that had once been part of a Tour de France course. This corresponds with Barnes' observation that, in case of the stereotype of 'The Disabled Person as Super Cripple': 'the disabled person is assigned super human almost magical abilities' (ibid.). The effort required for his recovery is severely downplayed in the film: thus, only a short episode at a doctor's office that depicts someone else doing exercises indicates that training is needed. The regularised physiotherapy required to learn to walk with an artificial limb, not to mention to ride a bike with one, is not shown. Interestingly, the crucial scenes in which Marc is still in intensive care are filmed with a blue-green colour filter, which visually marks the traumatic experience of Otherness.

Marc's sexual appetite despite heavy phantom pain also supports the 'supercrip' image. His body seems to be in perfect shape although the loss of his left leg should have had a negative effect on his body's muscles. Instead, it does not take long until he has sex with several women who pity him.

Shortly thereafter, he and his true love have sex as well and finally decide to begin a serious relationship. The film thus portrays a disabled body that seems to recover from physical trauma all too easily, maintaining the able-bodied standard of 'excellent shape' without much difficulty. Nevertheless, both *Phantomschmerz* and *Renn, wenn Du kannst* go further than many films have gone before in addressing the sexual lives of disabled characters in detail.

Conclusion

This chapter is intended only to give a brief impression of the stereotypes, myths and metaphors surrounding disability in contemporary German film. The selected films that appeared since 2005 show that in addition to narrative structures, camera or editing contribute to the close ties between norm(ality) and disability in films. These ties are interpreted in different ways depending on the individual film, director or character. Although disability is predominantly 'othered' in contemporary German film in various ways, there are cases in which films have attempted to go beyond this notion of 'other' – for example, in *Sommer vorm Balkon* or *Renn, wenn Du kannst*. Nevertheless, it is still more common to portray disabled characters through stereotypes that have been identified in disability studies scholarship in the Anglophone world – as shown, for example, in *Antikörper, Ich bin die Andere* or *Wo ist Fred?* Constructed as the 'Other', disabled characters are used to perpetuate binaries such as bad/good, evil/righteous, weak/strong that obscure the social norming of able-bodiedness.

Thus, it is actually not that surprising that – once again referring to Darke and Dederich – normality is the key to understanding the representation of disability in film. Considering Waldschmidt's idea that normality serves to assure able-bodied people of their reasonability – in this way, legitimising their participation in civil liberties – and Wendell's remarks on 'Othering', it can be noted that the close ties between norm(ality) and disability are not limited to fiction. In conclusion, it is worth remembering Darke's statement:

> Stereotypes are very useful in the identification of relations between social groups (the oppressed and the oppressor) and, as such, are both revealing of a wider social framework within which, in this case, disabled people are seen. Equally, stereotypes can be highly empowering and enjoyable for the oppressed in revealing the true nature and picture of their social relationships: I am right, society does see me in this way; I am not imagining it. Positive imagery, on the other hand

becomes a further threat to disabled people by making clear that to be accepted and valued by society one must be like this or that (i.e. normalised and educated). Thereby an equally false/arbitrary reality is created which many disabled people either cannot or do not want to emulate. (n.d.: n.p.)

This means that stereotypical (filmic) representations of disability need to be analysed and criticised, but also that they should neither be eliminated nor forbidden.

NOTES

1 Translations of quotes from films are mine.
2 Regarding the medical model of disability, see Wasserman et al. (2011) http://plato.stanford.edu/entries/disability, for example, in regard to German legislation see Section 2, Paragraph 1, Sentence 1 of the Social Code IX (§ 2, Abs. 1, Satz 1 des Neunten Buches Sozialgesetzbuch (SGB IX)). It says: 'Menschen sind behindert, wenn ihre körperliche Funktion, geistige Fähigkeit oder seelische Gesundheit mit hoher Wahrscheinlichkeit länger als sechs Monate von dem für das Lebensalter typischen Zustand abweichen und daher ihre Teilhabe am Leben in der Gesellschaft beeinträchtigt ist' ('People are disabled if their physical function, mental ability and psychological health most likely differs from the typical condition for more than six months and thus compromises their participation in society').

FILMOGRAPHY

Alvart, Christian (dir) (2005) *Antikörper* (*Antibodies*). 127 minutes. Kinowelt Filmproduktion/MedienKontor Movie GmbH. Germany.
Brüggemann, Dietrich (dir) (2010) *Renn, wenn Du kannst* (*Run, If You Can*). 112 minutes. Südwestrundfunk/Westdeutscher Rundfunk. Germany.
Dresen, Andreas (dir) (2005) *Sommer vorm Balkon* (*Summer in Berlin*). 107 minutes. Peter Rommel Productions/X-Filme Creative Pool. Germany.
Emcke, Matthias (dir) (2009) *Phantomschmerz* (*Phantom Pain*). 97 minutes. Film1/Neue Bioskop Film. Germany.
Huettner, Ralf (dir) (2010) *Vincent will Meer* (*Vincent wants to Sea*). 96 minutes. Olga Film GmbH. Germany.
Saul, Anno (dir) (2006) *Wo ist Fred?* (*Where is Fred?*). 107 minutes. Bioskop Film/H&V Entertainment. Germany.
Schweiger, Til (dir) (2005) *Barfuss* (*Barefoot*). 118 minutes. Buena Vista International Film Production/Filmstiftung Nordrhein-Westfalen. Germany.
Trotta, Margarethe von (dir) (2006) *Ich bin die Andere* (*I am the Other Woman*). 104 minutes. Clasart Film + TV Produktions GmbH. Germany.

BIBLIOGRAPHY

Anders, Petra-A. (2014) Behinderung und psychische Krankheit im zeigenössischen deutschen Spielfilm: Eine vergleichende Filmanalyse. Würzburg: Königshausen & Neumann.

Barnes, Colin (1992) 'Disabling Imagery and the Media: An Exploration of the Principles for Media Representations of Disabled People'. Krumlin, Halifax: The British Council of Organisations of Disabled People/Ryburn Publishing. Available at http://www.leeds.ac.uk/disability-studies/archiveuk/Barnes/disabling%20 imagery.pdf (accessed 24 November 2004).

Darke, Paul (1997) 'Everywhere: Disability on Film', in Ann Pointon and Chris Davies (eds) *Framed: Interrogating Disability in the Media*. London: British Film Institute, 10–14.

───── (n.d.) Introductory Essay on Normality Theory. Available at http://www.outside-centre.com/drake/mycv/writings/normtheo/normtheo.html (accessed 13 November 2004).

Dederich, Markus (2007) *Körper, Kultur und Behinderung: Eine Einführung in die Disability Studies*. Bielefeld: transcript.

Klobas, Lauri E. (1988) *Disability Drama in Television and Film*. Jefferson, NC: McFarland.

Lopez Levers, Lisa (2001) 'Representations of Psychiatric Disability in Fifty Years of Hollywood Film: An Ethnographic Content Analysis', *Theory & Science*. Available at http://theoryandscience.icaap.org/content/vol02.002/lopezlevers.html (accessed 25 June 2004).

Norden, Martin F. (2002) 'Disability', *St. James Encyclopedia of Pop Culture*. Available at http://www.findarticles.com/p/articles/mi_g1epc/is_tov/ai_2419100345 (accessed 1 December 2004).

Waldschmidt, Anne (2003) 'Selbstbestimmung als behindertenpolitisches Paradigma - Perspektiven der Disability Studies'. Aus Politik und Zeitgeschichte: Beilage zur Wochenzeitung Das Parlament, 13–20.

Wasserman, David, Asch, Adrienne, Blustein, Jeffrey & Putnam, Daniel (2011) 'Disability: Definitions, Models, Experience'. Available at http://plato.stanford.edu/entries/disability/ (accessed 8 April 2015)

Wendell, Susan (2006) 'Toward a Feminist Theory of Disability', in Lennard J. Davis (ed.) *The Disability Studies Reader*, 2nd ed. New York, NY: Routledge, 243–56.

The Other Body

Psychiatric Disability and Pedro Almodóvar (1988–2011)

Candace Skibba

In May 2015, the Prado Museum in Madrid opened an exhibit aimed at giving the visually impaired an opportunity to 'view' the collection. In the same month, the cultural organisation *La Casa Encendida*, also located in Madrid, inaugurated the second annual artistic project titled '¿Qué puede un cuerpo?' ('What Can a Body Do?'), which explored the possibility of the body in choreography and visual culture among many other activities.[1] These social and artistic efforts work toward increasing accessibility as well as normalising physical difference. And although these are definitely advances in social recognition and acceptance of difference, they do not take into consideration stigmas regarding mental illness.

As this chapter outlines, there are rapidly evolving analyses of physical disability within art history, and film and literary studies. More recently critics have also taken on the task of evaluating intellectual disability and its portrayal in film. What is lacking is a look at mental illness in an attempt to continue the effort at destigmatisation. This chapter enters into dialogue with established disability theories while adding to the discourse by including mental illness. First, it will be necessary to situate this chapter within disability studies. It will then be important to undertake a brief historical analysis of disability in Spain, focusing on mental illness while also introducing cultural studies critics whose works have informed this analysis. The study of three films by the acclaimed Spanish filmmaker Pedro Almodóvar – *Mujeres al borde de un ataque de nervios* (*Women on the Verge of a Nervous Breakdown*, 1988), *Átame!* (*Tie Me Up! Tie Me Down!*, 1990), and *La piel que habito* (*The Skin I Live In*, 2011) – sheds light on this area of disability studies that is just starting to emerge. Through this analysis I will show that including mental illness in an aesthetic that embraces difference reflects the actuality of human existence. According to the World Health Organization, 'One in four people in the world will be affected by mental or neurological disorders at some point in their lives' (Anon. 2001). Yet, the stigma remains. By creating an aesthetic of anti-normalisation, these three films by Pedro Almodóvar continue the trend he has set for exposing the abnormal and making it visible and normal.

In part, the brilliance in Almodóvar's work is his ability to bring to life the otherwise marginalised and dissident bodies under the decades-spanning dictatorship of Francisco Franco – women's bodies, homosexual bodies, transsexual bodies, etc. He came of age during a particularly transformative time in Spanish history following the death of the Franco in 1975. The director was part of the famed *movida* movement in Madrid in the early 1980s in which artists, musicians and designers took on the job of redefining Spanish identity following years of oppression. This was a time of growing pains in which the norms established in the post-war Western hemisphere – the binaries of man/woman, body/mind, socialism/capitalism, able-bodied/disabled, dictatorship/democracy – were being challenged and arguably surpassed in certain cultural and political circles within Spain. Almodóvar's first feature film, *Pepi, Luci, Bom y otras chicas del montón* (*Pepi, Luci, Bom and Other Average Girls*) was released in 1980 to mixed reviews. Since then, his work has grown to amass a total of nineteen films to date, two Academy Awards, six Goya Awards (the Spanish equivalent of the Academy Awards) and scores of other honours. The thematic nature of his films generally concentrates on interpersonal relationships, yet the nuanced character development, vibrant cinematography and references to Spanish political climate and history make his films unique, irreverent, emotional, compelling and, at times, polarising.

In the films of Almodóvar we are able to see a rhythmic portrayal of the human form and figure – the body in all of its various manifestations and versions. These are gender-bending bodies, stereotypical bodies, over-the-top bodies, violent bodies, etc – from the abused, fragmented, ill, dead, scarred and disfigured to the powerful, disguised and expressive. The bodies created through these works represent iconic cultural portrayals (such as nun, priest and bullfighter, to name just a few) and separation from societal expectations (transvestites, transsexuals, addicted, obsessed or inanimate). Throughout his oeuvre, Almodóvar has encouraged audiences to reconsider the body – perfection, classical beauty and heterosexual attraction (elements prevalent in mainstream Hollywood cinema, for example) do not constitute the norm in this cinematic world. Rather, imperfection, abnormality and strangeness remain constant.

Analysis of the socially marginal and abnormal in Almodóvar is extensive. Studies by Mark Allinson, Paul Julian Smith and Marsha Kinder, to name just a few, aptly outline the thematic framework that delineates the Almodóvar body as it relates to gender and sexuality. In *A Spanish Labyrinth: The Films of Pedro Almodóvar* (2008), Allinson determines that Almodóvar veers from the traditional cinematic tendencies that showcase and objectify women while privileging men's bodies and power through those bodies. Allinson's critical eye is also found in the anthology *All About Almodóvar: A Passion for Cinema* (2009), which provides a more in-depth analysis. An earlier article by one of the co-editors of that volume, Brad Epps (1995), further investigates endemic otherness such as queer identities, and overt and symbolic violence in three of the director's films. In *Blood Cinema* (1993) Marsha Kinder focuses on how violence, gore, the grotesque, fetish and patriarchal control serve as themes through which to explore Spanish identity. Although the body is not the main topic of discussion in Kinder's work, it is an implied component of her analysis. Paul Julian Smith also discusses the representation of the Spanish body within the context of fetish in *Desire Unlimited* (1994).

Part of the intent of disability studies is to shed light upon contemporary culture's penchant for giving precedence to normalcy. In so doing, it implores that society consider that 'normal' is simply constructed through media. Media images and advertisements perpetuate social norms and admonish those that are considered different due to physical embellishments (such as tattoos, piercings, hair dye), illness, disability and lifestyle choices. As illustrated by Sharon Snyder, Rosemarie Garland-Thomson and Brenda Jo Brueggemann in their introduction to the anthology *Disability Studies: Enabling the Humanities*, 'In stigmatizing and distancing ourselves from disability, we participate in late-capitalist culture's relentless attempt to standardize and stabilize the body. Such an effort effectively attempts to reduce both our individual particularities and our experience of bodily vulnerability' (2002: 2). Media saturated by such image standardisation facilitate consumption; and as current-day capitalism is based upon a consumer-structured economy, in exercising their purchasing power consumers are participating in stabilising such norms. In *Extraordinary Bodies* (1997), Garland-Thomson challenges not only the economic implications of prioritising the normal, but also political, medical and cultural. The body that is uncontrollable, abnormal and deviant is a threat to the organisation of society; however, it is attractive to characterisation within narrative. This social model established by Snyder, Garland-Thomson and Brueggemann serves as the point of departure for this analysis.

Disability studies is a compelling interdisciplinary field with various implications and applications. And although it has picked up quite a bit of momentum in the past twenty years, there are still some matters that require further analysis and discussion. As the field is continuing to grapple with types and categories of disabilities, their social definition, political resonance and intersection with a range of critical discourses, what is missing is the conversation regarding disability and mental illness. These conditions are difficult to diagnose and their categorisation can be challenging. This may be because the origination of the condition (i.e. genetic disposition, environment, physiological injury or malfunction, etc) can be difficult to pinpoint. Physical disability tends to be more visible than psychiatric disability – both in everyday life and as a subject within current work on disability studies. However, the possible psychological (mental health) issues that might accompany physical disabilities are less socially visible. By seeking to explore the ground common to mental health, psychiatric illness and social stigma/normalisation we can meaningfully expand the disability studies paradigm.

As the criteria presented in the *Diagnostic and Statistical Manual of Mental Disorders* (2013) (known as the *DSM V*) is widely used and accepted – although not without controversy – it will serve as our point of departure here. Mental illness is described there as 'a syndrome characterized by clinically significant disturbance in an individual's cognition, emotion regulation, or behavior that reflects a dysfunction in the psychological, biological, or developmental processes underlying mental functioning' (2013: 20). This is, in fact, an extremely wide diagnosis and includes a number of differential diagnoses. A model for the analysis of mental illness within cultural studies is provided by Elizabeth Donaldson, who has developed the discourse on mental illness, disability studies and the humanities. In 'The Corpus of the Madwoman', she astutely observes that while the medical model eschews social implications and the social/disability studies model often leaves out the body, 'feminist science studies and feminist examinations of the body can offer us the conceptual modes and the critical language to begin a rigorous denaturalization of impairment within disability studies' (2013: 29). She goes on to encourage a change in thought: 'It is possible, in other words, to begin with the premise that mental illness is a neurobiological disorder and still remain committed to a feminist and a disability studies agenda, and it is important that feminists and disability theorists begin to think about mental illness in these terms' (2013: 30). It is this perspective that I draw upon in order to situate representation of mental illness in these three films by Pedro Almodóvar.

It is necessary to briefly point out that scholars of disability in Spanish Peninsular studies have tended to emphasise cognitive disability along with physical disability and political concerns. Benjamin Fraser has looked at deaf cultural production, the politics of intellectual disability and its representation in film, and the social model of disability in Spain all culminating in his monograph *Disability Studies and Spanish Culture: Films, Novels, the Comic and Public Exhibition* (2013). Fraser's work not only discusses the content of the primary texts in which he engages, but it also highlights their formal elements adding yet another critical layer to his analysis. Another scholar, Julie Minich, looks at disability through the lens of identity politics in heteronormative social contexts. Matthew Marr tackles the topic of disability in *The Politics of Age and Disability in Contemporary Spanish Film: Plus Ultra Pluralism* (2013), highlighting various stages of human existence often left out of critical analysis of identity and subjectivity – adolescence, senescence and disability – themes used to organise the three sections of his book.[2] The chapters most relevant to my analysis are those regarding disability in Alejandro Amenábar's *Mar adentro* (*The Sea Inside*, 2004) and Pedro Almodóvar's *Los abrazos rotos* (*Broken Embraces*, 2009). In his analysis of *Mar adentro*, Marr points to a social disparity between physical and mental disability (2013: 100) and suggests that while some mental illnesses are frequently the topic of films due to their dramatic portrayal, depression and anxiety tend to be ignored (2013: 97, 117). *Mar adentro*, while focusing primarily on the main character's paralysis, also creatively contemplates the suggested bipolar disorder that either preempted or accompanies his current physical state. It is interesting to note that while mental illness is not referenced directly in this film, it is artistically displayed in the way the work is filmed.[3]

Yet another source bringing to the fore disability studies in the Spanish-speaking world is the special section of the *Arizona Journal of Hispanic Cultural Studies* edited by Encarnación Juárez Almendros (2013). In the introductory commentary, Juárez Almendros suggests that for many years, disability studies, 'seem to have been mostly associated with studies of culture and literature within the discipline of English' (2013: 153). However, the sheer existence of this section indicates that this is no longer the case. In fact, the article by Victoria Rivera-Cordero, 'Rebuilding the Wounded Self: Impairment and Trauma in Isabel Coixet's *The Secret Life of Words* and Pedro Almodóvar's *Los abrazos rotos*', is a telling example. In this article, the author references these two films for their portrayal of disabilities and their relationships to the trauma that led to the impairment. This novel connection between trauma studies and disability studies both sets her exploration apart and also connects with a broader tradition linking physical and psychological concerns in Spanish studies of disability.

Moreover, contemporary understandings of mental health in Spain must acknowledge the existence of mental hospitals in early Iberian history. Medical writings of that time acknowledged the existence of 'mania' and treated the illness in what has been documented as beautiful and centrally located environments. It is worth noting that this type of institution predates the onset of the European asylum. Jesús Pérez, Juan Undurraga, Ross J. Baldessarini and José Sánchez-Moreno further discuss the topic in their article 'Origins of Psychiatric Hospitalization in Medieval Spain' (2012), in which they distinguish the Islamic versus Christian traditions and how the medicalisation of mental illness came to be. According to them, 'Madness was widely conceived by the Islamic general public as being possessed by a spirit, elf, satyr, or genie (djinn or jinn). [...] The tradition of possession by a djinn continues to the present time in some Islamic cultures as a popular belief, and sometimes involves states resembling conversion reactions' (2012: 422). They acknowledge Greek traditions as contributing to increased medicalisation and objectification, and go on to state: 'However, this trend toward a medicalized view of mental illness struggled against social, legal, and religious interpretations and implications of such conditions, and continues to do so' (2012: 423). A study dealing with the development of psychoanalysis in Spain in the early twentieth century further assists an historical/cultural perspective. The author, Thomas Glick (1982), discusses the debate regarding Spanish reception of Freud. It is important to acknowledge this history as simply one piece of evidence to demonstrate the necessity to culturally contextualise studies of mental illness.

A turn to contemporary statistics will situate us in the current climate. FEAFES or the Confederación española de agrupaciones de familiares y enfermos mentales (Spanish Confederation of Groups of Families of Those with Mental Illness) defines mental illness thus: 'un trastorno o enfermedad mental como una alteración de tipo emocional, cognitivo y/o del comportamiento, en que quedan afectados procesos psicológicos básicos como son la emoción, la motivación, la cognición, la conciencia, la conducta, la percepción, la sensación, el aprendizaje, el lenguaje, etc. lo que dificulta a la persona su adaptación al entorno cultural y social en que vive y crea alguna forma de malestar subjetivo' ('an emotional, cognitive and/or behavior in which people whose basic psychological processes such as emotion, motivation, cognition, conscience, conduct, perception, sensation, learning styles, and language, etc suffer such that it is difficult to adapt to the social and cultural norms in which they live and this creates a poor way of living') (Anon. 2015b: 22).[4] An estimated 250,000 people suffer from some sort of mental illness in Spain and yet the types and significance (spiritual, personal, corporeal, medical and social) of the illnesses remains largely unknown (see Anon. 2015c). Among the most common illnesses, depression affects close to ten percent of the population and is projected to rise.[5] This analysis focuses on what is referred to in Spanish as 'trastorno de personalidad' ('personality disorders') and 'trastorno obsesivo compulsivo' ('obsessive compulsive disorder') – which is cited as affecting close to 2.5 per cent of the population.[6]

Before moving on to Almodóvar's films, it is useful to turn briefly to the argument laid out in Donaldson's article 'The Psychiatric Gaze: Deviance and Disability in Film' (2005). Even though she does not situate herself within scholarship on Spanish film, her comments on *Fight Club* (1999) as a film that represents psychiatric disability are relevant. In her estimation, this film does a good job of breaking stereotypes of mental illness and thus reducing stigma by: i) making the illness central to the narrative – rather than peripheral; and ii) by allowing the spectators a window into the world of mental illness: 'In addition to healing the wounds of spectators who witness severe mental illness, the psychiatric gaze is also marketed as a technology of normalcy' (2005: 43). Which then begs the questions: Are films that peripherally include mental illness able to reduce stigma? My analysis suggests that in many ways the films that include mental illness as simply a way of living and a 'normal' part of human existence are able to break down stereotypes and create a new normal.

Mujeres al borde de un ataque de nervios

This Academy Award-nominated film comes at an important time in Almodóvar's career in which he is thrust on the international scene. As per the loaded title, it is difficult to avoid the topic of mental illness in an analysis of this film. There is no 'normal' established in the film: or rather, almost all of the kitschy characters are eccentric in their own ways. This is a film about a break-up, family dynamics, misogyny, lust – all within a comical tone with a political backdrop. Shot in beautiful, bright colors that counteract the supposed sadness of heartbreak, the film presents the relatively simple story of a woman who is left abandoned by her lover. Pepa is portrayed as hysterical as she tries to recover after being left by Iván, the consummate Don Juan. And yet her connection to reality is much stronger than that of Iván's wife, Lucía, who has recently been released from a mental hospital.

The scene that captures Pepa's supposed hysteria begins with her ransacking the closet in which Iván's clothes are hanging. She is packing up a suitcase with his belongings as well as all of the items, gifts and knicknacks that remind her of him. As the scene begins, so too does the beautiful overture 'Capricho Español' by Nikolai Rimsky-Korsakov. As the harp gently plays, Pepa lights a cigarette and throws the matches on the bed, setting it alight. What follows is a 15-second shot of the fire burning. As the stringed instruments pick up tempo, so too does the rapidity of the transitions between shots: these visual and auditory cues intensify with the growing fire. And yet, Pepa's actions are still quite comical. Realising that the bed is on fire, she returns to her bedroom with a plastic flower, ostinsibly given to her by Iván. She stands staring at the fire as the phallic flower melts and wilts. It is unclear from Pepa's demeanour whether the fire initially proves gratifying, insprires fear, or simply provides entertainment.

There is no dramatic follow-up to the fire incident. Rather, the scene ends with Pepa sitting atop the suitcase containing Iván's belongings, her hysteria turned to sadness. This is normalisation of mental distress in that the camera does not inscribe judgement. In the crazy world that Almodóvar creates for his characters, lighting a match and setting fire to a mattress simply do not constitute cause for alarm.

In her aforementioned article, Donaldson references madness in the context of discussing *Jane Eyre*. She suggests that madness has been overly interpreted as rebellion – and that this metaphor has overshadowed the possible

Fig. 1: Pepa lights the bed on fire.

study of mental illness.[7] In particular, women, she says, have been affected by this oversight.

> I believe that the madness/rebellion configuration subtly reinforces what has become an almost monolithic way of reading mental illness within feminist literary criticism and perhaps in the larger culture of women's studies scholarship. This is undesirable … because this configuration of madness, if it remains widely accepted and uncontested, may limit our inquiry into madness/mental illness. (2005: 15)

In a similar way, hysteria is an affliction that has 'plagued' women, serving as a metaphor for all things out of the ordinary as expressed by a woman. Epps, who has written extensively about Almodóvar, connects the concept of hysteria and the genre melodrama saying, 'in Almodóvar's production of nervous, rattled women; in his depiction of passion, obsession, and repression; and in his self-reflexive play with voice, body, image, and movement there lies … the historical residue of hysteria, its discourses, and its spectacles' (1995: 101). We are left to question the representation of hysteria, madness and mental illness in this film. Does it perpetuate negative metaphors of women and mental illness? After all, the women in the film who drive the plot are also out of the ordinary. My suggestion is that, as in most things Almodóvar, the emphasis on madness in these women does not victimise or criticise them, but rather, by highlighting their abnormality, makes them real, accessible, pleasantly imperfect. In the end, the women overcome, and (at the risk of spoiling the plot), they survive.

Átame!

While in *Mujeres al borde de un ataque de nervios* Antonio Banderas plays a secondary role as Iván's prudish and nerdy son, in *Átame!*, he is the protagonist. This film follows the acclaim of *Mujeres al borde de un ataque de nervios* with controversy of a different type than the prestige of an Academy Award nomination. It caused so much polemic in the Hollywood rating system that it was involved in the initiation of the NC-17 rating. It is indeed a love story told unconventionally. The 'hero' is a formal patient at a mental institution. The 'heroine' is a former porn star and drug addict. Rather than the typical courtship, he kidnaps her and literally makes her fall in love with him.

The film opens with the image of an asylum. We are unfamiliar with the aesthetic. The lighting is subtle, not bright. There are organic elements – such as an indoor plant in the director's office – that portray the opposite of what is normally found in an asylum (white walls, sterility, inorganic). It is beautiful, yet sparce – hence destigmatised. It isn't clear that Banderas's character belongs to this community until it is understood that at this moment, he is to be released. The conversation that transpires between him and the woman who appears to be the director of the facility (and the first love interest we see) upon his release is as follows:

> Directora: 'Puedes incorporarte a la sociedad, Ricky' ('You can go reinsert yourself into society, Ricky').
> Ricky: '¿Cómo una persona normal?' ('Like a normal person?').
> Directora: 'Tú no eres una persona normal' ('You are not a normal person').

Through this interaction, we are told that Ricky is not normal. However, as the remaining cast members are introduced, it becomes apparent that Ricky is, in fact, one of the few normal people. In his search for love, he ends up in the world of film – porn stars, drug addicts, eccentric and egomaniacal characters. His insertion into the narrative thread – as a regular guy who might have been a bit of a pickpocket – serves as a clear juxtaposition to this eccentricity. The only element that leads the audience to suspect possible foul play is the extra-diegetic film score, which insinuates wrong-doing through discordance and rhythm.

Although mental illness forms the framework for the film, it is not a medical narrative. Through the development of the plot, Ricky is not meant

Fig. 2: Ricky meets with the director of the mental hospital.

to improve in his condition. His actions do not lead to a catharsis of character. In fact, his 'condition' of obsession and loss of clear footing in reality assists him in wooing his beloved Marina. At the end of the film, when the two lovers head off into the distance to begin their 'normal' lives together in the country, getting married and starting a family, the audience is left to contemplate their own sanity as they are impicated in the union of this strange couple.

La piel que habito

This third film is one of Almodóvar's most recent, in which the director reunites with Banderas to present a piece of filmmaking that questions the boundaries of science, gender and ethics. Banderas' character (Robert Ledgard) is a 'mad scientist' – driven mad by having withstood the tragic loss of his beloved wife. In the hope of refashioning a being in the likeliness of his spouse, his goal is the biological reproduction of skin. To carry out his experiment, he takes a 'subject' under his control – both literally and figuratively. This character (Vicente-Vera Cruz) is held in captivity for the duration of the experiment and frequently observed by her captor through the cameras he has installed. She is experimented upon not only through replacing her skin – proving the efficacy of Robert's work – but also in the scientist's sex reassignment surgery.

Dr. Ledgard's character is explored in detail through the opening scenes in which we find him: i) giving a lecture to a group of medical professionals; ii) working in the lab he has created in his estate in the country; and iii) carrying out everyday tasks, such as eating. The audience is made aware of his brilliance and precision but not yet introduced to his abnormality until thirteen minutes in to the film when it is understood that the work he has been conducting has led to the creation of artificial skin. The first introduction to the lab is a medium close-up in which we see Dr. Ledgard enter. The closeness of the camera shows the small size of the lab. The combination of glass/transparency with the natural sandstone arches communicates precision and softness, much like the scalpel that works with skin. Neutral colors of the doctor's suit, the walls and ceilings serve as background for the deep, saturated red of the blood sample that Ledgard removes from the receptacle. The lab setting is dark, extremely aseptic, unemotional and yet beautiful as the technical and technological elements are juxtaposed to the organic materials used to build the original structure which appears to be quite old. The combination of new and old, organic and inorganic, all lead to a feeling of sublime interest

Fig. 3: Dr. Ledgard enters the lab.

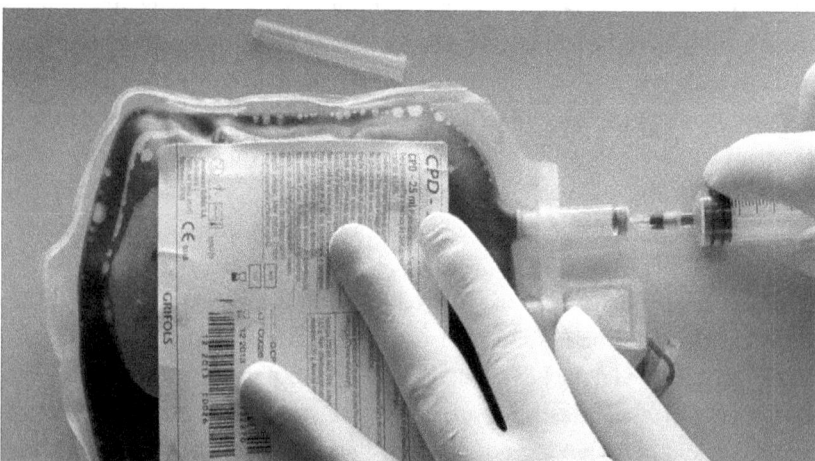

Fig. 4: A close-up of a blood sample.

for while it is obvious in a short amount of time that Dr. Ledgard is not 'normal', the audience is not yet led to feel disgust or abhorrence.

Evidence of the film's interest to mental illness scholars (in addition to film studies critics) is the fact that there is an entire section of the periodical *International Journal of Psychoanalysis* (2012) dedicated to this film. And, while it is not the purpose of my analysis to categorise nor medicalise the illnesses and characters presented in these films, it is nonetheless compelling to see how practicioners view mental illness in Almodóvar's artistic creation. Caron Harrang's diagnosis of rage focuses on how Dr. Ledgard's grief has affected his mental health: 'The result, as shown in the film when rage cannot be contained, is often disastrous' (2012: 1301). Domenico Di Ceglie suggests Dr. Ledgard has Asperger syndrome.

> Dr. Ledgard, as portrayed in the film, would appear to be an excellent systemizer but he has little empathy. [...] This style of thinking, characterized by average or above-average level of systemizing with a low level of empathy, is typical of people who present with autistic spectrum conditions and Asperger Syndrome. [...] These psychological aspects can offer an insight into some of the complex dynamics of the film. (2012: 1310)

The final diagnosis by Alessandra Lemma provides less of a diagnosis than a review of the possible implications or injuries leading to mental illness when one sustains trauma as did Dr. Ledgard: '*The Skin I Live In* is a rich exploration of central psychoanalytic themes: the psychic impact of trauma and the consequent perversion of loss when trauma and its associated losses cannot be faced, the survival of the good internal object as a mitigating factor in trauma and, finally, the relationship between the body and identity' (2012: 1293).

It is quite possible that three different practitioners would have yet another three different diagnoses to this particular character's affliction(s), which is to say that this type of examination is quite subjective, at best. At worst, it is simply a suggestion of abnormality. However, as opposed to the other characters mentioned in this chapter, the Ledgard character is not presented with the same amount of ambivalence as are the hysterical women of *Mujeres al borde de un ataque de nervios* and the love-sick, obsessed lover Ricky. The audience is led to be critical while inquisitive regarding his scientific talent, his objectification of his patients, and the detachment and sterility he experiences. Like most of Almodóvar's characters, he is a freak, existing outside of the norm. However, by skewing the norm, Almodóvar removes judgement.

In one of Pedro Almodóvar's most critically acclaimed films, *Hable con ella* (*Talk to Her*, 2002), the audience is led to both admire and admonish the protagonist Benigno. His apparent mental illness – that leads to the rape of one of his comatose patients, his subsequent incarceration and ultimately his suicide – is neither discussed in any depth nor clearly pathologised. What is strongly emphasised is the importance of communication, hence the title of the film. By communicating and portraying variations on normalcy and therefore breaking barriers of silence and stereotype, Almodóvar's films have encouraged audiences to consider alternative forms of existence, health and reality. In looking at these films, this analysis opens the discourse for further exploration of mental illness in Spanish film and literature. By seeing Almodóvar's films through a disability lens it is possible to dialogue with existing discourses of gender/sexuality and social marginalisation in his work from Spanish Peninsular studies while also working to correct the insufficient work on psychiatric disability in the wide interdisciplinary field of disabilty studies.

NOTES

1. '¿Qué puede un cuerpo? es un proyecto artístico vinculado a la escena en el que participan coreógrafos, teóricos, investigadores culturales y artistas locales e internacionales. El programa tiene una duración de dos semanas (del 9 al 22 de junio) e incluye laboratorios, encuentros y propuestas artísticas, que desde la coreografía, el movimiento, la cultura visual, la filosofía contemporánea y la teoría crítica desea reflexionar y experimentar en torno a la pregunta ¿qué puede un cuerpo?' ('What can a body do? Is an artistic project connected to the cultural scene including choreographers, critics, and researchers, as well as local and international artists. The program lasts for two weeks (from the 9th to the 22nd of June), and includes labs, meetings, and artistic projects through which choreography, movement, visual culture, contemporary philosophy and critical theory hope to reflect upon and create an experience that relates to the question: What can a body do?)' (Anon. 2015a: n.p.).
2. 'Therefore conceptualized as a response to, but also as a developmental amplification of, the aforesaid critical inclinations, the present study at the same time seeks to break genuinely new ground for Spanish cinema scholarship by fusing sustained close readings with analytical methodologies brought together from the allied fields of youth, aging, and disability studies. Moreover, this monograph consciously aspires to complement existing lines of inquiry in academic criticism's ongoing conversation regarding Spanish filmmakers' screening of marginalized forms of subjectivity' (Marr 2013: 5).
3. 'By this I mean to say that bipolar disorder is neither broached diegetically in dialogue, nor explicitly invoked as part and parcel of the movie's surface narrative. Rather, what I hope to show in this chapter is that it is inscribed onto the film through key aspects of performance, *mise-en-scène*, and the symbolic' (Marr 2013: 97).
4. My translation.
5. Statistics from a report presented during the XIV National Congress of Psychiatry in Barcelona, 2010.
6. See Knickerbocker (2003), who analyses obsessive-compulsive disorder in the works of Juan José Millás. His exploration, however, focuses on the mental illness aesthetic created by the formal elements of the texts and does not engage with the disability studies discipline. It is my hope that by embarking on this journey of analysis of mental illness, there will be a continuation of the discourse such that the field gains momentum.
7. Susan Sontag (1978) is often cited when discussing metaphors of illness. She illustrates her frustrations with metaphors of illness due to the multitude of negative associations employed in discussing the subject such as the word 'cancer' used within the framework of plague as well as the words used within the context of medical terminology

itself – 'fight cancer', 'the battle against cancer'. And although the examples she describes aptly defend her point of view, not all illness metaphors are deconstructive. David Mitchell and Sharon Snyder view this dependency on disability as narrative prosthesis or 'a stock feature of characterization and ... an opportunistic metaphor device' (2002: 15–16). In the chapter 'Narrative Prosthesis and the Materiality of Metaphor', they go on to explain the abuse of the abnormal characters as metaphor. 'The coinage of the phrase "narrative prosthesis" argues that disability has been used throughout history as a crutch on which literary narratives lean for their representational power, disruptive potentiality, and social critique. Yet, at the same time, literature avoids designating disability itself as a source for derisive social myths that need to be interrogated. Instead, disability plays host to a panoply of other social maladies that writers seek to address. Disabled bodies show up in literary narratives as dynamic entities that resist or refuse the cultural scripts assigned to them. The out-of-control body of literature has been historically used to identify the workings of dominant ideology in regard to nearly everything but the social construction of disability itself' (2002: 17).

FILMOGRAPHY

Almodóvar, Pedro (dir) (2011) *La piel que habito* (*The Skin I Live In*). 120 minutes. El Deseo/ Canal+ España. Spain.
____ (1990) *Átame!* (*Tie Me Up! Tie Me Down!*). 101 minutes. El Deseo. Spain.
____ (1988) *Mujeres al borde de un ataque de nervios* (*Women on the Verge of a Nervous Breakdown*). 90 minutes. El Deseo/Laurenfilm. Spain.

BIBLIOGRAPHY

Allinson, Mark (2008) *A Spanish Labyrinth: The Films of Pedro Almodóvar*. London: I.B. Tauris.
Anon. (2013) *Diagnostic and Statistical Manual of Mental Disorders*, 5th ed. Washington, DC: APA.
____ (2015a) ¿Qué puede un cuerpo? Available at http://www.lacasaencendida.es/es/grupo-eventos/%C2%BFque-puede-un-cuerpo-2015-sosteniendo-la-pregunta-4550 (accessed 7 September 2015).
____ (2015b) FEAFES - Confederación española de agrupaciones de familiares y enfermos mentales *Salud Mental y Medios de Comunicacion: Guía de estilo*. Available at https://consaludmental.org/publicaciones/GUIADEESTILOSEGUNDAEDICION.pdf (accessed 7 September 2015).
____ (2015c) *World Health Organization*. Available at http://www.who.int/whr/2001/media_centre/press_release/en/ (accessed 7 September 2015).
Di Ceglie, Domenico (2012) 'Identity and Inability to Mourn in *The Skin I Live In*', *International Journal of Psychoanalysis*, 93, 1308–12.
Donaldson, Elizabeth (2005) 'The Psychiatric Gaze: Deviance and Disability in Film', *Atenea*, 25, 1, 31-48.

_____ (2012) 'The Corpus of The Madwoman: Toward a Feminist Disability Studies Theory of Embodiment and Mental Illness', in David Bolt, Julia Miele Rodas and Elizabeth Donaldson (eds) *The Madwoman and the Blindman: Jayne Eyre, Discourse, Disability*. Columbus, OH: Ohio State University Press, 11–31.

Epps, Brad (1995) 'Figuring Hysteria: Disorder and Desire in Three Films of Pedro Almodóvar', in Kathleen M. Vernon and Barbara Morris (eds) *Post-Franco, Postmodern: The Films of Pedro Almodóvar*. London: Greenwood Press, 99–124.

Epps, Brad and Despina Kakoudaki (eds) (2009) *All About Almodóvar: A Passion for Cinema*. Minneapolis, MN: University of Minnesota Press.

Fraser, Benjamin (2013) *Disability Studies and Spanish Culture: Films, Novels, the Comic and Public Exhibition*. Liverpool: Liverpool University Press.

Garland-Thomson, Rosemarie (1997) *Extraordinary Bodies: Figuring Physical Disability in American Culture and Literature*. New York, NY: Columbia University Press.

Harrang, Caron (2012) 'Psychic Skin and Narcissistic Rage: Reflections on Almodóvar's *The Skin I Live In*', *International Journal of Psychoanalysis*, 93, 1301–8.

Glick, Thomas (1982) 'The Naked Science: Psychoanalysis in Spain, 1914–1948', *Comparative Studies in Society and History*, 24, 4, 533–71.

Juárez Almendros, Encarnación (2013) 'Disability Studies in the Hispanic World: Proposals and Methodologies', *Arizona Journal of Hispanic Cultural Studies*, 17, 153–60.

Kinder, Marsha (1993) *Blood Cinema: The Reconstruction of National Identity in Spain*, Berkeley, CA: University of California Press.

Knickerbocker, Dale (2003) *Juan José Millás: The Obsessive-Compulsive Aesthetic*. New York: Peter Lang.

Lemma, Alessandra (2012) 'A Perfectly Modern Frankenstein: Almodóvar's *The Skin I Live In* (2011, Sony Pictures Classics)', *International Journal of Psychoanalysis*, 93, 1291–1300.

Marr, Mathew (2012) *The Politics of Age and Disability in Contemporary Spanish Film: Plus Ultra Pluralism*. New York, NY: Routledge.

Mitchell, David T. and Sharon L. Snyder (2002) *Narrative Prosthesis: Disability and the Dependencies of Discourse*. Ann Arbor, MI: University of Michigan Press.

Minich, Julie A. (2010) 'Life on Wheels: Disability, Democracy, and Political Inclusion in *Live Flesh* and *The Sea Inside*', *Journal of Literary and Cultural Disability Studies*, 4, 1, 17–32.

Pérez, Jesús, Juan Undurraga, Ross J. Baldessarini and José Sánchez-Moreno (2012) 'Origins of Psychiatric Hospitalization in Medieval Spain', *Psychiatr Q*, 83, 4, 419–30.

Rivera-Cordero, Victoria (2013) 'Rebuilding the Wounded Self: Impairment and Trauma in Isabel Coixet's *The Secret Life of Words* and Pedro Almodóvar's *Los abrazos rotos*', *Arizona Journal of Hispanic Cultural Studies*, 17, 227–44.

Smith, Paul Julian (1994) *Desire Unlimited: The Cinema of Pedro Almodóvar*. London and New York, NY: Verso.

Sontag, Susan (1978) *Illness as Metaphor*. New York, NY: Farrar, Straus and Giroux.

Snyder, Sharon L., Rosemarie Garland-Thomson and Brenda Jo Brueggemann (eds) (2002) *Disability Studies: Enabling the Humanities*. New York, NY: Modern Language Association.

On the Road to Normalcy

European Road Movies and Disability (2002–2011)

Anna Grebe

In an article from 2010, published in the left-wing German weekly newspaper *Jungle World*, the German film reviewer and cineaste Georg Seeßlen attests the advent of a boom of mainstream movies about people with disabilities; beyond calling them 'appellative[s] feelgood movies [sic]', he identifies three important subgenres of this new genre: the 'Kriegsverletzten-Film' (veteran movie), the 'Behinderten-Thriller' (disability thriller), and the 'Behinderten-Roadmovie' (disability road movie).[1] These movies, according to Seeßlen, resemble the current public discourse on social and political inclusion and normalisation of disabled people, but also appear to refer to an allegedly overcome medical model of disability as criticised by disability studies. It is therefore fundamental to ask whether movies about disability not only depict disability, but rather also produce disability as a deviation or counterpart of a simultaneously produced 'normalcy' (see Ochsner and Grebe 2013).

Since the beginning of the twenty-first century, several of these 'disability road movies' have been made all over Europe. They have attracted a large audience in European movie theatres and film festivals. This chapter focuses on the relation between the narrative and aesthetic specifics of this new 'genre'. Moreover, it also situates this genre within the discourse of 'normalcy' as examined by disability studies scholars in Europe and the United States (see Waldschmidt 2006; Davis 2010). It connects issues concerning the definition of a genre by film scholars with an understanding of disability as a sociocultural product, with an analysis of these filmic narratives in selected Central European 'disability road movies' through a discussion of the dis/abled body as a starting point of the narration, where the disability is used as a 'prosthetic contrivance' (Mitchell and Snyder 2010: 99).

Defining the European Road Movie

Before turning towards the selected road movies in particular, we first have to get a picture of what is being discussed under the umbrella term 'European road movie'. A strong definition of the road movie as a genre in film is quite necessary, especially when comparing US-American and European movies, where the journey on the road is an essential part of the narration.[2] It is often pointed out that the road movie represents, especially in US-American culture, a genre highly related to the American Dream of self-realisation and the topographical overcoming of the Frontier (see Cohan and Hark 1997: 2; Sargeant and Watson 1999: 18). Scholars also stress that the European road movie should be assigned to the general classification of auteurist cinema. This view has been challenged by US-American and European scholars who worked particularly on finding a generic pattern of the road movie in general. David Laderman (2002), Ewa Mazierska and Laura Rascaroli (2006) and Sarah Bräutigam (2009) all emphasise the historical and socio-political interdependencies of American and Continental travel movies: while early film history features various examples focused on the movement itself as a cause for narration (Lumière, Méliès, etc), Mazierska and Rascaroli state: 'The European "road film" ... developed alongside the Hollywood road movie, being influenced by and influencing it at the same time' (2006: 4).

Most of the European road movies since Federico Fellini's *La strada* (*The Road*, 1954) and Ingmar Bergman's *Smultronstället* (*Wild Strawberries*, 1957), however, show particular attributes that are determined by the territorial constitution of Europe as a multiethnic continent and the European tradition of the travel film. In contrast to the US, Europe consists of 47 sovereign countries, and hence the probability of crossing national borders within the narration of a European road movie is subsequently much higher than in the US-American road movie (see Laderman 2002: 248; Mazierska and Rascaroli 2006: 5). In crossing borders, the protagonists not only trespass territorial limits, but also permeate boundaries between culture and language groups. These in turn imply a multitude of possibilities through which to move the narration forward, e.g. by misunderstandings, confusions or mistranslations. At the same time, sequences of driving are shorter in European than in US-American road movies, with a narrative focus on what stands between the driving sequences: pauses, stopovers and breakdowns on the way to the destination of the journey (see Risholm 2001: 124). By doing so, the cinematographic language of the European road movie produces fewer panorama views showing the speed of the car in a vast, empty landscape crossed by a paved highway. Instead, it focuses on shots of the car standing still and people moving around or in it (see Risholm 2001: 123; Bräutigam 2009: 155). The protagonists of European road movies are less frequently shown as outlaws or criminals choosing to 'hit the road', either to hide from the police or other authorities, and mostly lack a fixed destination or even a home to which they could return (see Laderman 2002: 247). Instead, they tend to be on their way to a more-or-less precise destination, driven by a certain idea or purpose and informed by practical considerations related to work, immigration or holidays. Therefore, the representation of European road movie protagonists tends to emphasise collective forms of life and practical necessities rather than the desire for absolute freedom or to escape from legal prosecution, which is then shot against the background of a long highway (see Mazierska and Rascaroli 2006: 5). Summing up these characteristics of the European road movie, Laderman states that 'the European road movie foregrounds the meaning of the quest journey more than the mode of transport; revelation and realization receive more focus than the act of driving' (2002: 248).

This study takes three German and Belgian films released since 2002 as representative examples: *Vincent will Meer* (*Vincent wants to Sea*, Germany 2010), *Hasta la Vista* (*Come as you are*, Belgium 2011) and *Verrückt nach Paris* (*Crazy About Paris*, Germany 2002). These movies identify themselves or are identified by film critics as 'road movies', staging people with disabilities as their protagonists.[3] What unites them in their narrative arc is a plotting in three parts: first, the point of departure, depicting the circumstances and the causes for the protagonists' decision to 'hit the road'; second, the escape from those circumstances and the road trip that follows the escape; third, the arrival at their (fixed or random) destination or place of longing. While this description of a typical road movie plot does not necessarily apply only to road movies including disabled people, I aim to show that in the subgenre of disability road movies, those three (probably heuristic) parts of the narrative arc are connected to an understanding of normalcy as a counterpart to non-normalcy. On the road these disabled protagonists confront and potentially transgress the social boundaries of the normalcy that governs their lives: but the question is whether these inner transformations and symbolic outer journeys will result in a wider social transformation.

Living in an Institution – Leaving the Institution

The similarities of these three selected European disability road movies – regarding their narrative arcs and their protagonists' constellation – make them extraordinary examples for discussing connections with the genre of the road movie and the core assumptions of disability studies. First of all, all protagonists from our three examples are living in 'total institutions' as defined in Erving Goffman's *Asylums* (1961). The concept of an institution refers to a social as well as a topographical dispositive that governs the life of an individual in all its aspects through control and confinement within an institution. All the inmates' activities are regulated and observed by a greater authority that rules through explicit and non-explicit norms. Monasteries, psychiatric hospitals and prisons are strong institutions that protect the individual from the community or vice versa; however, one could also include the family within the concept of a total institution.

In *Hasta la Vista*, the three young protagonists – Philip, Lars and Jozef from Belgium – are living with their families. Paraplegic Philip is his parents' only child and he depends on them in several ways: they take control of their son's whole life, including feeding, washing and dressing him – or even putting his palsied hand on his crutch when he goes to sleep. After another boring family vacation at the Northern Sea, he and his friends – terminally ill and wheelchair-using Lars and their almost blind friend Jozef – decide to go on a trip to Spain without their families, just as 'normal' youngsters their age would do. All three of them are represented as highly dependent on their families although living outside one of the 'classical' institutions as described by Goffman; nevertheless, their everyday life happens inside a given structure where their social function as 'son', combined with their respective disabilities, does not enable them to rebel against their parents. Therefore, their rebellion needs to be disguised: Philip, Lars and Jozef want to go to Spain, because they have heard of a brothel where female sex workers are not only very attractive, but also attending to men with disabilities. Under the pretext of a cultural and study trip, they initially book a fancy van including an experienced driver and male nurse, who cancels the trip when it is revealed that Lars' tumor is steadily growing, thus giving him only a few weeks to live. Unfortunately, Philip, Lars and Jozef cannot be too spontaneous in their intention of 'hitting the road': they can't drive themselves and need assistance for their daily necessities. Consequently, their breakout from their families is not only overcoming boundaries because of their wish to lose their virginity in a Spanish brothel (a 'normal' wish), but also because they realise their plan to leave their homes secretly and to start a road trip against their parents' will. In the end, they hire another driver and leave their homes early one morning with only Lars' little sister as a confidant.

In *Verrückt nach Paris*, Hilde, Karl and Philip are living in a home for people with (learning) disabilities in Bremen, Northern Germany. They live and work there, and the institution takes care of organising their everyday lives: the staff wake them up, feed them and plan their leisure time activities without letting them participate in those decisions. The three heroes are depicted as being frustrated because of their boring everyday life in the asylum and their monotonous work at a sheltered workshop, in addition to being disappointed in their assistant Enno. When Karl finds out that Enno prevented him from finding a job outside the institution, and Philip realises that his girlfriend is betraying him, they agree to their 70-year-old and quite adventurous friend Hilde's idea to take a short trip to Cologne without their caregivers, aided by a friend who works as a train guard. As they cannot drive by themselves, they take the train to Cologne and after a series of accidents manage to arrive in Paris, always followed by Enno, who is trying to bring them home. Hence, *Verrückt nach Paris* probably sketches the 'total institution' in the way that Goffman referred to as an 'asylum': that is, shared rooms with little personal belongings, all of them painted the same way; inmates whose lives are controlled by people to whom they are not even personally related; and the presence of a 'greater authority' that even decides how these inmates have to act around visitors. Additionally, their 'place of longing' is not an initially fixed destination. Karl, Philip and Hilde therefore form a trio that corresponds with the ideal of a classical road movie as they let themselves be led by the road itself instead of intending to meet a clear destination.

The protagonists Vincent, Marie and Alexander in *Vincent will Meer* also live in a total institution, even though they are not represented as physically but rather mentally disabled. Vincent's Tourette syndrome, named by his father as the reason for his mother's early death, is shown as something that deviates from normalcy, namely from what one would call 'decency' or 'modesty'. His stay at a clinic without a further specification is seemingly justified in the very first sequence of the film: while the people at his mother's funeral are sitting quietly and devoutly in the cemetery chapel, Vincent is not able to control his tics and starts quivering and swearing – something no one would do if he or she was 'normal'. Hence, the beginning of *Vincent will Meer* already establishes that Vincent is different. But he is not marked as 'disabled' until his angry father decides to get him 'cured' and brings him to the clinic, where he meets the obsessive-compulsive Alexander and anorexic and cardiac Marie. At the clinic everything is managed for the young inmates, who quickly become friends: mealtimes at the dining hall, therapies and shared dorms. A high fence surrounds the clinic; it separates and therefore divides the 'non-normal' people on the inside from the 'normal' people on the outside, and respectively the 'healthy' from the 'disabled'. For Vincent and Marie, the decision to flee these walls is easy: Marie tells Vincent that she 'found' a car after both of them had been admonished by their therapist for unreasonable behaviour. Vincent's late mother wanted to go to Italy right before she died, and Vincent was not able to fulfill her wish – although he had already packed her bags. Vincent therefore asks Marie to go to the Italian sea with him; Marie agrees and they secretly leave the clinic at night. Neurotic Alexander is following them, threatening them as he witnesses Marie and Vincent stealing the therapists' car, so they force him to come with them in the little red Saab, although he is reluctant and screaming for help. The road trip begins, this time bearing the typical European road movie feature of a fixed destination.

In each of these movies it is obvious that there is a difference between the protagonists and their surroundings. Moreover, this is a difference that is linked to a physical or mental confinement, or one made evident via the interaction between the protagonists and their surroundings, where blame is placed on individual bodies and not on the wider society in which disability takes shape as a social relationship. The exposition at the beginning of each movie establishes the institutionalisation of the protagonists and produces a governed normalcy for those inside the institution as well as a normalcy beyond the walls as physical and metaphorical limits – a normalcy that ironically marks the inside of the institution as something outside the norm. All protagonists are effectively in search of something – independence, (sexual) self-determination, adventure – and all of them are unsatisfied with their social role as 'non-normal' people. As in most road movies, this is not only about breaking out of the normalcy and routine inside the institution, but about a personal search of identity and meaning of life. This happens by means of a confrontation with what is outside the institution, an outside that paradoxically has marked the insiders as 'outsiders' (see Bräutigam 2009: 30). Nevertheless, they are no outlaws in the classical definition of being outside the law itself. The three movies and their cinematographic exposition instead are driven by an existentialist subject matter. They are 'quest road movies', in which the protagonists leave the places they were assigned to by society and start breaking the standards and expectations of society (see Bräutigam 2009: 45). Their produced deviation from 'normalcy', and their disability, becomes the cause for narration, 'a primary impetus of the storyteller's efforts' (Mitchell and Snyder 2010: 274). Their physical or mental divergence from a simultaneously produced normalcy becomes the background for a story precisely establishing this divide. The road trip thus begins as an adventure and as a transgression of visible and invisible boundaries (see Risholm 2001: 31).

The Trip Begins: On the Road to Normalcy

With the escape of our protagonists, the road movie starts with what it is identified as a genre: the journey on the road. Narrations about the life of individual heroes exist, these narrations are commonly and cross-culturally told by means of the imagery and symbolic meaning of the road itself (see Gerhard et al. 2001: 7). Curves, mountains, deserts, but also car breakdowns, disagreements over choosing the right way, heavy rains, etc are metaphorically charged and transposed into chapters of the inner process of the protagonists' transformations. These typical cinematographic features are mainly established in one of the three films, *Vincent will Meer*, probably because of the fact that the protagonists here are able to drive by themselves. Vincent, Marie and Alexander are crossing the Alps on a rural road instead of using the highway, fearing to be stopped by the *Autobahn* police. As a result they must negotiate curvy mountain passes and cross through green mountain pasture, representing the process of emotional dissolution from the clinic which they are leaving behind. Camera and montage, with long or extreme long shots establish the width of the filmic space – the efforts of a small vehicle trying to touch the horizon on seemingly endless roads. Cuts to the inside of the car and camera angles that allow a view through the front windshield or the side windows emphasise the distinction between an inside and an outside, again contrasting the monumentality of the landscape with the minor significance of the human being in the face of the imposing nature surrounding it (see Bräutigam 2009: 155).

For a 'normal' hero – as well as for the protagonists of *Vincent will Meer*, *Hasta la Vista* and *Verrückt nach Paris* – the journey on the road symbolically represents the feeling of absolute freedom and of having escaped from former lives. However, we have to pay attention to the divergences in disability road movies compared to the well-described genre of the non-disability road movie at this point: if the road movie carries the protagonist from his/her everyday life into a non-everyday life, the trip may end either with a refusal to return (for example, due to a desire to continue the journey or even death) or with a repatriation into society whereby the protagonist re-enters everyday life again. This development applies to our three filmic examples, which capture their protagonists fleeing from their respective institution to experience something new and different from their everyday life. But we have to critically evaluate if their journey under these circumstances should rather be understood as an escape from not-normalcy into normalcy (and maybe back into not-normalcy) oppositional to what Ellen Risholm would call a 'denormalization' (2001: 116). Referring to the German theorist of literature and culture Jürgen Link, Risholm describes the main narrative of the (non-disabled) road movie as a '(not) normal journey'. Initially, this denotation means to her that the journey in a road movie is opposed to a 'normal' everyday trip (i.e. to the supermarket) and is instead identified by crossing the limits of normalcy. This category does apply to Vincent, Marie and Alexander; to Karl, Philip and Hilde; and to Philip, Jozef and Lars – although with a twist. In their case, the escape from the institution as a transgression of the limits of normalcy facilitates that very sort of everyday life that passes for 'normalcy' in non-disabled road movies. Having dinner in a restaurant, going out, having sexual relations – the banality of these presumed everyday occurrences are nothing normal to these disabled characters. However, they subsequently also denote part of a process of normalisation instead of denormalisation: anorexic Marie starts eating again, seeing that outside the institution and its strict rules she can decide by herself whether and what to eat; the three guys from Belgium get so inebriated that they can barely find their way to their hotel rooms and eventually sleep in one bed; learning disabled Hilde pays with her own money for the train tickets to Paris, thus deciding where she wants to go instead of being patronised by the asylum's director. While those things would not be unusual occurrences in a well-developed scene in a 'normal' road movie, they are shown here as special in a world where normalcy and non-normalcy blur. Disability is thus produced as something extraordinary and as something that is worth being narrated as a response to the fear of the audience of being denormalised (see Waldschmidt 1998). However, the labelling as 'different' does not change due to the fact that the runaways are confronted on their journey with certain barriers in their environment whose overcoming is staged as a transgression of the impairment itself.

None of the three movies stages the protagonists as apparently pitiful creatures: paraplegic Philip in *Hasta la Vista* does not fit with the image of the 'good cripple' at all; instead, he is a cheeky and spoiled egomaniac who will not earn a lot of sympathy from the audience. He makes fun of his driver and assistant Claude, saying that she was a 'fat mammoth' when he thinks that she wouldn't understand him. But his behaviour changes towards her after Claude saves the life of blind Jozef, who has fallen into a river at a resting place at the side of the road. Philip realises that he depends on her, and tries to be nice, while still remaining insubordinate and brazen, almost provoking a fight with Dutch tourists in a vineyard. In *Verrückt nach Paris*, the three inmates of the asylum from Bremen on their way to Paris also do not endear themselves too much to the audience, replacing droll or pitiful traits with street-smart and stubbornness. And in *Vincent will Meer*, a conflict between Alexander and Vincent emerges after having climbed a mountain; Vincent hits Alexander multiple times in the face until he starts bleeding. Vincent later explains that he only did this out of affection and worries. All this would not be a problem for a road movie – but the filmic narration emphasises again and again how 'normal' these 'not normal' people were. In doing so, the films are acting against an explicit individual or medical model of disability which defines a person by his or her impairment and as an object of medical and therapeutic treatment. However, neither do they take a clear stand for a social or cultural model of disability as demanded and widely discussed by disability studies scholars. Consequently, the significance attributed to disability within the movies oscillates between a 'personal tragedy' model (see Barnes and Mercer 2003: 2) keeping the characters from realising their potential, and a constant repetition of the affirmation of 'normalcy' *à la* 'Look how normal these people are!' (see also the 'realistic mode'; Garland-Thomson 2001).

Remaining true to classic road movie narration, *Vincent will Meer*, *Verrückt nach Paris* and *Hasta la Vista* all feature the character of a chaser or persecutor trying to track the heroes down, acting as an antagonist. In classical US-American road movies such as *Thelma and Louise* (USA, 1991) or *Easy Rider* (USA, 1969), this antagonistic force is embodied in the police or legal authorities, who try to hunt down the protagonists – also by car – in order to capture them and seemingly re-establish social norms. In disability road movies, this role is taken up by the parents or staff from the clinic or asylum, who try to bring the escaped characters back into the institution – of course, seemingly for their own good – thus reaffirming the medical model of disability that sees disabled characters as a problem to be fixed or contained. Because the escape from the institution has usually occurred in secret, the chasers first have to find out where the fugitives are going. Consequently, road movies are full of mysteries, clues and red herrings, but also sudden encounters, wild car chases and narrow escapes. During the journey, not only do the protagonists undergo transformation by negotiating their identity along the distance traveled, their persecutors also pass through a kind of *rite de passage*, and may start to reflect on their own role as parents or assistants to the fugitive protagonists.

The persecutors of the three adventurous youngsters from Belgium in *Hasta la Vista* only appear once – and quite suddenly, for both the boys and the audience – during the trip to Spain: Driver and assistant Claude is forced to arrange a meeting between them and their parents at a French hotel to avoid her own persecution by law (she is still on parole). The clash of Philip, Lars and Jozef gets very emotional; Lars' parents are afraid that he might die during the journey because of his progressive disease. But the boys' handicaps makes it impossible to flee from this situation, to run back to the car and start the engine to continue their trip to Spain. Luckily, they manage to convince their parents that this road trip is of major importance to them and necessary to obtain a certain range of personal freedom as disabled persons (of course, they neglect to inform their parents of their wish to lose their virginity during the trip). Enno, the assistant in *Verrückt nach Paris*, who started pursuing Karl, Philip and Hilde filled with anger and a lack of understanding for their wishes and needs, initially is more motivated by trying to keep his job rather than bring the escapees home safely. By virtue of the journey to Paris, Enno not only meets the love of his life, he also realises that he had behaved badly towards the three heroes and starts to get seriously worried about their well-being. And in *Vincent will Meer*, the protagonist's father, who not only thinks that his son is disabled, stupid and abnormal, but also blames him for his failed marriage with the late mother, experiences a sudden change of mind through an argument with Vincent's therapist. When he and the therapist start following Vincent, Marie and Alexander on the road to Italy, he is primarily interested in salvaging his reputation as a politician, clearing up a situation in which the three fugitives left a gas station without paying their bill. During the trip, he realises that he cannot blame Vincent for his own mistakes and that Tourettes is not a disease that can be treated or cured; instead, he and his son need to find a way to live with the syndrome.

Their journeys continue. But where will they end?

Destination: Re-entering the Institution?

The three Belgian protagonists of *Hasta la Vista* lose their virginity in Spain; Hilde, Karl and Philip experience some great adventures in an African community in Paris; and Vincent finally makes his way to the sea. But the filmic narration has not come to its end yet: what comes next is a re-encounter between fugitive and persecutor, one that will require a readjustment of the relation between normalcy and non-normalcy.

According to Risholm, the majority of the 'normal' road movies lead to an irreversible denormalisation. However, she also recognises that there is a possibility that not-normal journeys could bring the heroes of a road movie back to normalcy or at least to social territories in which lifestyles that differ minimally from normalcy are accepted (2001: 122). A happy ending is just as feasible as a tragic ending, depending on the perspective from which the story is told. Yet for the disability road movie, Georg Seeßlen states that at the end of this exceptional genre only a re-entering of the institution is imaginable, although this might be on a 'higher level'. This is determined by the fact that neither in film nor in reality would there be a place where people with disabilities could find happiness, seeing that society has not found a place for them. In the case of *Hasta la Vista*, the return to the institution is not questioned at all: Lars dies after his 'successful' visit to the brothel. For Philip, the trip finds an end when his parents take him home to Belgium again. Only for Jozef does the potential of future freedom exist as he gets into Claude's van, and it remains unclear whether they take the road back home or keep on travelling.

Verrückt nach Paris tries a similar gesture, although the utopian character of the movie becomes apparent at this point: Karl, Philip and Hilde and their assistant Enno find their way back to Bremen at the German coast of the Northern Sea. It seems as if due to their experience gained on a self-determined road trip and their re-won freedom a long-term dissolution from the institution might be possible. But presumably because of their learning (and in Philip's case also severe physical) disability, they are only granted a limited freedom: Karl opens a crêpes stall, Philip gets back his girlfriend and Hilde keeps on working in the kitchen – but they remain as inmates in the institution. The institutionalisation is not criticised at all in this case; instead, it appears that they now live under 'better' circumstances due to their supposed participation in these decisions.

In *Vincent will Meer* the arrival at the seaside is not only connected within the dramatisation of the title character encountering his father and his therapist again; it also coincides with the breakdown of anorexic and cardiac patient Marie, who has to be admitted to the hospital. While she is in the emergency unit, Vincent gets into the car with his morally cleansed father who intends to take the road back to Germany. When Vincent asks his father to let him get out of the car so that he can go back to the hospitalised Marie, the movie aesthetically and narratively depicts the fundamental openness to a life outside the institution: as Vincent and Alexander start walking back towards the Italian town where Marie is, the camera turns to the left and zooms out. It shows a seemingly never ending width of horizon over the sea – a symbol for the renewed opportunity that Vincent and Alexander might have to direct their lives on their own terms. Consequently, the movie does not end with establishing institutionalisation as Seeßlen predicted; instead, it makes an effort to stress the autonomy of the decisions of its protagonists. It remains unclear, however, whether Vincent is taken back to the clinic or if he and his father are going to start all over again outside the institution.

If re-entering of the institution on a 'higher level' is plausible, as Seeßlen mentioned, this must take place under the presumption posed by Risholm that alternative lifestyles are thoroughly possible within the limits of normalcy. One must ask, however, if the protagonists of these films can truly enjoy self-determined lives when their freedoms are necessarily conditioned by former persecutors. Overall, the films' critiques of the discourse of disability is limited: the institution and its power do not dissolve but instead extend their scope of responsibility. This happens not by marking the protagonists as 'normal' but showing their possibilities of compatibility with the simultaneously produced normalcy. Instead of making a stronger argument for full inclusion and a stronger criticism of the discourse of social normalcy, we have a weaker argument for potential integration. The labelling as 'disabled' continues, the protagonists are only able to act inside the territory of normalcy as enforced by the putative majority of the non-disabled people. It remains to be seen whether our protagonists will find a place in society where they feel a kind of relative freedom.

NOTES

1 See http://jungle-world.com/artikel/2010/34/41609.html (accessed 9 June 2015).
2 As in several South American countries the genre of the road movie is intertwined with discourses of (postcolonial) identity and a specific aesthetics due to the vast landscapes of e.g. Patagonia, I am using the prefix 'US' to flag this distinction between North and South American qualities of the road movie. For an overview, see García Ochoa (2009).
3 Other disability road movies from Europe are, for example, *Aaltra* (Belgium, 2004), *Erbsen auf halb 6* (*Peas at 5:30*, Germany, 2004) or *Gran Paradiso* (Germany, 2000).

FILMOGRAPHY

Bahlke, Pago and Eike Besuden (dirs) (2002) *Verrückt nach Paris* (*Crazy About Paris*). 90 minutes. Geisberg Studios/Norddeutscher Rundfunk. Germany.
Bergman, Ingmar (dir) (1957) *Smultronstället* (*Wild Strawberries*). 91 minutes. Sweden.
Enthoven, Geoffrey (dir) (2011) *Hasta La Vista*. 115 minutes. Fobic Films/K2. Belgium.
Fellini, Federico (dir) (1954) *La strada* (*The Road*). 108 minutes. Ponti-De Laurentiis Cinematografica. Italy.
Huettner, Ralf (dir) (2010) *Vincent will Meer* (*Vincent wants to Sea*). 96 minutes. Olga Film GmbH. Germany.
Hopper, Dennis (dir) (1969) *Easy Rider*. 95 minutes. Pando Company/Raybert Productions. USA.
Scott, Ridley (dir) (1991) *Thelma and Louise*. 130 minutes. Pathé Entertainment/Metro-Goldwyn-Mayer. USA.

BIBLIOGRAPHY

Barnes, Colin and Geof Mercer (2003) *Disability*. Cambridge: Polity Press.
Bräutigam, Sarah (2009) 'Transatlantische Bewegungen im Roadmovie. Eine Analyse des Filmgenres Roadmovie unter Berücksichtigung seiner kulturellen und ästhetischen Verbindungen zu Europa', unpublished PhD thesis. Available at http://docserv.uni-duesseldorf.de/servlets/DerivateServlet/Derivate-18392/Dissertation_Finalversion_2011.pdf (accessed 6 July 2015).
Cohan, Steven and Ina Rae Hark (eds) (1997) *The Road Movie Book*. London and New York, NY: Routledge.
García Ochoa, Santiago (2009) 'Algunas notas sobre la aplicación de la categoría de género cinematográfico a la Road Movie', *Liño*, 15, 187–96.
Garland-Thomson, Rosemarie (2001) 'Seeing the Disabled. Visual Rhetorics of Disability in Popular Photography', in Paul K. Longmore and Lauri Umansky (eds) *The New Disability History: American Perspectives*. New York: New York University Press, 335–74.
Gerhard, Ute, Walter Grünzweig, Jürgen Link and Rolf Parr (eds) (2001) *Nicht normale Fahrten. Faszination eines modernen Narrationstyps*. Heidelberg: Synchron.
Goffman, Erving (1961) *Asylums: Essays on the Social Situations of Mental Patients and other Inmates*. Chicago, IL: Aldine.
Laderman, David (2002) *Driving Visions: Exploring the Road Movie*. Austin, TX: University of Texas Press.
Mazierska, Ewa and Laura Rascaroli (2006) *Crossing New Europe: Postmodern Travel and the European Road Movie*. London and New York, NY: Wallflower Press.
Mitchell, David T. and Sharon L. Snyder (2010) 'Narrative Prosthesis', in Lennard J. Davis (ed.) *The Disability Studies Reader*. New York, NY: Routledge, 274–87.
Ochsner, Beate and Anna Grebe (2013) *Andere Bilder. Zur Produktion von Behinderung in der visuellen Kultur*. Bielefeld: transcript.
Risholm, Ellen (2001) '(Nicht) normale Fahrten US-amerikanischer und deutscher Road Movies', in Ute Gerhard, Walter Grünzweig, Jürgen Link and Rolf Parr (eds) *Nicht*

normale Fahrten. Faszination eines modernen Narrationstyps. Heidelberg: Synchron, 107–32.

Sargeant, Jack and Stephanie Watson (eds) (1999) *Lost Highways. An Illustrated History of Road Movies.* London: Creation Books.

Waldschmidt, Anne (1998) 'Flexible Normalisierung oder stabile Ausgrenzung: Veränderungen im Verhältnis Behinderung und Normalität', *Soziale Probleme*, 9, 1, 3–35.

____ (2006) 'Die Macht der Normalität. Mit Foucault " Nicht-) Behinderung" neu denken', in Roland Anhorn, Frank Bettinger, and Johannes Stehr (eds), *Foucaults Machtanalytik und Soziale Arbeit. Eine kritische Einführung und Bestandsaufnahme.* Wiesbaden: VS Verlag für Sozialwissenschaften, 119–133.

Re-envisioning Italy's 'New Man' in *Bella non piangere!* (1955)

Jennifer S. Griffiths

In 1916 the September/October issue of the illustrated Italian periodical *La Domenica del Corriere* featured a cover by artist Achille Beltrame, which pictured a *bersagliere*, or member of the Italian infantry, leading a charge out of the trenches against Italy's Austrian opponents of World War I. Leaning on a rifle in his left hand and brandishing a crutch in his raised right, the soldier lunges forward on his single right leg. The image caption beneath explained, 'L'eroica fine del mutilato Enrico Toti: ferito per la terza volta, si alza e scaglia la sua gruccia contro il nemico in fuga' ('The heroic end of amputee Enrico Toti: wounded for the third time, he rises and hurls his crutch at the retreating enemy'). Following Enrico Toti's death at the sixth battle of Isonzo on 6 August 1916, this image of Toti as an unlikely soldier making the supreme sacrifice for his country was widely disseminated despite the dubious nature of the account: he was never officially admitted to the infantry corps and was unlikely to have been leading any charge. Propagating the belief that he had been at the frontlines of the fighting, Beltrame's illustration went a long way toward furthering his status as one of Italy's most important war heroes and martyrs. Toti's legacy was taken up first by the Italian monarchy and then by the newly established Fascist regime to unite and strengthen popular nationalist sentiment, but the popularity of his story continued after Liberation Day. If the leadership cults of Garibaldi or Mussolini served to unite public support for what has been called the political myth of the Italian nation or the political religion of the state, then a similar cult took shape around the image of Enrico Toti as the epitome of the noble citizen upon whose martyrdom the young nation state depended.[1] His remains were paraded back to Rome and ceremonially buried in the cemetery of Verano in May 1922; his name was resurrected during inter- and post-war periods via a series of streets, piazzas and monuments; and, nearly fifty years after his death, his legend was still compelling enough to inspire the feature-length film that is the subject of this chapter.

Body Politics

Given the ubiquity of the body politic metaphor, it is not surprising that bodies have been important surfaces for the inscription of national identity in post-Risorgimento Italy (see Polezzi and Ross 2007). In the making of Italy the identification of the ideal masculine body with the ideal nation became indispensable (see Bonetta 1990; Mosse 1996; Benadusi 2012). Prior to 1915, Italian authors like Enrico Corradini espoused notions of *mens sana in corpore sano* ('sound mind in sound body') as key features of masculinity and, under the regime, this model of the perfect male specimen became the metaphor for Fascist society (see Benadusi 2012: 15). 'Against the fragmentation and anomie of modern mass society', it has been said that Fascism advocated 'the harmony, belonging, and identity of the national community' (Koon 1985: 3). It generally promoted these ideals in productions of visual culture like the marble athletes at the Stadio dei Marmi in the Foro Italico sports complex in Rome, which was completed in 1928. If these youthful, aestheticised and proportioned bodies recalled classical sculpture and served to evoke an idealised model of Italy's unified cultural history, then the tortured bodies of Christian saints in medieval or renaissance painting are a closer point of resonance with common images of Toti, whose body came to represent a political martyrdom rather than a religious one. He exemplifies how, in the Italian context, disabled bodies after 1916 came to symbolise the national community and its struggle toward victory (see Bracco 2011) while the manipulation of his story and image under Fascism demonstrates that the symbolism of the disabled veteran continued to be exploited (see Salvante 2013).

It is difficult to find examples of disabled bodies being constructed in heroic terms before World War I, but recent historians have argued that the specific circumstances of the Great War provoked reformulations of masculinity in relation to disability in both Britain and the United States (see Bourke 1996; Carden-Coyne 2009). If masculinity, as George Mosse wrote in his pivotal study of the subject, had thus far been regarded as 'of one piece from its very beginning ... one harmonious whole, a perfect construct where every part is in its place' (1996: 5), then in response to the numerous visibly fragmented male bodies it produced, the conflict forced a rethinking of masculinity in terms of a flawless bodily specimen. When David Carbonari's film *Bella non piangere!* (*Don't Cry, Beautiful!*, 1955) opens, Toti, the main protagonist, is represented as the quintessential male lead who embodies the attributes of 'new manhood': virility, courage and vigor.[2] When he loses his leg as a result of an act of selfless heroism, he regains his manhood and reconstructs his lost masculinity in the forge of battle only by making the ultimate sacrifice for his country. No longer whole in either body or soul, the story of the film suggests that like the fragmented territories of Italy, war will make him whole again and like the ruins of Rome, his corpse will testify to his former glory. Toti's body is used as a surface onto which a moralising rhetoric of masculine sacrifice in the service of nationalism is inscribed. It is perhaps because of the timeless and universal appeal of this message that his legacy survived both Giolitti's Liberal government and the subsequent Fascist regime in Italy, not only as the protagonist of Carbonari's film, but as an enduring symbol of national sacrifice to whom the most recent monument was dedicated in 2008.[3]

Man and Myth

As the factual details of Enrico Toti's life have been forgotten and/or manipulated in lieu of successive fictionalised or exaggerated accounts, the man has become more of a national myth. Lucio Fabi, the major authority on his life story, described the task of untangling fact from fiction as like navigating a historical labyrinth (1993: 10). What is known is that he was born in Rome in 1882 and enlisted in the navy at fourteen years of age, serving for eight years until 1905. A year after taking a job as a stoker with the railways, he lost his left leg in a work-related accident that dragged him beneath a locomotive. Instead of conforming to social expectations of the period with regard to disability, he set about using modern media to establish himself as a *personaggio*, or public personality (see Fabi 1993: 20). He took on a number of impressive athletic challenges, including an international swimming competition across the Tiber River and a world bicycle tour during which he reportedly traversed 20,000 kilometres across Europe and Africa.[4]

Toti advocated Italy's intervention in the war and shortly after its May 1915 entry into the conflict he set off on his bicycle with a homemade uniform for the front. Turned away on numerous occasions, he was back to Rome in August of that year where he presented repeated requests to various ministries for permission to return to the front. The would-be soldier was supposedly granted this permission thanks to the intervention of Prince Emanuele Filiberto Duca d'Aosta, to whom he had written in an undated letter, 'Le guiro che ho del fegato e qualunque impresa la più difficile, se mi venisse ordinata, la eseguirei senza indugio' ('I swear to you that I have nerve and I would execute without hesitation even the most difficult challenge that might be assigned to me') (quoted in Sillani 1924: 50). Toti's eventual assignment was as an auxiliary volunteer, obliging him to stay well behind the front lines *without* a weapon. He later appears to have been able to obtain a transfer to the Third Battalion of *bersaglieri* cyclists under Major Paride Razzini, where he may have been tasked with monitoring lines of communication, retrieving weaponry and identifying the dead.

Yet there is confusion surrounding Toti that arises as a result of conflicting accounts and his subsequent politicisation as a national hero. His personal letters are full of frequent exaggeration and fantasy and it is according to them that he received permission to be in the war zone. Unfortunately there is no official record of his claims (see Fabi 1993: 40–4) and *post facto* military accounts placing him at the front of the attack on 6 August 1916 do not match those of contemporary biographers who report how he suffered from being disallowed to follow the 'glorious battalion' (Fabi 1993: 58). Despite the possibility that it was complete invention, the story of the heroic figure who threw his crutch at the Austrian enemy was celebrated by the monarchy and then held aloft and elaborated upon during the interwar period. Benito Mussolini advocated his place as the epitome of the Italian patriot; Fascist youth, he affirmed, would be trained to idolise him as the quintessential emblem of the self-sacrificing citizen (see Fabi 1993: 10–11). The regime even went so far as to expand on the scant existing details of events leading up to his death with newly elaborate and emotive official accounts twenty years after the fact (see Fabi 1993: 13).

The specific nature of Toti's apparent determination and defiance captured Italy's contempt for what would be termed their 'vittoria mutilata', or mutilated victory, against the Austrians. During the Risorgimento, or Italian unification, Italy undertook a series of Wars of Independence from Austria (1848, 1859, 1866); when it joined World War I in May 1915, it had been an independent nation state for only 45 years. Like David up against Goliath, it was a young, small, poor nation when it decided to confront the wealth and power of the Austro-Hungarian Empire yet again. This time Italians would be humiliated at the Battle of Caporetto in 1917 and bankrupted by what was said to be 'the war to end all wars'. Italy entered the war reassured by British,

French and Russian promises in the Treaty of London that it would acquire new territories, including Tyrol and Dalmatia. However, following the war, Italy's allies failed to deliver on those promises in the Treaty of Versailles and much of the nation felt doubly victimised. For Italian nationalists, the government's failure to confront the Entente powers (America, Britain, Russia and France) was unforgivable. Added to the economic consequences of World War I, these events fueled the nationalist sentiments that eventually led to the rise of Fascist radicals. Enrico Toti may have found himself at a physical disadvantage, but he refused to give up in the face of certain defeat and his final gesture proved he had more backbone than either the elite ruling classes of Prime Minister Giovanni Giolitti's Liberal government or the Austrian enemy. His manly act of 'sprezzatura', or indifference, in the face of death, came to symbolise Italy's attitude toward their 'mutilated victory' while the war hero's injured body could be identified directly with that of the proud, if disgraced, nation.

Bella non piangere!

While film critic Morando Morandini panned David Carbonari's post-war film in his *Dizionario del Film*, describing it as a 'patriotic tear-jerker, one of the most feeble B-movies of the 1950s', *Bella non piangere!* illustrates that the allure of Italy's one-legged hero endured well beyond the historic trenches of World War I or the Fascist era and into the post-war period. If Neorealist film of the 1940s represented an overturning of the patriotic idols and ideals held up under the Fascist regime by Italian leftist intellectuals, then this film is emblematic of what has been termed the 'crisis' of Neorealism at the beginning of the 1950s.[5] The immediate post-war generation may have looked upon the patriotic self-sacrifices of the war with justifiable cynicism, but by 1955 Italy's future was viewed with new optimism and the sacrifices of both world wars appeared to have been less in vain. Adopting a conservative spirit and a more popular Hollywood feel, the plot returns filmgoers to the heroic, patriotic themes of the interwar era and represents a new embrace of nationalist sentiment at the dawn of Italy's Economic Miracle.[6]

Deviating from factual accounts, screenwriter Duilio Coletti and director Carbonari created filmic appeal in *Bella non piangere!* by adding a love interest and introducing new elements to exaggerate the protagonist's adventurous spirit and utterly self-sacrificing character. Thus in this film version of the story, Enrico Toti is a macho man's man, an intrepid traveller and sportsman, an action hero who never stays home for long, but will go to any length in order to defend it. By embellishing the heroic aspects of his narrative, the filmmakers characterise him as a modern *superuomo*, or superman, reviving key elements of Fascist dogma related to what Emilio Gentile has described as the myth of a 'Greater Italy' populated by 'New Men' (2003: 5–6). The film is emblematic of an ideology that subordinates individual and political liberties to the perceived needs of the nation, which is conceived as a cohesive body. By juxtaposing the hero's physical drama with cityscapes of Rome and landscapes of war, the creators of the film utilise a strategy common to all nationalisms wherein the physical and moral health of the human body is metaphorically related with that of the country.[7] In this case, the parallel suggests that his personal moral triumph is a collective, national one and in this respect the film likely resonated with Italy's post-war generation, for whom the man and his defiant act continued to represent, in a most singular fashion, the admirable principle of self-sacrificing military heroism (see Fabi 1993: 7).[8] They had, after all, grown up under the influence of Italy's imagined 'New Man' who, with his attitude of *sprezzatura*, was capable of spitting in the face of injury or death, and Toti was envisioned as having defied both.

Views of Italy's capital in the first half of the film are a recurrent backdrop that activate the Eternal cityscape as a visual metaphor for broader conceptions of shared cultural heritage, national belonging and the Italian homeland. Key moments of intimacy unfold against carefully selected views of the city that frame Toti within romantically ruined visions of Rome and suggest a meaningful connection between the iconic fragments of the city's glorious past and the hero's own fragmented and fated body. Genuine World War I footage from Italy's Istituto Luce (L'Unione Cinematografica Educativa) appears in the latter half of the film, conveying the destruction of the Italian countryside beyond the capital. Scenes of train travel then mediate between the safe inner spaces of Toti's Roman home and the chaotic fringes of the front, implying that the struggles of the faraway conflict are ultimately in defence of Rome, at the heart of Italy, an emblem of the nation's hard-won national unity in 1870.[9]

Bella non piangere! opens with a written message projected onto the rooftops of Rome, which reads: 'Questo film e dedicato ad Enrico Toti, fulgido esempio di eroismo, ed a tutti coloro che in tutte le guerre, donando tutto ciò che potterano donare sacarificarono se stessi per la libertà della Patria' ('This film is dedicated to Enrico Toti, shining example of heroism, and to all those who in all the wars, giving all that they could give, sacrificed themselves for the liberty of the homeland'). The story begins when Enrico returns home to his mother and love interest, Nina, after a long stint abroad with the merchant marines. 'Non ci so stare fermo' ('I don't know how to stay still'), he tells them. Reunited and embracing on the banks of the Tiber River, Nina begs him to stay and find an administrative job so that they can at last be married. In the background of their intimate encounter looms the infamous Pons Aemilius, known to contemporary Romans as the 'Ponte Rotto', or broken bridge. The ancient, ruined bridge foreshadows both Enrico's ensuing accident and the inevitable collapse of their love.

Although he is reluctant, Enrico agrees to interview for a government office job where two slow-moving old men hover over dusty bookshelves. Feeling trapped in this stuffy room, Toti tugs at his collar and tries to open the window onto the Roman fountain in the piazza below, but the men cry, 'No, no, it's been five years since we opened it'. The ageing ministers inside their suffocatingly small room, surrounded by their piles of paperwork, are contrasted with the youthful and energetic Enrico, whose evident need for fresh air and open space remind us that he is a man in his prime. The scenario reiterates the protagonist's status as a 'New Man' who is youthful, active and strong. Here the film draws out Fascist definitions of new manhood, which exalted youthfulness, manly vigour and physical fitness.[10] Yet it also draws on attitudes that were common among the avant-gardes, which envisioned the 'New Man' as repudiating ivory-tower intellectualism to actively construct Italy's future.[11] The scene identifies the awkward and ageing clerks with an Italy of the past and Enrico with its modern future. He flees the interview, refusing to be emasculated or enervated inside the restrictive office interior.

Having disappointed her, Enrico tries and fails to win back Nina's affections by serenading her at her bedroom window, but she responds by dumping a bucket of water on him from above. The piggybacking of the two scenes implies that if Nina's place is inside the home, his is not. When he later observes Nina in the marketplace of the ruined Portico of Octavia, being wooed by Fernando the barber, he decides to head off again, this time on a cycling adventure. After returning as the victor of a long haul race, Enrico is reunited with Nina and, as before on the picturesque banks of the Tiber, she asks him to take a day job in Rome. This time she suggests a more modern one attuned to his nature with the newly instituted railways. Here we see Enrico's character making the first of a series of self-sacrificing choices as he curbs his active lifestyle for the woman he loves. Yet in its staging of events the film suggests that, in ceding to Nina's pleas, the protagonist is relinquishing his previously unrestricted freedoms and weakening his masculine resolve. The suggestion seems to be that, in the tradition of Greek tragedy, his accident is predestined by such a disjunction of body and soul.

In Carbonari's version of the story, Enrico Toti loses his leg on the job while saving a child vagrant who is found hiding in the rail cars and flees the authorities across the tracks. The moment of its loss is a heroic precursor and will become the catalyst for a new unparalleled level of masculine heroism linked to the ultimate physical sacrifice he makes for the national cause. Initially, however, the trauma of the injury results in an emotional breakdown. When he wakes up in the small hospital room and looks down at his amputated leg, Enrico declares, 'So' finito. Era meglio che morivo, se il treno mi ammazava subito' ('I'm finished. Better I had died, that the train had just killed me'). Rather than face Nina, he tells her that while his injury is insignificant he has decided that he doesn't want to marry her. As he struggles to recover some mobility with the use of a crutch in the confines of home beside his mother, war is declared outside his window in the streets below. Although he attempts to enlist, he is turned away because of his disability. Determined to get to the front, Enrico then writes his historic letter to the Duke of Aosta and recruits the help of the young beggar whose life he saved at the railroad tracks. Having previously snuck in to visit his heroic saviour in the hospital, the boy is happy to devote himself to the older man's service and procures him the fabric for a homemade uniform. He even manages to find him an illustriously feathered *bersagliere* hat, the iconic symbol of the Italian light infantry corp. However, when the boy ignores his warnings and follows him onto the train to join him on his clandestine bid to make it to the front, their cover is blown and they are detained by high command. About to be sent ignominiously back to Rome, the Duke of Aosta intervenes on Enrico's behalf. The Prince's reputed real-life intervention is thus embellished and transformed into a personal encounter wherein the monarch says he received all of his letters and decrees that he will be assigned the dangerous task of delivering mail to troops via bicycle along the frontline. 'Poche cose sono più importanti che le notizie dalla famiglia' ('Few things are as important as news from the family'), a soldier receiving his mail in the trenches tells him in following scene. As the frontline courier Enrico becomes the connective tissue between homeland and borderland.

After a bridging shot of weaponry and transports at the front, Enrico is seen returning home where he seeks Nina out to tell her, 'La guerra mi ha insegnato che in fondo anche senza una gamba si può essere lo stesso un soldato, un uomo. Posso sposarti lo stesso. Ho paura' ('The war has taught me that, even without a leg, one can be a soldier, a man. I can marry you after all'). In defence of Italy, Enrico believes he has regained his manhood and become whole once more. But, as the audience is already aware, it is too late for them: Nina has married Fernando the barber, who is abusive, but with whom she now has a baby. When Enrico hears of the abuse, he confronts Fernando at the barbershop to defend her, demonstrating once again his superior kind of selfless manhood.

In a rather contrived scene as he heads back to the front Enrico looks through a classroom window where young children are being taught a geography lesson. The teacher explains the war as part of the fight to liberate Italian comrades and reunite the rest of Italy with the lost Italian territories of the north. Once again the window is used as an effective, even if simplistic, visual device, which mediates between interior and exterior space, and metaphorically suggests the contested national borders that delineate the safety of the Italian homeland from the foreign exterior. If ageing ministers, beloved Nina, and the young schoolchildren belong within its sheltered interior, Enrico Toti stands on guard at its periphery. Meanwhile a map of the Italian peninsula, nicknamed 'Lo stivale' for its boot-like shape, hangs on the classroom wall, linking Toti's physique and his lost limb in particular with the anthropomorphic configuration of Italy's geographic boundaries. Introducing the concept of the body politic through dialogue and imagery, the scene suggests a parallel between Italy's lost territories and Toti's lost limb. War, it is implied, offers the means by which to heal both the nation and the man. This connection between war and the regeneration of masculinity and national honour has a particular resonance in Italian experience, exemplified by the name of the Italian movement for unification itself ('Risorgimento' means 'resurgence'). If for centuries Italians were slandered with stereotypes of effeminacy and cowardice, then, as Lucy Riall (2012) has demonstrated, leaders of the unification viewed war as a way to redeem the honour of Italian masculinity. In this historical sense the map summons up a long-term national discourse of lost honour and draws out an association between Toti's damaged masculine body and the fragmented, and once again dishonored, Italian nation.

The love triangle between Enrico, Fernando and Nina unravels toward the end of the film as a result of the events of the war. Fernando also departs for the front, but only after he bids farewell to Nina and his son, Petruccio, a seemingly transformed and nobler man by virtue of his new role in the fighting. He is fatally injured almost immediately, however, and in the course of being transported to a war hospital, is reconciled with Enrico to whom he confesses 'Non sono mai stato un buon marito...' ('I was never a good husband...'); but despite this fact he swears he always loved Nina and the child. Unlike their love for the same woman, which drew them apart, here the two men are seen to be brought together by a mutual love of country, united as brothers in arms. Enrico writes to tell Nina of Fernando's condition and she boards a train for the front where she is able to hear his dying words: 'Sono stato un mascalzone. Non meritavo una donna come te' ('I was a scoundrel. I didn't deserve a woman like you. I am afraid'). Fernando's dramatic character shift and the reconciliation between the two men are events that solidify the film's advocacy of war as an act of masculine redemption. In their last moments together, Enrico sees Nina off at the train station with a group of singing, injured soldiers who are likewise heading home to Rome. Enrico stands on the platform wishing her 'Addio' multiple times as his voice trails off and his darkened figure moves into the distance as the camera pulls away with Nina's train. Here the shot conveys the hallowed status of the hero who is backlit and thus framed by a halo of light. As Nina returns home to Petruccio, Enrico returns to the trenches of the frontlines where we already know he will die.

Genuine footage of bombs, gunfire and smoke from World War I is used to make it clear that the Italian situation is deteriorating at this point in the film. Under serious fire from the enemy, the Lieutenant tells high command that it is impossible under current conditions to send out a dispatch. Nevertheless Enrico volunteers and, when he is ordered not to go, defies these instructions to crawl over the walls, through barbed wire and gunfire, and into the adjacent trenches. The bombardment intensifies, forcing Enrico to take up one of the abandoned machine guns and begin firing into the night. The hero's final moments take place at dawn when his bullets finally run out and he crawls out of the trench. Standing alone on the hilltop, backlit once again like a saint, he is shot once, tosses a stone, is shot again, and hurls his crutch before finally collapsing. If, in previous scenes, the crutch was a cipher for curtailed or truncated manhood, then in this final act it becomes a declaration of manhood reclaimed, made whole once again through bravery and voluntary sacrifice. In death all difference and disability disappear as he joins the numerous other war dead whose broken bodies are somehow the price to pay for Italian redemption. As the camera pans over the ground, which is scattered with the bodies of fallen soldiers, a new wave of *bersaglieri* come charging over the hill and the trumpet declaring victory sounds. Italy and the Allies have defeated Austria, but not before Enrico Toti has made the ultimate sacrifice. There follows another series of historic film reels depicting cavalry, cycling battalions and convoys of army trucks returning home. With two final images the film cuts from Enrico's smiling corpse to a shredded Italian flag waving in the wind, his postmortem smile presumably signifying the individual and collective moral victories that his death represents. This closing melodramatic juxtaposition confirms Toti's identification with the 'New Man' that was supposed to build a 'Greater' Italy and reaffirms the metaphor of the body politic. Like the flag, the protagonist's broken, but ennobled, body becomes an emblem of Italy, his individual story incorporated into a grand, national narrative of devotion, responsibility and sacrifice.

NOTES

1 On Garibaldi see Riall (2007); on Mussolini, see, for example, Gundle *et al.* (2015); on Fascism as a political religion, see Gentile (1996).
2 Thanks to the Scuola Nazionale di Cinema – Cineteca Nazionale (formerly the Centro Sperimentale di Cinematografia) of Rome for providing me the means to view the film. All transcriptions and translations of the dialogue are my own.
3 A bronze monument of Toti executed by artist Egidio Ambrosetti stands in Cassino's eponymous central piazza. On Enrico Toti's representation in commemorative national monuments, see Griffiths 2015.
4 On Toti and his cycling career, see Foot (2011).
5 On the politics of Neorealism, see Pastina (2000) or Bondanella (2003).
6 The term Economic Miracle has been used to describe the sustained period of economic growth that transformed Italy from a predominantly rural nation into an industrialised power in the 1950s and 1960s.
7 For more on the Italian context, see Bonetta (1990).
8 'La figura di Toti, per la generazione dei quarantenni e per quelli che hanno qualche anno in più, reassume in maniera singolare uno dei principi stereotipi dell'eroismo bellico, il soldato che suggella con un estremo gesto bellicoso il sacrificio supremo per la Patria' ('For a generation in their forties, or those a few years older, the figure of Toti sums up in a singular manner one of the stereotypical principles of military heroism, the soldier who seals his supreme sacrifice for the Fatherland with an extreme warlike gesture').
9 Rome became part of the rest of Italy only in 1870 after a series of failed attempts to take the city from Papal rule. Giuseppe Garibaldi's famous rallying cry during the Risorgimento was 'Roma o morte – Rome or death', a slogan now inscribed on his monumental equestrian statue in Rome's Piazza Garibaldi; on the symbolic significance of Rome for the Fascist regime, see Kallis (2014).
10 On the Fascist cult of youth, see Malvano (1994); on Fascist distinctions of new manhood, see Benadusi (2012).
11 On various views of the 'New Man' by F. T. Marinetti, Giovanni Papini or Giuseppe Prezzolini, for example, see Gentile (2003) or Benadusi (2012).

FILMOGRAPHY

Carbonari, David (dir) (1955) *Bella non piangere!* (*Don't Cry, Beautiful!*). 84 minutes. Excelsia Film. Italy.

BIBLIOGRAPHY

Benadusi, Lorenzo (2012) *The Enemy of the New Man: Homosexuality in Fascist Italy*. Madison, WS: University of Wisconsin Press.

Bonetta, Gaetano (1990) *Corpo e nazione: L'educazione, igienica e sessuale nell'Italia liberale*. Milan: Franco Angeli.

Bourke, Joanna (1996) *Dismembering the Male*. Chicago, IL: University of Chicago Press.

Bondanella, Peter (2003) 'From Italian Neorealism to the Golden Age of Cinecittà', in Elizabeth Ezra (ed.) *European Cinema*. Oxford: Oxford University Press, 119–38.

Bonetta, Gaetano (1990) *Corpo e nazione: L'educazione ginnastica, igienica e sessuale nell'Italia liberale*. Milan: Franco Angeli.

Bracco, Barbara (2011) 'Il mutilato di guerra in Italia: polisemie di un luogo crudele', *Memoria e Ricerca*, 38, 9–24.

Carden-Coyne, Ana (2009) *Reconstructing the Body: Classicism, Modernism and the First World War*. Oxford: Oxford University Press.

Fabi, Lucio (1993) *La Vera Storia di Enrico Toti*. Gorizia: Edizioni della Laguna.

Foot, John (2011) *Pedalare! Pedalare!: A History of Italian Cycling*. London: Bloomsbury.

Gentile, Emilio (1996) *The Sacralization of Politics in Fascist Italy*, trans. Keith Botsford. Cambridge, MA: Harvard University Press.

____ (2003) *The Struggle for Modernity: Nationalism, Futurism and Fascism*. London: Praeger.

Griffiths, Jennifer S. (2015) 'Enrico Toti: A New Man for Italy's Mutilated Victory', in Luca Somigli and Simona Storchi (eds) *Annali d'Italianistica: The Great War and the Modernist Imagination in Italy*, 33, 345–59.

Gundle, Stephen, Christopher Duggan and Giuliana Pieri (2013) *The Cult of the Duce*. Manchester: Manchester University Press.

Kallis, Aristotle (2014) *The Third Rome 1922–43*. London: Palgrave Macmillan.

Koon, Tracey H. (1985) *Believe, Obey, Fight: Political Socialization of Youth in Fascist Italy*. Chapel Hill, NC: University of North Carolina Press.

Malvano, Laura (1994) 'Il mito della giovinezza attraverso l'immagine: il fascismo italiano', in G. Levi and J. C. Schmitt (eds) *Storia dei giovani: L'età contemporanea*. Rome: Laterza, 311–48.

Mosse, George (1996) *The Image of Man: The Creation of Modern Masculinity*. Oxford: Oxford University Press.

Pastina, Daniela (2000) 'Opera and Neorealism: The Function of L'Elisir d'Amore in Visconti's Belissima', in Rebecca West (ed.) *Pagina Pellicola Pratica: studi sul cinema Italiano*. Ravenna: Longo, 85–96.

Polezzi, Loredana and Charlotte Ross (eds) (2007) *In Corpore: Bodies in Post-unification Italy*. Cranbury, NJ: Associated University Presses.

Riall, Lucy (2007) *Garibaldi: Invention of a Hero*. New Haven, CT: Yale University Press.

____ (2012) 'Men at War: Masculinity and Military Ideals in the Risorgimento', in Silvana Patriarca and Lucy Riall (eds) *The Risorgimento Revisited: Nationalism and Culture in Nineteenth-Century Italy*. London: Palgrave Macmillan.

Salvante, Martina (2013) 'Italian Disabled Veterans between Experience and Representation', in Steven McVeigh and Nicola Cooper (eds) *Men After War*. New York, NY:

Routledge, 111–29.
Scarry, Elaine (1985) *The Body in Pain: The Making and Unmaking of the World*. New York: Oxford University Press.
Sillani, Tommaso (ed.) (1924) *Lettere di Enrico Toti*. Firenze: Edizioni Bemporad.

'Get Your Legs Back'

Avatar (2009) and the Re-booting of American Individualism

Susan Flynn

One cannot consider contemporary American film without thinking of Hollywood's ambiguous bodies that escape human imperfection by the fusion of biotechnology with the body. Enacting 'American-ness', the bodies on film are now jostled and coerced into a conspicuous optimisation; one that is the duty of each citizen, be it for power, profit or beauty. This somatic duty is the new form of ableism in Hollywood film.

American identity, rather than depending on a common ethnicity or language, seems to be defined by faith in a set of ideologies. American-ness is embodied by the Hollywood characters who espouse a range of perceived American traits: individualism, equality, liberty, democracy and American exceptionalism. Americans focus on these specific ideas of themselves to justify their lifestyles, plans and projects (see Crothers 2010) and the Hollywood film industry buttresses these internalised cultural beliefs. Individualism, an ideology which purports that each individual is responsible for himself and ought to utilise the capacity to improve his own circumstances, may be characterised by self-governance, self-determination, autonomy and progress (see Garland-Thomson 1997). Woven into culture and social institutions, individualism symbolises the freedom of the American way of life; rather than being static, economic political and cultural shifts continuously shape the notion of individualism (see Greene 2008: 118). Disparate threads may be identified that still share common structural antecedents and over-arching outcomes; although individualistic beliefs vary across social class, location and various identities, the notion of self-reliance is paramount. This chapter assumes a Marxist approach: individualism buttresses capitalism by fostering self-interest, inspiring the masses to hard work, while encouraging them to focus on their own material desires (see Marx and Engels 1978).

It was in the United States that individualism became a symbolic catchword of immense significance, celebrating capitalism and liberal democracy, free enterprise and the American Dream, and came to be seen as incompatible with the opposing claims of socialism and communism (see Lukes 1971). Propagated along with the new liberal nation, America embraced individualism as a corrective to the social hierarchies that immigrants left behind in Europe; the notion of social responsibility is also eschewed by this individualism: 'Compared with the more socially minded Europeans, Americans are thought to place a higher value on self-reliance and individual initiative and to recoil from the idea of government responsibility for individuals' well being' (Gilens 2009: 32). Hollywood dresses itself in these ideological clothes, acting as a global transmitter which garners public fascination in the mythical notion of an individualist, free democracy where each citizen has the ability to improve their social standing by virtue of hard work (see Garland-Thomson 1997; Snyder and Mitchell 2006). The Jeffersonian notion of the individual's self-direction and autonomy is still deeply rooted.

> The view of America as 'the land of the free' refers to individuals unencumbered by political or religious tyranny. 'Land of opportunity' myths allude to autonomous individuals finding pathways to wealth, success, status, and the like. The bald eagle – a solitary hunter – is depicted as the official national symbol of a country of free, autonomous individuals. (Greene 2008: 122)

Furthermore, in this paradigm, each citizen is a microcosm of the American nation (see Garland-Thomson 1997). 'Good' citizens, then, are those who enact the correct amount of self-drive and determination, to improve their own position and the overall position of the nation. However, that depends upon a body that is fit and able: a neutral instrument of the individual will. The disabled figure complicates this fantasy (ibid.). The economic sphere is fraught with competition and celebrates the 'survival of the fittest', which literally and figuratively places people with disabilities at a disadvantage. The notion extolled by individualism whereby each citizen has the same potential for success, is predicated on the assumption that every citizen has the same material condition. Individualism, therefore, has a predilection for 'normal' bodies and so seeks to reject or 'normalise' those outside the realm of what is considered normal. American democracy, citizenship and majority consent depend on and assume a heterogeneous and autonomous subject who exercises free will for the betterment of himself and consequently all others.

America has long imagined itself as a technological leader and industrial power, moving from an agrarian society to a leading industrial power by the 1800s. Industry became central to the world image of America as a dynamic inventive culture and throughout the twentieth century technology became the hallmark of America's modernism (see Clark 2006). The significance of industrial work and inventiveness is central to the mythology and perception of American-ness. Ideologies of what such work is, and who performs it, lead it to a critical juncture at which American-ness meets individualism. This focus leaves no room for persons with differing abilities. Films made in Hollywood, primarily for an American audience, reflect this centrality of individualised work: '[Mass media] are the cultural arms of the industrial order from which they spring. Mass media policies reflect and cultivate not only the general structure of social relations but also specific types of institutional and industrial organization and control' (Gerbner 2000: 144). Mike Oliver (1990) suggests that the ideologies of individualism, medicalisation and normalisation are linked to capitalism's rise and have shaped contemporary understandings of disability; the capitalist system established a hegemony of fully functioning bodies that has continued to perpetuate ableism in mainstream employment. Social critics posit that individualism justifies inequalities by suggesting that barriers to economic success are due to the psyches of individuals, rather than to social structures (see Greene 2008). Encouraging autonomy, individualism assumes each person is capable of rational and vigorous self-improvement. The assumption that every person has the ability to improve their social position leaves no room for those who may need care or assistance and perpetuates the myth of self-sufficiency, constructing some as dependent and others as autonomous (see White and Tronto 2004). A person's 'disability', then, is his or her own responsibility. A neoliberal ethos prevails, which incurs a high degree of body management; those who do not sufficiently maintain their own bodies are held responsible for their non-well-being (see Mitchell 2014: 4). The political resonances of these ideologies have far-reaching consequences for people with disabilities. Constrained within its own system, Hollywood fails to provide a broad range of representations of disability. Any deviation from ideologies of individualism and equal opportunity is considered unseemly (see Kolker 1983).

Hollywood and the Reconstitution of Ideology

Much has been written about *Avatar* (James Cameron, 2009), perhaps due – at the time of writing – to its status as the most financially successful film of all time (see Bennett 2013). This film is an interesting example of biotechnology occupying a discursive position which facilitates American individualism; providing the opportunity to escape from the imperfect body, while making optimisation of the body a duty of individualism. In situating the disabled character in a diegesis which privileges able characters, the film recirculates medical model ideologies of the disabled character in need of diagnosis, intervention, cure or rehabilitation. Furthermore, in positioning biotechnical optimisation as the duty of the disabled citizen, *Avatar* enacts a drama of individualism where to 'get on' you must 'get fixed'. The film celebrates the optimising potential which is provided by biotechnology, even though it confesses that not everyone will have access to its transformative 'solutions'. In the opening voiceover Sully (Sam Worthington) reveals 'they can fix a spine if you got the money. But not on *vet* benefits, not in this economy'. In dealing with the financial exigency by suggesting hard work and determination will allow every disabled person to acquire the necessary finances for biotechnical intervention, the film reconstitutes the ideology of individualism, using Sully's body as a disturbing commentary on perceptions of disabled people's lives.

Rather than society having responsibility for creating disability, the onus is on that person to improve their life prospects. From a Marxist perspective Hollywood films such as this contribute to the reproduction of the capitalist system and maintain the existing social structure. American individualism is visible in the conviction that everyman can 'succeed'; attain professional, personal and romantic success by hard work and bravery. In fact, lack of success is suggested to stem from indolence and lack of moral citizenship, as is shown in the *mise-en-scène*; the differing depictions of Sully before and after he takes up his position with the corporation are visible in costume, performance and staging. The apparently apathetic former marine with his despondent slouch and casual 'hoodie' is transformed into a soldier with 'potential' when he takes the job on Pandora. Troubling for disability rights, as it removes any responsibility from society to better accommodate differing abilities, individualism also makes the disability a personal tragedy which must be overcome, and so is tied up with Medical Model ideology.

As the film makes clear, cures need cash, and so it is possible to surmise that even in the scientifically advanced future, there will still be disability and a class structure that will preclude medical 'cures' for the have-nots. *Avatar* not only suggests that individualism is the answer to this problem but that moral worth equates with the willingness to become 'able': 'American individualism is most clearly manifest in the conviction that economic autonomy results from hard work and virtue, while poverty stems from indolence and moral inferiority' (Garland-Thomson 1997: 47). The film suggests that if one can be 'fixed' one *must* desire and pursue that outcome; narrative closure depends on it. The happy ending emphasises the importance of the individual in determining his own future prospects, thereby managing to undermine the role of class, education or fate (see Crothers 2010).

Sully's heroism testifies to American exceptionalism, an ideology bound up with individualism; the American working-class hero is the fair, if uneducated, everyman who brings peace. Sully's innate sense of right and wrong apparently come from his humble beginnings in the US. When he orates to the Na'vi and encourages them to engage in a war to restore their freedom, he espouses the American notions of 'fighting for freedom' and caters 'to the audience's seemingly bottomless thirst for imagining themselves the heroes of world history' (Reider 2011: 49). Re-hashing the rhetoric of the Bush administration, *Avatar*'s Colonel Quarritch channels the American policies of 'shock and awe' and 'pre-emptive strikes' that articulate the national ethos of strong, assertive aggression. American exceptionalism is exposed in the narrative closure, which sees Neytiri's rightful claim to power neutralised by the strong white American male. The 'forces of good' instilled in Sully during his military training, the supposed benevolent intent of US marines, arm him with the characteristics of the perfect American lone hero, saving the world, conquering lands and people; things he apparently could not do in his disabled state. The emphasis on nation and national fitness obviously plays into the metaphor of the body and the metaphor of the marine. If individual citizens are not fit and able, if they do not fit in, then the national body will not be fit (see Davis 1995). In most cinematic versions of American exceptionalism, the US is portrayed as having the good of the world as its primary concern, displaying a generous foreign policy that confirms the US as the leader of the 'free world'.[1]

The Lone Hero and the Frontier

At the beginning of the narrative Sully is a disabled veteran, seemingly no longer an active member of society. There is no suggestion that a return to active duty in the forces is imminent. The death of his identical twin has provided the opportunity to gain employment, replacing him in the avatar programme. He is notably unqualified and in this sense he is an outsider and very much alone. 'Frequently, a disabled body is represented as a metaphor for emotional or spiritual deficiency. Unlike normative filmic bodies that literally advance the plot, the disabled body often exists primarily as a metaphor for a body that is unable to do so' (Chivers and Markotic 2010: 2). In order to advance the plot, Sully must seize the optimising potential on offer and become re-abled, thus driving forward the narrative and simultaneously enacting and celebrating individualism.

As a renegade avatar, he acts against his military and corporate superiors, raging against their colonialist attitudes to the destruction and plunder of Pandora. Lone heroes in this sense act against entire power systems, in a recognisable convention of 'everyman' rejecting the chains that bind him to his social position. In this way the lone hero often has a tenuous relationship with authority; flaunting it when he sees it does not represent the common good. *Avatar*'s 'lone hero' can only enact his hero status as an 'able' avatar; he becomes the cowboy at the frontier once he has thrown off the shackles of his disabled body. In this way his disabled body becomes the surface upon which the story of American individualism is written. The sturdy individualism of the cowboy with his disregard for convention defines a necessarily 'able' hero. Existing by and for himself, he lives at the borders of civilisation where 'unconstrained by civil mores, he is able to restore morality with his six-guns and by doing things no civilized man dare' (Kaulingfreks *et al.* 2009: 152). Cowboys embody a vision of American liberal ideology; seeking the greater good despite a disregard for social conventions, the cowboy works alone to benefit society.

The western as a genre appeals to American individualism simply because the triumph of good over evil justifies liberal politics which depend on self-reliance and independence (see Nichols 2008). The benefits of the cowboy's individual action are shared by the community in a morality tale of self-reliance and duty to the common good. But the West, as the old adage says, is no country for old men; neither, as *Avatar* would have us believe, is it a country for people with disabilities. Crucial to the ideology of American individualism, the frontier fed the fantasy of the good life that every citizen could attain. The western genre enacted a mythical manhood that was built on strength, virility and individualism, a notion of the autonomous individual with the strength to survive and vanquish the indigenous 'savages'. Professional intervention allows Sully to become such a hero; medical model ideologies and the spirit of capitalism in this way fortuitously allow him to be reborn as an able avatar.

In a classically ableist construction Sully is apparently alone, unemployed and unable to find love as a disabled man. In this way disability is portrayed as the symptom of individual attributes; the effect of his impairment. In scene one his apparent indolence and apathetic slouch add to the image of him as despondent and alone, human 'waste' that the military-industrial complex can recoup due to the shared DNA of his dead twin. As an 'able' avatar he finds love and furthermore reinforces traditional gender roles, as Neytiri's rightful claim to power is diffused by her marriage to the American (able) man. Traditional gender roles are thus reestablished by Sully's re-ableing. The frontiers of the uncivilised lands of Pandora provide the arena for the re-abled hero to reassert his manhood. The frontier has traditionally held a romantic attraction in American culture: 'In marrying a native woman, the metaphorical symbol of the landscape, the white male literally marries the frontier, subordinating it to the patriarchal will' (Wherry 2013: 2). In this way, Pandora thus becomes the conquered land and stands as a testament to individualism; the 'he who dares wins' mentality.

Giving Disability 'The Boot'

At the beginning of scene two an extended close up of Colonel Quarritch's boots acts as an establishing shot which alludes to the strict military regime that is goal-driven and highly organised.

The starkness of the shot alludes to the importance of feet and (able) bodies in the narrative as well as providing a contrast with Sully's feet. Focusing

Fig. 1: Quarritch enters discussing the strict military regime.

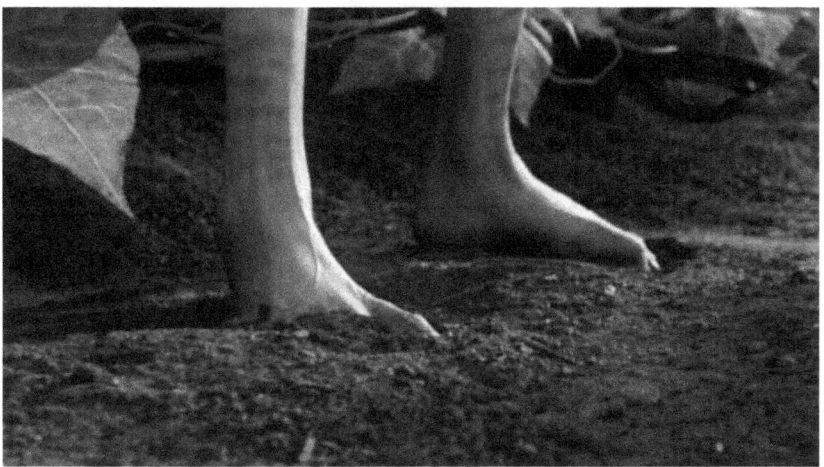

Fig. 2: Sully's avatar feet caress the earth on Pandora for the first time.

on a body feature to define the characteristics of a character inevitably invokes cultural or ideological notions about such body parts and their efficacy. Quarritch promises to help Sully 'get his legs back', a prospect so far denied to him because of financial constraints. This is Sully's motivation, a plan that will require a return journey to another planet and take six years of cryo sleep each way. Accepting such a deal reveals not only that Sully had nothing of importance to do on Earth, but those twelve years of sleep is a fair price to pay for 'new legs'.

Sully's new feet are at the forefront of the shot when he awakens as an avatar for the first time. Now an 'able' avatar, he enacts a thrilled fascination with his feet, which become the symbol of his new mobility. Shunning the cautions of the lab workers, he escapes outside, joyously running through the lush open spaces of Pandora. Sully's new feet, the symbol of the 'able' body, enact both celebration and spectacle. The shot of the new feet caressing the brown earth alludes to the new-found mastery of the body.

The 'working' feet, a source of excessive sensation, articulate the worth of the new body. The editing of the shots, which draws attention to specific body parts, is thus complicit in a judgement, as the sub-division of the body into a set of discontinuous functions speaks to a 'fetishistic fragmentation of the embodied person' (Shildrick 1997: 53). This fragmentation allows the (able) feet to become a motif of the narrative, their blue fleshiness a panacea to the Earthly ills that have apparently caused, among other ills, the 'problem' of disability. In this very Foucauldian sense, the body is the canvas upon which history is written; molded by regimes of power. The singularity of the ineffective (disabled) feet divorces Sully from the shared identity of American-ness; the disability cannot be accommodated by American individualism and so it must be left behind.

Science and the Duty of 'Cure'

Sully is objectified by scrutiny and intervention, subjected to normalising judgement which constitutes impairment as a deficit; as such he occupies an in-valid social position. As is the tradition of Hollywood disability films, 'capitalism is introduced as a system that facilitates the successful re-integration of the characters into society' (Fore 2011: 5). Seizing the opportunities that biotechnology offers thus becomes Sully's American duty.

It is indisputable that new technologies are radicalising social life while also mediating personhood. Biotechnological advances now propose individualised 'solutions' and proclaim disability 'as a designation for the non-(re)constructed bodies of the Old World' (Kumari Campbell 2009: 45). *Avatar* glorifies the solutions that biotechnology offers through the marriage of individualism with the transformative potential offered to Sully. To 'get his legs back' he must seize the opportunity to transform; the return to normalcy thus depends on his own actions. Furthermore, when Sully becomes an able Na'vi, he joins a tribe connected to one another, plugged-in to a healing force which enables each of them to upload information from each other and from a central source; a simple metaphor for the power of technology to reboot and re-enable broken bodies. The need to plug-in suggests that one must get 'fixed' to be part of the community.

Sully's avatar bears only a trace of the disabled human; deeply encoded in the avatar's performativity are the longing to be 'able' while enacting the uncertain borders between human and unhuman. Modern audiences, sold on the notion that everything is fixable, are lulled into this vision of the repairable body. Through such narratives, biotechnology may be seen as the servant of American individualism; the body is a site at which new technologies radicalise opportunities, making the spoils of mythic America open to self-service. The price is scrutiny; surveillance is internalised in the disabled body as 'cure' is provided, functionality is restored as internal privacy is lost. Disabled bodies are thus seen as matter that biotechnology can recoup.

The film is morally unambiguous; Sully must optimise to repair the difficulties in his own micro world and consequently in the macro world of the earth/Pandora struggle. Hostile forces can only be brought to heel by the enactment of individualism which inculcates intervention and control;

the normalising judgement of professional opinion and supposedly rational intervention. In this way, the individualist position incurs professional interference at the most intimate level, drawing the professional into the body and the mind of the disabled character, quantifying, measuring and logging both physical and mental activity while the disabled subject is sealed in his sarcophogeal control booth.

Avatar's vision of the future is replete with modulations of the body. The intersection of physiology and technology result in a quintessential postmodern fantasy of instantaneous transmission, a radicalisation of mind and matter and of organic and mechanical. This raises questions about how we see the future of disability and its representation, how we align our hopes for a medically and scientifically advanced future with the reality of imperfect bodies. In the dystopian future of *Avatar*, the disabled body is viewed as waste that a military industrial complex can recoup. Sully is given the ability to acquire a prosthetic alien-soldier body not as compensation for his disability but in spite of it; his genomic capital as the twin of his dead scientist brother makes him the only possible match for the cloned body, a technology far more expensive than his own 'defective' body. This disturbing disruption of bodily integrity and mental privacy upsets the concept of personal identity but also commodifies the human body. In this case, a disabled one is 'colonised' by the military corporation, becoming 'whole' through its surrender to the colonising forces. The transcendent qualities of CGI and biotechnology here pose a troubling solution to the delicate human organism. The film's vision of the future as enveloped in genetic fundamentalism is thus a frightening development of the current fascination with genomic capital. This fetishising of DNA has a dangerous consequence for disability; it suggests that 'defective' genes that lead to an impairment may be screened out, leading to a dehumanisation of the individual where he or she is reduced to a quantifiable set of molecules.

Avatar's alien culture features an alternative ecological-economic model; a symbiotic network where peripherals such as plants and animals can interface with each other. In Pandora, the natural world is considered as a single living organism, as opposed to the capitalist agenda of Earth, with the competing interests of individuals and corporations. The collapse of boundaries between abled and disabled, human and machine is representative of film's move towards a Baudrillardian postmodern uncertainty; due to the competitive individualist logic and paternalistic ethos of biotechnology and its conspicuous largesse. Biotechnology's ability to reconstitute normality is thus a heavily loaded anthropophagic strategy.

The Politics of the Body

When we consider the body which occupies Hollywood film, we consider a deeply politicised space, as film bodies enact difference or docility. Contemporary Hollywood films trade on the post-eugenic fashion of extreme efforts to fix people with disabilities, in this way alleviating the need for society to be more inclusive (see Snyder and Mitchell 2010). That the body is a site of power is not a new notion, but contemporary Hollywood film enacts a new representation of subjectivity that is open to manipulation at the material and somatic level. The bodies of film now transform and transcend; social control is achieved through them in internal surveillance. The massive success of the science fiction genre and its use of surveillance and control of bodies illustrates that such subject matter captivates the social imaginary. Surveillance, once the gloomy Orwellian nightmare of the future, is now omnipresent in our filmic visions of the future (see Flynn 2015). In our cultural imaginings, and consequently in film, bodies are now 'open' to intervention and at this nexus individualism creates a duty. The twenty-first century has brought a multiplicity of life-optimising technologies: 'These new forms of life, these new ideas of what kind of persons we are and could or should become, are emerging at the multiple intersections between the imperatives of the market and the drive for shareholder value, the new imaginations of the body and its processes'; the new imaginations of the body 'must be understood as hybrid assemblages oriented towards the goal of optimisation' (Rose 2007: 105, 17).

Hollywood films of this century enact these new imaginations of the body, as they depict its need of biotechnical intervention, its transformation and its transcendence of the human/machine boundary. This is played out most spectacularly in films like *Avatar* which place 'life' somewhere at the boundary of human/machine, reducing life to a series of codes.

> Biology is now inextricably linked with information technology and has become in its own right a science of information. It is not interested in man, but rather in his elementary components, apparently without concern for the negative consequences of this conception of the human, given that it dissolves the subject, and perhaps even the human condition itself. (Le Breton 2004: 2)

Life is now seen as a sum of information; reducible to numbers, our humanity is calculable, alterable and reducible. This century's vision of life is data; images of coding sequences and DNA form the contemporary view of life itself, privileging the order and sequence of the imagined pattern of 'life'. Scenes of computerised diagnostics and highly complex gene sequencing feature in Hollywood's science fiction narratives (*Source Code*, 2011; *Elysium*, 2013; *Transcendence*, 2014), as well as contemporary crime dramas where 'proof' is envisaged at the molecular level, such as the 'scientific' close-ups of the *C.S.I.* television franchise. This view of 'molecular' life also opens up the human to scrutiny; 'flaws' become disjunctures where intervention is necessitated and ontology becomes mediated.

As can be seen in *Avatar* the enactment of individualism and of 'good citizenship' thus incurs a vision of oneself as eminently malleable at the molecular level. 'Thus we can see that in advanced liberal democracies, where individuals are enjoined to think of themselves as actively shaping their life course through acts of choice in the name of a better future, "biology" will not easily be accepted as fate or responded to with impotence' (Rose 2007: 26). Hollywood films reject the state of 'disabled', instead instilling a duty in the disabled character to individualise, thus enacting a biopower which places the onus on the individual to garner biomedical/techno scientific assistance. Genomic sequences are now seen to transcend life itself (*Transcendence*) while life is made 'manageable' by pharmaceuticals (*Love and Other Drugs*, 2011; *Dallas Buyers Club*, 2013). Family medical histories and genealogies become open to expert opinion and adjustment as though 'good parenting' depends on preventing the birth of a 'defective' child (*Gattaca*, 1989). Finding cures for disabled or ill children becomes the duty of the parent (*Elysium*). Individualised solutions to diegetic crises dull the responsibility of society and incur medicalising discourses.

Avatar is intimately concerned with the molecular; Sully qualifies for the job on Pandora only through the shared DNA of the dead twin. The film fantasises 'geneticism': the allure of the imagined power of the gene. Sully's project of 'getting his real legs back' (one can imagine that these will be somehow scientifically created), incurs the necessity to submit to the hyper intrusive process of transformation. This vision of genetics in the film is implicated in the salvation of humanity.

> It involves a radical identification of evil in biological terms, along with a ruthless drive to eliminate it, not by social or political means but by employing an array of genetic tests and suitable means of biological engineering. This uncompromising vision of genetics is one expression of a powerful imaginary current that runs through our contemporary societies. (Le Breton 2004: 4)

The genetic potential of the film colludes in the creation of Sully's disability as abject. Sully's diegetic imperative is to acquiesce to the transformation potential of science; firstly into an avatar and then in the plan of getting back to earth and retrieve his 'real legs'. The individualised solution to Sully's disability is the commitment to the programme which transforms him into an avatar and hence eventually transforming back into his 'able' self.

Individualism beyond the Diegesis

As this discussion has shown, *Avatar* places an individualist duty on the disabled character to 'better' his prospects, in line with American ideology. Beyond this diegesis, the 3D spectacle and 'performance capture' technology produce a kinetic aesthetic that draws audiences into a peculiar 'gaming' subjectivity, further inculcating individualism. Drawn individually into the cinematic experience, the spectator is now swallowed up by the digital world and must identify with the (dis)abled protagonist, existing vicariously through him because, as in the gaming ethos, we want the character to win; virtual digital bodies exceed their limitations and are encouraged to do so. Hollywood's 3D technology thus facilitates the spectator's longing to live through an avatar as a heightened active self: 'The aspiration to reach the most controllable cinematic image is motivated by the desire to enhance the virtual heroic action-body performance in order to dramatize the progress, failure, and success of its journey towards mastery through a spectacle of physical endurance and control' (Cohen 2014: 57).

The technological novelty engages the cinematic scopic gaze, forces the spectator to look at the digitally enhanced character as a single character removed from the social system in which he exists. This suits the normative regime of American individualism; the sensory impact and spectacle are heightened and the spectator is drawn to the individual's action, rather than any social or cultural context. Society is conveniently discharged from any responsibility and the heroic able body is produced as solution. In this way, 'the display of heroic physicality by the iconic body provides a vision of an empowered human functioning at the extremes' (Cohen 2014: 58). *Avatar's* 3D technology thus privileges physical supremacy and within the narrative of purportedly positive transformation, the disabled body is expelled from the diegesis in favour of the digital body.

The CG bodies of the (able) Na'vi move fluidly through the digitally created landscape enacting a freedom from the constraints of the human body. Although digitised, the Na'vi enacts spectacular corporeality in contrast to the relative stasis of the humans. Audience sympathy is thus invested in these supremely able bodies. Cameron's use of the avatar as a device central to the story eases and facilitates the transfer of audience sympathy toward the CG body. This identification causes the (normative) audience to empathise with Sully's motivation.

Almost every culture sees disability as a problem in need of a solution (see Mitchell 2002: 15). American film, however, utilises disability as a crux to drive forward a normalising and optimising logic, incurring the American notion of individualism to inspire people with disabilities to fix themselves. In a screen age where military misadventures create disabilities, disability is seen as the challenge that the individual must overcome. Biotechnology fortuitously offers the pacifying lure of repair and reboot. Such narratives heighten mainstream culture's discomfort with disability, providing sanitised, simplistic models of its eradication.

America's cultural ambivalence toward people with disabilities, visible in popular film, can be seen as a symptom of the aggressive logic of a capitalist nation. The ubiquitous American body, depicted as a site of cultural, ideological and financial investment, chooses transmutation over disability, is subjugated and is remade in the name of the land of opportunity. This chapter has proposed that American individualism is manifest in the depictions of disability as a personal obstacle, one which may be overcome by the biotech solutions on offer in this new millennium. Failing to interrogate disability as a social issue, *Avatar* places disability in an isolated body, an individual psyche. The complexities and intersections with society and culture go unexamined in this fiction of repair and re-boot.

NOTE

1   'The concept of a benevolent US foreign policy emerges from the widespread historical belief in 'American exceptionalism', which describes the belief that the US is an extraordinary nation with a special role to play in human history; that is, America is not only unique but also superior among nations' (Alford 2010: 21).

FILMOGRAPHY

Blomkamp, Neill (dir) (2013) *Elysium*. 109 minutes. TriStar Pictures/Media Rights Capital. USA.

Cameron, James (dir) (2009) *Avatar*. 162 minutes. Twentieth Century Fox Film Corporation/Dune Entertainment. USA.

Jones, Duncan (dir) (2011) *Source Code*. 93 minutes. Vendome Pictures/Mark Gordon Company. USA.

Niccol, Andrew (dir) (1997) *Gattacca*. 106 minutes. Columbia Pictures/Jersey Films. USA.

Pfister, Wally (dir) (2014) *Transcendence*. 119 minutes. Alcon Entertainment/Straight Up Films. USA.

Vallée, Jean-Marc (dir) (2013) *Dallas Buyers Club*. 117 minutes. Truth Entertainment/Voltage Pictures. USA.

Zwick, Edward (dir) (2010) *Love and Other Drugs*. 112 minutes. Fox 2000/Regency Enterprises. USA.

BIBLIOGRAPHY

Alford, Matthew (2010) *Reel Power: Hollywood Cinema and American Supremacy*. London: Pluto Press.

Bennett, Bruce (2013) 'The Normality of 3D: Cinematic Journeys, "Imperial Visuality" and Unchained Cameras', *Jump Cut: A Review of Contemporary Media*, 55. Available at http://ejumpcut.org/archive/jc55.2013/Bennett-3D/index.html (accessed 4 April 2015).

Chivers, Sally and Nicole Markotic (eds) (2010) *The Problem Body: Projecting Disability on Film*. Columbus, OH: Ohio State University Press.

Clark, Christopher (2006) 'Industry and Technology', in Howard Temperley and Christopher Bigsby (eds) *A New Introduction to American Studies*. New York, NY: Routledge, 198–219.

Cohen, Orit Fussfeld (2014) 'The New Language of the Digital Film', *Journal of Popular Film and Television*, 42, 1, 47–58.

Crothers, Lane (2010) *Globalization and American Popular Culture*, 2nd ed. Lanham, MD: Rowman & Littlefield.

Davis, Lennard J. (1995) *Enforcing Normalcy: Disability, Deafness, and the Body*. New York, NY: Verso.

Flynn, Susan (2015) 'New Poetics of the Film Body: Docility, Molecular Fundamentalism and Twenty First Century Destiny', *ABC: American, British and Canadian Studies Journal*, 24, 5–23.

Fore, Dana (2011) 'The Tracks of Sully's Tears: Disability in James Cameron's *Avatar*', *Jump Cut: A Review of Contemporary Media*, 53. Available at http://www.ejumpcut.org/archive/jc53.2011/foreAvatar/text.html (accessed on 20 March 2015).

Garland-Thomson, Rosemarie (1997) *Extraordinary Bodies Figuring Physical Disability in American Culture and Literature*. New York, NY: Columbia University Press.

Gerbner, George (2000) 'Mass Media Discourse: Message System Analysis as a Component of Cultural Indicators', in John Hartley and Roberta E. Pearson (eds) *American Cultural Studies: A Reader*. Oxford: Oxford University Press, 141–51.

Gilens, Martin (2009) *Why Americans Hate Welfare: Race, Media and the Politics of Antipoverty Policy*. Chicago, IL: University of Chicago Press.

Greene, T. William (2008) 'Three Ideologies of Individualism: Toward Assimilating a Theory of Individualisms and their Consequences', *Critical Sociology*, 34, 1, 117–37.

Kaulingfreks, Ruud, Geoff Lightfoot and Hugo Letiche (2009) 'The Man in the Black Hat', *Culture and Organization*, 15, 2, 151–65.

Kolker, Robert Phillip (1988) A *Cinema of Loneliness*. Oxford: Oxford University Press.

Kumari Campbell, Fiona (2009) *Contours of Ableism*. London: Palgrave Macmillan.

Le Breton, David (2004) 'Genetic Fundamentalism or the Cult of the Gene', *Body & Society*, 10, 4, 1–20.

Lukes, Steven (1971) 'The Meanings of Individualism', *Journal of the History of Ideas*, 32, 1, 45–66.

Marx, Karl and Frederick Engels (1978) *The Marx-Engels Reader*, 2nd ed., ed. Robert C. Tucker. New York, NY: W. W. Norton.

Mitchell, David T. (2002) 'Narrative Prosthesis and the Materiality of Metaphor', in Snyder, Sharon L, Bruegermann, Brenda J. and Garland-Thomson, Rosemarie (eds.) *Disability Studies: Enabling the Humanities*. New York: Modern Language Association, 15–30.

____ (2014) 'Gay Pasts and Disability Future Tenses', *Journal of Literary and Cultural Disability Studies*, 8, 1, 1–16.

Nichols, Mary P. (2008) 'Revisiting Heroism and Community in Contemporary Westerns', *Perspectives on Political Science*, 37, 4, 207–15.

Oliver, Mike (1990) *The Politics of Disablement*. London: Macmillan.

Reider, John (2011) 'Race and Revenge Fantasies in *Avatar*, *District 9* and *Inglorious Basterds*', *Science Fiction Film and Television*, 4, 1, 41–56.

Rose, Nikolas (2007) *The Politics of Life Itself*. Princeton, NJ: Princeton University Press.

Shildrick, Margrit (1997) *Leaky Bodies and Boundaries: Feminism, Postmodernism, and (Bio)ethics*. London: Routledge.

Snyder, Sharon L. and David T. Mitchell (2006) *Cultural Locations of Disability*. Chicago, IL: University of Chicago Press.

____ (2010) 'Body Genres', in Sally Chivers and Nicole Markotic (eds) *The Problem Body: Projecting Disability on Film*. Columbus, OH: Ohio State University Press, 178–204.

Wherry, Maryan (2013) 'Introduction: Love and Romance in American Culture', *The Journal of American Culture*, 36, 1, 1–5.

White, Julie A. and Joan C. Tronto (2004) 'Political Practices of Care: Needs and Rights', *Ratio Juris*, 17, 4, 425–53.

Through the Disability Lens

Revisiting Ousmane Sembène's *Xala* (1975) and *Camp de Thiaroye* (1988)

Ken Junior Lipenga

Film scholar Manthia Diawara observes that one of the main trends in African filmmaking has been the recovery of various chapters of the continent's history. In this fashion, African filmmakers have set on a journey of reclamation, re-presenting parts of the continent's history with fresh perspectives. For most parts of the continent, this past is of the colonial encounter, and is therefore a source of bitterness, particularly due to the fact that this is a period whose records mostly exist in the form of archives created by the former colonisers. African filmmaking therefore has the potential to provide a counter-narrative to these often skewed versions of history. Diawara observes that many inhabitants of the continent view these films 'with a sense of pride and satisfaction with a history finally written from an African point of view' (1992: 152). Through the film medium, African filmmakers are able to revisit parts of their continent's history that had previously been misrepresented or otherwise ignored.

Ousmane Sembène is one of the filmmakers whose output over the years has mainly been geared towards portraying various parts of African life that may not get the attention of Hollywood productions. In one interview, he expresses his hope that 'young filmmakers assume their social responsibilities, that they become the voices of their peoples, of their time' (in Niang *et al.* 1995: 177). I read this advice as being inclusive of the filmmaker's responsibility for articulating the voice of those who are often unheard in their societies, including the oppressed or marginalised, the poor and the disabled. Sembène has done it with Pays in *Camp de Thiaroye* (*The Camp at Thiaroye*, 1988). Djibril Diop Mambéty has also done the same with the young Sili Laam in *La petite vendeuse de soileil* (*The Little Girl Who Sold the Sun*, 1999).

This chapter examines Sembène's *Xala* (1975) and *Camp de Thiaroye*, focusing on the disabled figure in these films. *Xala* was first released as a film, followed by the novel in 1976. The plot of the two forms is similar to a large extent, with a few minor differences in that the novel features much more detailed characterisation – and a greater range of extra characters – than the film. As a result, although the main focus of this chapter is the film, I also include from the novel a few passages that emphasise points omitted in the film version. In *Xala*, the filmmaker employs the trope of disability as a tool for critiquing the neo-colonialist African leadership, whereas in *Camp de Thiaroye*, the disabled character presented is the sole individual whose perception of reality is clearer than that of his colleagues. A comparative study of the two films reveals Sembène's portrayal of disability as at once a complex human experience, marked (and at times defined) by intersections with various historical and cultural phenomena – but also as a human experience that affords a novel reading of humanity on the continent.

The Disabled Body in African Film

From Martin F. Norden's *The Cinema of Isolation: A History of Disability in the Movies* (1994) to the most recent edition of the *Disability Studies Reader* (2013), one would observe that scholars in the field hardly acknowledge that there is a huge output of African films that also serves as a platform for the representation of disability. The focus has been almost entirely on Hollywood as the source of filmmaking that deserves scholarly attention. This unfortunate neglect of non-Hollywood productions coincidentally mirrors the observation made by Chris Bell, who in his Swiftian satirical piece, points out that disability studies tends to focus on a limited field of works, which, through the attention by scholars in the field, are quickly forming into what might very well become a disability studies canon; the field 'by and large focuses on the work of white individuals and is itself largely produced by a corps of white scholars and activists' (2006: 275). These are the texts that to be found in various syllabi, programmes and readers of disability studies.

I would argue for the necessity of shifting the lens of disability studies towards African film because as a literary medium, cinema has the potential to do two things. Firstly, the filmic medium presents an opportunity to appreciate attitudes towards disability in various African communities, as they are reflected through the filmmaker's vision. Patrick Devlieger argues that the ways in which various disabilities are understood in Africa is often surprising to scholars in the west, who often mistakenly assume a similarity in experiences of disability at a global level. He argues that in most African societies, disability is more of an 'embedded concept', to be understood not as being an individual experience, but rather one associated with the natural order, the social order and the cosmological order (2006: 695). In this regard, the causes of disability are often traced to relationships with 'cosmologies and social worlds' (Devlieger 1995: 104). This is a helpful way of thinking about the diversity of conceptions of disablement, and I will therefore return to it in the course of the discussion.

The second reason for this proposed shift in focus is that the work of some of these filmmakers challenges predominant misconceptions and stereotypes about disability. The close of the last decade saw the publication of two special issue journals that hint towards this shift. In 2007, there was a special issue of *Wagadu*, devoted to 'Intersecting Gender and Disability Perspectives in Rethinking Postcolonial identities'. The other publication is the special issue of the *Journal of Literary and Cultural Disability Studies* (2010), which carried a number of articles and reviews devoted to exploring, among other things, the representation of disability in postcolonial spaces. These two journals mark a shift from a fixation on Western-produced texts, an indication of the realisation that the representation of disability is not limited to the Global North alone. This is a worthwhile endeavour, although there still remains a relative dearth on the analysis of filmic representation. Through theme, characterisation and style, African filmmakers have challenged the perpetuation of negative stereotypes that is often to be found in traditional forms, and have instead propagated a more contemporary vision that recognises the worth of the disabled individual as a person. The more recent the films, the more obvious this observation is, as is seen in films such as Raman Suleman's *Zulu Love Letter* (2004) and Mahamat-Saleh Haroun's *GriGris* (2013).

There are a number of African films that have employed disabled characters as a way of advancing the social mission of the directors. In her study, Jori de Coster makes this observation – focusing on semiotics – with respect to five films, including *Xala, Wend Kuuni* (*God's Gift*, 1982), *Gombele* (1994), *Keita* (1995), *La Petite Vendeuse de Soleil* (1998) and *Khorma (la betise)* (*Khorma: Stupidity*, 2002). These five films merely represent the tip of the iceberg. There are yet many more which continue to highlight the links of disablement to the cosmic realm.[1]

Xala: Impotence and the Disabled Body

Sembène's *Xala* traces the plight of El Hadji Abdou Kader Beye, who is struck by the *xala* moments after marrying his third wife. It traces his downfall as he seeks a cure for the affliction of sexual impotence. For most critics, this downfall mirrors the failure of African leadership, which has been characterised by corruption, nepotism and greed. The world of *Xala*'s Dakar is therefore a microcosmic representation of the plight of many African countries at the dawn of independence.

Xala has gained its place in the canon of African literature and film not only due to its style and language, but also importantly for its treatment of a theme that had currency at the time of its release, when many countries had gained independence, and a few were just beginning to experience the disillusionment from their dreams of a better world. This issue has often been highlighted and has become so commonplace in the continent that it can hardly be commented on anymore. Fortunately a revisitation of the film in the light of emerging concerns such as the representation of disability brings to light new reasons for retaining it in the canon. The film is among the earliest representations of disability on the African continent, and this alone, in my opinion, merits a re-examination of the narrative.

My reading of *Xala* focuses on two levels of disablement. The first is El Hadji's impotence, for which he becomes reviled by his family and colleagues. The second level of disablement is one which only has presence later in the film. This is the disablement that is shown in a group of beggars who hang around the city, and who are later presented as El Hadji's direct antagonists and potential saviours. These are othered figures that are nevertheless empowered by the filmmaker.

Impotence is not a condition that is normally associated with disability. In most cases, it is regarded as a condition that can be remedied with various over-the-counter drugs and exercise regimens. In *Xala*, however, we can read it as a disability due to the way it affects El Hadji's existence in the social environment. The social model of disability lays emphasis on the life of the individual within their society. Its very definition of disability has to do with the quality of life of the individual within this social environment. Due to his bodily condition, El Hadji finds himself othered in various ways in his community.

Various scholars have already identified the symbolic function of disability in Sembène's works, including *Xala*. El Hadji's impotence is often said to represent the impotence of the bourgeoisie who take over power from the colonials (see Gugler and Diop 1998: 147; Harrow 2004: 129; Mushengyezi 2004: 51). However, through an overlapping of disability with other concerns, bodily difference takes on additional significance that enables the reader/viewer to appreciate how commonly held attitudes about disability give birth to other beliefs that affect our appreciation of the humanity of others. This chapter considers the supernatural dimensions implied in the film, in connection with disability. Within Africa, the evidence of disability as an embedded concept comes from its connection to the social order through 'links between social behaviour and misfortune, e.g. through sorcery and witchcraft systems of belief, and marriage regulations' (Devlieger 2006: 695). In the film, impotence is seen as a disability that is passed on in the form of a curse. This immediately links it to the supernatural order.

The film begins with the celebration of El Hadji's third marriage. He is a successful businessman, a husband of two (soon to become three) wives, a father of a brood of children and an African who had played a key role in the ousting of the colonisers. These multiple roles serve to emphasise his position as an able-bodied individual in both the personal and social sense, which are important in this particular community. His children attest to his physical and sexual well-being. His generosity towards his wives and friends emphasises his role as a social benefactor. And although it appears to be at face value, his taking on of a third wife illustrates his position as a devout Muslim.

The first indication of the connection of the *xala* to the supernatural world appears in attempts to avoid it. On the wedding night, El Hadji is advised to undergo the traditional ritual of sitting on a mortar, with a pestle between his legs, a process which is meant to ensure his virility. This ritual must be understood as one of many that are usually meant to ward off malignant forces that might bring about undesirable bodily conditions. In this case, El Hadji is being encouraged to undergo a ritual that would ensure that he is not 'disabled' in the one part of his body that is deemed most crucial on his wedding night. Disability in this case then, is something that is partially defined by drawing on a Butlerian performative function. He must *act* in a particular way in order to prove his able-bodied stature. Incidentally, El Hadji is a man who regards himself as being civilised. As a result, he refuses to take part in the ritual, spurning it as a 'ridiculous belief'. Describing this moment in the novel, Sembène writes that El Hadji 'was sufficiently Westernized not to have any faith in all this superstition' (1976: 20). The fact that he fails to achieve an erection soon afterward links – in the mind of the viewer – the two events. His failure to abide by traditional practice, which is linked to a long respected and observed social etiquette, is thus linked to the 'malfunctioning' of his body.

This association of the disability with supernatural powers gains more credence as various characters muse on the possible causes of the *xala*. The new wife's aunt is the first to suggest that El Hadji could have been cursed by one of his older wives, jealous at his latest marriage. In a society that believes in witchcraft, such a possibility is not farfetched.

With these suspicions that the cause of the disablement is rooted in the supernatural, the next logical step is to seek countermeasures within the same realm. Modern disability studies does not promote the idea of 'curing' disabilities. Instead, the dominant rhetoric encourages addressing societies to take into account bodily differences and ensure access to various spaces that are available to other citizens. In many African communities, on the other hand, the rhetoric of cure is common. And the authorities in this field are the *n'gangas, marabouts, sangomas* and various other healers, most of whom profess a connection to a world beyond the earthly one. It is from this world that they derive powers with which they can reverse various human ailments and conditions. In the film, El Hadji consults a number of such healers, the first being one who divines with the help of cowrie shells.[2] This healer prescribes 'holy water' with which to bathe, a beadstring to wear around the waist, and an enchanted band to wear on the wrist. This prescription does not work, unsurprisingly, mostly because El Hadji's new wife reacts in horror at the sight of her husband crawling towards her thus accoutred, an amulet firmly held between his teeth. The second marabout visited in the film is Serigne Mada. Again this description of the marabout as a holy person indicates the connection of disablement to the supernatural world. The possibility that the *xala* may be a psychological phenomenon is not entertained. Instead, the belief is that it is a condition which requires some form of divine intervention.

In considering the portrayal of disability in *Xala*, we must also turn to the beggars, most of whom have physical disabilities. These are a group of characters who are referred to as 'human rubbish' by El Hadji and as 'undesirables' by the police at the end of the film. The President of the Chamber of Commerce regards them as being 'bad for tourism'. Sembène's portrayal of these characters serves two functions. On the one hand, through them, he criticises the polarisation of modern society based on class and bodily appearance. In this regard, the beggars are closest in ideology and practice to Sembène himself, playing the role of 'choric commentators or … surrogates for the filmmaker' (Landy 1984: 42). They are means by which he conveys a critique not only of the postcolonial state, but also of ableist attitudes. On the other hand, Sembène unwittingly entrenches an association of disablement with villainy, since all suggestions point to the fact that the disabled person cursed El Hadji with the *xala*. This is where the portrayal of disability in the film coincidentally mirrors that of some earlier Hollywood films, in presenting the disabled character as having a link to dark, supernatural forces.

In *Enforcing Normalcy*, Lennard J. Davis observes that in most societies, the 'able body is the body of a citizen' whereas 'deformed, deafened, amputated, obese, female, perverse, crippled, maimed, blinded bodies do not make up the body politic' (1995: 71). Regarding the ways in which anomalous bodies are removed from the public space in *Xala*, sometimes violently, Davis's argument indeed rings true. In this society, citizenship is marked by ability, and the police are there to guard against incursion into these ableist spaces. The image of the beggars in procession towards El Hadji's home at the end of the film is therefore a powerfully projected challenge to this idea of citizenship. Within the public space, the disabled are deemed as not belonging, as misfits, confirming Rosemarie Garland-Thomson's argument that 'to misfit in the public sphere is to be denied full citizenship' (2011: 601).

Sembène's empowering of the disabled beggars occurs in tandem with their acquiring of greater and more forceful narrative presence. After they are deported from the city (at El Hadji's behest), they make the long trek back to Dakar. This is one of the most moving scenes in the film, especially since it shows socio-economic differences by being in contrast with the opulence displayed in both the motorcade of the members of the Chamber of Commerce and the one that is part of El Hadji's wedding procession (see Lindfors 1997: 69). The scene is additionally significant because it is one of those moments when the camera does not focus on El Hadji or anyone directly connected to him. It is also a scene only present in the film version of the narrative (see Gugler and Diop 1998: 150). Their return to the city is a long, drawn out series of shots where Sembène again permits the viewer to stare unreservedly at the disabled figures as they crest sand dunes, assisting each other, until they once again return to the city. This is one moment when an advantage of the film mode over the textual mode becomes evident – as Vartan Messier observes: 'the visceral aesthetics of the film utilises the affective power of images to produce a lasting impression that transcends the immediacy of the represented historical context' (2011: 2). Their return to the public spheres of the city mirrors their insertion into the visual field by Sembène, and significantly, their attaining of a vital level of primacy in the narrative. Just as the population of Dakar has to acknowledge the humanity of these characters, the viewer too is made to realise their presence and see their lives and social presence as significant.

Finally, we have to look to the figure of the beggar as one who confirms the supernatural nature of disablement in the film. At the end of the film, the leader of the beggars, Gorgui, reveals himself as the cause of the *xala*. He claims to have inflicted it on El Hadji, and consequently has the power to reverse it. This is a claim he makes after he leads his colleagues in a rather memorably dramatic entry into El Hadji's home:

> Leading the way, [Gorgui] pushed open the door, followed by his retinue [...]. A legless cripple, his palms and knees covered with black soil from the garden, printed a black trail on the floor like a giant snail. Another with a maggoty face and a hole where his nose had been, his deformed, scarred body visible through his rags, grabbed a white shirt and putting it on admired himself in a mirror, roaring with laughter at the reflection of his antics. A woman with twins, emboldened by the others, tore open a cushion on the settee and wrapped one of her babies in the material. On the other cushion she rested a foot with a cloven heel and stunted toes. (1976: 108)

This claim, and the consequent belief, by most of the cast, confirms the supernatural element. According to Thomas Lynn, 'if the beggar does impose the *xala* on El Hadji, he possesses a trait typically associated with folkloric and mythic tricksters, a trait that some other contemporary literary tricksters possess: magical power' (2003: 186). The manifestation of such power takes place in the equally memorable scene where the disabled beggars spit on El Hadji as a way of curing him of the *xala*. This moment is identified as one of 'ritual cleansing' (see Pfaff 1982; Gugler and Diop 1998: 151). More significantly, it indicates a Bakhtinian inversion of authority, an unsettling of socially constructed difference, when 'Sembène reminds the viewer of the fact that the modern and traditional, power and vulnerability, rich and poor, are intricately intertwined' (Devlieger and de Coster 2009: 160). As a gesture with 'spiritual, moral and physical regenerative function – a rite of passage from one state of being to another' (Pfaff 1982: n.p.), the saliva 'bathing' can be interpreted as a type of christening or initiation, establishing an inescapable link between him and them.

There is an obvious problem with the characterisation of the beggars as the source of the disablement here. Sembène is in a way promoting the association of physical disability with villainy and/or supernatural power. In *Camp de Thiaroye*, on the other hand, his portrayal of disability takes on a different level of significance, mostly due to the intertwining of disability and racism.

Camp de Thiaroye: Disability as Special Insight

Ato Quayson's book, *Aesthetic Nervousness* (2007), always brings to mind Vladimir Propp's attempt to establish a classification which would reflect the rules on which Russian fairy tales were constructed. Similarly, Quayson devises a 'thematic typology of the numerous representations of disability, both physical and otherwise, that obtain in literature' (2007: 36). He observes that one of the most common images of disabled characters is of them 'as bearers of superior insight … disability as inarticulable and enigmatic tragic insight' (2007: 49). The association of disability with special insight or vision is to be found in various other societies. What is fresh in Quayson's analysis is the recognition of the failure to articulate such insight. This is an observation that rings true with the portrayal of Pays in Sembène's *Camp de Thiaroye*.

In a similar fashion to *Xala*, *Camp de Thiaroye* is a film that has had appeal mainly as a postcolonial text. It is based on an episode of colonial history, depicting the French massacre of African soldiers – *les tirailleurs sénégalais* – during their stay at a demobilisation camp in Senegal on their return from fighting for and with the French in World War II. Sembène's primary aim in the film is to bring to light a part of history previously kept hidden from the world – 'to make sure people knew [his] history right' (Gadjigo 2010: 68). The film unveils the racism that characterised French colonial policy. In *Camp de Thiaroye*, this racism is seen in the conversations of most of the French soldiers, in the unjust payment of the African soldiers' wages, in the contemptuous treatment of the *tirailleurs* and ultimately in the decision by French authorities to shell the camp.

Pays is not necessarily the central character in the film. However, his presence and experiences make him a focaliser for various threads of discrimination witnessed in the film, including the implied violence that the soldiers have experienced in the war, and the racist violence that they endure. In spite of being labelled the mad man, 'his derangement, however agonizing to him, has locked onto the truth in a way that not one of the other African protagonists [in the film] has succeeded in doing' (Downing 1996: 210). This is why Quayson's notion of disability as tragic insight is extremely relevant. Pays is privy to a truth that he only shares with the viewer, thus deepening the emotional tie constructed with this particular character.

What makes the portrayal of this character even more tragic are the ableist attitudes expressed by Pays' colleagues. In their presence, Pays finds filial acceptance, reflecting the argument that in colonial societies, 'the need to objectify and distance the "Other" in the form of the madman or the leper, was less urgent in a situation in which every colonial person was in some sense, already "Other"' (Vaughan 1991: 10). In spite of their acceptance of him as one of their own, the other soldiers nevertheless speak of Pays as a 'cracked' individual, referring to his mental instability. This shows that their acceptance of him is tainted by an ableist mentality, and this attitude disables him more than anything else. All these soldiers have experienced violence on the battlefield. Pays, however, has suffered even more, having lost his faculty of speech, and according to most of his colleagues, his mind. Violence is therefore central to his disablement, and possibly also contributes to his mistrust of the white man. As the end of the film indicates, this mistrust is well-founded.

The special position accorded to the disabled character in this film can be further appreciated through a close look at his name. Sembène's choice for this character's name is deliberate, and further illustrates his centrality to the narrative. The word *pays* means 'country' or 'land' in French. Sembène explains in an interview that it is actually meant to refer to the entire continent:

> Pays is Africa. He has been abused and traumatized. He can't talk. He is alive, he can look and see, he can touch, and he can see the future. He is the beholder of the drama of the past, on the concentration camps of colonization, very disciplined, very alone, very solitary, but he can't express it. (in Owoo 2008: 29)

The name therefore has connotations of homeland. It indicates how Pays strengthens the theme of belonging that is evoked by the soldiers' presence in Dakar. The greatest irony is reflected in the fact that the one person whose name is associated with home is the one who is the most restless at the camp, the one who feels least at home. In one memorable scene, Corporal Diarra attempts to allay Pays' fears by pouring soil into his hand and telling him: 'Here we are on African soil, you are no longer a prisoner.' Seen in this light, Pays' name is ironic, since the camp strongly evokes memories of imprisonment in him. Another dimension of this irony emerges from the realisation that Pays is the only black soldier with a French name. The French policy of assimilation ideally extended citizenship to its colonial subjects. The name 'Pays' evokes this idea of citizenship, with France as the mother country. Having a French name would naturally suggest that Pays is the most likely to identify France as the mother country, yet he is the one bearing the deepest mistrust of the French – a point that is also reflected in his defiant donning of the German SS helmet, a visual motif with which he 'effectively "dons" the mantle of opposition to French rule in Africa' (Murphy 2000: 164). The disabled Pays embodies the trauma of the African people caused by colonialism; the continent that has been 'abused and traumatised'. Representing all of them, he nevertheless remains the most isolated.

Pays' disablement has occurred as a result of horrors witnessed at Buchenwald, a fact that is made evident to the viewer on Pays' first appearance. In this scene, he seems shocked by the similarity of the camp at Thiaroye to the concentration camp at Buchenwald. Fear is clearly indicated on his face, even as he traces his fingers along the wire fence, as if to confirm this unwelcome reality. The comparison is cemented later by flashbacks of people shot and killed whilst attempting escape from German concentration camps. With regard to the material nature of his disability (as opposed to its symbolic significance), Pays is among those that Cindy LaCom calls 'doubly colonized' (2002: 138). She decries postcolonial scholarship's disregard for 'that colonized subject who is Other in terms of body and voice ... made doubly Other by means of her disability' (ibid.). LaCom's focus is on characters like Pays, and it is significant that she notes the two spheres of oppression that affect such characters. Pays' body, therefore, is a site upon which various kinds of disablement are constructed.

In the colonised and disabled person, one finds a character potentially facing different types of marginalised experience. Such is the position of Pays. On the one hand, Pays is 'different' on the basis of his mental disability, and on the other, he is the quintessential African othered by people like Captain Labrousse and the other white French officers. LaCom offers one unique way of reading the colonised disabled body. Drawing on Homi Bhabha's *The Location of Culture*, LaCom interprets such bodies as crucially informing what Bhabha calls 'the third dimension', which is the *in-between* region that emerges once the Self/Other binary opposite is disrupted. She argues that 'the disabled body multiplies the possible terms of disavowal for both the colonizer and the colonized; because disability can be a more evident signifier even than the color of one's skin, it becomes a visual means by which to define normalcy and, by extension, nation' (2002: 140). This is a compelling argument, emphasising the point that disability is sometimes used to define normalcy. But in this case, it is not only the disability that is the visual marker of difference – the man's skin colour is also visible. This perspective therefore highlights the 'doubly colonised' position that the disabled character occupies in the colonial state.

LaCom's perspective can still be applied to a reading of Pays' position in *Camp de Thiaroye*. As one of the *tirailleurs*, he is among those 'ambiguous figures ... viewed both as agents of French colonialism ... and also as its victims, especially in relation to World War I and II, in which the *tirailleurs* gave their lives for the metropolitan "homeland", only to discover their status as mere colonial subjects once the war was over' (Murphy 2007: 57–8). Existing in this already ambiguous role, Pays' position is further rendered ambivalent by his relationship with his colleagues, which is simultaneously one of acceptance and denigration. For this reason, Pays experiences a unique form of disablement from his fellow soldiers. Although he is not fully one of them, his presence as a 'cracked' person enables his colleagues to affirm their normalcy (their 'wholeness'), and by extension, their humanity and dignity against their oppressors. Pays' ambivalent position therefore reflects the complexity of the character's role, while also problematising any attempt to categorise him in the neat slot of 'colonial subject', since – as Ania Loomba observes – madness is 'a transgression of supposed group identities' (1998: 139).

This discussion of *Camp de Thiaroye* is an attempt to locate the film among other texts that can be seen as depicting 'the transgressive potential of different bodies' (LaCom 2002: 138). Interestingly, it is not Pays who changes in the film, but rather the viewer's assessment of him. As opposed to other film protagonists who develop in the course of the narrative, Pays' steadfast position, even as he is ridiculed by both his colleagues and the white French officers, remains in the mind of the viewer even after the credits have rolled past. His body is thus positioned as a site where different spaces of marginalisation are played out and challenged. This is because, due to his vigilance and ambivalent position, Sembène portrays him as perhaps the most 'able' character in the film, forcing the viewer to re-examine assumptions associated with disability. Just like he does with *Xala*, Sembène presents a memorable climax to *Camp de Thiaroye*. In the latter film, this moment occurs when the soldiers are massacred in a spectacular example of overkill at the end, when tanks and artillery are used to suppress the *tirailleurs*' uprising. It is a scene that reveals an uncanny similarity to *Xala* in the depiction of an attempt to erase the marginalised body from 'legitimate' spaces.

Focusing on Pays in the discussion of this film, and unveiling the way in which his character draws attention to several variant themes of the narrative, affords a more intimate look at the tragic events of 1 December 1944. He is the first character the viewer empathises with, as the realisation sinks in that he is not as 'cracked' as his colleagues assume, but is instead the only one in their midst to recognise the camp for what it really is – the place of their death. And it is this character's death that is the most tragic, since he had tried to warn his colleagues of the danger they were in. In the treatment of Pays we find a fusion of racist discrimination, colonial violence as well as ableism. The unexpected twist is that Sembène uses the disabled, voiceless character to counter racist and ableist assumptions. In the end it is this character's presence (and death) that endures in the mind.

NOTES

1   As the fastest growing film industry in Africa, Nollywood has played a huge role in the portrayal of disability in connection with the supernatural world. Witchcraft is a dominant theme in Nollywood productions. There are a lot of cases where such witchcraft is connected to disabled persons. This appears to echo a trend which has occurred for a long time in Hollywood films, where villainy has often been connected to bodily or mental difference.
2   The novel indicates that El Hadji visited numerous marabouts. The film only features two.

FILMOGRAPHY

Sembène, Ousmane (dir) (1975) *Xala*. 123 minutes. Films Domireew. Senegal.

____ (dir) (1988) *Camp de Thiaroye*. 157 minutes. Enaproc/Films Domireew. Senegal/Algeria/Tunisia.

BIBLIOGRAPHY

Bell, Chris (2006) 'Introducing White Disability Studies: A Modest Proposal', in Lennard J. Davis (ed.) *The Disability Studies Reader*, 2nd ed. New York, NY: Routledge, 275–82.

Davis, Lennard J. (1995) *Enforcing Normalcy: Disability, Deafness and the Body*. London: Verso.

de Coster, Jori (2007) 'Culturele representations van mensen met een handicap in Afrikaanse films', unpublished MA thesis, KU Leuven.

Devlieger, Patrick (1995) 'Why Disabled? The Cultural Understanding of Physical Disability in an African Society', in Benedicte Ingstad and Susan Reynolds Whyte (eds) *Disability and Culture*. Berkeley, CA: University of California Press, 94–106.

____ (2006) 'Experience of Disability: Sub-Saharan Africa', in Gary L. Albrecht (ed.) *Encyclopedia of Disability*, vol. II. Thousand Oaks, CA: Sage, 693–6.

Diawara, Manthia (1992) *African Cinema: Politics and Culture*. Bloomington, IN: Indiana University Press.

Devlieger, Patrick and Jori de Coster (2009) 'Disability in African Films: A Semiotic Analysis', *Semiotica*, 174, 145–64.

Downing, John D. H. (1996) 'Post-Tricolor African Cinema: Toward a Richer Vision', in Dina Sherzer (ed.) *Cinema, Colonialism, Postcolonialism: Perspectives from the French and Francophone World*. Austin, TX: University of Texas Press, 189–228.

Gadjigo, Samba (2010) *Ousmane Sembène: The Making of a Militant Artist*, trans. Moustapha Diop. Bloomington, IN: Indiana University Press.

Garland-Thomson, Rosemarie (2011) 'Misfits: A Feminist Materialist Disability Concept', *Hypatia*, 26, 3, 591–609.

Gugler, Josef and Oumar Cherif Diop (1998) 'Ousmane Sembène's "Xala": The Novel, the Film, and Their Audiences', *Research in African Literatures*, 29, 2, 147–58.

Harrow, Kenneth W. (2004) 'The Failed Trickster', in Françoise Pfaff (ed.) *Focus on African Films*. Bloomington, IN: Indiana University Press, 124–42.

LaCom, Cindy (2002) 'Revising the Subject: Disability as "Third Dimension" in *Clear Light of Day* and *You Have Come Back*', *NWSA Journal*, 14, 3, 138–54.

Landy, Marcia (1984) 'Political Allegory and "Engaged Cinema": Sembène's "Xala"', *Cinema Journal*, 23, 3, 31–46.

Lindfors, Bernth (1997) 'Penetrating Xala', *International Fiction Review*, 24, 1/2, 65–9.

Loomba, Ania (1998) *Colonialism/Postcolonialism*. New York, NY: Routledge.

Lynn, Thomas (2003) 'Politics, Plunder, and Postcolonial Tricksters: Ousmane Sembène's *Xala*', *International Journal of Francophone Studies*, 6, 3, 183–96.

Messier, Vartan (2011) 'Decolonizing National Consciousness Redux: Ousmane Sembène's *Xala* as Transhistorical Critique', *Postcolonial Text*, 6, 4, 1–21.

Murphy, David (2000) *Sembène: Imagining Alternatives in Film & Fiction*. Oxford: James Currey.

____ (2007) 'Fighting for the Homeland? The Second World War in the Films of Ousmane Sembène', *L'Esprit Créateur*, 47, 1, 56-67.

Mushengyezi, Aaron (2004) 'Reimaging Gender and African Tradition? Ousmane Sembène's *Xala* Revisited', *Africa Today*, 51, 1, 47–62.

Niang, Sada, Samba Gadjigo and Ousmane Sembène (1995) 'Interview with Ousmane Sembène', *Research in African Literatures*, 26, 3, 174–78.

Norden, Martin F. (1994) *The Cinema of Isolation: A History of Physical Disability in the Movies*. New Brunswick, NJ: Rutgers University Press.

Owoo, Kwate Nee (2008) 'The Language of Real Life: Interview with Ousmane Sembène', *Framework: The Journal of Cinema and Media*, 49, 1, 27–9.

Pfaff, Françoise (1982) 'Three Faces of Africa Women in *Xala*', *Jump Cut*, 27. Available at http://www.ejumpcut.org/archive/onlinessays/JC27folder/XalaPfaff.html (accessed 22 November 2012).

Quayson, Ato (2007) *Aesthetic Nervousness: Disability and the Crisis of Representation*. New York, NY: Columbia University Press.

Sembène, Ousmane (1976) *Xala*, trans. Clive Wake. London: Heinemann.

Vaughan, Megan (1991) *Curing Their Ills: Colonial Power and African Illness*. Cambridge: Polity Press.

Homes Wretched and Wrecked

Disability as Social Dis-ease in Kurosawa's *Dodes'ka-den* (1970)

James A. Wren

'Only when lions have historians will hunters cease to be heroes.'
African proverb

Pervasive appeals and 'citizens' movements' (*shimin undo*) opposing US occupation of Okinawa; an International Exposition indulging an insatiable curiosity for the neoteric impertinence that defined Osaka; a fetid landfill on Tokyo Bay concealed within the extravagance of a man-made 'Island of Dreams' (*Yumenoshima*) ... Japan's mad rush from its past forward in pursuit of the wild abandon of economic boom and an incipient sense of liberalisation and social reform in the late 1960s is, doubtless, characterised by trappings of modernist values of progress, productivity and excess. Such public construction projects, promising a larger reconfiguration of traditional society, heralded the arrival of the post-war period. And whilst standards of living improved during this epochal shift and rapid industrialisation, traditional familial hierarchies and social structures were eroded. Privileging short-term gains over long-term values, excess inscribed an all-encroaching sense of alienation, as well as a concomitant embrace of ethical irresponsibility and moral degradation that soon followed.

Such is the historical moment within which director and auteur Akira Kurosawa (1910–1998) adapted *The Town Without Seasons* (*Kisetsu no nai machi*, 1962), a novel by Yamamoto Shūgorō (1903–1967), for the screen. An enthralling and richly textured portrait of the downtrodden, Kurosawa's *Dodes'ka-den* (1970, onomatopoeia suggesting the English equivalent 'clickety-clack') exposed the unsavory side of a 'new' Japan. Essential to the larger overarching nature of his exposé, his use of vibrant colour, dynamic editing and complex compositions underscored the waste of conspicuous opulence in a toxic world within which people, once abandoned, struggle to survive (see Cowie 2010). An at-times brash, violent and humorous voice emerging above longstanding silences and the void forced viewers to confront the exploitive nature of representations of *disability* (see Yoshimoto 2000).

Disability, Home and Nation

From the earliest quasi-historical accounts in the *Kojiki* (712), for example, when the female goddess Izanami circled the pillar, made a sexual advance toward her brother, Izanagi, and in due course birthed a 'leech' child without limbs and boneless, anything less than 'normal' was defined as 'inviable' and, thus, abandoned in a boat made of reeds and set adrift. A second severely deformed offspring went unmentioned, removed from sight and all but erased from the creation mythology. Similarly, those unable to help themselves were 'excised' from society, through deliberate acts of physical and emotional abuse, abandoned to the elements or euthanised. All such instances of 'first wave' identity were fixed by oppression and a mythologised absence of ability (see Peters 1996; Davis 2006). However much physical disability (*shintai shōgai*) was deemed shocking, even horrific; intellectual (*chinō shōgai*) and mental (*seihaku*) disabilities were seen as far more so.[1] Acutely sensitive to issues of *ethos*, status and deviation, distinctions between 'native behaviours within the group' (*uchi*) and 'foreign behaviours beyond the group' (*soto*), 'true feelings' (*honne*) and 'public persona' (*tatemae*), fundamental to any understanding of Japanese social values, perpetuated an unchallenged difference between self and society (see Creighton 1997).

Essential to this distinction is the ubiquitous concept of *home*. With a renewed interest in home as a geographical site but also as an imaginary social construct dependent upon a shared sense of national belonging, Kurosawa privileged symbolic representation, inviting a wider examination of some of the less savoury recesses of modern culture and unleashing a barrage of subliminal social and political commentary on the times. Doubtless, employing his conventional hero to combat social evils left unresolved by the actions of individuals, he reconfigured modern cultural values in terms of home, wretched or wrecked. As material and cultural artifact, *Dodes'kaden* is an amalgamation of concrete examples of the displacement and abolition: the destruction and subversion of such locational-identity terms as *shusshin* (family origins), *furusato* (birthplace), and *ie* (the family unit as house) abound, especially in the impotence of the 'ideological construct of the "family-state"' (*kazoku kokka*). We question, that we might regain our ability to feel and feel deeply.[2] In fact, the related concept, Japanese 'nationalism' (*kokka shugi*) – the Japan family unit inscribed within and by the nation – signifies the construction of legitimating and mediating narratives across time. The nation of family and the ideology it espoused, for familial relationships and their vocabulary are nothing if not essential to the cultural modernity of Japanese society (see Kawamura 1980).

Hitherto, inflammatory rhetoric the likes of 'revere the Emperor, expel the barbarians' (*sonnō jōi*) and 'rich country, strong military' (*fukoku kyōhei*), had by the mid-Meiji period (see Gluck 1986; Hirai 1987) given way to other, equally incendiary catchphrases, amongst them 'selfless devotion and sacrifice to your country' (*messhi hōkō*), 'loyalty to the Emperor and patriotism' (*chûkun aikoku*) and 'Japanese spirit, Western techniques' (*wakon yosai*). Far more demagogic and overtly paternalistic vocabulary described an idealised Japan, the 'family-state' (*kazoku kokka*) and 'worship and governance are one' (*saisei itchi*), for example. Indeed, by the mid-1930s, all such rhetoric nuanced a patriotic allegiance to the Emperor as head of a Japan increasingly configured along wholly familial lines. It comes as no surprise, then, that as World War II ended in surrender on 15 August 1945, the nation turned in unison to the Emperor and apologised for *their* defeat (*ichioku sōzange*). The political vocabulary further demonstrates the process by which the ruling elite took liberty in memories of some illusory 'traditional' past in order to maintain autocratic control.

As a commentary on an emerging State-erected, aggressively patriarchal and widely encroaching monolithic modernity, this film preserves and ensures an increased awareness of the exclusionary nature of *difference*, disability included. Stripped of romanticised indulgence, disability as an iconic construct signifies a refusal to glorify the familial, even as it excludes those who are rendered devoid of humanity and deemed incapable of normative social function. The 'family registration' (*koseki*) – institutional recognition of national identity by which births, deaths, marriages and divorces of *all* Japanese citizenry are recorded – were routinely tainted by the inclusion of such individuals.

In certain instances, 'shame' (*haji*) as a cultural trait necessitated exclusion (see Rosen 2001). For familial reputation directly correlates with degrees of 'public humiliation' (*haji wo kaku*). Of equal consequence, any mention of disability by its nature is unsettling insofar as it contradicts any collective sense of group 'harmony' (*wa*), implying peaceful unity and ensuing conformity. Its perceived disruption by the mentally ill, for example, severely curtails any serious efforts to address the Japanese construct of disability, laden as it is with moralistic judgements. Metaphorical associations readily projected onto difference subsist in a quotidian understanding of disability as a pathology tantamount to 'punitive or sentimental fantasies' (Sontag 1978: 3). By definition a cultural phenomenon, any discussion of the benign, if anastomosing, nature of specific examples, then, can result only *after* that of the malignant and metastasising role of social disease. However difficult to articulate, even a tacit awareness of disability within dominant discursive practices of necessity requires a resisting subject who nonetheless is marginalised, disenfranchised, rendered invisible (see Hannerz 1989; Sullivan 2005).[3]

Understanding Kurosawa's Images

Against such an ideological background, Kurosawa thought of his modern dramas (*gendai-geki*), not as social melodrama but as social criticism, addressing issues germane to post-war Japanese society. When we read *Dodes'kaden* as a text – beyond and beneath the lyrical surface into the oppositional values struggling to find articulation – we distinguish larger discourses of power at the heart of the familial ideology and its national metaphors. Any attempt to address difference becomes an affront to the homogeneity of the nation-state and its self-legitimising meta-narratives (see Doak 2001). We must reconcile, eventually, that the very details comprising values and practices have (d)evolved historically from a post-war nationalist ideology of *national* unity and cultural *identity*. In concrete terms, the disabled are shunned. Or fear they will be at some point. As spectators, we share in common with his characters our own disabilities. The recognition of the privations of disabilities necessarily opens up a representational space from where the hegemonic discourse of the State can be purposefully challenged and cultural differences foregrounded.

Kurosawa suggests that little has changed either in the post-war era or with the unfolding economic boom of the late 1960s. In fact, the metaphor of the nation-as-family is exposed as a commercial enterprise, and the political, as synonymous with the economic.[4] Bourgeois domesticity becomes yet another form of institutional injustice working to sustain economic and social inequality. *Dodes'ka-den* offers instances of the Lacanian real and *jouissance* (see Yoo 2012) to depict in kind how the rules for the family-state necessarily break down when self-identity is questioned.[5] Incidences of violence (e.g.

rape, attempted suicide) and death (e.g. the poisoning of the street urchin) are the expected result.

Until recently, Japanese society relied on a sense of discipline originating within and imposed throughout the collective consciousness to maintain social order (see Foucault 1995; Turner 1996; Horne 2000; Sullivan 2005). As individual subjects were constructed and, thereafter, classified according to their function within a self-aggrandising socioeconomic system, the disabled in particular were perceived in and by the absence of normalcy. As objects of *ab-normality*, they were judged, manipulated by those *able* to exercise power, for purview of the State is reducible to its maintenance of a viable work force in support of the economic (see Foucault 1991; Sullivan 2005; Tremain 2005). Furthermore, to recognise the social construction of disability is to analyse oppressive and marginalising practices whereby corporeality *is* difference (see Foucault 1995: 138; Nussbaum 2007: 134), where impairment, as a conflict between body and culture, is routinely neglected (see Titchkosky 2003; Miceli 2010). Precisely because the disabled cannot experience impairment and disability separately, for the act of living in an impaired body, calling forth issues of stigma and prejudice, any representation remains a culturally mediated social construction whereby negative beliefs and societal barriers within the Japanese mindset *impose* rather than *embody* any deficiency residing with the individual (see Garrison 2007: 9). Disability then is performative (see Hughes and Paterson 1997; Hughes 2009).

Beyond his careful crafting of *mise-en-scène* and blocking, his discriminating cinematographic techniques (e.g. his reliance upon long-lens shots and unusual angles, multiple cameras and widescreen visuals) and his dramatisation of confined spaces and relationships fraught with tension and imbalances of power, how, then, does Kurosawa communicate such complexities in meaning within his pertinacious, sumptuously anointed, often self-indulgent filmic images? Certainly, since the mid-1960s, an increasingly critical attitude toward functionalist modernism has led to a spread of revisionist thinking and a growing concern for historicism, symbolism and meaning. With the recognition that a single image may reflect and ground identity, the search for ways to represent local, national and regional traditions through the mediated image began anew. Following this understanding, the question might better be re-contextualised thus: to what extent might contemporary readings of image better characterise the problematic reality of disability?

Our answer, at least in part, lies in discerning the three dimensions within which the filmic code itself operates. First, meaning may originate from a performer's activities, be they linguistic or paralinguistic, kinesics or proxemics. Kurosawa's ironic use of sound, for example, is hardly limited to music: the very title itself, *Dodes'ka-den* – the only sound the young trolley master utters, from early morning to night – mimics that sound made as his car runs along its tracks. Or consider the at-times metaphysical nature of the diction society fashions to describe diseases and those infirmed. In each instance, the richness of new terms signifies the universal, nation-building function and the claims attached to language in general. Likewise, the particularly violent nature of such language abuses is synonymous with a generalised denial of other specificities and differences in the process of identifying 'part', 'whole' and 'outside' within a homogeneous nation of Japan (see Gottlieb 1998).

On the most fundamental of levels, idiomatic usage and the metaphors they generate represent *beings*. Yet, in works the focus of which is disability, they portray events in an *ableist* fashion (see Vidali 2010: 42). As a semiotic practice, the classification of individuals into regimes of normalcy facilitates, enflames and enjoins others in an opportunity to know who 'we' are. A societal problem, definition rests on the deviance of bodies in need of remediation or cure. Stigmatisation, then, results as a normalising practice objectifying the experience of the disabled in a world where ability fixes humanity (see Otsubo and Bartholomew 1998; Griffiths *et al.* 2006: 21). Recognising the prominent place and function of social hierarchies in which the able-bodied dominate, therefore, delimits the normal (see Titchkosky 2003), and definition is exposed as no more than the summation of cultural practices rife with political and social implications.

Perhaps nowhere is this clearer than with the linguistic expressions used to describe corporeality (see Lee 2014; Mitchell and Synder 2015), as the idioms *kibun ga warui hito* ('weak' person), *atama ga warui hito* ('stupid' person – literally, 'the head is bad') or *me ga fujiyū* ('blind') illustrate. The visually impaired are defined by a single experience – or lack thereof: their encounter with the world in the absence of sight. In fact, the more colloquial expression, *me ga warui hito* ('a person whose eyes are bad') attributes the acquisition of knowledge with sight and excludes, denying entrance into a reality only accessible to the 'able-bodied'. Similarly, the hearing-impaired, as the idiom *mimi ga tooi hito* ('person whose ears are distant') suggests that sound is essential to apprehending reality. These conventions challenge cognitive ability. As widely-held metaphors, they locate and re-evaluate in ways as much descriptive as oppressive (see Flaugh 2010: 294) and abject (see Pheasant-Kelly 2013). The identification of disability given currency exercises control over, classifies and determines who is eligible to receive goods and services.

Second, meaning may arise in relation to the appearance and accoutrements of a performer. The young trolley master wears – appropriate to his age, lest we recall that certain disabilities often precluded educational opportunities – the standard state-sanctioned student uniform, and as he does so, he is re-framed as the perverted symbol of a moral fervour that ought otherwise enable his rise above endemic poverty and beyond the reaches of despair (see Kurosawa 1983: 51–2; Prince 1999: 302; Cardullo 2008: 167).

And third, meaning may be conveyed by the performance space itself. Beyond the desolation of the slum and the surrealistic landscape, the mother's graphically adorned room as a shrine to her son's misdirected potential and delusions, and the sparsely-furnished shanties or abandoned Volkswagen-cum-shelter, we saturate location with issues of place-making that in no other way could be considered anything but marginal. In fact, these locations that unfold over time and across space are constituted by and can be understood across societal boundaries. In each instance, however, the audience is left to interrogate the meaning of margins – as well as its role in such place making. And as we confront movement toward the erasure of both spatial and temporal difference, we paradoxically bolster the boundaries of the nation. As such, the disabled subject must be repeatedly inscribed; and the (d)enunciatory act of inscription erases in order to maintain that subject, in precisely the same manner in which collective, national – able-bodied and participating – subjects must trace and retrace their spatial and temporal boundaries and the identity of part and whole and past and present in order to remain in circulation. The disabled occupy not the border but a place beyond and without, an entirely alien location where they are outcasts (see Mogi 1992; Nicolas 1996). Here, authentic lives are never clearly articulated, not once understood. They elude representation (see Minich 2010: 38). Kurosawa's disabled characters are never fully developed on a personal level but, instead, are trapped in that 'between' place understood as *becoming*, the performance of which remains nonetheless contingent on hegemonic structures and language that problematise and re-contextualise them as Other (see Ogami 1997; Otake 2006; Snyder and Mitchell 2010).

Whereas it is widely accepted that Kurosawa employs fragmentation to sustain emotional effect (see Kurosawa 1983; Richie 1999; Cowie 2010), this same technique is almost never mentioned with regard to his development of character. But perhaps nowhere is division more obvious. His representation of the disabled and the ill meant to challenge preconceptions of 'national subjects', the audience is quickly bombarded in succession by a series of haunting, hunted images of the 'scraps, patches, and rags of daily life' (Bhabha

1990: 297). More to the point, such an observation provides a context within which we might better understand the various characters strewn over the landscape.

Disability and Illness in *Dodes'ka-den*

The film opens with a driver in action: he is a mentally-challenged young man, who makes his daily rounds through the slums. He perceives his run as his job and identifies strongly with it, and his work is in and of itself honorable (see Tsurumi 1993), if we accept that dynamics of his reality comprise a wandering and sedentary life. The relationship between his own 'sacred sites' and the weak of society might be described as one of pursuit, including higher levels of sacredness. Well before his imagined departure, he inspects his illusory car. So meticulous is his scrutiny that *we* hear the clangs of doors. We enter his delusions as we engage with his dance, as he moves with agility across the surrealistic, often phantasmagoric terrain, all the time mimicking the incessant mechanical sounds that are his journey. His is a world where boundaries shift whimsical and where the imposition of hegemonic structures further alienate and confuse. In this diasporic existence, he ceases to

Fig. 1: Kurosawa's character repeats the onomatopoeia 'dodes'ka-den' as he drives his illusory vehicle.

be a citizen, for he has no culture other than that bound in ableist, normative discourse (see McDermott and Varenne 1995). He lives with his mother in a house bordered by a trolley line in front and in back a long stretch of rubble extending through the shantytown and connected to it by what may have once been trolley run.

In addition to the material context, there exists a disturbing personal conflict between mother and child as she responds to her own challenges. Clearly distraught as much by her son's much-maligned behaviour as by the taunts made by other children, she prays. We approach their relationship with a sense of the mother's utter lack of power to do anything but survive. Alone and seated before an altar, she has succumbed to despair and her own delusions, that of Buddhism and possible salvation from the sufferings and hardships of this world. Following the teachings of the Buddhist monk Nichiren (1222–1282), she enjoins in a ritual chanting of the mantra, *nam'myōhō renge kyō* ('Glory Be to the Lotus Sutra'), as if to awaken her Buddha nature and tap into the deepest levels of existence where lives and the universe are one. As she invokes a state of mindfulness, ideally she would surrender to the compassions of the Buddha and the Lotus Sutra (the source of her chant). But her fervent adherence to the tenets of her religious faith renders her ineffective. Her unanswered prayers, once meant to bring about healing through self-enlightenment, now offer neither solace nor solution.

Confounding the rapport between parent and child (*oyako*) is another, a rigidly hierarchical relationship defined by longstanding institutional norms and discourses prescribing their interactions. She in fact expects the outside world to understand her needs without having to make them explicit. Her efforts in effect trap her in a world that strongly emphasises the powerful position of outside society over them. Like her son, she experiences – in fact, she labours under – a heightened sense of alienation brought on both by the stigma associated with intellectual disability and mental illness and by a lack of social understanding about its causes and manifestation (see Ohnuki-Tierney 1984). As she surrenders herself to the emotional, rather than to the tangibly concrete realities of her situation, she redefines the stress of her situation solely in terms that capitulate to it.

Her prayers point to an even larger conflict. Amidst a post-war transformation where the sacredness of *now* is readily accessible, they have become less about 'prayer' and giving, more about receiving and 'profit'. Furthermore, the associated transformation of travel to sacred locations is reducible to a sense of inviolability, increasingly voyeuristic and cheapened (see Yamanaka et al. 2007: 1–2; Hulko 2009). And just as the trolley 'travels' and carries its driver along a path between home and the slums, so too are we transported. Along the way, he encounters a series of 'missed' stops, and with each passing we witness other recognisable disabilities, among which are those who have collapsed under alcoholism or sexual violation, families who disintegrate into abuse or a lack of genuine affection, and young children who must protect their inattentive parents. Each image resituates that sense of fragmentation and the incompleteness of its socially and politically disenfranchised subject. Reflecting ultimately a sense of melancholic fatalism, the disturbing echoes of the trolley and its driver, the mother's prayers and the cacophony of disturbances along the way magnify the unremitting susceptibility of language to communicative breakdown. In general, these sounds 'diagnose' a metaphorical stutter, symptomatic of some observable flaw in character (see Coriat 1943; Bobrick 1995) and no less subject to the process of punitive metaphorisation (see Sontag 1978: 3). In particular, the ineffectual nature of language itself proves an obstacle dividing inner self from outer world. As important, the pathology of this disorder is neither terminal, nor outwardly visible, but occupies a certain liminal position (see Pollack 1985: 395). Of the two operative metaphors, the first with the lack of fluency offers a less punitive representation, given that it acts inclusively. But the second, blurring rigid distinctions between pervasive speech, sets an impossible standard for all acts of language and metaphysical 'languaging'.

Related to such interruptions and breaks, failures ensue in the breakdown of society around them. Central to the slum and the chaos and action of the area, for example, are two oft-inebriated factory workers and their wives who seek solace from the squander within bouts of drinking and forays into sexual excess: they periodically switch wives – an activity that 'births' gossip within the community. They violate the normative system of values found in the world beyond and hence obfuscate the process of subjectification (see Foucault 1995; Lyon 2001, 2002; Kuppers and Overboe 2009; Mercieca and Mercieca 2010). Rather than a command of normative values, however, the gossip functions in its meticulous and distanced observation, to monitor – but not to curtail – social order. The ultimate fusion and dissolution of any sense of social identity emerges in expressions of unpleasant ambiguity or worse, hellish chaos.

Also along the way are other families, extended but equally dysfunctional and defined by their daily routines. Each labours to craft their wares under modes of oppression wholly incompatible with production. A young girl makes paper flowers to be sold in the city, and her work is every bit a violation as her actual penetration and rape by her step-uncle against a crimson bed of her own making. A perversion of her duty to repay familial debt, she instead becomes pregnant. In an uninitiated act of procreativity, she loses her emotional self, as her family expresses outrage and disdain. Any sense of familial obligation pales before her anger, confusion and despair. Nowhere is the overt linking of monetary and sexual exploitation more poignant perhaps than when later she inadvertently strikes at a *sake* peddler, the only person to show any concern for her. In the one scene where she speaks, she suggests that her irrational rage and confusion arose from an attempt at suicide. Meaningful conversation is met with silence, as he offers her food and rides off on his bike. Once more abandoned, she lacks any positive relationship that might supplant her personal negation. Stripped of power and worth at every turn, she is powerless to change her circumstances.

Thereafter, we come across a small, seemingly idyllic family. The father appears quite productive as he crafts doll after doll to earn a living. His wife, however, proves far more industrious: unfaithful to him, she churns out her own bastardised products, six or so children who are not his. The illusion of family and procreation within the bond of matrimony intact, he nonetheless proves impotent, capable only to fashion dolls. Able only to perpetuate misconceptions, he reassures the children that he is their father not if, but because they love him best and believe him to be so. The children themselves fall prey to his illusions as he evades reality to validate a lie with the carefully crafted artifice of rhetoric.

Alongside these thriving cottage workers are a crippled, twitching and inarticulate *salariman* and his thieving, ever-abusive wife. Beyond any dystopic implications inherent to their monstrous physical and uncontrollable moral bent (see Inahara 2009), their relationship to employment not only insulates; it segregates them from others in the area and from mainstream society. They are the subject both of bio-power and of its absence (see Foucault 1995). They are of no value, save their capacity to contribute (see Conroy and Hayes-Conroy 2010).

But perhaps the most agonising images involve the homeless father and his urchin-son who reside in what had once been a Volkswagen. As the child moves with a singular focus from alley-way kitchens and restaurants in search of food, his father imagines building a house, beginning with the gate and fence and later revisions in a new porch, a new colour. His delusions are but the folly of whim.

And it is whim, not any actual memory, that facilitates the father's connection to a world beyond the slums. His imagination likewise denies his son any kind of objective existence. The overt effacement of paternal responsibility, mirroring a larger, society-wide breakdown of those values characteristically espoused within a family and in their place the substitution of the State and its particular ideologies, illustrates that moment within which the traditional family unit struggles with change and reconfiguration. Parental bonding gives way as the son assumes the role as caretaker and titular 'head' of his household. As an orphan, he subsists beyond the purview of any moral guide (see Abberley 1987). His perseverance in the face of enormous obstacles, his assumption of responsibility and his existential loneliness are all that define him.

But even this image is itself disabled, perverted, as the 'orphan' orphans his father. The inordinate emphasis on sustenance subverts any sense of nourishment. They suffer from food poisoning, and when his son grows sicker, his father clings to the illusion that all will be well and rejects any offer of help. Awakened to find his son blue-faced and stiff amongst the filth of their abandoned Volkswagen, he defers the consequences. A wholly impotent man with an omnipotent imagination, he can but stand over the cremated remains placed within an unmarked grave. What he projects onto this scene is all that we see – a gigantic swimming pool, the final touch to his imagined house. Home as a highly complex nexus between the intellectual, the material and the spiritual locus, a place by definition where a family is meant to prosper and thrive, proves equally illusive. No hopeful image of what might be, here and now, or well into the future, despair becomes the only reality.

Thus, to engage with the representation of the disabled subject is simultaneously to question how normalising discourses about beings and their humanity have shaped our apprehensions of meaning itself (see Karatani 1980). Distinctions between subject and object are irrelevant, being exists against a backdrop of nature, and with this placement, humanity is relegated to the transience of post-war sensibilities. A larger endless cycle of disappointment and heartache is perpetuated in their personal emotional and psychological suffering and denies them any sense of conclusion. They persist and subsist if only because they can do nothing less.

Disability, then, is fetishised, as a symbol of disorder, of an alienation that disrupts the normative view of life. Because normalcy articulates a subjectivity conforming to idealised formations and because the commodification of its opposite reduces individuals to spectacle, it is hardly surprising that Kurosawa would reconsider the value of a life disabled by circumstance.

By problematising the very images widely circulating as clichéd sociocultural contradictions and institutional dilemmas, he essentially addresses disability as part of a cultural space wherein normalcy can be questioned and culture can be diagnosed. In the absence of possibility, he relegates those disabled to an in-between-space of alterity, conditioned by decay and exile.

All such representations speak to the disarray we equate with identity in post-war Japan. The lack of any tangible home or family symptomatic of an overt pathology of social disability and an overwhelming sense of foreboding and disease, unleashed upon the land, is met with moral descent and physical degeneration. Absence plunges us into a world wrought with abandonment, rent by continuing delusions, themselves little more than naive, sentimental idealisations (see Matsubara 1998). The meta-narrative of identity becomes a false idol behind any unifying nation-state as family. Home, family and national identity amount to nought in a world where ambiguous reality perpetuated either and neither, all and nothing.

NOTES

1. Japanese documentary filmmaker Sōda Kazuhiro, employing the style of *cinéma vérité*, investigates this taboo in *Seishin* (2008) and draws our attentions to issues of mental health (see Stevenson 2009).
2. Recall how the family-state is figuratively dismembered, with the image of a severed hand wedged between the teeth of a mangy cur (*Yōjinbō*, 1961).
3. The series *Anime de wakaru shinryōunaika* (also translated as 'Comical Psychosomatic Medicine'), first airing on 13 February 2015, features psychologist and his cheerful nurse as they explain in a series of jokes, puns and references to pop culture the validity, prevalence and origins of mental disorders, and address specific disorders.
4. Research often neglects socio-cultural factors in shaping familial response to disability (see Kalyanpur and Harry 1999), this in spite of recognising that certain cultural characteristics make life especially difficult for the estimated seven million registered disabled people in Japan.
5. One of the earliest recognisable ironies of metaphor of the family-state used to consolidate the Japanese empire is that the empire itself laid waste to the traditional familial hierarchy – with fathers never returned from the war, mothers forced into sexual labour (see Mizoguchi Kenji's *Street of Shame* [*Akasen chitai*], 1956) and children denied a childhood (see Shinoda Masahiro's *Macarthur's Children* [*Setouchi shōnen yakyū-dan*], 1984).

FILMOGRAPHY

Hirofumi, Ogira (dir) (2015) *Anime de wakaru shinryōunaika*. Animated television series (20 episodes). Japan.

Kurosawa, Akira (dir) (1970) *Dodes'ka-den* (*Clickety-Clack*). 140 minutes. Toho Company/Yonki-no-Kai Productions. Japan.

____ (dir) (1961) *Yōjinbō*. 110 minutes. Kurosawa Production Company/Toho Company. Japan.

Sōda, Kazuhiro (dir) (2008) *Seishin (Mental)*. 135 minutes. Laboratory X. Japan.

BIBLIOGRAPHY

Abberley, Paul (1987) 'The Concept of Oppression and the Development of a Social Theory of Disability', *Disability, Handicap, and Society*, 2, 1, 5–19.

Bhabha, Homi (1990) *Nation and Narration*. London: Routledge.

Bobrick, Benson (1995) *Knotted Tongues: Stuttering in History and the Quest for a Cure*. New York, NY: Kōdansha.

Cardullo, Bert (ed.) (2008) *Akira Kurosawa: Interviews (Conversations with Filmmakers)*. Jackson, MS: University of Mississippi Press.

Coriat, Isador H. (1943) 'The Psychoanalytic Conception of Stammering', *The Nervous Child*, 2, 2, 167–71.

Cowie, Peter (2010) *Akira Kurosawa: Master of Cinema*. New York, NY: Rizzoli.

Creighton, Millie (1997) '*Soto* Others and *Uchi* Others: Imagining Racial Diversity, Imagining Homogeneous Japan', in Michael Weiner (ed.) *Japan's Minorities: The Illusion of Homogeneity*. London: Routledge, 211–38.

Davis, Lennard J. (2006) *The Disability Studies Reader*. London: Routledge.

Doak, Kevin M. (2001) 'Building National Identity through Ethnicity: Ethnology in Wartime Japan and After', *Journal of Japanese Studies*, 27, 1, 1–39.

Flaugh, Christian (2010) 'Of Colonized Mind and Matter: The Dis/Abilities of Negritude in Aime Cesaire's *Cahier d'un retour au pays natal*', *Journal of Literary and Cultural Disabilities Studies*, 4, 3, 291–308.

Foucault, M. (1991) 'Governmentality', in Graham Burchell, Colin Gordon and Peter Miller (eds) *The Foucault Effect: Studies in Governmentality*, trans. Rosi Braidotti. Chicago, IL: University of Chicago Press, 87–104.

____ (1995) *Discipline and Punish: The Birth of the Prison*. New York, NY: Vintage Books.

Garrison, Heather (2008) 'Adolescent Perceptions of the Sociocultural Construct of Disability When Responding to Literature of Mice and Men', Unpublished Dissertation, New York, Fordham University.

Gluck, Carol (1986) *Japan's Modern Myths: Ideology in the Late Meiji Period*. Princeton, NJ: Princeton University Press.

Gottlieb, Nanette (1998) 'Discriminatory Language in Japan: *Burakumin*, the Disabled and Women', *Asian Studies Review*, 22, 2, 157–73.

Kathleen M Griffiths, Yoshibumi Nakane, Helen Christensen (2006) 'Stigma in Response to Mental Disorders: A Comparison of Australia and Japan', *BMC Psychiatry*, 6, 21.

Hannerz, Ulf (1989) 'Culture Between Center and Periphery', *Ethos*, 54, 3/4, 200–16.

Hayes-Conroy, Jessica and Allison Hayes-Conroy (2010) 'Visceral Geographies: Mattering, Relating, and Defying', *Geography Compass*, 4, 9, 1273–83.

Hirai, Atsuko (1987) 'The State and Ideology in Meiji Japan', *Journal of Asian Studies*, 46, 1, 89–103.

Horne, John (2000) 'Understanding Sport and Body Culture in Japan', *Body & Society*, 6, 2, 73–86.

Hughes, Bill (2009) 'Wounded/Monstrous/Abject: A Critique of the Disabled Body in the Sociological Imaginary', *Disability and Society*, 24, 4, 399–410.

Hughes, Bill and Kevin Paterson (1997) 'The Social Model of Disability and the Disappearing Body: Towards a Sociology of Impairment', *Disability and Society*, 12, 3, 325–40.

Hulko, Wendy (2009) 'The Time- and Context-Contingent Nature of Intersectionality and Interlocking Oppressions', *Affilia*, 24, 4, 44–55.

Inahara, Minae (2009) 'This Body Which Is Not One: The Body, Femininity and Disability', *Body and Society*, 15, 1, 47–62.

Kalyanpur, Maya and Beth Harry (1999) *Culture in Special Education: Building Reciprocal Family-Professional Relationships*. Baltimore, MD: Brookes.

Karatani, Kōjin (1980) *Nihon kindai bungaku no kigen*. Tokyo: Kōdansha.

Kawamura, Nozomu (1980) 'The Historical Background of Arguments Emphasizing the Uniqueness of Japanese Society', *Social Analysis*, 5/6, 44–62.

Kuppers, Petra and James Overboe (2009) 'Introduction: Deleuze, Disability, and Difference', *Journal of Literary and Cultural Disability Studies*, 3, 3, 217–20.

Kurosawa, Akira (1983) *Something Like an Autobiography*, trans. Audie E. Bock. New York, NY: Vintage Books.

____ (1999) *Yume wa tensai de aru*. Tokyo: Bungei shunjū.

Lee, Rachel C. (2014) *The Exquisite Corpse of Asian America: Biopolitics, Biosociality, and Posthuman Ecologies*. New York, NY: New York University Press.

Lyon, David (2001) *Surveillance Society: Monitoring Everyday Life*. Buckingham: Open University Press.

____ (2002) 'Everyday Surveillance: Personal Data and Social Classifications', *Information, Communication & Society*, 5, 2, 242–57.

Matsubara, Yoko (1998) 'The Enactment of Japan's Sterilization Laws in the 1940's: A Prelude to Post-war Eugenic Policy', *Historia Scientiarum*, 8, 2, 187–201.

McDermott, Ray and Herve Varenne (1995) 'Culture as Disability', *Anthropology and Education Quarterly*, 26, 323–48.

Mercieca, Daniela and Duncan Mercieca (2010) 'Opening Research to Intensities: Rethinking Disability Research with Deleuze and Guattari', *Journal of Philosophy of Education*, 44, 1, 79–92.

Miceli, Michael (2010) 'The Disavowal of the Body as a Source of Inquiry in Critical Disability Studies: The Return Of Impairment?', *Critical Disability Discourse*, 2, 1–14.

Minich, Julie (2010) 'Disabling *La Frontera*: Disability, Border Subjectivity, and Masculinity in *Big Jessie, Little Jessie* by Oscar Casares', *Melus*, 35, 1, 35–52.

Mitchell, David T. and Sharon L. Snyder (2015) *The Biopolitics of Disability: Neoliberalism, Ablenationalism, and Peripheral Embodiment*, Ann Arbor, MI: University of Michigan Press.

Mogi, Toshihiko (1992) 'The Disabled in Society', *Japan Quarterly*, 39, 440-8.

Nicolas, Kristof (1996) 'Outcast Status Worsens Pain of Japan's Disabled', *New York Times*, 7 April.

Nozawa, Kazuhiro and Hajime Kitamura (eds) (2006) *Hatatsushōgai to media*. Tokyo: Gendai jinbunsha.

Nussbaum, Martha (2007) *Frontiers of Justice: Disability, Nationality, Species Membership*. Cambridge, MA: Belknap Press.

Ogami, Kōji (1997) 'Shōgaisha mondai Seminar', *Tomoni ikiyō, rakuni ikiyō*. Tokyo: Akashi shoten.

Ohnuki-Tierney, Emiko (1984) *Illness and Culture in Contemporary Japan: An Anthropological View*. Cambridge: Cambridge University Press.

Otake, Tomoko (2006) 'Is "Disability" Still a Dirty Word in Japan?', *Japan Times*, 27 August.

Otsubo, Sumiko and James R. Bartholomew (1998) 'Eugenics in Japan: Some Ironies of Modernity, 1883-1945', *Science in Context*, 11, 3/4, 545–65.

Peters, Susan (1996) 'The Politics of Disability Identity', in Len Barton (ed.) *Disability and Society: Emerging Issues and Insight*. London: Longman, 215–34.

Pheasant-Kelly, Frances (2013) *Abject Spaces in American Cinema: Institutional Settings, Identity and Psychoanalysis in Film*. London: I.B. Tauris.

Pollack, David (1985) 'Action as Fitting Match to Knowledge: Language and Symbol in Mishima's *Kinkakuji*', *Monumenta Nipponica*, 40, 4, 387–398.

Prince, Stephen (1999) *The Warrior's Camera: The Cinema of Akira Kurosawa*, Princeton, NJ: Princeton University Press.

Richie, Donald (1999) *The Films of Akira Kurosawa*. Berkeley, CA: University of California Press.

Rosen, Erica (2001) 'The Influence of Culture on Mental Health and Psychopathology in Japan', presentation at Washington University in St. Louis: Arts and Sciences, 29 November.

Snyder, Sharon L. and David T. Mitchell (2010) 'Introduction: Ablenationalism and the Geo-Politics of Disability', *Journal of Literary and Cultural Disability Studies*, 4, 2, 113–25.

Sontag, Susan (1978) *Illness as Metaphor*. New York: Farrar, Straus and Giroux.

Stevenson, Elena (2009) 'Getting "Mental" in Japan: Interview with Kazuhiro Soda', *Ningin.com*, 9 January (accessed 16 April 2015).

Sullivan, Martin (2005) 'Subjected Bodies: Paraplegia, Rehabilitation, and the Politics of Movement', in Shelley Tremain (ed.) *Foucault and the Government of Disability*. Ann Arbor, MI: University of Michigan Press, 27–44.

Titchkosky, Tanya (2003) *Disability, Self, and Society*. Toronto: University of Toronto Press.

Tremain, Shelley (2006) 'Foucault and the Government of Disability', *Scandinavian Journal of Disability Research*, 8, 1, 75–7.

Tsurumi, Kazuko (1993) *Hyōhaku to teijū to – Yanagita Kunio no shakai hendōron*. Tokyo: Chikuma shobō.

Turner, Bryan S. (1996) *The Body and Society: Explorations in Social Theory*. London: Sage.

Vidali, Amy (2010) 'Seeing What We Know: Disability and Theories of Metaphor', *Journal of Literary and Cultural Disability Studies*, 4, 1, 33–54.

Yamanaka, Hiroshi *et al.* (2007) '"Basho no seisei" no henyō', *Saikōchiku to tsūrizumu ni kansuru sōgōteki kenkyū*, 1–2.

Yoshimoto, Mitsuhiro (2000) *Kurosawa: Film Studies and Japanese Cinema*. Durham, NC: Duke University Press.

Yoo, Hyon Joo (2012) *Cinema at the Crossroads: Nation and the Subject in East Asian Cinema*. Lanham, MD: Lexington.

Leprosy and the Dialectical Body in Forugh Farrokhzad's *The House is Black* (1964)

Rosa Holman

In her documentary, *Khaneh siah ast* (*The House is Black*, 1964), Forugh Farrokhzad adopts the poetic voice-over and the rhythmic soundscape as a way of evoking a lyrical and dialectical understanding of human existence, and in particular the experiences of embodiment. Despite the images of physical suffering in Farrokhzad's short black-and-white film about leprosy, it is the voice-over and the use of sound that redefine the experiences of those who have had their bodies characterised as abject and contaminated. The 'lived body' that emerges in Farrokhzad's documentary is both a site of profound banality and poetic beauty. With Farrokhzad's legacy persisting in the poetic realism of contemporary Iranian cinema, so too representations of disability continue to be informed by the strategies of lyricism, ambivalence and the innovative use of sound and voice.

Farrokhzad's influence on pre- and post-revolutionary Iranian cinema has been widely recognised in the scholarship on the poet and filmmaker (see Rosenbaum 2005; Dabashi 2007; Naficy 2011). Her poetry and documentary, as part of a broader movement of Iranian literary modernism and New Wave cinema, have powerfully shaped the reality aesthetic of contemporary Iranian cinema and infused it with a particular kind of Persian lyricism. But Farrokhzad's influence has not only extended stylistically, but also in the continuing foregrounding of physical disability in poetically realist Iranian art cinema.

Disability was a recurrent theme in the films of the 1980s and 1990s, with the eight-year-long Iran/Iraq war represented as leaving a legacy of physical and psychological damage. Children in particular were portrayed as bearing the brunt of such turmoil, struggling with impairment, poverty and, frequently, the absence of any real parental support.[1] Certainly in the films of Majid Majidi and Mohsen Makhmalbaf children with disabilities were frequently forced into homelessness and institutionalisation. The experiences of young boys with blindness in particular were centralised in Makhmalbaf's *Sokut* (*Silence*, 1998) and Majidi's *Rang-e Khoda* (*The Colour of Paradise*, 1998). In both cases the vision-impaired youth were portrayed as possessing an acute awareness and gifted understanding of sound, emanating from both the natural world and musical instruments. While such films certainly need to be interrogated for their representations of vulnerability, like *The House is Black*, they also attempt to redefine notions of 'ability' and 'debility'. For it is not the children themselves who are portrayed as being incapacitated by their blindness, but society at large that is shown to be suffering from its own form of myopia. Such a misrecognition and mismanagement of what is perceived to be 'disability' incarcerates individuals in oppressive 'house(s) of blackness' and deprives them of the most basic human rights.

This chapter is interested in contextualising Farrokhzad's film as an example of Iranian New Wave cinema and in examining how her poetry underpins the documentary, thus maintaining a dialogue between Farrokhzad's written oeuvre and her cinematic production. It proposes that Farrokhzad's use of rhythm in *The House is Black* situates leprosy, not as an 'individual pathology' to be endured in isolation, but rather as a symptom of a 'discriminatory environment' (Ellis 2008: 3). While so much critical discourse has focused its analysis on the 'abject' visuals in Farrokhzad's film, this chapter contends that the filmmaker persistently privileges sound as a means of representing the rhythms and cycles of the body, irrespective of the body's apparent status as 'disabled' or 'diseased'.

Situating *The House is Black*

Forugh Farrokhzad was born in 1935 in Tehran to a middle-class family, marrying her second cousin, Parviz Shapur, at sixteen and a year later giving birth to their son, Kamyar. When the couple divorced after three years Farrokhzad lost custody of Kamyar and was denied all contact after the separation (see

Milani 1992). In 1955 Farrokhzad was hospitalised following a nervous breakdown, the same year her first collection of poetry, *Asir* (*Captive*), was published. Thereafter Farrokhzad made several trips to Europe (in 1956, 1960 and 1964) where she continued to write poems, short stories and letters, taking employment as a translator in Munich. She published two more collections of poetry between her sojourns, *Divar* (*The Wall*) in 1956 and *Esyan* (*Rebellion*) in 1958. At this time she also began working at the Golestan Film Workshop, first as a secretary, and later as an assistant, an editor and finally as the director of *The House is Black*. Once filming had concluded on the documentary Farrokhzad permanently adopted one of the children appearing in it, Hossein Mansouri. Farrokhzad's fourth and most famous collection, *Tavallodi digar* (*Another Birth*, 1964), was seen as a major turning point in the poet's career and established her as a key contributor to Iranian modernist poetry. Tragically Farrokhzad died in a car accident on 14 February 1967, aged 32. Her final volume of poetry, entitled *Imam biyavarim be aghaz-e fasl-e sard* (*Let Us Believe in the Beginning of the Cold Season*), was posthumously published in 1974. Her poetry has been persistently hailed as radical and innovative in part because of its representation of the female body and women's desire. Against the intersecting programmes of State-prescribed liberalism and ingrained traditionalism, Farrokhzad's poetry reclaims the body, not as a projection for male-orientated fantasies of eroticism or purity, but as a vehicle for autonomy and agency.

Farrokhzad's poetry emerged in the 1950s and 1960s as part of a larger movement of cultural modernity in Iran. After the disposal of the popularly elected Prime Minister, Dr Mohammad Mossadegh, in 1953, Muhammad Reza Shah consolidated Iran's diplomatic ties with the United States, encouraging industrialisation and attempting to quash leftist political parties and liberal dissidents (see Afary 2009: 202).[2] In 1957 the Shah increased the powers of the secret police (the SAVAK) and created a culture of brutal intolerance towards political opposition. As part of the State-devised White Revolution launched in 1963, the government instituted various land reforms and expanded women's civil rights. Such developments were influenced in part by the increasing pressure from the Kennedy administration to democratise Iran. As many scholars are quick to note, the conflicting narratives regarding the Shah's programme of modernisation make it impossible to either entirely applaud or condemn the process of liberalisation (see Kia 2005; Afary 2009; Degroot 2010). Women were certainly enfranchised by reforms to education, health and increased access to the workplace, with eight women even being admitted to Parliament in September 1963 (see Afary 2009: 207). And despite the centralised and often circumscribed nature of women's organisations under the Shah, various scholars still emphasise the important legislation introduced during this period, which extended women's legal rights in marriage and divorce (see Kia 2005; Afary 2009). While many intellectuals supported aspects of the Shah's modernisation, there was still much suspicion and opposition to the monarchy's dictatorial approach and tight reign over Iranian cultural life. To depict the poverty or misery that many Iranians suffered during this time was completely at odds with the Shah's aims of projecting a democratic and modernised national image. Artists and intellectuals were subjected to harsh penalties for contravening the State's programme of censorship and repression. Freedom of expression thus became a central concern for the intellectuals, artists and writers of this period who were caught between the opposing programmes of liberalism and cultural prescription.

Cinema was no exception and several films in the 1960s representing the 'realistic portrayal of the underside of institutionalised disability and their political contexts' were interpreted as 'direct attacks on the government and its failed social service programs' (Naficy 2011: 127). Interestingly, Farrockhzad's documentary was favourably received by the State, even attracting the 'royal seal of approval' (Naficy 2011: 87). The Shah's wife, the Empress Farah Pahlavi, was a patron for the Society to Assist Patients of Leprosy and a special screening of the film was organised for the monarch. But despite the Empress's interest in the cause and charitable support for the organisation, leprosy remained a disease associated with social stigmatisation and isolation in Iran during the 1950s and 1960s. *Mycobacterium leprae,* which causes the disease, is transmitted through breathing, a fact that only served to heighten fears concerning contagion and physical contact with leprosy sufferers. However, unlike tuberculosis, most individuals have a genetic immunity to leprosy and 'prolonged and intimate contact with a contagious individual is required for a susceptible person to acquire the disease' (see Sehgal *et al.* 2006: 9). There are also varying strains, degrees of severity and forms of leprosy. Sufferers may experience skin lesions with eventual loss of sensation, which in some cases causes damage to the peripheral nerves. The introduction of sulpha drugs in the 1940s temporarily offered the first 'effective medical cure'; however, by the 1960s a drug-resistant strain of leprosy returned and it was again thought to be an incurable and 'intractable illness' (Buckingham 2006: 959). With the loss of nerve sensation, limbs become susceptible to accidental damage, deterioration and ulceration, and in severe cases, require amputation. Untreated leprosy may also eventually damage the eyes, nose and palate, resulting in the loss of speech, sight or hearing.

It is the association of leprosy with deformity and contagion that has resulted in the historical isolation, institutionalisation and stigmatisation of leprosy sufferers worldwide. Leprosy sufferers were often relegated to 'asylums' in the nineteenth and twentieth centuries, and it is their confinement and ostracism that Farrokhzad interrogates in her short film. The original Persian word used to describe leprosy, *khoreh*, meant 'something which eats or destroys the tissues, indicating the destructive character of the disease' (Azizi and Bahadori 2011: 426). The Arabic term *jozam* has long since been substituted as the word for leprosy. Records from the *Qajar* period (1785–1925) indicate that leprosy sufferers were encouraged to live in their own colonies outside of major cities and that 'by 1920, there were three leper colonies in Iran, in Arpadarrassi and Khalkhal in Azarbaijan (northeastern Iran) and near Mashhad, Khorasan Province (northwestern Iran)' (Azizi and Bahadori 2011: 427). By 1933 the Bababaghi leprosarium in Azarbaijan province was well established and became a place of permanent settlement for sufferers around Iran. In 1957 the Anjoman-e Komak be Jozamian (Society for Assistance to Lepers) was established in nearby Tabriz to assist those in the Bababaghi leprosarium. It was this charity that commissioned and partly funded *The House is Black,* at a time when conditions were at their worst.

Farrokhzad conducted an initial research trip during July 1962, accompanied by Dr Abdolhossein Radji, the head of the charitable society for supporting lepers (see Milani 2014: 146). She returned to Bababaghi three months later to begin production. The documentary was filmed over twelve days with a small crew, including its producer, Ebrahim Golestan, and director of photography, Soleiman Miasian. It was apparently made without any shot list or script (see Ghorbankarimi 2002), although certain scenes have been obviously staged (see Rosenbaum 2005: 15; Naficy 2011: 85). The film won the Grand Prize at the Oberhausen Film Festival in 1963 and was shown at the Pesaro Film Festival in 1966. It received only a limited release in Iran but attracted generally positive reviews (see Naficy 2011: 87). However, despite its critical acclaim within contemporary scholarship, Farrokhzad's film was initially not influential within Iran. Its impact and elevation as a modernist Iranian cinematic work came later and was due to the screenings and scholarship carried out after the 1979 Revolution, both in Iran and within the diaspora.

Filmed in black and white and running for just over twenty minutes, *The House is Black* opens with a close-up of a woman with significant facial deformity, gazing at herself in the mirror. This is followed by scenes of leprosy sufferers involved in all the prosaic activities of everyday life: eating, resting, engaged in conversation, brushing their hair and so on, while Farrokhzad's voice-over melancholically recites her own poetry and various biblical quotations. There is a distinct shift early in the film when a male voice-over (often identified as Golestan's) provides more factual information on the condition of leprosy and its treatments, while individuals are shown being examined by doctors and undergoing various forms of physical therapy. The film then reverts to its previous mode with disjointed scenes of the leprosy colony, with Farrokhzad's voice-over again reciting poetry.

Various scholars (for example, Rahimieh 2010; Naficy 2011; Jahed 2012) have attested to the importance of Farrokhzad's relationship with the producer, Ebrahim Golestan. In particular Hamid Naficy argues that Farrokhzad's development of cinematic poetic realism was significantly influenced by Golestan's own production practices and his collaborative approach with other writers and filmmakers. Working as an activist, writer, translator and then filmmaker, Ebrahim Golestan formed the Golestan Film Workshop (GFW) in 1955. Naficy writes, 'The GFW became a lively intellectual salon where employees and fellow intellectuals … would read and discuss poetry and other matters late into the night' (2011: 79). With little scripting, the blurring of documentary and fictional film modes and the recording of synchronous sound, Golestan's works broke new cinematic ground with their heightened reality aesthetic and lyrical quality. Farrokhzad was first employed as a secretary at the GFW in 1956, but was soon working as an assistant, actress and editor on various projects. Her first experience of working directly with film was editing Golestan's documentary *Yek atash (A Fire,* 1958–61). She also co-directed and co-edited *Ab va garma (Water and Heat,* 1961).

While Naficy's identification of a 'GFW house style' must be taken into consideration when examining Farrokhzad's development as a filmmaker, it may also be worth noting the more international cinematic developments in avant-garde and modernist cinema. There has been some debate regarding the degree of influence that cinematic movements such as the French New Wave and Italian Neo-Realism have had on the emergence of a national form of cinematic poetic realism in Iran, both in terms of the 1960s New Wave cinema and the New Iranian cinema that emerged in post-revolutionary Iran during the 1990s and 2000s (see Chaudhuri and Finn 2003; Naficy 2011; Jahed 2012). In making the link between European avant-garde filmmaking traditions and Farrokhzad's own filmmaking practices in the 1960s it is important to avoid re-instating the centrality or hegemony of Western filmmaking theory and practice. Instead, it may be valuable to observe how *The House is Black* emerged in correspondence or dialogue with other modernist cinematic practices. The fact that Farrokhzad's film won the Grand Prize at the Oberhausen Film Festival in 1963, at a time when German cinema was undergoing its own cultural and formal transformation, is arguably significant. The recognition that *The House is Black* received in Europe later implies that Farrokhzad was working not only as a key member of the Iranian New Wave, but was also contributing to the emergence of a more global, transnational form of cinematic modernism.

The affinity between the Iranian New Wave cinema of the 1960s and its European counterparts is marked both in terms of the production processes and the interdependence of film criticism and practice. Parviz Jahed contends that like the French filmmakers who began their careers as critics and intellectuals, documenting their conceptual innovations in journals such as *Cahiers du cinéma*, so too filmmakers such as Golestan, Farrokh Ghafferi and Houshang Kavousi also published scholarly reviews and railed against the status quo of the popular *film farsi* before embarking on their careers as practitioners of art cinema (2012: 86). The fact that several filmmakers of this period trained in France and incorporated the practices of casting children and non-professional actors, also contributed to the 'hybrid form that involved fictional and documentary elements' (Naficy 2011: 128). In relation to the 'avant-garde documentaries' of the New Wave, filmmakers also began experimenting with 'editing timed to music' (Naficy 2011: 129) as a means of breaking with the official style of documentary-making. Similarly, Farrokhzad was also beginning to investigate the use of rhythm and music in *Water and Heat* (1961). As Naficy writes, 'the differences between the section she directed on heat and the section on water, which Golestan directed, revealed her keen sense of rhythm and her affinity for sound, an affinity she amply demonstrated in designing the sound for *Water and Heat*, which included her own voice singing a lullaby' (2011: 81). He thus points not only to Golestan's influence in the context of particular production practices, but also to the way in which Farrokhzad differentiates herself from Golestan's style and consolidates her distinct brand of poetically realist cinema, in which the treatment of sound is central.

The House is Black is most frequently described as a 'poetic documentary'. (Rosenbaum 2005: 15). Hamid Dabashi states that the 'poetic realist' mode of documentary ties together 'fact' and 'fantasy' (2007: 61). He is careful to assert that by using the term 'poetic' he does not refer to light-heartedness or sentimentality, rather he is referring to what is intellectually and philosophically informed; 'poetic truth is thus no mere aesthetic claim. It posits an epistemic claim, a theorem of its own; it possesses a thematic autonomy that defines its particular take on reality' (2007: 62). Dabashi asserts that *The House is Black* is a form of visual poetry, an argument taken up by various critics who contend that Farrokhzad uses a kind of editing to generate this form of visual lyricism. Maryam Ghorbankarimi argues that the 'medical' part of the documentary is edited with a conventional 'narrative edit', 'creating a sense of continuity in a linear, sequential series of images' (2010: 141). Alternatively, the rest of the film employs a faster-paced montage technique, favouring jump cuts and tight close-ups. There is a detectable tension at work in this cinematic mode between Farrokhzad's self-portraiture and the desire to document the external, socio-cultural world. *The House is Black* is thus invested in both subjective, personalised enunciation of Farrokhzad's poetry and the collective, located world of inhabitants of the leprosy colony.

Voice and the Rhythmic Body in *The House is Black*

Farrokhzad begins *The House is Black* with a blank, dark screen, with a male voice-over warning the spectator: 'On this screen will appear an image of ugliness, a vision of pain no human should ignore.' Despite the fact that the voice-over problematically refers to 'naghsi az yek zeshti' ('an image of ugliness'), the film as a whole generally works against prescribed and regressive notions of beauty/ugliness and disease/health. The strategy of beginning with a blank screen and a voice-over arguably points to the limits and confines of the image and underscores the more evocative and dignifying power of the voice to conjure the experiences of 'pain' and suffering. Nasrin Rahimieh astutely observes that as a film, *The House is Black* is acutely aware of its parameters, that it 'records its own limitations and captures a remarkable self-awareness on the part of the artist' (2010: 128). Susan McCabe also argues a similar case in her analysis of modernist cinema and its paradoxical desire to both employ cinema as a means of 'corporeality', 'bodily rhythms' and the 'movement of the lived body', while simultaneously recognising the 'unavailability' of the bodily experience as mediated through 'mechanical reproduction' (2005: 3, 4). McCabe goes on to argue that the use of montage editing in modernist film ultimately 'ruptures fantasies of wholeness' and gestures towards the modern malaise of hysteria. Farrokhzad is undoubtedly cognisant of the constraints of cinematic reproduction, but more specifically she draws our attention to the limits of the *visual image*. Farrokhzad privileges the cinematic voice as the more powerful and poetic medium, capable of suggesting the corporeality of the body. In contrast to McCabe's understanding of modernist cinema, where montage ruptures the coherence of the body, Farrokhzad's own employment of montage and jump-cuts, far from suggesting fragmentation and hysteria, actually points to the rhythms of the 'lived body' – the beating of the heart, the whisper of the breath, the thumping of a foot against the earth. The use of poetic voicing and a rhythmic soundscape enables Farrokhzad to more purposefully evoke her central 'epistemic claim' (to employ Dabashi's phrase) that the human body – irrespective of gender, class, ethnicity or ability – is suffused with the experiences of suffering and joy. Disability precludes neither beauty nor enjoyment of life. While often the source of pain, frailty and immobility, the (disabled) body is also centralised as the foundation of pleasure, desire and catharsis.

But Farrokhzad's film avoids sentimentality through its central dichotomy: a tension between darkness and light, suffering and pleasure. Reciting her own poetry and fragments of biblical text, Farrokhzad's off-screen voice often intones plaintively and mournfully over the images of daily life at Bababaghi leper colony. An early classroom scene in which boys are shown solemnly praising God, is reminiscent of Farrokhzad's poem 'Jomeh' ('Friday') in *Tavallodi digar (Another Birth*, 1964), in which the speaker despairs of their isolation and imprisonment.

> An empty house
> A depressing house
> House with doors barred to the onrush of youth
> House of darkness and dreams of the sun
> House of solitude, divination and doubt
> House of closets, curtains, pictures and books. (2010: 65)

There are parallels between this poem and the documentary, most obviously the phrase, 'khaneye tariki' ('house of darkness'), which closely resembles the film's title, *Khaneh siah ast (The House is Black)*. The house, or rather the classroom and the leprosy colony more generally, is characterised in this section of the film by its gloom, dimness and atmosphere of despondency. Farrokhzad's voice can then be heard intoning; 'Who is this in hell praising you, O'Lord? Who is this in hell?' The classroom also appears to be a space completely 'barred to the onrush of youth' and pervaded by 'darkness', 'divination and doubt'. It is not the disease, but rather the prevailing socio-cultural discourses and practices relating to leprosy that sequester these young boys into a 'hell', forcing them to perform 'empty' rituals and maintain their 'depressing' isolation. Just as Michael Oliver's ground-breaking work on the definition of disability demonstrated the necessity of reframing impairment as 'a particular form of social oppression' (1996: 22), so too Farrokhzad points to the social construction of leprosy, and the manner in which the systemic segregation of its sufferers imprisons them in a 'house of darkness'.

One of the most striking examples of the use of sound in the film immediately follows the first classroom scene, when a man is shown singing, creating his own accompaniment through the clicking of his fingers and the tapping of his bare foot on the paving stones. The camera begins with a close-up of the man's twisted and deformed foot beating the ground and gradually pans up his body, only very slowly revealing the source of the powerful chanting, when the camera arrives and frames the singer's face. Despite the manner in which leprosy has transformed the body, the forceful and evocative sounds emanating from the singer reveal how oral forms of self-expression, such as singing and chanting, allow the social actors to reclaim their identity outside the discourses of disease and pathology. The man's chanting continues as a sonic thread through the film, sometimes as a rhythmic accompaniment to the other scenes of daily life at the colony. At other times Farrokhzad repeats the scene, splicing it between static scenes of leprosy suffers, centralising it as a key cinematic moment. Farrokhzad undoubtedly employs montage-editing techniques in *The House is Black*, but she uses such devices not to infer the fragmented nature of subjectivity, but to evoke the very corporeal rhythms and cycles of the human body. She evokes this sense of bodily rhythm not only through the use of voice, but also via the twang of a string being continually pulled, the squeak of a wheelbarrow and the repetitive thud of a ball hitting the earth.

In *The House is Black*, Farrokhzad represents the bodies of the leprosy sufferers, not simply as abject sites of suffering and existential malaise, but as vehicles of ordinary pleasure, love and enjoyment. A young girl, already evidencing the first signs of disease via a rash of lesions across her angelic face, smiles as an older woman vigorously brushes her luxurious thick hair. In another scene, a significantly deformed woman applies make-up before she is presented in a marital ritual. The intense drumming and singing in this scene shifts the emphasis to the emotion and pleasure of this familiar rite. In another scene a boy grabs a crutch and guilelessly uses it as a toy with which to play with another child. In all of the abovementioned scenes, disease and disability are ever-present but do not preclude the possibilities of pleasure, play and fulfilment. This is not to say that Farrokhzad sanitises or conceals the suffering of the leprosy inhabitants, only that she refutes the notion of the 'abject' body and refuses to represent the individuals as 'contaminated' and thus undesirable. As Nasrin Rahimieh writes, Farrokhzad's film interrogates the 'practice of mistreating those who have been disabled as a result of disease, even worse, condoning mistreatment and ostracization as culturally normative' (2010: 129). The 'abject' is thus reframed by Farrohzad, in that it becomes the marker of the prejudicial and regressive attitudes towards disease and disablement. Just as Farrokhzad railed against the notion that women's bodies must be segregated, veiled and pathologised in her poetry, so too her film interrogates the policy of quarantining leprosy sufferers and assigning them the role of the impure 'other'. *The House is Black* thus treads a delicate line, at once trying to redefine the experience of leprosy, while also demonstrating the inhumanity with which it sufferers have been treated.

Poetic Ambivalence: The House is Both Black and White

One of the most critically analysed scenes of *The House is Black* depicts a man pacing an alleyway, almost obsessively touching the window ledges as he strides to and fro. Farrokhzad's voice can be gradually discerned naming the days of the week. While this scene certainly reveals the claustrophobic, monotonous and severely quotidian nature of existence inside the leprosy colony, it also introduces the notion of temporal structures: the length of a day, a week, the passing of the seasons.

Fig. 1: A man is depicted pacing back and forth, while Farrokhzad is heard reciting the days of the week.

This emphasis on the cyclical and repetitive nature of human existence becomes most pointed when Farrokhzad interchanges two scenes; one showing a woman breastfeeding her baby, the other depicting a dog carrying a puppy in its mouth. Farrokhzad's voice-over is heard: 'Leave me, leave me, my days are but breath. Leave me before I set out for the land of no return, the land of infinite darkness.' Several short scenes follow, edited together as a montage: children devising a game with crutches, birds flying in a sweeping arc overhead, two men playfully wrestling, before Farrokhzad's voice-over continues: 'Oh God, remember my life is wind and you have given me a time of idleness, and around me the song of happiness, and the sound of the windmill, and the brightness of the light have vanished.' When we return to the man pacing the alleyway, Farrokhzad continues: 'Lucky are those who are harvesting now and their hands are picking sheaves of wheat.' Interestingly, there is tension at play in these scenes, where the voice-over works against the assumed meaning of the visuals. Instead of celebrating 'new life' in those scenes of the baby breastfeeding and the puppy being held by its mother, Farrokhzad intones about 'the land of infinite darkness'. Instead of finding joy in the two children inventing a game with an implement like the crutches, Farrokhzad's voice-over dwells on the 'light' that has vanished. Overlaying such scenes with a deeply melancholic voice-over demonstrates that sound and image need not work harmoniously towards one unifying form of meaning, but may operate dialectically. Sound is thus not used as a supplementary medium supporting the dominance of the visuals in *The House is Black*, but as a powerful medium in its own right, which creates additional, subtle and often paradoxical layers of meaning.

Farrokhzad appears to be pointing here to the impermanence of human existence and the fact that all life must end in death. Her melancholic voice-over evokes the opening line of the poem *Tavallodi digar* ('Another birth') in which the speaker laments: 'Hame hasti man ayeh tarik-ast' ('All my existence is a dark chant'). Certainly towards the end of the film both the visual and the verbal references to 'tariki' ('darkness') intensify, becoming more frequent and pressing. In one of the final scenes, a man walks on crutches through an orchard towards the spectator. As his body nears and eventually merges with the frame, total darkness engulfs the screen and nothing is heard but the rhythmic clump of his crutches hitting the ground. Accompanying this scene is the female voice-over, which is heard once again dwelling on the transience of human existence and the futility of seeking freedom and fulfilment: 'Maanande fakhteh baraye ensaaf minaalim va nist Entezaare nur mikeshim va inak zolmat ast' ('Like doves we cry for justice and there is none. We wait for light, and

Fig. 2: A man on crutches walks through the orchard at the Bababaghi leprosarium.

darkness reigns').[3] Pessimism and existential despair dominate this scene with both the literal frame and the metaphoric allusions of the voice-over pointing to the hopelessness, confinement and suffering of the colony's inhabitants.

Farrokhzad resists, however, presenting a totalising and nihilistic vision of disability in *The House is Black*. The rhythmic thumping of the crutch once again infuses the scene with a sense of the body's powerful perseverance, even in the face of debility and the inevitability of death. And after several beats while the screen remains dark, a boy's voice is heard off-screen, reading from a text in which the luminosity of Venus is discussed. The screen is then filled with the natural daylight of the classroom, which appears particularly bright after the intermission of darkness. The teacher asks a student: 'Chera baayad baraye daashtane pedar va maadar khoda ra shokr kard? Tou begu' ('Why should we thank God for having a father and mother? You answer'), to which the boy poignantly replies, 'Man nemidanam. Man hich kodam nadaram' ('I don't know, I have neither'). The teacher then turns to Hossein Mansouri (the boy Farrokhzad went on to adopt) and instructs him, 'Tou esme chand ta chize ghashang ra begu' ('You, give me the name of four beautiful things') to which Hossein answers: 'mah, khorshid, gol, bazi' ('moon, sun, flower, game'). Hossein's response again centralises the notion of a cinematic poeticism. The onomatopoeia of the four words spoken by the boy, 'mah, khorshid, gol, bazi', become a form of spontaneous, elliptical and oral poetry.

Whether the boy was instructed to speak the words by Farrokhzad, or the answer was voluntarily and spontaneously devised, is not important. What is central here is the tension between the constraints of the traditional documentary structure and the possibilities of a different form of cinema, in which poetry 'underpins' the structure and maintains the dialogue between Farrokhzad's written oeuvre and her cinematic production. The teacher then instructs a different student to write a sentence with the word 'khaneh' ('house') in it. The boy's anxious contemplation is interrupted by a scene in which a crowd of leprosy sufferers approach the camera, only to be suddenly enclosed by gates, on which is written 'jozam-khaneh' ('leprosy colony'). The final scene of the film then concludes with the boy carefully writing 'Khaneh siah ast' ('The house is black') on the blackboard. And while the film is inevitably preoccupied by blackness, the experience of suffering and the curtailment of human rights, each time *The House is Black* appears to be inclining towards complete existential and aesthetic 'darkness' Farrokhzad reintroduces 'light' both cinematically and metaphorically. This cinematic tension between 'suffering' and 'beauty' relate directly to Farrokhzad's own poetry and her consistent interest in dignifying and complicating the experiences of the human body.

Eschewing the visual polarities of 'darkness' and 'light', impurity and purity, disease and health, Farrokhzad uses sound as a means of pointing to a third and more dialectical understanding of human embodiment. Unable to totally surrender her film to the 'darkness' of existential despair or the optimism of a 'saccharine' 'humanism' (see Dabashi 2011), Farrokhzad positions *The House is Black* within the realms of poetic ambivalence. Most importantly her ongoing identification with her subjects and her desire to represent their experiences via the practices of poetry and the lyrical voice-over, demonstrates the manner in which such institutionalised 'house(s) of blackness' deprive leprosy sufferers of their rights to dignity, freedom and social inclusion.

NOTES

1   See, for example, Pouran Derakhshandeh's *Mute Contact* (1986), *Little Bird of Happiness* (1987), Mohsen Makhmalbaf's *The Peddler* (1987) and *The Silence* (1998), Samira Makhmalbaf's *The Apple* (1998), Majid Majidi's *Children of Heaven* (1997) and *The Colour of Paradise* (1999).
2   Dr Mohammad Mossadegh had been popularly elected as the Iranian Prime Minister in 1951 and had passed the Nationalisation Law, through which his government intended

to reclaim total control of Iranian oil resources. Refusing to bow to compensation for their previous exploitation through the Anglo-Iranian Oil Company, by 1952 Iran's diplomatic ties with the United Kingdom were severely compromised. Mossadegh also challenged the authority of the Shah to choose the Minister of War, in a move to recoup Prime Ministerial powers as outlined in the 1906 constitution (see Momayesi 2000). However, Mossadegh's attempts at nationalisation and democratic reform threatened both Western interests and Iran's monarchical power structure. The Truman administration, attempting to protect their own oil interests, quickly became involved and attempted to mediate a solution between Iran and the United Kingdom. When talks failed the new Republican government, headed by President Eisenhower, assisted the Shah in staging a coup and removing Mossadegh (see Ruehsen 1993).

3   This chapter quotes the official subtitles as they appear in the production widely distributed by Facets Video, although it is acknowledged that there are frequent discontinuities between the English translation and Persian transliteration of the dialogue provided here.

FILMOGRAPHY

Farrokhzad, Forugh (dir) (1964) *Khaneh siah ast* (*The House is Black*). 20 minutes. Studio Golestan. Iran.

BIBLIOGRAPHY

Afary, Janet (2009) *Sexual Politics in Modern Iran*. Cambridge: Cambridge University Press.
Azizi, Mohammad Hossein and Moslem Bahadori (2011) 'A History of Leprosy in Iran during the 19th and 20th Centuries', *Archives of Iranian Medicine*, 14, 6, 425–30.
Buckingham, Jane (2006) 'Leprosy and Disability', in Gary L. Albrech (ed.) *Encyclopedia of Disability*. London: Sage, 959–63.
Chaudhuri, Shohini and Howard Finn (2003) 'The Open Image: Poetic Realism and the New Iranian Cinema'. *Screen*, 44, 1, 38-57.
Dabashi, Hamid (2007) *Masters and Masterpieces of Iranian Cinema*. Odenton, MD: Mage.
Degroot, Joanna (2010) 'Feminism is Another Language: Learning from "Feminist" Histories of Iran and/or from Histories of Iranian Feminism since 1830', *Women: A Cultural Review*, 21, 3, 251–65.
Ellis, Kate (2008) *Disabling Diversity: The Social Construction of Disability in 1990s Australian National Cinema*. Saarbrucken: VDM Verlag.
Farrokhzad, Forugh (1955) *Asir*. Tehran: Amir Kabir.
____ (1956) *Divar*. Tehran: Amir Kabir.
____ (1958) *Esyan*. Tehran: Amir Kabir.
____ (1964) *Tavallodi digar*. Tehran: Amir Kabir.
____ (1974) *Imam biyavarim be aghaz-e fasl-e sard*. Tehran: Morvarid.

___ (2010) *Another Birth and Other Poems*, trans. Hasan Javadi, Susan Sallee. Odenton, MD: Mage.

Ghorbankarami, Maryam (2010) 'A Timeless Visual Essay', in Nasrin Rahimieh and Dominic Brookshaw (eds) *Forough Farrokhzad, Poet of Modern Iran: Iconic Woman and Feminine Pioneer of the New Persian Poetry*. London: I.B. Tauris: 137–48.

Jahed, Parviz (2012) *Directory of World Cinema: Iran*. Bristol: Intellect.

Kia, Mana (2005) 'Negotiating Women's Rights: Activism, Class and Modernization in Pahlavi Iran', *Comparative Studies of South Asia, Africa and the Middle East*, 25, 1, 227–44.

McCabe, Susan (2005) *Cinematic Modernism: Modernist Poetry and Film*. Cambridge: Cambridge University Press.

Milani, Farzaneh (1992) *Veils and Words: The Emerging Voices of Iranian Women Writers*. New York, NY: Syracuse University Press.

___ (2014) *Words, Not Swords: Iranian Women Writers and the Freedom of Movement*. New York, NY: Syracuse University Press.

Momayesi, Nassar (2000) 'Iran's Struggle for Democracy', *International Journal on World Peace*, 17, 4, 41–70.

Naficy, Hamid (2011) *A Social History of Iranian Cinema, Volume 1: The Artisanal Era, 1897– 1941*. Durham, NC: Duke University Press.

___ (2012) *A Social History of Iranian Cinema, Volume 4: The Globalizing Era, 1984 – 2010*. Durham, NC: Duke University Press.

Oliver, Michael (1996) *Understanding Disability: From Theory to Practice*. London: Palgrave Macmillan.

Rahimieh, Nasrin (2010) 'Capturing the Abject of the Nation in "The House is Black'", in Nasrin Rahimieh and Dominic Brookshaw (eds) *Forough Farrokhzad, Poet of Modern Iran: Iconic Woman and Feminine Pioneer of the New Persian Poetry*. London: I.B. Tauris, 125–36.

Ruehsen, Moyara deMoraes (1993) 'Operation "Ajax" Revisited: Iran, 1953', *Middle Eastern Studies*, 29, 3, 467–86.

Rosenbaum, Jonathan (2005) 'Radical Humanism and the Co-Existence of Film and Poetry in "The House is Black'", *Goodbye Cinema, Hello Cinephilia: Film Culture in Transition*. Chicago, IL: University of Chicago Press, 260–5.

Alfica Sehgal, Edward I. Alcamo, David Heymann (2006) *Leprosy*. New York, NY: Chelsea House.

Index

Aaltra 97–9, 106n.1, 184n.3
Abel 100
ableism 5, 13, 21, 200, 202, 227
ablenationalism 4, 9, 50
abnormality 11, 82–4, 151, 159, 165, 167
About Love see O Lubvi
abrazos rotos, Los 161–2
Ab va garma see Water and Heat
Academy Awards 66, 158
Addlakha, Renu 13n.1, 74
Acevedo-Muñoz, Ernesto 80–1, 90n.5
aesthetics 184n.2; of anti-normalisation 158; and disability 4; grotesque corporeal aesthetics 79; surrealism-inflected aesthetics 89; visceral aesthetics 222
African films 216–28, 228n.1
Allinson, Mark 159
Almodóvar, Pedro 12, 157–70
Alvart, Christian 141, 143
Amenábar, Alejandro 161
American democracy 202
American Dream 174, 201
American exceptionalism 200, 204, 213n.1
American identity 200
American individualism 12, 200–13
American-ness 200, 202, 208
Amsterdamned 102

Anand, Shilpa 74
Anglophone audiences 13–14n.3
Anglophone disability cinema/films 3, 9, 11, 12
Anglophone Disability Studies 4, 9
anorexia 101, 147, 177, 180, 183
Another Birth see Tavallodi digar
Antibodies see Antikörper
Antikörper 141–2, 144, 154
Anton's Right Here 11, 110–23; *see also* autism
Anton's Right Here Centre 122
Anton tut riadom see Anton's Right Here
Arkus, Lyubov 110–22, 123–124n.6, 124n.n.11,12
ASD 128–9
Asperger syndrome 103, 139, 169
Asylums 176
Átame! 12, 157, 165–7
Autism 11, 94, 103–5, 101–23, 123n.1, 124n.9, 126–39; non-autistic actors 134
Autisme Centraal 104
avant-garde 80, 193, 252, 253; European avant-garde 252
Avatar 12, 200–13; *see also* biotechnology

Bakha Satang see Peppermint Candy
Balabanov, Alexei 112

Balthazar, Nic 103, 104
Barefoot see Barfuss
Barfuss 145–7
beggar 82, 90n.4, 194, 219, 221–3
Belgian films 12, 98, 99, 106n.1, 175
Bella non piangere! 12, 187–97; *see also* New Man
Beltrame, Achille 187
Ben X 103–5; *see also* autism
Bergman, Ingmar 174
Berocca 24–5
biotechnology 12, 200, 203, 208–9, 213
bipolar disorder 161, 170n.3
blackness 248, 260
Black, Rhonda 100, 129, 130, 133
black soldier 225
Blind Child see Blind Kind
Blind Kind 95
blindness 79, 84, 86–9, 248
bodies: able-bodied 1, 6, 10, 20, 23, 25, 26, 28, 29, 34, 37, 59, 67, 132, 134, 141, 143–52, 154, 158, 220, 235, 236; anomalous bodies 20, 222; bodies on film 200; disabled body 6, 12, 23–4, 28–9, 67, 106, 170–171n.7, 188, 208; idealised body 65, 97; lived body 247, 254, 255; representation of 5; transsexual bodies 158; women's bodies 158, 257
Bolden, Oriana 22
Bollywood Cinema 11, 63–6, 75n.1
Bombay cinema 64
Broken Embraces see abrazos rotos, Los
Brüggemann, Dietrich 151
Buñuel, Luis 11, 78–83, 85, 89, 90n.5

Cahiers du cinéma 253
Cameron, James 203, 213
Camp at Thiaroye, The see Camp de Thiaroye
Camp de Thiaroye 12, 216–17, 223, 224–7
Camphill Village Svetlana 118
Campos Artigas, Alfonso 83, 84, 90n.10
cancer 93–5, 111, 170–171n.7

capitalism 72, 114, 158, 159, 201, 202, 205, 208
Carbonari, David 189, 191, 194
Carey, Allison C. 50
Castells, Manuel 38, 40, 42
cerebral palsy 10, 24, 34, 40, 41
Chang-dong, Lee 10, 33–40, 42–4
chien andalou, Un 81
Chorok Mulgogi 33
Christianity 23, 143; Orthodox Christianity 124n.11
chromosomal mismatch 59
Ciske de Rat 95
citizenship 47–51, 58, 60, 202, 203, 211, 222, 225
citizens movements 230
Clínica de la Conducta 82–5
cognitive code of reality 1, 5–8
Coixet, Isabel 161
Cold Blood see Sang Froid
Coletti, Duilio 191
colonialism: British colonialism 63, 70, 71, 73; doubly colonized 226; French colonialism 70, 216, 220, 224–7; neo-colonialist 217; postcolonial Africa 12, 218, 221, 224, 226; postcolonial spaces 218
Colour of Paradise, The see Rang-e Khoda
Come As You Are see Hasta la Vista
communism 201
Confederación española de agrupaciones de familiares y enfermos mentales see FEAFES
Cost of Living, The 28
counter-narratives 93
Crazy About Paris see Verrückt nach Paris
crippled 81, 95, 145, 222, 223, 240; bad cripple 150; good cripple 150, 180; super cripple 153
cross-cultural 1, 4, 36, 179

Daglicht 103–5; *see also* autism
Dallas Buyers Club 211
Danes, Claire 126–7, 132–3; *see also*

Temple Grandin
Davis, Lennard J.   3, 82, 173, 204, 222, 231
Daylight see Daglicht
deafness   23, 61, 81, 84, 161, 222; Anglophone work on   4; deaf culture in Spain   3; deaf vampires   23
debility   248, 259
Debrauwer, Lieven   99
deformity   222, 223, 231, 251, 256
Deléfine, Benoit   97
dementia   149
denormalization   180
depression   68, 161, 163; *see* mental illness
destigmatisation   157, 166
Diawara, Manthia   216
Dick, Maas   102
disability: cinematic representation   2, 4, 7–9, 12, 143; disability culture   1, 4, 27–8; disability dance   28; disability documentary   10, 18, 22; disability drag   11, 126–7, 131–2, 134; disability identities   104; disabled children   21, 118; disabled evildoer   141–5; disabled women   19; as embedded concept   12, 218, 220; for global audiences   9; historical exclusion of   20; intellectual disability   11, 47–50, 52, 55–7, 61n.6, 69, 75n.3, 100, 157, 161, 238; media representation of   129; narratives of   6, 12, 106, 126, 129; negative images of   2 ; in non-Anglophone contexts   2; non-disabled actors   9; positive imagery of   154; in post-industrialised wester   19; representations of   2, 5, 11, 63, 65, 79, 93, 99, 103, 126, 132, 141, 143, 148, 155, 202, 219, 224, 231, 247; in Russia   111, 113, 122, 123n.1; social disability   242
disability film festivals   18, 19, 22, 24, 27, 29, 30, 31; DisArts Film Festival   19
disability rights movement   30, 203; in post-Soviet Russia   111, 122

disability road movie   12, 173–84, 184n.3; and non-disability road movie   179
disablism   147
disfigurement   102, 158
Diop Mambéty, Djibril   217
Dizionario del Film   191
Dodes'ka-den   13, 230–42
Dolgopolov, Greg   110, 116, 119, 123n.2
Donaldson, Elizabeth   160, 163, 164
Don't Cry, Beautiful! see Bella non piangere!
Down syndrome   6, 10, 19, 47–60, 61n.7, 99; *see also* and sexuality
Dresen, Andreas   148–9
Dutch Cinema: non-disabled actors   99; New Wave-influenced crime   95; Postwar   11, 93–106
Dutch Film Canon *see* Nederlands Film Festival
dyscalculia   69
dyslexia   11, 63–75, 75n.3

Easy Rider   181
echolalia   112
edad de oro, La   81
Eighth Day, The see huitième jour, Le
Elysium   211
Emcke, Matthias   151, 152
Enthoven, Geoffrey   97
eroticism   52, 56, 61n.8, 249
epilepsy   85, 90n.10
eugenics   19, 66–8, 85, 90n.7; post-eugenic   210
European road movie   12, 97, 173–84, 184n.3; *see also* disability road movie
Ex Drummer   102

Farrokhzad, Forugh   13, 247–60
Fascism   187–93, 197n.n.9,10
FEAFES   162
Fellini, Federico   174
Fight Club   163
Film Krant (magazine)   97
Fire, A see Yek atash

INDEX   265

first-person narrator 142
Flaherty, Robert J. 5
Foucault, Michel 74, 207, 234, 239, 240
Franco, Francisco 158
French New Wave 252
Freud, Sigmund 162
Fuentes, Carlos 78

Garland-Thomson, Rosemarie 13n.2, 30, 35, 67, 159–60, 181, 200, 201, 204, 222
Gattaca 211
Gehlawat, Ajay 64
German films 141–55
GFW 249, 252
Ghafferi, Farrokh 253
Global North 1, 218
God's Gift see *Wend Kuuni*
Goffman, Erving 176, 177
Golden Age, The see *edad de oro, La*
Golestan, Ebrahim 251–3
Golestan Film Workshop see GFW
Gombele 218
goodnight, liberation 22
Goya Awards 158
Green Fish see *Chorok Mulgogi*
GriGris 218
Grimm 101
Gwangju Uprising 33

Hable con ella 169
Haroun, Mahamat-Saleh 218
Hasta la Vista 99, 105, 175–6, 179–83
heroism 189, 192, 194, 197n.8, 204; able hero 205; American lone hero 204–6
Higiene Mental Escolar 85
Hindi film industry 64
Hollywood cinema 14n.5, 64, 99, 102, 145, 159, 165, 174, 191, 200–2, 203–4, 210, 211, 216–17, 222, 228n.1; disability films 208; Hollywood's 3D technology 212
homeland 192, 194, 195, 225, 227, 240
homelessness 248

homosexuality 48, 49, 96, 158
House is Black, The 13, 247–60; see also leprosy
Huettner, Ralf 146
huitième jour, Le 99, 100
human rights 49, 51, 248, 260; Human Rights Watch 123n.3
hysteria 164–5, 254, 255

I am the Other Woman see *Ich bin die Andere*
Ich bin die Andere 144, 154
Imam biyavarim be aghaz-e fasl-e sard 249
I'm in Away From Here 25; see also autism
impotence 13, 33, 211, 219–23
impure modernism 79
Indian education system 70; see also colonialism
Inside I'm Dancing 97
integration 7, 9, 51, 74, 106, 184, 208
Introduction to My Disability 22–3
Invitation to Dance 29–30
Iranian cinema 13, 247–60; Iranian New Wave cinema 13, 248, 253; New Iranian cinema 252
isolation 11, 23, 57, 68, 69, 75, 97, 104, 118, 123n.1, 136, 248, 250, 251, 255
Italian Neo-Realism 191, 252
Ivanovo detsvo 112
Ivan's Childhood see *Ivanovo detsvo*

Jackson, Mick 11, 126–8, 132–3; see also autism
Japan 9, 29, 23–5, 242n.n.n.1,4,5; Japanese nationalism 232; linguistic expressions 235; new Japan 13, 213; post-war era 233, 242
Journal of Literary and Cultural Disability Studies 4, 218
Juárez Almendros, Encarnación 14n.5, 161
Jungle World (newspaper) 173
Kafer, Alison 24, 29

Katie Tippel see *Keetje Tippel*
Kavousi, Houshang 253
Keetje Tippel 95
Keita 218
Kenau 102
Kerverne, Gustave 97
Khamidkhodzhayev, Alisher 111, 113, 116
Khaneh siah ast see *House is Black, The*
Khorma (la betise) (Khorma: Stupidity) 218
Kim, Eunjung 34, 36, 39
Kim, Young-jin 36
Kinder, Marsha 159
Kisetsu no nai machi see *Town Without Seasons, The*
Kiss, The 6–7
Kleine Teun 100
Kojiki 231
Korean New Wave 10, 33–44
Kracauer, Siegfried 5
Kurosawa, Akira 13, 230–42

Laaste Dagen van Emma Blank, De 101
LaCom, Cindy 226, 227
Lance, Stephen 19
Last Days of Emma Blank, The see *Laaste Dagen van Emma Blank, De*
legless 81, 85, 90n.4, 223
leprosy 13, 247–60
Lermontov, Mikhail 112
Let Us Believe in the Beginning of the Cold Season see *Imam biyavarim be aghaz-e fasl-e sard*
Levinson, Barry 103
liberalism 249, 250
Like Stars on Earth see *Taare Zameen Par*
Link, Jürgen 180
Linton, Simi 29
Little Girl Who Sold the Sun, The see *petite vendeuse de soileil, La*
Little Teun see *Kleine Teun*
Love and Other Drugs 211
Lumière and Company see *Lumière et compagnie*
Lumière brothers 5, 6, 174

Lumière et compagnie 6
Lyotard, Jean-François 44

Macaulay, Lord Thomas 70, 75
madness 145, 162, 164–5, 227
Majidi, Majid 248, 260n.1
Makhmalbaf, Mohsen 248, 260n.1
Man of Aran 5
Mar adentro 161
martyrdom 12, 187–8
Marxism 10, 12, 201, 203
masculinity 47–60; alternative masculinities 96; disabled masculinity 10, 12, 47; heterosexual masculinity 47, 53; individual masculinity 33; lost masculinity 189; male trauma 33; male anxiety 33; masculine heroism 194; mythical manhood 205; narratives of athletic masculinity 106; reformulations of masculinity 188
mass media 124n.12, 131, 202
McCabe, Susan 254
melodrama 19, 34, 64, 165, 233
mental disability 111, 115, 161, 226
mental hygiene 85
mental illness 85, 93, 143, 157–70, 170n.6, 238
meta-narratives 233
metaphor 7, 44, 63, 65, 82, 87, 103, 116, 122, 141, 149, 154, 164, 178, 179, 192, 195, 205, 208, 233, 239, 259, 260; body politic metaphor 188–9, 197, 204, 205; of illness 170–171n.7; ironies of 242n.5; metaphor of the door 126, 127, 135–8; as a national 233, 235; women as a 165, 206
Me too see *Yo, también*
Milky Way, The see *voie lactée, La*
Milyang see *Secret Sunshine*
mise-en-scène 65, 170n.3, 203, 234
mobility 31, 194, 207, 255
Monchamps, Eugénie 84
Mortier, Koen 102
moving images 2

Mujeres al borde de un ataque de nervios
 12, 157, 163,165,169
Murderball 96
Mussolini, Benito 187, 190
muteness 24
mutilated victory 190-1
myth 141, 149, 154, 189-92, 202, 208, 223; historical myth 12; individualist myth 12, 201; manhood myth 205; national myth 189; political myth 187; of self-sufficiency 202; social myth 170-171n.7
mythology 231

Naficy, Hamid 247, 250-3
Naharro, Antonio 47, 57
national identity 80, 188, 232, 242
National Institute of Psychopedagogy 85
nationhood 1, 8
Nederlands Film Festival 94, 101
neoliberalism 21, 31
Neorealism *see* Italian Neo-Realism
new *hallyu see* Korean New Wave
new Japan 13, 231
New Man 12, 187-97
Nollywood 13, 228n.1
Noordelingen, De 101
normalcy 12, 66, 159, 163, 173-84, 208, 222, 226, 227, 234, 235, 241; non-normalcy 175, 180, 183
normality 38, 141, 143-4, 147, 154, 209
Northerners, The see Noordelingen, De

Oasieu see Oasis
Oasis 10, 33-44
Ober 101
Oberhausen Film Festival 251, 253
objects of curiosity 145
obsessive-compulsive disorder 147, 170n.6
O'Donnell, Damien 97
O Lubvi 20-1
olvidados, Los 11, 78-89, 89n.3, 90n.n.n.4,5,6

Onega camps 115
On Freaks and People see Pro urodov i liudei
Other 11-12, 35, 67, 141-55, 225-6, 236, 257; Self/Other 141, 226
Otherness 43, 104, 153, 159

paraplegia 95, 96, 151, 176, 180
Pasolini, Pier Paolo 5, 7, 8; *see also* cognitive code of reality
Pastor, Álvaro 47
Patiño Rojas, Dr. José Luis 82-4, 90n.10
Paul-Boncour, Georges 84
Pauline and Paulette 99, 100
Pepi, Luci, Bom y otras chicas del montón 158
Peppermint Candy 33
Pesaro Film Festival 251
petite vendeuse de soileil, La 217
Phantom Pain see Phantomschmerz
Phantomschmerz 151-2, 154
picaresque 81, 89n.3
piel que habito, La 169
Pineda, Pablo 47, 49
Poetry 33, 37
popular culture 2, 65
post-war Italian nationalism 12
poverty 20, 31, 82, 84, 204, 236, 248, 250
Pro urodov i liudei 112
psychoanalysis 162
Putin, Vladimir 11, 21, 111-18, 121

Quayson, Ato 224

racism 13, 223, 224
Radji, Dr. Abdolhossein 251
Rain Man 103, 120, 127
Rajadhyaksha, Ashish 64
Rang-e Khoda 248
realism 95, 150; poetic realism 13, 247, 252; social realism 80
Renn, wenn Du kannst 151, 154
Risholm, Ellen 175, 179, 180, 183, 184

Road, The see *strada, La*
Rubin, Henry 96
Rue des Invalides 98, 99, 105, 106
Rukojć, Katarzyna 34, 36, 37
Run if you can see *Renn, wenn Du kannst*
Rutten, Gerard 95

Sánchez Vidal, Agustín 78, 81, 89n.3, 90n.4
Sandahl, Carrie 28
Sanders, Mari 98–9, 106
Sang Froid 23
Santamarina, Dr. Rafael 84
Sassen, Saskia 44
Saul, Anno 147
savantism 114, 127–8
Schweiger, Til 145
Sea Inside, The see *Mar adentro*
Secret Life see *Vida secreta*
Secret Life of Words, The 161
Secret Sunshine 33, 37
Seeßlen, Georg 173, 183, 184
Sembène, Ousmane 12, 216–28
sexism 65, 134
sexuality 6, 10, 19, 32, 35, 36, 40, 47–60, 97, 141, 150–4, 159; discourses of gender/sexuality 12, 13n.1, 170; expressions of 51; sexual abnormality 150, 151; sexual activity 47, 56–60, 61n.6; sexual agency 56; sexual desire 53, 55, 57; sexual disinhibition 95; sexual impotence 219; sexual minorities 49; sexual oppression 19; sexual politics 34; sexual prohibition 19–20, 56, 61n.8; sexual rights 10, 49, 58, 60; sexuality of disabled characters 150; sexually abnormal 142
Shapiro, Dana 96
Shi see *Poetry*
Siebers, Tobin 4, 7, 9, 19, 110, 126, 132
Silence see *Sokut*
Skin I Live In, The see *piel que habito, La*
Smith, Paul Julian 159
Smultronstrället 174

socialism 158, 201
Society of Disability Studies 29
Society to Assist Patients of Leprosy 250
Sokurov, Alexander 114, 123–124n.6
Sokut 248
Sommer vorm Balkon 148–50, 154
Source Code 211
South Korean society 37, 43
space/place 1
Spanish Confederation of Groups of Families of Those with Mental Illness see FEAFES spectatorship 2, 7
Spetters 95–6
Splatters see *Spetters*
Staudte, Wolfgang 95
stereotypes 98, 130, 141, 144, 149, 154, 195, 218; breaking stereotypes 163; of extraordinary ability 115; negative stereotypes 218; neurotypical stereotypes 113; of The Disabled Person as Super Cripple 153
sterilisation 50
stigmatisation 35, 42, 157, 235, 250, 251
strada, La 174
Suleman, Raman 218
Summer in Berlin see *Sommer vorm Balkon*
supercrip 11, 74, 98, 126, 127–32, 134, 139, 152–3
surrealism 81, 89

Taare Zameen Par 11, 63–75, 75n.3; see also dyslexia
taboos 30, 242n.1
Talk to Her see *Hable con ella*
Tarkovsky, Andrei 112
Tavallodi digar 249, 255, 258
Taylor, Martin 24
Temple Grandin 11, 126–39; see also autism
Thelma and Louise 181
thinking in pictures 11, 126, 134–6
Tie Me Up! Tie Me Down! see *Átame!*
Toti, Enrico 12, 187–97, 197n.n.3,8

Tourette syndrome   146–7, 153, 177, 182
Town without Seasons, The   230
Transcendence   211
trauma   6, 33, 112, 113, 147, 153–4, 161–2, 169, 194, 225, 226
Treurniet, Maarten   102
Turkish Delight see Turks Fruit
Turks Fruit   94

UNCRPD   51, 60
United Nations Convention on the Rights of Persons with Disabilities *see* UNCRPD
US-American road movies   174–5, 181

Valiant Kunal see Veer Kunal
Van der Keuken, Johan   95
van Dormael, Jaco   6–8, 99
van Rooijen, Diedrik   103
van Warmerdam, Alex   94, 100–2
Veer Kunal   65
Verhoeven, Paul   94–6
Verrückt nach Paris   175, 177, 179, 181–3
Vertov, Dziga   119–20
Vida secreta   81, 90n.4
Viel, Dr. Benjamin   78–80
Vincent Wants to Sea see Vincent will Meer
Vincent will Meer   146, 175, 177, 179, 181–4
Viridiana   81
vittoria mutilata *see* mutilated victory
voice-over   112, 115, 120–1, 247, 252, 254, 258–60
voie lactée, La   81
Von Tippelskirch, Christian   29
von Trotta, Margarethe   144, 145

Waiter see Ober
Wagadu (journal)   14n.9, 218
Waldschmidt, Anne   143, 154, 173, 180
Water and Heat   252, 253
Wend Kuuni   218
Werkema, Lotte   98
What It Is Like To Be My Mother   26
wheelchair   25, 31, 34, 41, 94–9, 143–5, 148, 151–3, 176
White Revolution   249
Wild Strawberries see Smultronstrället
Wo ist Fred?   147, 154
Women on the Verge of a Nervous Breakdown see Mujeres al borde de un ataque de nervios
Wonderful Life of Willem Parel, The see Wonderlijk Leven van Willem Parel, Het
Wonderlijk Leven van Willem Parel, Het   95
world cinema   1, 9–13
World Health Organization   158
World War I   187–92, 196, 227
World War II   224, 227, 232

Xala   12, 216–18, 219–24, 227

Yek atash   252
Yolk   19
Yo, también   10, 47–60, 61n.6
Young and the Damned, The see olvidados, Los
youth-culture   105

Zulu Love Letter   218

GPSR Authorized Representative: Easy Access System Europe, Mustamäe tee
50, 10621 Tallinn, Estonia, gpsr.requests@easproject.com

www.ingramcontent.com/pod-product-compliance
Lightning Source LLC
Chambersburg PA
CBHW051352290426
44108CB00015B/1983